To EB
from d ♡
P9-DXC-604

# A Fortune in the Junk Pile

BY THE SAME AUTHOR:

# A Fortune
# in the Junk Pile

*a guide to valuable antiques*

By DOROTHY H. JENKINS

CROWN PUBLISHERS, INC.
New York

© 1963 BY DOROTHY H. JENKINS
LIBRARY OF CONGRESS CATALOG CARD NUMBER: 63-12065
PRINTED IN THE UNITED STATES OF AMERICA

*Seventeenth Printing, February, 1972*

PHOTO CREDITS

ALL PHOTOGRAPHS, EXCEPT WHERE OTHER CREDIT HAS BEEN GIVEN, WERE TAKEN BY GOTTSCHO-SCHLEISNER. CREDIT ALSO HAS BEEN GIVEN WITH THE PHOTOGRAPHS OF THOSE ANTIQUES THAT BELONG TO A RESTORATION OR MUSEUM. THE MAJORITY OF THE ANTIQUES THAT HAVE BEEN PHOTOGRAPHED ARE PRIVATELY OWNED AND USED OR DISPLAYED IN THE HOMES OF THE FOLLOWING: MR. AND MRS. W. E. KYLE IN VIRGINIA; MR. AND MRS. S. D. HATHAWAY AND MR. AND MRS. RICHARD HEMMENWAY OF NEW JERSEY; MISS HELEN BATTENBERG IN PENNSYLVANIA; MR. AND MRS. ROBERT ADAMS, MRS. EARL JOCKERS, MRS. WILLIAM H. SCHLEISNER, MR. AND MRS. GEORGE SENGELAUB, AND MRS. WILLIAM STICKLES ON LONG ISLAND; MR. AND MRS. E. A. AXELSON, MR. AND MRS. ROBERT BARTLETT, MR. AND MRS. RALPH EARLE, MR. AND MRS. DONALD E. HARRISON, MRS. FREDERICK A. MORLEY, MRS. WILBUR F. PRESTON, MR. AND MRS. GEORGE P. TILLEY, MR. AND MRS. PAUL VAUTRIN, MR. AND MRS. CHARLES F. YUNG, MISS OLIVE E. ALLEN AND THE AUTHOR IN CONNECTICUT. TO ALL OF THEM AS WELL AS TO THE PRINCIPAL PHOTOGRAPHERS—GOTTSCHO-SCHLEISNER, AND TED EASTWOOD OF THE *New Haven Register*—GO SPECIAL THANKS FOR THEIR COOPERATION AND PATIENCE.

To

*M. E. M.*

and

*H. B.*

because they instilled appreciation
of family heritage

# Contents

# 1

# *What is an Antique?*

A CUP WITHOUT A HANDLE but with two saucers, a salt crock to hang on a kitchen wall, a cream pitcher in the form of a cow with luster spots over its white pottery body, an amber bottle shaped like a fish, a satiny rose bowl whose glowing color belies its prim roundness—all these were useful and probably treasured possessions in homes 85 to 150 years ago. Today, eyebrows would be raised if tea were served in a cup without a handle, and the salt crock would be considered unsanitary. Their value lies in their being antiques. As such, they are as genuine as the brass lantern with beveled glass sides that hangs in the hall of the Governor's Palace, restored to its eighteenth-century splendor, in Williamsburg, Virginia.

Antiques command more attention today than they ever have. So widespread is the interest that the amber bottle which held Dr. Fisch's bitters when it

was purchased for a few coins in the early 1800's is regarded as respectfully as the hanging lantern, which was expensive even by present-day standards, when it was bought in the 1700's. Nothing that was of personal or household use during the last 300 years is too minor for consideration in this century. Yet hundreds of simple everyday articles that once were indispensable now are left to gather dust or are unrecognized for what they are.

An antique, according to the dictionary, is "a piece of furniture, tableware or the like, made at a much earlier period than the present." It is not, however, necessarily out-of-date or old-fashioned. A chair that was built soundly from good hardwood around 1820 and is comfortable to sit on is never out-of-date. A 7½-inch-high octagonal teapot of blue Staffordshire is monstrous in comparison to contemporary streamlined pots, but it makes as good tea as it did more than a century ago.

How many years old must a chair, a plate, a trivet, a fan, or a clock be to warrant its being called an antique without anyone's arguing the point? Some people insist on a precise number of years, such as 80 or 100. The 80-year span is justified on the basis of two generations, each one covering 40 years. Yet a watch that is only 75 years old is likely to look old-fashioned, and so perhaps it also is an antique. Certainly anything that is 100 years old deserves the label.

An official definition of an antique is stated in the Tariff Act of 1930. According to Paragraph 1811 of that Act, antiques are "works of art (except rugs and carpets made after the year 1700), collections in illustration of the progress of the arts, works in bronze, marble, terra cotta, parian, pottery or porcelain, artistic antiquities and objects of ornamental character or educational value which shall have been produced prior to the year 1830."

This statement is clear in its application to imports and the payment of duty on them. But the year 1830 is more than an arbitrary date in the classification of American antiques. It was about this time that mass production and factory manufacture began to displace the making of individual pieces entirely by hand. Glass began to be pressed into forms by machine instead of being hand-blown. Chairs were the first piece of furniture to which assembly line methods were applied. Although the cabinetmaker, the glassblower, the blacksmith, and other craftsmen were not put out of business immediately, each succeeding decade brought an increase in mass manufacturing.

The fact that a chair or table was made by a cabinetmaker before 1830 does not necessarily make it a more valuable antique than one made thereafter. All the cabinetmakers in any period were not equally skillful; many of them turned out mediocre pieces. But in every craft that contributed to daily living, some workmen produced wares that made their names famous.

The painted side chair with stencil decoration and rush seat was produced in quantity and sold cheaply during the 1820's because Lambert Hitchcock turned his Connecticut workroom into a factory where the parts were cut and turned, assembled, and then decorated, so that many more chairs were completed in a day than if a workman had concentrated on one from start to finish. The Hitchcock chair now is as undeniably an antique as a mahogany fiddle-back Empire chair or a Chippendale ladder-back made many years earlier by cabinetmakers. So also are a steeple clock of the 1860's, a pressed glass lamp that burned whale oil during the 1840's or a brass student lamp that burned kerosene in the 1880's, and the cut glass wedding presents of the 1890's.

The quest for antiques can be as successful in one region of the country as another. In the Southwest, the oldest traditions and antiques are Spanish in origin, although people there share with the rest of the United States a rich Victorian background. Louisiana is one of several notable areas in the United States and Canada where the influence was primarily French. In the Northwest and in the north central states, descendants of Scandinavian settlers are proud of handsome carved bedsteads and equally handsome household linens.

Except for small districts where certain nationalities tended to settle during the nineteenth century, the eastern, southeastern, and midwestern states reflect in their antiques a predominantly English influence. Household and family goods brought to this country, imported during Colonial days, and later produced here in great quantity followed trends and living habits established in England. The Orient also placed its stamp on eastern towns that thrived as seaports in the late 1700's and much of the 1800's, just as it did on England. To such centers as Salem and New Bedford, Massachusetts, Baltimore, Maryland, and Norfolk, Virginia, came Canton tableware, Kashmir shawls, teakwood chests and tables.

Not a day goes by but that someone in one of the fifty states glances at some object and fails to recognize it as an antique. For example, how many young women know a sewing bird when they see one, and how to use it? They are likely to be baffled even when a small velvet pincushion is attached. The sewing bird, usually of metal, is an ornamental clamp to be fastened to a table. It holds fabric in its beak to facilitate hemming, and was a great aid when all sewing was done at home. It's fun to use because the beak is closed by a spring and can be opened by a tail lever.

Many similar homely things are packed away in trunks, chests, and cupboards or are gathering dust in attics and cellars. More often than not, things of greater value than a sewing bird are found. In New Hampshire one summer while looking over the attic of his boyhood home, a man was curious enough to chip the paint off an inconspicuous spot on a case piece with two drawers and cupboards. Since he suspected it might have been made of good hardwood, he removed the paint —several coats in various colors topped by an ugly green one—and discovered that he had a small mahogany sideboard with more graceful proportions than much of the furniture made during the American Empire period (1815-40) during which it had been made.

Clearing out a house in which one family has lived for a long time or disposing of the possessions of an elderly relative is almost certain to be rewarded with the discovery of some antiques. Few of the articles may be of museum quality. Some will have

**4**

greater sentimental or nostalgic than monetary value. However, not even the stacks of magazines, the scrapbooks put together 75 or more years ago, or the clutter of dusty bottles should be tossed aside for the trash collector. At the very least, publications and clippings represent valuable research material for people in many fields of work today. If there's time to go through them, you may find one issue of a magazine, a lithograph in a scrapbook, or a historical flask among the old canning jars and milk bottles that will bring hard cash in the antique market.

It is a fact that any antique you come across that has no appeal for you or suggests no use to you is likely to be a treasure to someone else, who will gladly pay for it. Ten to one, the person who buys is a collector. A small percentage of the men and women who collect antiques have catholic tastes and will buy almost anything that strikes their fancy. The really zealous collector is the one who specializes. Preferences range from such popular things as pressed glass, some type of pottery, clocks, lamps, coins, coin banks, bottles, souvenir spoons, and guns to oddments such as butter pats, hatpin-holders, mustache cups, cut glass knife rests, and toothpicks. Nothing is too small, too unimportant, or too queer but that someone somewhere collects it.

Many collectors, including those who buy relatively inexpensive items such as hatpin-holders, gradually assemble a group that becomes valuable in terms

of money. In contrast, there are people who literally buy antiques as an investment which they expect to increase in value. Such things as authentic Queen Anne and Philadelphia Chippendale furniture made here during the 1700's, Meissen figurines, and Lowestoft china are currently expensive examples of sound investments. Less costly now, but almost certain to increase in value during the next twenty years, are furniture made between 1785 and 1820, eighteenth- and early-nineteenth-century brass, early-nineteenth-century china, Tiffany glass, and—probably—cut glass.

People with money to invest seldom buy without the advice of a reliable antique dealer. Collectors, both those who rely on an expert and those who do not, are bound eventually to learn a good deal about their field and most of them become shrewd buyers. In self-defense, therefore, a person who owns or finds antiques must learn something about them before offering them for sale. It is not enough to be halfway convinced that the iridescent, marigold-hued glass bowl that you've kept in the cupboard because it came from home, but have never liked or used, is carnival or taffeta glass. When you attempt to make certain that it is, you undoubtedly will hear that there is at present a brisk market for this glass, which is hardly old enough yet to be antique. Because of the current demand, the bowl which may have been acquired by your grandmother as a premium can be sold now for several dollars.

Carnival glass does not have the name of the manufacturer or the butcher who gave it away worked in with the design, nor does any pressed glass that was obtained as a premium. Many other things displaying the name of the manufacturer or merchant that were given away between 1850 and 1900 are worth money today. If you find any fans, spoons, calendars, paper dolls (printing on the backs), a bootjack, or tin containers emblazoned with firm or trade names, they need not be discarded as trash.

Anyone who is in a hurry to sell the antiques found in an old house is probably wise to ask a reliable dealer to come in and look them over. He may be willing to handle the sale of some or all of them on the usual commission basis. Or, for a small fee, he may merely advise on the value and salability of the entire lot. Remember, antique dealers have customers, whereas you must find an interested buyer before you can dispose of anything, however rare, odd, or valuable it may seem.

If selling is not urgent, there are several ways a person can learn to recognize and, eventually, evaluate an antique. Visits to antique shops and occasional attendance at an auction in a city gallery or on a rural green are means of learning what is being offered for sale, what people are buying, and what prices are being paid. The ability to recognize antiques is aided greatly by viewing a restored house or village. More of them are being opened to the public every year, and almost every state now has at least one. Because restorations show how people lived, they are full of everyday things. More than one restoration visitor has been reminded of a nineteenth-century duplicate consigned to a cupboard at home as too ordinary to be considered an antique but too good to throw away. Fully as enlightening are the specialized exhibits at the Clock Museum in Bristol, Connecticut, the Farmers' Museum in Cooperstown, New York, the Maritime Museum in San Francisco, California, and Henry Ford Museum and Dearborn Village in Dearborn, Michigan, to mention only a few. Many fine arts museums have exhibits of china, silver, glass, and the like.

If any member of your church or community is a collector, by all means accept an invitation to see the display. A collector may be willing to pass judgment on some piece you have found that belongs within his special field. However, it's best not to mistake willingness to advise for willingness to buy. A local historical society, if there is one, can be a source of knowledge through its members, its displays, its meetings and speakers, as well as its library.

Books, as a matter of fact, are perhaps the easiest way to sharpen recognition and aid in the identification of antiques. The primary purpose of this one is to be a guide to antiques, major and minor. There also are books on subjects as specific as milk glass, paperweights, and pewter.

Once an antique has been identified, its characteristics will have to be evaluated. Its approximate age, workmanship, the quality of the materials, present condition, and rarity all have a bearing on both its intrinsic and market values. Repair or restoration may downgrade an antique. A piece of pressed glass that can be authenticated as having been made at the Boston and Sandwich Glass Company's factory in Sandwich, Massachusetts, is to be prized or sold for a good price. However, there's no excuse for jumping to the conclusion that any piece of pressed glass is Sandwich glass, for many excellent as well as beautiful pieces came from factories elsewhere in New England and in Pennsylvania, West Virginia, and Ohio.

Owners often carelessly fool themselves into believing that an antique is older than it actually is. The Queen Anne style in furniture, for example, was made everywhere in America between 1725 and 1750. Its distinguishing details continued to be followed, particularly in rural areas, for many years after other styles had come into fashion. Thus, a tea table made in New Hampshire in the early 1800's may well have some distinctly Queen Anne characteristics.

There is a tendency also among owners who are not familiar with the antique market to set an inflated valuation on anything they wish to sell. Pride and sentiment have nothing to do with selling prices. The appraised value of an antique, stated after careful examination by a qualified expert, may well be higher than current market value. In antiques as in everything else, the selling price is determined by supply and demand. Pressed glass brings much higher prices now than it did thirty years ago when collecting it first became popular. Ten years ago cranberry glass was selling for excellent prices, and it would have been difficult to give away a piece of late-nineteenth-century Tiffany or cut glass. Recently, collectors have become wary of cranberry glass, but Tiffany glass sells reasonably fast and well and cut glass is beginning to find a market, in some areas.

Every year adds both prestige and value to nineteenth-century antiques. It will take longer, because more of everything was made during the 1800's, but sooner or later the number of nineteenth-century pieces will be reduced just as eighteenth-century antiques have been—by collectors, investors, and those who enjoy living with antiques. The increasing number of folk museums and restorations is another drain, for such places may sell reproductions but not authentic pieces. If not this week, then some day, the Double Nine-Patch quilt handstitched about 1810 and other equally unpretentious furnishings and belongings are certain to rank as important inheritances. And a second look at utensils from a nineteenth-century kitchen may prove them to be as worthwhile from an antique standpoint as the parlor furniture.

# 2

# Furniture and its Background

ANTIQUE FURNITURE all too often is
held in considerable awe. A card table
or a sideboard that has been handed
down through four or five generations
of the same family deserves respect.
In all likelihood, such a piece is still in
excellent condition and can be used
almost as confidently now as it was
150 years ago. Until about 100 years
ago, furniture was made by hand in
cabinetmakers' shops or by carpenters
in new settlements hacked out of the
wilderness. These craftsmen worked
with durable hardwoods, joined them
carefully, and when a more sophisticated society demanded furniture with
decoration, made veneer many times
thicker and stronger than the accepta-
bly good veneer of the present time.

Some antique furniture is worth no
more than the wood out of which it
was made. Age is not necessarily synonymous with quality. There are excellent pieces of 200-year-old furniture in

museums, restorations, and private collections as well as some almost as old
that belong to descendants of the families for whom they were made. Then
again, Great-great-Aunt Abigail's needlepoint footstool or Great-Uncle
Henry's office chair is likely to have
much more sentimental than financial
or museum value.

In one way, it seems as if there should
be a great deal more antique furniture.
Tables, chairs and benches, beds, and
chests and cupboards are the oldest
pieces in general use, and had been
made in one form or another for centuries before Columbus discovered
America. However, the *Mayflower* and
all the ships that brought settlers to
North America during the seventeenth
century had little room for furniture.
Personal necessities were much more
important. As a result, furniture had
to be made in this country from the
earliest days of the Virginia and Massa-

chusetts settlements. This furniture naturally copied the styles with which the settlers had been familiar in the land of their origin.

As the Colonies grew and flourished, furniture was imported from England and, in lesser amounts, from France. English furniture styles always have been most influential in this country. Yet, although the skilled cabinetmakers who emigrated to the Colonies followed current styles in England and Europe, they did not copy them exactly. America has its own heritage of furniture of which it can be proud.

A *walnut table (25½ inches in diameter, 24 inches high) made in New England about 150 years ago shows many characteristics of Queen Anne furniture. The grandmother of the present owner used it as her tea table.*—Ted Eastwood

It is improbable that anyone now will chance upon furniture made in the seventeenth century, and almost as improbable that any eighteenth-century pieces are still to be found and identified. A good many pieces made in the late eighteenth century and in the first half of the nineteenth century are still being used in private homes. By far the greatest amount of eighteenth-century furniture is in museums, restorations, and private collections. Although you are not likely to make such a valuable find, it is desirable to understand the various styles of furniture that predominated after 1650.

Comfortable and graceful Queen Anne furniture was made in England chiefly from 1702 to 1720 and in this country from about 1725 to 1750. However, it is possible to find a tea table or other occasional piece in the style of Queen Anne that was made in this

country as late as the 1850's and 1860's. And, of course, the famous eighteenth-century styles are still being reproduced or adapted by today's furniture manufacturers. A very late Queen Anne piece undoubtedly is the product of a cabinetmaker who produced individual pieces to order in his shop. There are still a few cabinetmakers scattered around the country who make excellent reproductions and do reliable restoring of genuinely old pieces, but by about 1850 furniture began to be mass-produced in factories.

Political events, economics (including prosperity at home and trade with other countries), and the freedom to travel from one country to another influenced the styles of furniture as well as the amount considered essential in a home. Every so often, also, a great furniture designer who introduced new and different-looking pieces established a style and set a period. Between 1700 and 1800, five distinctly different furniture styles prevailed in England and America. The names attached to these styles or periods were sometimes those of the reigning monarchs, sometimes of a furniture designer.

Furniture made in the American Colonies prior to 1700 was influenced by the Jacobean (1603–88) and the William and Mary (1688–1702) periods in England. In this country the William and Mary influence extended to about 1725. Then the Queen Anne style took over until about 1750. By that time

*This walnut side chair, made in New York State before 1800, borrowed its vase-shaped splat from the English Queen Anne style. The straight legs and uprights and the rush seat are typically American.*

Thomas Chippendale's new and different-looking chairs and tables were the vogue in England, but it was at least 1755 before any of Chippendale's designs were copied here, just as it had been about 1725 before the Queen Anne style, popular in England by 1705, was introduced in this country.

The seventeenth-century Jacobean and William and Mary furniture tended to be heavy, almost ponderous. It was made in both England and this country of solid wood, especially oak, although walnut became quite fashionable for William and Mary pieces. Simplicity of structure, straight lines, and squat proportions were typical. Legs were firmly braced with stretchers.

Carving was preferred to inlay and veneer for decoration. Many a Jacobean piece appeared weighted down by its carving. Typical were panels, as on the doors of chests, carved in geometric designs. A variation was strapwork consisting of thin, flat pieces of wood. The backs of chairs also often were solid wood, carved. However, seats might be upholstered with leather or woven pads in England. In this country rush seats were more common.

Beds were monstrous, although how much of this effect was due to the bedstead and how much to the hangings is a question. Never before or since were beds so high as between 1600 and 1660. Hangings were important, and could be drawn to cover the four sides of a bed. Their purpose was to shut out the cold. Truckle or trundle beds, which were low and on wheels so they could be pushed under a bedstead, were made for children and servants. Daybeds were quite another thing and were the forerunners of reclining couches.

Tables were long. The trestle, which is the oldest style of table and goes back to Medieval times, began to have some competition. The gateleg table, a style still popular, was made first during the Jacobean period. Cricket tables with three legs were also new.

Stools perhaps were even more common than chairs. They were made in great numbers and doubled as seats and tables. They were about the height of a chair seat.

Side chairs and armchairs, which were really side chairs with wood arms attached, offered little choice when it came to comfort. In addition to solid-backs, there were slat-back chairs, which had three or more wide and usually shaped wooden pieces horizontally across the back. The banister-back chair had fairly wide vertical slats surmounted by a crest or top rail. Some of these top rails, as well as the banisters, were more richly carved than others.

The latter part of the seventeenth century, technically known as the Restoration period in England, followed by William and Mary, brought lighter and more adaptable furniture. Special turnings, scrolled and more elaborate stretchers, became fashionable. Decorations expanded to include lacquer, marquetry, and some inlay.

The wing chair appeared before 1700; it was probably the first comfortable one and certainly the first upholstered one. The wings attached to the frame of the back served the same purpose as hangings on a bed—that is, they cut off drafts. Earlier, settees had been no

*The banister-back chair gets its name from the upright rails in the high back. The style was popular in the early 1700's; the rockers probably were added around 1800.*

more than wood benches with arms and backs. Between 1660 and 1690, sofas began to have covered arms and backs.

Chairs of all kinds became more important than stools because the new styles transformed them into movable, decorative furniture instead of simple seats. From this time forward, to identify the period to which side chairs or armchairs belong, the characteristics of certain parts must be noted. The shape of the front legs, also the back legs, and the kind of feet were usually typical. Stretchers and their placement are almost as important. Stretchers disappeared during some periods—Chippendale, for instance. The back of a chair and particularly the vertical or horizontal pieces (splats)

*The mahogany desk box shown here, made about 1780, is 19 inches long when opened. The glass shaker for sand (upper left corner) has a silver cover; the inkwell next to it is covered with leather. A similar desk box believed to have belonged to Thomas Jefferson is in the Norfolk (Virginia) Museum.*

and the crest rail were subject to many changes, and are perhaps easiest to keep in mind.

The first desks made during the 1600's were not the furniture that we recognize by that name. Instead, they were large, heavy, slant-top boxes in which writing materials were stored and which provided a writing surface. Desk boxes had a revival in the nineteenth century, when smaller ones were much used by Victorian ladies. The writing or desk box was placed on a stool or small table.

It was 1700 before desks were made to any extent as separate pieces of furniture. First to appear, between 1688 and 1700, was the familiar slant-top desk with a chest of drawers under the hinged top that could be lowered for a writing surface. Then in quick succession came the secretary, which consisted of a slant-top desk topped with a bookcase or cupboard having wood or glass doors, and the kneehole desk with a recess in the center and tiers of drawers on either side.

Secret drawers were built into desks and secretaries. They did not advertise themselves as drawers. The most likely places to discover them are behind the arched tops of pigeonholes, above the center area and concealed by an apron, in the panels or pilasters that flank the open area or behind a small removable cabinet there, or behind pigeonholes and small drawers. To find these hidden compartments, sometimes a sliding panel must be touched. Then again, if a small secret drawer is actually a pilaster flanking the open center area, it need only be pulled out gently.

Chests and cupboards were essential for storage. They were made in great variety, some of the cupboards small enough to hang on the wall. A cupboard is a cabinet, open or closed, for displaying or storing, cups and other articles for household use or ornament. In 1690 the small chests with lids that could be lifted were still important, but the early cupboard was beginning to be superseded by a chest of drawers. This was the forerunner of the bureau as we know it. Chests were made in

*Some mahogany secretaries of the 1750-80 period followed the older custom of having wood instead of glass doors on the cupboard.*

one or two sections, the latter type often called a chest-on-chest. Some chests were on frames with legs that held them well above the floor. Both cupboards and chests often combined drawers and cupboards in one case piece.

The highboy and the lowboy were something new. Highboys and lowboys often resembled each other, but were not always made as matching pieces. Both were made originally for bedrooms. Lowboys originally were dressing tables, but nowadays are as often placed elsewhere in a house.

The highboy consisted of two parts —a chest of drawers and a stand of drawers on legs. The top section of a real highboy was slightly narrower and shallower than the lower part so that it fit inside the raised molding around the top of the base. If there is no molding on the lower section, the two parts were not made as one piece. The lowboy was similar to the base of a highboy, but there is a difference in construction. A real lowboy had a tabletop without the raised molding that was essential to the lower section of a highboy. A true lowboy was smaller, too, and as it was developed to a high art during the 1700's, it became a case piece with a flat surface under which were one to three drawers, the whole mounted on comparatively high legs.

The wing chair, the gateleg table, the highboy, and the lowboy are a few of

**13**

for comfort, and as the century grew older more kinds of furniture were made, more kinds of wood were used, and decoration became more varied. Many of the new styles of tables— they included tea, Pembroke, tripod, card, sewing, serving, and bedside tables, and candlestands — continue to be popular to this day. Innovations appeared in cupboards and chests, and all case pieces — cupboards, chests, wardrobes, highboys, lowboys, desks, and secretaries — were important. Chairs were not only comfortable but also beautiful in a diversity of styles.

The early years from 1702 to 1720 are known as the Queen Anne period. In quick succession followed great furniture designers: Thomas Chippendale (1745–70), George Hepplewhite (1780–90), the Adam brothers (1765–95), and Thomas Sheraton (1790–1810). (The dates are those of their dominance in England.) Each brought distinctive changes in style. Their influence was felt a few years later in this country and continued longer, with American cabinetmakers putting their own individual stamp on the borrowed styles.

*A walnut lowboy made in New England, probably in the early 1800's, by a not-too-skilled craftsman. The style resembles Queen Anne, popular here until 1750, but the type of hardware (oval mounts) is that used after 1790. The mirror is American Empire with turned half-columns.*

the furnishings that can be traced back to seventeenth-century England. The eighteenth century made a great many more contributions. Starting shortly after 1702, furniture began to be made

Queen Anne furniture was lighter in appearance and much more graceful-looking than the ponderous seventeenth-century pieces. Furniture remained functional, however, and also became comfortable. Lines were simple, with emphasis on the curvilinear. The single most important decoration of Queen Anne furniture was

*Slant-top desk of mahogany with fan or shell carving and brass willow mounts was made in Massachusetts in 1802, according to the date written by the cabinetmaker in one of the secret drawers.*
—Ted Eastwood

the carved cockle or scallop shell. Often, one large shell was carved on the slant top of a desk or on the front of a highboy, lowboy, or chest. A smaller shell sometimes was carved on the knee of a cabriole leg and—with or without carving on the legs—to top the splat of a chair or daybed. The shell motif emphasized the curvilinear element. On some pieces, this carved motif is more clearly recognizable as a fan or a sunburst.

Legs on chairs, tables, and case pieces, instead of being turned, were largely cabriole—that is, the leg had an out-curved knee and an incurved ankle. Feet were likely to be the simple pad or Dutch foot, occasionally the drake foot, which was carved with three toes, or the Spanish foot, which curved gracefully and showed rectangular lines

of carving. Stretchers were omitted or else not particularly noticeable. The kettle or bombé base, which swelled outward at sides and front, appeared on cupboards and some other case pieces.

Oak was still widely used in England but walnut became the preferred wood in both England and America. After walnut, cherry and maple rather than oak were the choices in this country. Regardless of the wood, some small amount of Queen Anne furniture was painted white and gilded.

A radically different style of chair appeared that was called the corner or roundabout chair. (It is still being made.) This had a low back that encircled two sides of the seat, the latter placed diagonally so that it formed a right-angled corner. All chairs had a softly curving structure, for they were shaped to fit the body. Side chairs and wooden armchairs often had a high, shaped back with one wide, vase-shaped splat. Such stools as were made followed the styles of chairs.

The drop-leaf table, either oval, round, or rectangular, replaced the trestle table for dining. Dropping the leaves, of course, saved space when they were not in use. Rectangular tables with marble tops were made for dining rooms because, so far, no one had thought of making a sideboard.

Small tables really came into their own. As stools were made less and less, small tables for various purposes came into general use. Work table was a general classification and sewing table, bedside table, serving table, and candlestand were among the specific designations. The corner table was just that, for with the drop leaf lowered the surface was triangular. The half-round table did not have a drop leaf, but it was most convenient alongside a chair or close to a wall.

The new custom of drinking tea, brought from the Orient, made necessary a table to hold the equipment. Some Queen Anne tea tables were rectangular with cabriole legs only slightly swollen at the knees. Other tea tables were low and round with pad feet.

Card or gaming tables were another Queen Anne innovation that continued to be popular for more than a century. By the mid-1700's in this country, it was not uncommon for a household to own a half-dozen or more fine examples of card tables. Each one was well made of selected hardwood and was handsome, for it was part of the furniture of the room at all times. No comparison is possible between this style of table, which has become a classic, and the collapsible bridge table so common today.

All of these card tables, now bonafide antiques, had tops consisting of two leaves that were hinged so that one could be folded on top of the other or be supported against a wall when the table was not in use. Of the

four or occasionally five legs, one was movable to support the folding leaf when the table was opened to full size. The square table with a top 36 to 38 inches when opened flat usually had outrounded corners to hold candlesticks to light the gaming. Some tables also had four oval saucers, one at each player's left, for coins. Occasionally there was a drawer under the top.

The tripod or pedestal table became popular immediately and continued to be so in this country for many years. It had a comparatively small top, usually round or oval, rarely square, supported by a tall pedestal with three feet terminating curving legs. The smallest

*A mahogany tilt table, made in this country before 1800, was put together with handmade nails and has a handmade clamp to adjust the top.*

tripod table became indispensable was that its top usually could be tilted so that the table could be pushed against the wall when it was not needed, and thus save space. Before long, some tripod tables were made with a device under the top that permitted them to be turned or rotated as well as tilted; these were known as "tip and turn" tables.

Chests and cupboards continued to be made in two sections, although single-section ones were still in wide use. In addition to straight cupboards to line up parallel to a wall, the corner cupboard now made its debut. Most of the large cupboards had doors but some had open shelves at least in the top

*After more than 175 years of use in Virginia homes, this mahogany candlestand with its characteristic tripod legs is remarkably unscarred.*

tripod tables became known as candle-stands. Perhaps one reason why the

*Originally intended to serve as a tea table, this tilt-and-turn table with piecrust edge and carved legs ending in claw-and-ball feet is a Chippendale design, made in this country between 1755 and 1790. A rear view shows the mechanism under the top that permits it to be rotated as well as turned.*

section. Highboys and lowboys were made in quantity, usually with cabriole legs and shell carving somewhere.

Desks and secretaries were graceful and often fairly small. Like chests and highboys, they often consisted of two parts. The bureau desk and the desk mounted on a frame with cabriole legs both were fashionable.

The variety of tables, chairs, desks, secretaries, and the like that ornamented the Queen Anne period increased with the emergence of the furniture designers. The most important innovations of the eighteenth century were so soundly and gracefully designed that they are still being copied and reproduced.

Thomas Chippendale's book *The Gentleman and Cabinet Maker's Director,* first published in 1754, was the most important collection of furniture designs that had been issued in England. His furniture enriched England from 1745 to 1770, and his influence was strong in this country from 1755 to 1790. Chippendale brought new and fresh ideas, but above all, his furniture was always carefully fitted and joined. Mahogany, which appeared about 1750, became his favorite wood. At first, it was often finished to resemble walnut, the fashionable wood after 1702.

Chippendale's designs fall into four general styles. One, using such motifs as lions, masques, eggs, and darts, might be called English. For a time, too, many

of Chippendale's pieces borrowed from the rococo appearance of French Louis XV furniture and were really an embellishment of the simpler Queen Anne style by means of elaborate lines and touches. There were also Chippendale pieces that reflected the Chinese, with pagoda motifs, bamboo turnings, the claw-and-ball foot, carved latticework, and considerable lacquering. Others showed the Gothic influence, which was distinguished by pointed arches, quatrefoils, and the fretwork leg.

Carving, which was excellent—deep and sharp—was the chief decorative technique. It was not limited to shell carving but extended to elaborate scrolls, foliage, and gadroons. Gilding, some veneer, and fretwork galleries around small tables and the tops of cabinet pieces were other forms of decoration.

Under Thomas Chippendale's guidance, bedsteads became less pretentious although still handsome. This was the age of the four-post bed, and in this country at least the hangings were not quite so all-enveloping. A short valance began to replace floor-length draperies. Sometimes there was a curtain across the back of the bed and perhaps side curtains at the two rear posts. These beds became known as tester or canopy beds. Sometimes a headboard came into sight.

Chippendale secretaries and desks were handsome. The slant-top desk was made with straight or serpentine front.

**18**

Between 1760 and 1790 in this country, fine cabinetmakers produced kneehole desks and secretaries as well as other case pieces that were truly Chippendale yet had one characteristic that no Chippendale furniture made in England ever had. These were the block fronts, so called because the straight line was broken by large raised panels or blocks rising the full height of the piece. Many of these blocks terminated in a large carved shell the width of the projecting block.

Highboys and corner cupboards as

*This secretary, which could have been made in any prosperous city along the Eastern seaboard between 1760 and 1830, shows Chippendale's influence in the fretwork pediment and willow mounts. Its square bracket feet are as typical as claw-and-ball feet. (The center finial is missing.)*

A *bonnet-top highboy made in New England between 1740 and 1780 has shell carving and willow mounts on the drawers. It is an outstanding example of good proportion and workmanship.*

These as well as other case pieces were as likely to have square bracket feet as claw-and-ball feet. Pitch pediments replaced the flat tops on earlier pieces. These pediments often were elaborately scrolled, as in the bonnet top, or had framed fretwork.

made in this country between 1760 and 1790 established an American Chippendale style. Lowboys were handsome too, but seem not to have been made in equal quantity. At about this time, drawers instead of cupboards were made for the lower section of a cupboard, and the upper section had glass doors. Corner cupboards were made in great quantity here until about 1840.

Dining tables followed the style of those already in use, namely either oval or rectangular drop-leaf. Now they were likely to have cabriole legs ending in claw-and-ball feet. In addition, elaborate rectangular tables with tops of wood or marble and four to six legs also appeared in dining rooms. These were serving tables, for there were no sideboards. Card tables became more common and, if possible, even more handsome when made of mahogany or cherry with Chippendale details. Tea

tables were made in variety. The pedestal or tripod table was likely to be more elaborate, often with carving on the legs and with a molded edge. When the molding was scrolled, the piece was called a piecrust table.

The Pembroke table was first designed by Chippendale. This was an individual style of drop-leaf with an oblong or rectangular fixed center piece with a drawer beneath, and two comparatively narrow drop leaves, either squared or shaped. Still another innovation in small tables on which china was displayed was the fretwork gallery.

Side chairs and armchairs were Chippendale's masterpieces. No one ever did so many things to make them look different. Unbelievable versatility distinguished the backs, which always had a distinctive pattern, and both the vertical-splat back and the ladder back (horizontal splats) came in for new

*The two mahogany side chairs shown here are fine enough to have been made in Philadelphia between 1750 and 1780. The one at the left has details characteristic of Chippendale furniture, but the simplicity of the earlier Queen Anne style distinguishes the one at the right.*

treatment. Some of his elegantly carved ladder-backs are called ribbon-backs. Pierced splats were sometimes carved to produce a distinctly Gothic impression of arches and pillars; others were so intricately carved as to be almost lacy-looking. Uprights were flat, molded, fluted, or carved. The top rail or crest was scrolled and came to points or "ears" at the corners.

Legs of these chairs were cabriole, straight, or fretted. Cabriole legs were at the front; square, outward slanting legs at the rear. Claw-and-ball feet were his great favorite, but he also made a leaf-carved foot. Stretchers disappeared, or if they were used, were recessed. Square seats and rectilinear backs were also Chippendale characteristics.

All Chippendale furniture had a solidity that came from careful fitting and joining. However, decorative details kept it from looking heavy.

The Adam brothers (1765–95) brought a return to the classic lines and classic motifs of Greece and Italy. Robert Adam, the eldest of the four brothers, was primarily an architect. He believed that architecture should be firmly linked with the furniture and decoration of a building, and so it was natural that he design the furniture cabinetmakers made for his buildings. Adam interiors were light, delicate, and graceful, with refined and finished detail. So also was the furniture. The wreath, fan, and honeysuckle, and urns and columns were employed as ornamentation; all were handled with delicate grace. Adam is best remembered in this country for mantels rather than furniture.

In his respect for and handling of classic details, Adam influenced two other great furniture designers—George Hepplewhite (1780–1800) and Thomas Sheraton (1790–1810). Both men published books of designs for their light and delicate-looking yet sturdy pieces. Their ascendency coincided with that of the new United States, where cabinetmakers adapted their ideas with evident enthusiasm.

Hepplewhite created his own hallmarks and contributed certain new pieces to the many homes here that now were quite luxuriously furnished. So did Sheraton. Both designers worked with mahogany, but exotic woods such as satinwood and rosewood appealed to them. Both favored inlay and veneers for decoration. Hepplewhite particularly made exceptional use of inlay. The latter was so firmly applied that it is not unusual to find pieces made about 1800 with little or no inlay missing. By the same token, veneer was so thick that it was slow to blister or crack.

However distinct were certain characteristics—and however individual the contributions—of each of these late-eighteenth-century designers, their styles tended to blend together. Often, details from the designs of both were combined in one piece in America.

Contributing to the grace of Hepplewhite furniture were the square, tapering legs. The shield-shaped back on chairs was one of his trademarks; in some cases, the back was nearly heart-shaped. The graceful oval was almost as typical a Hepplewhite characteristic. Card tables, for example, which heretofore had been square, now became oval. The drop-leaf table not only was longer but also opened to an oval shape. The half-round table, which had been introduced years before, became a work of art. Serpentine fronts were typical on tables and case pieces.

Richly colored mahogany pieces in the Hepplewhite manner were set off with inlay of the lighter-colored satinwood. Thin lines on either side of the square legs or bordering a table were sometimes accented by a simple bellflower motif. Hepplewhite used a good deal

*This mahogany card table, made before 1800, is a New England interpretation of Hepplewhite. Inlay strings the tapering legs and the edge of the top. Light-colored veneer bands the apron and matches the inlaid medallions. The left rear leg swings out to support the leaf when it is lowered.*

*A mahogany side chair, probably made in or near Boston about 1875, has the shield-shaped back with urn and drapery carving typical of Hepplewhite.*

of veneer too. With Sheraton, the carving of mahogany replaced inlay.

Sheraton's designs leaned more toward the rectilinear without losing any delicacy. The backs of his chairs, though no higher than Chippendale's, were rectangular with a carved splat that showed a great deal of openwork or three or four carved columns. A later chair was equally distinctive, for it had a wide top rail and one wide, carved horizontal splat. This sort of chair had what are called saber legs, that is, the front ones flare forward, the rear ones backward. A lyre or drapery—on chairs made in this country, an eagle—frequently was the carved motif.

The pedestals of Sheraton tables were often carved to a lyre or vase shape. Legs were likely to be turned and reeded, and on case pieces half-round pilasters were reeded, or carved in narrow, rounded, vertical and parallel lines, as decoration.

The days of Hepplewhite and Sheraton brought to both England and the United States not only the large dining-room table, usually oval with drop leaves, but also the first sideboards. Sideboards so long that they required

*An American Empire octagonal sewing table (1810-40) has outcurving legs tipped with brass paw mounts. The lower drawer is so finely reeded that it resembles tambour.*

*The half-round table was made of different woods in the city and the country. Country ones were usually pine or maple. This elegant example (24 inches long, 12¼ deep, and 23¾ high) was made of mahogany with inlay of lighter colored wood, after the manner of Hepplewhite.* —Ted Eastwood

eight legs often displayed a pair of carved wood urns. These were for storing the silver tableware when not in use. A knife box, also for silver storage, had a top or lid with a slanting front. Urns and knife boxes were generally made of mahogany. The urns were so difficult to carve that only the finest craftsmen could attempt them, and fewer were made in this country than in England.

Hepplewhite and Sheraton continued to make all the kinds of tables that had been introduced earlier in the century, but with their own particular style marks. Card tables were made in greater number than ever before, and

the array of other small tables was increased by their introduction of what became known as a work table and in particular a sewing table. Several quite distinct types of sewing tables appeared in this country starting about 1800. These small tables were oval, rectangular, or octagonal, with two or more drawers, often a top that lifted, and sometimes with a tambour front. After 1800, a few sewing tables had a silk bag fastened to the underside. Bedside tables were much simpler but ever so convenient.

Sheraton also was responsible for the drum table, a style still popular. This was a pedestal table with a round deep top in which there were drawers.

The tambour, which appeared on some sewing tables after 1800, was first introduced by Hepplewhite on a desk. A tambour is a flexible sliding shutter made of slender strips of wood, rounded

*A tambour desk, made early in the 1800's in the Hepplewhite style, has a hinged leaf that is supported by slides flanking the top drawer when it is opened for writing. Note the corner chair with cabriole legs* (at the left) *and the sewing table with a bag underneath* (at the right).

on the face, which have been glued to a coarse fabric or canvas backing. (A wood strip may occasionally fall off an old tambour, but it can be glued firmly in place with a modern adhesive.) Hepplewhite's desk had a tambour that concealed the cabinet above the writing surface. Instead of a slant top that could be lowered, the tambour desk had a flat leaf that folded over, and could be supported on slides when opened to provide an adequate writing surface. Secretaries also were made with tambours. Much larger were the bookcases with drawers or drawers and cupboards beneath, and three or four glass doors above to protect the shelves of books.

A graceful tambour roll-top desk also appeared, but few examples remain, chiefly those made in Philadelphia and Baltimore. The cylinder-top desk or secretary, which had been introduced in England early in the century, was made to some extent in America at this time but never became really popular here until Victorian days.

Still another new and different type of desk was the fall-front bureau desk. When closed, this looked as though it were a chest of drawers. What appeared to be the top and deepest drawer was a hinged front that could be let down for a writing surface. Pigeonholes and small drawers were arranged behind the fall front. The drawers below the writing leaf might be graduated in size.

Sheraton also made use of tambours,

*A bureau-desk, with a fall-front top "drawer" that makes a writing surface. It is a Hepplewhite style made in this country between 1795 and 1815.*

but a credit that is wholly his own is the chest of drawers with an attached mirror. This, of course, is still being made although not always in as graceful a manner as Sheraton's. It has been said that Sheraton was responsible for twin beds. Be that as it may, both Hepplewhite and Sheraton continued to make canopy beds.

In France, furniture had been changing almost as much as in England and often along the same lines. French periods are differentiated according to monarchs. Thus, Louis XIV (1643–1715) was grand and massive, as was Jacobean furniture in England. It was carved, gilded, and displayed marquetry. Louis XV (1715–74) was a rococo period with its curves, scrolls, and bold

decoration. Chippendale borrowed some of his rococo effects from this furniture. Louis XVI (1774–93) made use of straighter lines and classic motifs, as did Adam and Hepplewhite in England, but the French versions were much more elaborate.

French Provincial furniture incorp rated characteristics and offered piec of the Louis XV period. It was ir way a simple adaptation of elabor; court furniture. Instead of the exo woods such as mahogany used to ma furniture for palaces, Provincial pie were made of native woods, includi fruitwoods such as cherry or pear. T Louis XV cabriole leg became a simpl one on Provincial furniture, usually lacking the carving. Elaborate brass or bronze decoration was reduced to simple grilles on Provincial pieces, mar quetry and inlay were not seen, ar hand decoration in gilt or pastel colc gave way to white, gray, or pas; paint.

Upholstery, soft and luxurious, was typical of Provincial as of other Frer furniture. The upholstered chair w arms and back in one piece, called bergère, and the chair with open ar and upholstered back and seat, know as a fauteuil, were found in both Lo XV and Provincial. So were the chai longue, the closed secretary and fla writing table, and the commode that also could serve as a table.

During the 1700's, some cabinetmakers in America made such unusually fine pieces of furniture that their names still live. They did not originate a style in the sense that Chippendale, Hepplewhite, or Sheraton did, but they did adapt the current English designs, as these were imported here, to their clients' way of living and the available materials. If one word can distinguish American period furniture from the English, it is simplicity. These American cabinetmakers, who had learned their trade in their native countries, would—and did—carve perfect shells, graceful, ribbon-back chairs, and bonnet-top pediments. However, the decoration as well as the lines of the pieces made here inclined toward simplification.

Mahogany, which was made popular by Chippendale, was used in this country too after about 1750. Walnut continued to be used, and toward the end of the century cherry became a favorite. Curly maple made handsome veneer.

Beds perhaps illustrate better than any other piece of furniture the simplicity that became characteristic of even the finest style here. However much carving was done on chair backs and chests, beds were relatively simple. In the small, new houses that settlers built there was no room for towering beds with heavy hangings. A bed was likely to have fairly plain posts and even a headboard. As cities and even settlements became prosperous and some citizens quite wealthy, larger and more handsomely equipped houses were built. By 1750, more of the tall four-post beds were being made. Posts were more slender even though they were modestly carved in the Queen Anne or Chippendale manner. The pencil-post bed was a New England contribution which had quite plain and very slender, tapering posts.

Between 1740 and 1780, Philadelphia was the wealthiest city in the Colonies. It is not surprising that it was here the field or tent bed with its arching canopy was made first. Later this style also was made in New England. Excellent furniture was made in Philadelphia again during the Federal period. At this time Henry Connolly and Ephraim Haines produced pieces distinctly influenced by Sheraton, notably with reeded legs. Their furniture was

*A mahogany bed with low, pineapple-topped carved posts, spirally turned legs, and spiral carving on the headboard and footboard is American Empire, made after 1825. This bed was purchased at a sale held at Monticello in Charlottesville, Virginia, in the 1890's to aid in the restoration of Thomas Jefferson's home.*

as fine, although less has been heard about it, as Duncan Phyfe's furniture made in New York. Yet the style points on furniture made in the two cities were quite different.

Philadelphia first became famous for its furniture because such skilled cabinetmakers as Benjamin Randolph and William Savery maintained business there between 1750 and 1780. The highboys from their shops incorporated Chippendale characteristics and were as handsome as anything that was made by Chippendale himself. In fact, Philadelphia highboys set a new standard for this piece of furniture.

Highboys continued to be made in America throughout the eighteenth century, although they had fallen out of favor in England during the days of Chippendale. Chest-on-chests also were popular in this country and cabinetmakers in every locality made them. No one could ever count the number of corner cupboards made in America, and many of them, in their excellence of proportion and detail, rank with the Philadelphia highboys.

*A walnut corner cupboard like this one, made in New England about 1800, could have been made anywhere east of the Mississippi River. Rat-tail hinges secure the glass door, H-hinges the wooden doors.*

Case pieces with block fronts were never made in England. They originated in New England. Many of these are credited to John Goddard, a cabinetmaker in Newport, Rhode Island, between 1748 and 1783, and the Townsend family who worked in Newport from 1700 until 1765. After the Revolution, Newport's prosperity declined while that of Boston and Salem, Massachusetts, and Portsmouth, New Hampshire, increased. So in the last years of the eighteenth century, it was in these places that outstanding furniture was produced. Samuel McIntire, who worked in Salem, was both an architect and a carver; Benjamin Frothingham

The solid-wood drawer fronts on this maple bureau made in western Massachusetts around 1800 were doubtless chosen for their interesting grain. The corners of the top are outcurved to fit over the spirally and vertically reeded legs, which extend the full height. Similar bureaus sometimes have only the front legs reeded.

was a cabinetmaker worth remembering in Charlestown, Massachusetts.

Distinguished furniture was made in New England throughout the 1700's, starting with restrained pieces in the Queen Anne style. And furniture production was not confined to the seacoast cities. In the previous century Nicholas Disbrowe had made a name for himself in Hartford, Connecticut, and not far away in East Windsor, after the Revolution, the Chapins were at work. Middletown was another well-known Connecticut furniture center. In western Massachusetts, William Lloyd produced inlaid sideboards that were as fine as those made in Baltimore. Cherry was a favorite wood of

Connecticut cabinetmakers throughout the eighteenth century, and when inlay became fashionable toward its close, boxwood and satinwood were combined with the cherry.

Albany, New York, and Lancaster, Pennsylvania, were other notable inland centers. After 1790, the Hepplewhite and Sheraton influences on furniture-making appeared in Ohio and west to the Mississippi River.

Wealthy planters in Virginia and other southern states probably imported more furniture then did those who lived farther north. Some amount also was made on their own plantations.

A mahogany bureau with an overhanging top drawer and columns flanking the three drawers underneath. The three small drawers recessed on the top are 4¼ inches high and 11¾ inches deep. This piece was made in New England during the American Empire period (1815-40); although the willow mounts belong to an earlier period, they are the original ones on the bureau.—Ted Eastwood

However, Thomas Elfe, another follower of Chippendale, worked in Charleston, South Carolina, between 1755 and 1775.

*Cherry drop-leaf dining table (1820-40) with spiral and ring turnings on the legs. There is a drawer underneath at one end.*

Baltimore and Annapolis sparked an interest in fine furniture by Maryland craftsmen from about 1790 to 1815. Of the many cabinetmakers kept busy in this area, John Shaw is one of the few whose name is still recognized. Furniture made for Maryland families followed the styles of Hepplewhite and Sheraton and was rich with inlay. It was here that the petaled bellflower was used so much to accent the lines of light-colored wood inlay. Sideboards and card tables were made of mahogany and inlaid with light-colored box-

wood and holly. Considerable satinwood inlay and veneer also were used. The secretaries and desks were notable.

By the 1790's, the young United States began to use furniture that was distinctly American and is now generally referred to as Federal. From 1790, give or take a year or two, to about 1820 furniture made here derived from both Hepplewhite and Sheraton as well as from the Regency period (1810–30) in England. Then, about 1805, for the first time, French furniture styles became influential here. After all, France had supported the Colonies during the Revolution. The Directoire (1795–1805) and Empire (to 1815), which brought great changes in France, brought changes here too.

Whatever the name given to the period in each of the three countries, the furniture in all of them showed classic lines and motifs. Darker woods and brass trim became noticeable. In this country the eagle — carved, painted, gilded, or inlaid—crowned all possible pieces. Yet the three feathers of the Prince of Wales were sometimes the

*A cordial chest, made not later than 1800, with deep drawers for bottles flanking the cupboard for storing glasses. The wood is mahogany, with light-colored veneer around the drawers, the cupboard, and above the legs, and with inlay stringing on the legs.*

motif for carving, borrowed from the Regency in England. Sheraton's straight lines dominated the early Federal period from the 1790's to about 1815. Thereafter, until 1840, Federal pieces took on the heavier aspect of French Empire.

The Directoire years in France were inspired by ancient Greece. Legs of both tables and chairs were abruptly curved and usually splayed. The arms and backs of sofas and settees followed the scroll line. Columns, turned or reeded, were incorporated into beds, bureaus, and sideboards. Decorative motifs were classical in origin—the lyre and the swan, for instance. Brass mounts, feet, and ornaments also became stylish.

During the ten years of the Empire period in France, furniture became heavier, almost massive. Napoleon's personal insignia—the bee, the crown, the laurel wreath, and the letter "N" —were worked in somehow as ornaments. A new style of draping beds followed the crown motif. Tables were supported by heavy pedestals, turned or carved to represent a lyre. The columns on tables and case pieces were bronze, marble, or wood (usually wood in America). Ornament often was wood carved and gilded to look like metal.

One of this country's finest cabinetmakers, Duncan Phyfe, who worked in New York City from about 1790 to 1847, illustrates the transition from true Federal (1800 to 1815) to American Empire (to 1840). Phyfe is one

*The corner cupboard of cherry shown here, made in Ohio between 1815 and 1840, is wider, heavier, and less well-proportioned than many. The small cupboards below have brass knobs.*

American cabinetmaker whose name is still a household word. Today, it is often applied to reproductions that follow the general lines of the original furniture he made.

Duncan Phyfe's furniture always showed excellent workmanship with fine woods. (Mahogany, incidentally, was the chief wood of the Federal and Empire periods, with cherry a close second in this country.) Typical of all his work were simple and often scrolled lines, carved eagles and classic ornaments such as the lyre and acanthus leaf, and metal mounts. Brass stars were another of his decorations.

Phyfe's tables and sofas are perhaps best remembered and most often reproduced. Both his drop-leaf and card tables might be supported by an eagle with outspread wings, a lyre, or a substantial pedestal base. The splats in the backs of side chairs and armchairs and the arms of chairs and sofas often were carved with lyres. The backs of side chairs usually curved.

Sometimes Duncan Phyfe is credited mistakenly with furniture that actually was made by Charles Honoré Lannuier, a French émigré who worked in New

*Found in an attic in the 1920's, this mahogany sideboard was covered by seven coats of paint of various colors. It was made in New Hampshire around 1830 or 1840. Note the spirally turned half-columns flanking the cupboard doors.*

York City from 1805 to 1819. Lannuier followed French Directoire patterns much more closely than did Phyfe. For one thing, he used considerably more brass and gilded ornament, even on card tables.

Many other excellent cabinetmakers were kept busy in New York after 1800, for this now was a bustling place. Furniture almost as excellent as that of Phyfe and Lannuier was turned out by Michael Allison, George Woodruff, and John Dolan, among others. They also made use of the eagle, lyre, carved drapery, and the acanthus. Sofas with carved panels and chairs with carved backs reflected the slender lines of Sheraton, with classic decoration. Like Phyfe, these other cabinetmakers turned out tables of various kinds in profusion, with card, drum, and Pembroke styles most popular.

The Empire style pretty much took over the United States during the 1820's and 1830's. Chairs never did become as massive as the true Empire ones in France, but other pieces became heavier and more imposing-looking. The darkness of mahogany and mahogany veneer contributed to the look of weightiness. So did the addition of half-columns and ogee moldings for decoration. Bureaus and sideboards featured an overhanging drawer, with columns or molding flanking the two or three recessed drawers below it.

Empire armchairs had scrolled or curved arms. Legs were much simpler

*A miniature mahogany chest (circa 1830) with the top drawer overhanging the lower ones may have been a journeyman cabinetmaker's sample or a piece of toy furniture. It is 14 inches high by 14¾ inches wide and 8½ inches deep.*—Ted Eastwood

*Casters have replaced the original feet on a chest of mahogany veneer made in Prince Edward County, Virginia, around 1840. New drawer pulls also were added. The American Empire mirror with mahogany frame has new, not the original, glass.*

than during the eighteenth century, but often they were saber legs. Sometimes legs were spirally reeded or acanthus-carved. Brass paw mounts often tipped legs of chairs and tables. One typical side chair had a wide, solid splat that was fiddle-shaped. The curule chair or bench, patterned after a camp stool with curved legs, was an innovation in the Empire period of France and Regency of England and was copied to some extent here.

In Empire beds, headboards and footboards were the same height. Low posts instead of high posts made their appearance. Some beds were built with only two posts, which were on the side away from the wall. This style in France usually had crown draping. In the United States, the sleigh bed was a simpler version of the elaborate Napoleon bed. The sleigh bed had headboard and footboard of the same height, and followed the outlines of the horse-drawn sleigh.

*An Empire side chair of Honduras mahogany with fiddle-shaped splat, made in New England between 1830 and 1840.*

*This small table with top, leaves, pedestal, and plinth of solid mahogany and curved drawer fronts of mahogany veneer is an Empire style made in the 1830's. Simple refinishing brought it to its present gleaming condition.*—Ted Eastwood

The hardware used on furniture of the American Empire period was as different as that of each of the eighteenth-century periods or styles. Wooden knobs were common on drawers and cupboards made in America, but brasses were typical of both seventeenth- and eighteenth-century furniture. For example, William and Mary pieces had, attached to the wood, a small brass plate or escutcheon from which hung a small brass drop to be used as a pull. During the Queen Anne period, the brass plate became larger and a metal loop or bail was attached to it. Some of these plates are called "bat's wing" because of their shape.

Chippendale hardware, as befitted his furniture, was more decorative. One style widely used in America as well

as in England was the "willow" plate with a scrolled outline. Bails were attached by means of two small round or oval plates.

The hardware used on Hepplewhite and Sheraton as well as Federal pieces consisted of an oval or octagonal plate stamped with a design. Oval mounts had shallowly curved bails, and octagonal mounts had shaped bails, which were usually six-sided. The oval plates sometimes were plain with a molded rim and a molded oval medallion in the center. Plain ovals sometimes had a beaded edge. Then again, oval mounts would have an embossed design, most often of an eagle with stars or perhaps a sheaf of wheat or

*Spirally turned legs distinguish a small drop-leaf table, circa 1820. It was used by its original owners as a sewing table.*

an acorn with oak leaves. The eagle with stars also was the favorite design for octagonal mounts.

Two rosettes holding a bail were used in New England and elsewhere from 1750 onward. Rosettes were either plain or scrolled.

The French influence, which began here in the early nineteenth century, brought in pendent ring pulls. These were brass and consisted either of a rosette or a lion's head with a ring hanging from it. By the 1820's, knobs were coming back into fashion. On heavy mahogany pieces with Empire lines, large polished wooden knobs were appropriate. Knobs of brass and of pressed glass also were used to some extent here.

It has often been said that cabinetmakers occasionally dated their furniture by means of the hardware—that

is, by the oval or octagonal plates decorated with an eagle or stars. Count the number of stars, each one representing a state; the piece of furniture is said to have been made during the years when there were that many states in the Union. In truth, an eagle with thirteen stars was used decoratively for many years longer than there were only thirteen states.

On the other hand, more than thirteen stars may well date the furniture. A sideboard in the Hepplewhite manner with oval plates embossed with an eagle and fifteen stars could well have been made between the years 1792 and 1796.

The number of panes of glass in the doors of a cupboard is also said to be a clue to the time when it was made, but there is little basis for believing this. Cupboards with thirteen panes of glass in each door, presumably indi-

*A brass drawer pull displaying an eagle and fifteen stars, which was used on a sideboard made in the Hepplewhite style, in western Massachusetts. Oval mounts with or without designs were common from 1785 to 1800 or a little later.*

*A drawer pull from a high chest made in New Hampshire. Notice the eagle surmounted by thirteen stars; also the shaped bail or loop. Pulls like this one were commonly used from 1785 into the 1830's.*

cating that they were made during the years when there were thirteen colonies or states, are less common than case pieces with thirteen stars on the hardware. The arrangement of small panes in various geometrical shapes started with as few as six or eight panes and went on to eleven, twelve, and up to seventeen. If there were only six or eight panes, they were likely to be square ones. When the number was larger, the panes were cut in various shapes to work out intricate arrangements.

Hinges are less noticeable than other hardware. However, some of them are worth noticing. The strap hinge was an early design used on the outside of cupboards and the inside of chests. Butterfly hinges were early too, and may be found on cupboards, slant-top desks, and tables. Look also for rat-tail hinges on cupboards. The name came from the shape of the long supporting bracket for a simple hinge leaf. Incidentally, on furniture made before 1815 the screws were handmade.

Once in a while, a family changed the hardware on a piece of furniture to conform to the latest style. Where this was done, the holes for the original hardware can usually still be detected, even though they were filled in at the time. At the present, all period styles of brasses and hinges are being reproduced carefully.

Often, furniture is believed by its owners to be much older than it actually is.

In some instances pieces have come to be accepted as originals. A case in point is a desk donated for the current restoration of the White House in Washington, D.C., which was revealed in 1962 to have been misdated. When it was accepted, the desk was believed to be an early-nineteenth-century piece made by a Baltimore cabinetmaker. It took close and repeated examination by a group of experts in antique furniture to decide that it was a skillful copy, made *circa* 1880, of an earlier style of desk. It is still an antique and still valuable, although it has been downgraded, particularly in price.

A few misnomers are being used constantly. It's hard to say how or why these incorrect names were acquired, but habit has pretty well fixed them now. A prime example is the Governor Winthrop desk. The term "Governor Winthrop" is generally applied to a good-sized slant-top desk, often with brass willow mounts. The slant-top desk was being made in England, but probably not in America, in 1707 when the last of three Colonial governors named Winthrop died. The Martha Washington sewing table really should be classified as Sheraton or perhaps Federal; it is even quite possible that it was made in this country too late for Martha Washington to have owned one. This is the table with semicircular ends flanking the legs and with the top hinged so that it can be opened at the ends. Reproductions often have plain wood sides, but the originals made around 1800 were either reeded wood or covered with silk. On the other hand, the Martha Washington chair takes its name from a chair with upholstered back and seat and open wooden arms that was in her home, Mount Vernon.

It takes years of experience, observation, study, and training to differentiate between an antique and a faithful reproduction. Some characteristics, however, cannot be reproduced. Perhaps the most unmistakable one is patina. This is a mellowing of the surface acquired by wood through age, use, dusting, and polishing. True patina is nonexistent on furniture only a few years old. Although fine mahogany, cherry, or maple, recently milled, may look handsome, they lack the glow that comes with a century or more of use. The tone or color of course varies

*An old mahogany drop-leaf table makes a handsome end table today. The drawer, its front shaped to an ogee curve, has no pull but is opened by means of the groove carved beneath it.*

with the wood, but the bloom grows with age and handling. Restoring and refinishing always must be done carefully to avoid damaging the patina.

The natural aging of wood contributes greatly to its patina. Backboards and drawers made of soft woods also color as they age. When they are taken out, the upper drawers may still be light-colored because they were protected. But the backboards and the bottom of the lowest drawer, which have been exposed, will have darkened and mellowed to a soft shade of brown. Again, this darkening cannot be reproduced or faked by applying stain.

Normal signs of wear, which are to be expected, do not reduce the value of antique furniture. Loose bits of veneer, inlay, or molding, for instance, are not unusual. Carving done long ago will not be as sharp as it was originally, and the edges of a piece, particularly at the corners, will be slightly round instead of angled. Any surface may have been scarred inadvertently by dusting or polishing. Tabletops as well as feet and legs may show dents and bruises, and stretchers of chairs undoubtedly will be worn down across the top. Table leaves that were made of single boards will have warped and the circular tops of tilt tables shrunk.

The existence of these and other signs of wear are a pretty good indication that a piece of furniture is old and probably antique. When the sum total amounts to no more than minor damage, the value remains high. Excessive damage naturally reduces the possible selling price.

When it came to construction, cabinetmakers worked pretty much in the same way. Easiest to recognize are their methods of joining, in particular the mortise and tenon and the dovetail. Widely used as they were, these two vary in quality of workmanship. Allowance must be made, however, for the fact that the individual parts of joinings were larger and fitted more loosely before about 1725. The more general use of glue thereafter permitted smaller units and tighter fitting. Regionally, the most skilled of cabinetmakers varied somewhat in their methods of joining.

Marks made by certain tools also aid in the identification of antiques. If the slight ridges and hollows made by a hand plane cannot be seen, they can sometimes be felt. Saw marks looking like parallel scratches may still be evident on backboards and the interior of drawers that were left rough-finished. Flat and curved gouging chisels left their traces on the undersides of tables, on the framework of upholstered chairs and sofas, and on certain types of side chairs. The scribing awl, used to lay out work, also left its traces. All of these are unmistakable to the person who knows what to look for!

To sum up: A piece of genuinely antique furniture certainly will show some signs of wear. The details of its construction and any tool marks are important clues, at least to whether it was produced by a cabinetmaker during the 1700's or by machinery after 1850. Above all, the wood of antique furniture will show a patina that is both mellow and softly gleaming.

After these four points—patina, normal signs of wear, construction, and tool marks—have been noted, the state of preservation should also be considered, for it too contributes to the value of a piece. The need for major restoration diminishes value. A few of the restorations rated as major, which often are needed, are replacement of feet, legs, interior drawers, the top or any leaves of a table. Also major would be an almost complete restoration of veneer or a great deal of inlay. You may wish to have any such necessary work done by a qualified cabinetmaker. However, the amount, kind, and quality of the restoration work affects the value when you sell.

Combining a top and base that were not made originally to go together is another example of downgrading and reduction in value. Construction details will easily prove whether the two sections belong together. This kind of thing occurs with highboys, corner cupboards, chest-on-chests, and other two-piece units.

The general tendency is to overvalue antiques—except by those people who wouldn't have a piece of antique furniture in their homes at any price. Well-known names enhance value: A highboy authenticated as having been made by Benjamin Randolph of Philadelphia is considerably more valuable than one by an unknown cabinet-maker, however good his work, across the river in Trenton. A Philadelphia highboy would be appraised at—and could be sold for—several thousand dollars. In fact, any eighteenth-century highboy would have to be in awfully bad condition to be worth less than $500.

A sideboard made by William Lloyd in Springfield, Massachusetts, probably could be valued at as much as $3,000. On the other hand, a sideboard made at approximately the same time by a less gifted cabinetmaker in western Massachusetts or southern New Hampshire is likely to be worth somewhere between $500 and $1,000. Both sideboards are almost certain to have square, tapering legs and inlay in the manner of Hepplewhite, but the one by the unknown cabinetmaker undoubtedly would have poorer over-all proportions and less skillfully wrought details. However good the condition of an American Empire sideboard, this later piece will fall somewhere between $300 and $1,000.

Excellent examples of American Chippendale chairs may be valued at $1,000 or more, but a crude one may be worth less than $100. An American Empire side chair may be worth anything from a few dollars to about $150. All of them are salable.

The antique dealer who offers you $3,000 for a Lloyd sideboard probably has a customer in mind who would be interested in buying it. Should you postpone selling and approach him a few months later, his offer may no longer be open simply because the customer has found something else, or he may ask for time to interest someone in the piece. The appraised valuation of any piece of antique furniture is a sound one if it has been stated by an expert in the style of furniture. By all means, ask the expert to write out and date his appraisal. However, it is not always possible to sell in the open market for the same amount.

Since American Empire furniture is not considered stylish at present (1963), the market for it is so poor that it's hard to obtain any prices for it. In spite of the fact that many pieces are distinguished as well as practical, and were made from handsome mahogany or cherry, they would probably have to be sold now for much less than their appraised value. This picture can change at a whim in a few years.

On the other hand, Jacobean furniture imported from England finds a ready market. It sells for considerably less than eighteenth-century furniture made in this country after the fashions of Chippendale and Hepplewhite.

| PERIOD | CHARACTERISTICS | NEW PIECES |
|---|---|---|
| Jacobean<br>   1603–60<br>Restoration<br>   1660–88 | Heavy and ponderous<br>Straight lines<br>Squat proportions<br>Carving, strapwork, and<br>  paneling | Gateleg table |
| William and Mary<br>   1688–1702<br>United States<br>   1700–1725 | Turnings<br>Scrolling<br>Lacquer<br>Marquetry<br>Inlay | Wing chair<br>Slant-top desk<br>Secretary<br>Highboy and Lowboy<br>2-section chests |
| Queen Anne<br>   1702–20<br>United States<br>   1725–50 | Curvilinear and graceful<br>Shell or fan carving<br>Cabriole leg | Kneehole desk<br>Corner chair<br>Tables: drop leaf, tea, corner,<br>  card, tripod |
| Chippendale<br>   1745–70<br>United States<br>   1755–90 | Excellent construction<br>Varied carving<br>Veneer, gilding, and fretwork<br>Pitched pediment on tall pieces<br>Cabriole legs, often carved<br>Claw-and-ball, also bracket feet | Block-front desks, secretaries,<br>  etc. (America only)<br>Pembroke table |
| Hepplewhite<br>   1780–90<br>United States<br>   1785–1800 | Graceful with emphasis on the<br>  oval<br>Serpentine fronts on tables and<br>  case pieces<br>Square tapering legs<br>Inlay and veneer | Large dining tables<br>Sideboards<br>Desks: fall-front and tambour<br>Sewing table, bedside and<br>  other small tables<br>Field or tent bed |
| Sheraton<br>   1790–1810<br>United States<br>   1795–1815 | Rectilinear and graceful<br>Veneer<br>Carving more important than<br>  inlay<br>Reeding, especially of legs, and<br>  half-round columns | Drum table<br>Chest of drawers with<br>  attached mirror |
| United States:<br>   Federal: 1800–1815<br>England: Regency<br>   1810–30<br>France: Directoire<br>   1795–1805<br>   Empire: 1804–14 | Classic lines and motifs<br>Brass trim, including feet<br>Eagle, stars, three feathers,<br>  chief decorations here | Pier tables |

| CHANGES IN OLD | CHAIRS | HARDWARE |
|---|---|---|
| Stools more common than chairs | Slat-back with horizontal, shaped splats<br>Banister-back with vertical, turned spindles<br>Solid carved back<br>Stout stretchers | Wood knobs |
| Chairs became important<br>Lighter and more adaptable<br>Chests of drawers as important as cupboards | High backs<br>Some banister-backs, others upholstered | Wood knobs<br>Small brass plate, drop pulls |
| Stools less common<br>Comfort stressed<br>Kettle base on cupboards and case pieces<br>Tripod tables had tilt tops | Shaped back and arms<br>High backs<br>One wide splat, vase-shaped | Brass plates, some bat's wing<br>Metal loops |
| Bedsteads less pretentious, 4-post<br>Serpentine front<br>Piecrust edge on tripod tables<br>Fretwork, galleries, on small tables<br>Stretchers less important | Back most distinctive and varied: carved and pierced splat, ribbon-backs, fret-back, Gothic arch<br>Crest rail scrolled, with "ears"<br>Seat square, back rectangular | Scrolled "willow" plate or fretted plate<br>Brass loop<br>Rosettes with bail |
| Card tables oval rather than rectangular | Backs shield-shaped, less often heart-shaped or oval<br>Openwork carving includes drapery, urn, eagle, vines | Oval plates, plain or with beaded edge<br>Molded oval medallion or design of eagle, stars, sheaf of wheat<br>Metal loops |
| Card tables rectangular, many with pedestal bases<br>Diversity of small tables<br>Upholstered sofas with wood back panel and arms | Backs rectangular with carved vertical or horizontal splat<br>Carving: drapery, urn, lyre, eagle<br>Saber legs | Octagonal brass plates<br>Designs as above<br>Shaped handles |
| Tables supported by eagle or lyre pedestal<br>Sofas with scrolled arms | Backs curved outward<br>Back splats carved | Octagonal plates as above<br>Rosettes or lion's head with brass ring |

| PERIOD | CHARACTERISTICS | NEW PIECES |
|---|---|---|
| American Empire 1815–40 | Ball feet or brass paws Columns and molding for decoration | Curule chairs Sleigh bed |

# GLOSSARY

*Apron:* also called a skirt; a crosspiece of wood placed at the bottom of bureaus, chests, and other case pieces, also under a tabletop between the legs, and under the seats of chairs.

*Bergère:* an armchair with arms and back in one piece.

*Cabinetmaker:* a craftsman whose occupation is the making of fine furniture.

*Cabriole:* a leg curved outward at the knee, inward above the ornamental foot.

*Canopy:* the covering fixed over a bed and attached to the four posts.

*Cant:* the angle, slant, or slope as of a chair leg.

*Case pieces:* furniture with a case or frame, such as chests, bureaus, desks, highboys, and the like.

*Chair:* a movable seat, usually for one person. The parts of a chair are the seat, legs and possibly stretchers between the legs, the back with spindles or splats and a top or crest rail. A chair may or may not have arms.

*Crest:* the top rail of a chair back, or the highest part as of a mirror frame.

*Escutcheon:* the protective metal which is applied to a surface.

shield, usually ornamental, around a keyhole or serving as the back plate of a handle.

*Fauteuil:* an armchair with open arms and upholstered back and seat.

*Finial:* the ornament (often urn-shaped) that tops an architectural detail such as a pediment or the uprights of the back of a chair.

*Fretwork:* wood cut in an ornamental openwork pattern.

*Gadroon:* an ornamental edging made by carving a rounded molding, for instance with fluting.

*Gallery:* a railing of metal or wood, usually ornamental.

*Hardware:* the metal parts on a piece of furniture, also known as mounts. It includes handles or drawer pulls, which consist of a brass plate or escutcheon fastened to the wood, from which hangs either a drop or a metal loop called a bail. Also included are keyhole escutcheons and the metal mounts, if any, on feet.

*Inlay:* light-colored wood inserted into a surface for decoration.

*Kettle:* outward curving, as of sides and front of case pieces; also Bombé.

*Marquetry:* a decorative design of inlay in more than one color of wood.

*Skirt:* see Apron.

| CHANGES IN OLD | CHAIRS | HARDWARE |
|---|---|---|
| Beds: headboards and footboards same height<br>Tables: heavily carved pedestals<br>Chests and sideboards with overhanging top drawer and corner columns | Scrolled or curved arms<br>Legs reeded, acanthus carved; also saber<br>Side chairs with fiddle-back | Rosettes or lion's head with ring<br>Wooden knobs<br>Brass paw mounts tipped the legs |

*Mounts:* the decorative metal details on furniture (see Hardware).

*Pedestal:* a central support, as for a table.

*Pediment:* the ornamental, pitched top on a high piece of furniture such as a corner cupboard. It may have a scrolled or triangular outline, broken in the center.

*Piecrust table:* table with a raised rim that is carved and scrolled.

*Pilaster:* a rectangular or half-round column attached as an upright.

*Plinth:* the lowest member of a base, as the block of wood between the pedestal and feet on a table.

*Rail:* a horizontal connecting and supporting piece.

*Rake:* the inclination, slope, or angle of a chair leg.

*Reeding:* carving in a series of small, convex moldings.

*Rung:* one of the rounds of a chair or ladder.

*Saber:* descriptive term for the legs of a chair whose front legs curve forward, rear legs curve back.

*Slat:* a thin, narrow horizontal piece.

*Splats:* the flat thin pieces of a chair back, either vertical or horizontal.

*Stile:* an upright piece in framing or paneling into which secondary pieces are joined.

*Strapwork:* narrow bands of wood applied as ornament.

*Stretcher:* a horizontal piece connecting and supporting the legs of a chair or table.

*Stringing:* the arrangement of inlay in straight, parallel lines.

*Tambour:* a flexible, sliding shutter of slender strips of wood glued to coarse fabric.

*Tester:* the canopy over a bed.

*Turning:* the shaping of wood, often to display such decorative forms as ring, vase, etc.

*Uprights:* the vertical parts of a chair back, particularly the two outer pieces of wood.

*Veneer:* a thin sheet of wood, often chosen for its grain or markings, glued onto other wood for a decorative surface.

## FOR FURTHER INFORMATION:

AMERICAN FURNITURE by Helen Comstock. New York: Viking Press (A Studio Book).

FIELD GUIDE TO EARLY AMERICAN FURNITURE by Thomas F. Ormsbee. New York: Bantam Books.

FINE POINTS OF FURNITURE (*Early American*) by Albert Sack. New York: Crown Publishers, Inc.

# 3

## Country Furniture

IT HARDLY SEEMS possible that there were as many cobbler's benches in use between 1700 and 1900 as are serving as coffee tables nowadays. Their popularity is a good omen for the simpler types of old tables, as well as the appealing painted chairs and interesting cupboards, that everyone finds sometime and somewhere. Look again at the rather battered side chair with peeling paint at your summer home or the long table brought from grandmother's and consigned to the cellar as a toolbench. Either one of these and many other utilitarian, taken-for-granted pieces of furniture are quite likely to be negotiable.

Call this sort of furniture Country, Cottage or Primitive, Shaker, Pennsylvania Dutch, or New England—depending on its decoration or lack of it. It's all good Americana, and in the 1960's Americana is fashionable. And if you know for certain that a chair, table, or bedstead, plain as it is, was made for Great-great-grandfather or Great-aunt Sally, someone will be willing to buy it before you can turn around.

Country furniture, all of it very simple, consists of essential household furnishings. Some of it, particularly the chairs, is reminiscent of elegant mahogany and cherry pieces modeled on Queen Anne, Chippendale, and Sheraton styles and made by cabinetmakers for urban homes. The country pieces, however, were of maple, hickory, chestnut, pine, and other native woods. With a few exceptions country furniture lacked decoration, having neither inlay nor veneer. Carving, when there was time or inclination to do any, was modest, and turnings plain. Paint was about as far as these practical, rural furniture-makers went in the matter of further embellishment, and often a piece was painted merely to disguise

*A small rocker* (left) *with cane seat and back and a spindle armchair* (right) *are comfortable if undistinguished examples of furniture made in the late 1800's.*—Ted Eastwood.

the fact that it was built of two or three kinds of wood.

All country furniture was practical and sturdy. Sometimes, in their emphasis on sturdiness, the makers lost sight of proportions and made chests and cupboards that looked topheavy, tables that were sound enough but ungainly in appearance. In new settlements and rural towns, cabinetmakers were a rarity. Carpenters and handymen made most of the furniture, and skillful as they were at cutting boards and driving nails, the results were hardly polished, even though acceptable.

You need not live in New England to be the unsuspecting owner of country furniture made between 1800 and 1900. Of course the very first pieces date from the days when Massachusetts Bay Colony and Providence Plantation, in what is now Rhode Island, were being settled, but country furniture continued to be made through

the years of exploring and settling the country, first in the Western Reserve, which is now part of Ohio and Indiana, then across the Mississippi River, and, finally, in Oregon and Washington. Anywhere a person lives, the possibilities of discovering country furniture are good. Tables similar to early Colonial tavern and trestle tables were made as late as the 1850's and perhaps the 1870's. Women who cooked meals and cared for their families in isolated houses with no neighbors within hailing distance were grateful to have a trestle table on which to spread the food. Even if a woman knew that Duncan Phyfe in New York City was turning out tables with carved eagle pedestals, she realized not only that it would be foolish to try to bring one across the mountains and prairies, but that such a table would look too fancy in her raw new house.

The trestle and tavern tables, and the Windsor, the slat-back, and the rocking chairs so popular along the East Coast were copied as best the workmen could remember, as settlers moved westward. Thus, distinct styles in country furniture developed in different regions.

Pennsylvania Dutch or, correctly, German furniture came from a small area in southeastern Pennsylvania where rich farmland was cultivated long before the Revolution by settlers from the Palatinate. These people loved color and produced distinctive designs incorporating hearts, flowers, birds, angels, unicorns, and knights in vivid colors. Or they carved and then painted such designs on chests and other large pieces.

Not as well known is the brightly painted decoration typical of the Swedes who early settled along the Delaware River and the Scandinavians who later made their homes in Minnesota and the northwestern states. If these people did not bring their own chests, cupboards, and bedsteads with them, they made new ones as much like them as possible. Their painted decorations were gay but not as strikingly individual as those of the Pennsylvania Dutch.

The Dutch families from the Netherlands who developed the Hudson River Valley were somewhat more sophisticated than the Germans in Pennsylvania. Their furniture was heavy and stable. Great chests and wardrobes might be carved but not painted in gay designs.

In the southeastern states, a great deal of fine furniture was imported from England or commissioned from local cabinetmakers. Probably at least an equal amount was made on plantations. Much of this was patterned after the best furniture in the main house, but some of it disregarded the fashion of the moment.

Shaker furniture was the plainest and most functional of all. A group of Shakers first came to New York City in 1774, and by 1874 had established fifty-eight centers of communal living in New York State, Massachusetts, Connecticut, New Hampshire, Kentucky, Ohio, Indiana, and later, briefly, in Florida. They used light-colored woods such as maple, birch, and pine almost exclusively. Sometimes their chair uprights were given simply carved finials, but drawer pulls were plain wood knobs and ornament was strictly forbidden. Chair seats were rush, cane, or woven splint or tape. Occasionally chairs were painted red or blue. Chairs, boxes, and their ingenious cupboards and chests are probably best known. The Shakers made all the furniture for their communities, which were self-supporting, and by the late nineteenth century sold a certain amount to outsiders.

Whether it bears a regional or ethnic stamp or could have been made anywhere from New Jersey to Nebraska and Oregon, all country furniture is functional. This necessity brought about innovations that are still usable and copied. Lazy Susans to be placed

*The owner of this chair bought it at an auction for ten cents, and then devoted about fifty dollars' worth of his time to gluing and refinishing the frame and putting in a rush seat. The legs and stretchers are pegged; the curved slats make it easy to pick up and move this small chair.*

in the center of the table were common in the South and Midwest. Milk and pie safes with pierced tin doors, spice boxes to place on shelves, and hanging wall cupboards and boxes were other practical ideas. The dough tray or kneading table with a flat removable top, now sometimes used as a small table, was patterned by the Pennsylvania Dutch after similar ones in their homeland. Dry sinks and benches, which were made to stand in a kitchen

and hold a washbowl and pitcher, are not always as appropriately used today.

Nothing could be more functional and practical than the settle chair, made entirely of wood without upholstery and padding, to stand at right angles to the fireplace. The high, solid back and the wings flanking it were protection against drafts. The seat often was the lid of a chest, although some settles had small drawers underneath the seat instead. An equally practical space-saver was the chair or hutch table, which belonged in the kitchen or main room of a house. When the hinged top of a chair table was raised, it became the broad and protective back of a roomy seat. The arms of the seat supported the back when it was lowered for a tabletop, and also permitted the seat to be pulled up to the fire. The top might be either circular or rectangular.

Whereas the settle and probably the hutch table were chiefly Colonial pieces, little made after 1800, trestle and tavern tables were long a staple of country furniture. A well-made one —and these country ones were sturdy —is as good today after refinishing as when it was first made. Various styles of trestle and tavern tables used during the 1800's are fairly plentiful now. The trestle table is easily recognized. It is a plain rectangular table with two to four braced legs, the number depending on its length. The legs, an inverted T shape, are correctly known as trestles. This table goes back to Medieval days in Europe and England, and was made until at least 1850 in rural parts of the United States. The finest examples had the top cut from one board, although two or three boards were frequently employed. Two or more kinds of wood, such as an oak frame and a maple top, were common. A variation was the sawbuck table, so called because its trestles formed an X like the rack known as a sawhorse or sawbuck, on which wood is laid to be cut.

A long narrow type called a harvest table is featured among current reproductions. Its shape and size are typical of the trestle table, but it usually has conventional legs and narrow drop-leaves.

By the early 1800's, good-sized drop-leaf tables were becoming more common than trestle tables in kitchens. The drop leaves could be raised and leaves also could be inserted in the center of the table to accommodate however many persons were to sit down to a meal. Afterward, the table could be closed to save space. If you find such a drop-leaf table, search until you find the leaves to extend it. Oval and rectangular drop-leaf tables seem to have been preferred to the round, but none of these commodious tables was made with any frills. Their sturdy legs might be round, square, or six-sided, with little or no turning and certainly no skillful turning.

Because of the day-in, day-out use of these drop-leaf tables, the finish now is often marred, scarred, and unattractive. A careful cleaning frequently reveals that the top and leaves are one wood, such as hard ash, the legs and base another, such as maple or pine.

Gateleg tables were made in New England during the late 1600's. These, however, are not as commonly found among country furniture as the drop-leaf, probably because the gateleg was more difficult to make.

The small tavern and butterfly tables never lack for buyers. A great many of these were made during the nineteenth century, although the style goes back to the late 1600's, and many are still waiting to be recognized. Less commonly found now are little half-round tables of pine.

The tavern table had plain or turned

*The drop-leaf table shown here was made for a farmhouse kitchen between 1850 and 1880. The top of ash is lighter colored and coarser grained than the maple legs. Extra leaves can be inserted to make a surface 73 inches long.—Ted Eastwood*

*Country furniture more than a century old still looks attractive and homelike in a present-day living room: a maple rocking chair* (left), *a tavern table with drop leaf* (center), *and a maple slat-back armchair.*

legs braced by stretchers. Tops were rectangular, round, or occasionally oval, and ranged from about 30 inches in length or diameter to 4 or 5 feet. The smallest ones were really good-sized stools or benches. Once in a while, a tavern table with one drop leaf or a drawer is discovered. An interesting variation was the round table on three legs braced with stretchers forming a triangle, but this again is a very old style, little made during the 1800's.

A cross between the tavern table and the gateleg table was the butterfly table. This small type with drop leaves was strictly American and took its name from the shape of the swinging brackets or supports for the drop leaves. The brackets extended from the top to the stretchers.

Tavern and butterfly tables were made of all kinds of wood. They are rated not only according to their state of preservation but also by their proportions, the quality of the turnings on legs and stretchers, and the rake of the legs. Tavern tables, incidentally, not only are reproduced but also are faked cleverly by putting together the base of an antique tavern table and the top of a later drop-leaf.

Plain, rather angular legs and feet, by no means as graceful as on cabinet-makers' examples, distinguished country-made tripod tables. A Shaker candlestand, for example, had a plain, round pedestal and three canted legs under an ungraceful rectangular top. The height of simplicity was the cross-base candlestand with pieces of thick wood forming an X base into which the pedestal was secured. Practicality and ingenuity, so typical of the Shakers, were shown in a worktable built for use by two persons. Under the rectangular top were two drawers, one on either side of the tripod support.

Butterfly tables were made first in New England about 1700. So were Windsor chairs. They became the chair of the eighteenth century and were made in more variations than any other style of chair except the rocker. Prior to this, both side chairs and armchairs had either banister backs (vertical splats with a carved crest rail) or slat backs

*A small hickory-wood rocker with acorn finials made in New Hampshire about a century ago. The rush seat is new.*

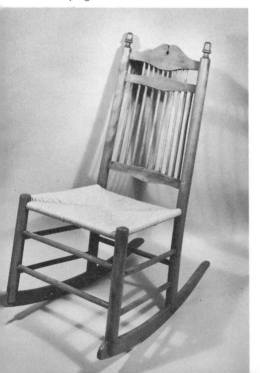

(simple but shaped horizontal splats). The uprights of both banister-backs and slat-backs usually were topped with finials.

Slat-back chairs continued to be a popular country style almost throughout the nineteenth century. Made mostly with light-colored native woods and often combining two different kinds, these country slat-backs were a very different chair from the elegantly carved ribbon-backs made in cities. The height of the seat and the height of the back varied, but almost always the uprights had simple finials. The slats varied not only in number but also in width and shaping. Seats were rush or woven splint. Slat-backs and particularly the high ladder-backs are not the most comfortable chairs to sit in.

Like slat-backs, Windsor chairs were made all over the country. They still are, although in fewer variations than during the 1700's and 1800's. The best examples of antique Windsors were polished, but many good ones were painted, usually black or green.

This all-wood chair originated in England, but when made in this country, became quite different-looking. The outstanding characteristic of the American Windsor chair was the spindles that form the back and arms and gave rise to the term "stick" construction. In England, this style of chair had a carved or shaped splat and hence fewer spindles, various styles of legs including

the cabriole, and thinner seats. In America, Windsor chairs had shaped seats made of a thick solid piece of wood, turned legs with a decided rake, and two, three, or four turned stretchers.

Turnings of legs and stretchers varied from simple cylinder to vase and ring. Certain individualities of turning enable experts to place a chair as having been made in a specific region such as New England, New York, or Pennsylvania. The majority of Windsors had spindles that tapered at either end. However, in the early 1800's, a change came about in the tapering and turning of cylinders in the manner of bamboo. Although comparatively few Windsor chairs, in view of the great number made, had bamboo turnings, this style cannot be pinpointed to any one locality.

Bamboo turning was used chiefly for chairs and settees with a double crest rail. Bamboo spindles were fitted into the lower part of the back, and thinner, plain round spindles between the double rail. Legs and stretchers, much thicker than the spindles, also were bamboo turned. This chair with its rectangular back showed the influence of Sheraton. In New England, it is often referred to as a Broken Chicken-Coop chair.

Before this unusual type, Windsor side chairs and armchairs had been made in many shapes. The names were derived from the shape of the back.

*The Windsor side chair with double-rail back and bamboo turnings was made from New England to the Carolinas from 1800 to 1815. It is known as a Sheraton-type bamboo Windsor, and—in New England—as Broken Chicken-Coop.*

Bow-back, hoop-back, fan-back, arch-back, loop-back, and rod-back were the chief variations. Bow-back and arch-back types often had two extra spindles to brace the back from crest to seat. The fan-back had its top rail brought out into ears, as did elegant Chippendale chairs.

Comb-back Windsors were chiefly armchairs and rockers. The "comb" was added to the low back to provide a headrest and hence more comfort. Several types, including bow-back and arch-back, commonly had combs added. Combs are not always in good proportion to the back or to the chair as a whole.

A *Windsor rocking chair with a comb back is an indifferent example of a style popular for 200 years. Windsor armchairs, like side and rocking chairs (the latter a latecomer), are named for the shape of their backs.*

Rocking chairs were latecomers among the Windsor types. It is obvious that rockers were added to some armchairs instead of being part of the original construction. Any number of Windsor forms were made as rockers.

Some armchairs had a flat table or writing box attached to the right arm. So popular was the stick construction of Windsors that it was used for high chairs for babies, small chairs for children, cradles, love seats, and settees. The latter, whether low-back, bow-back, comb-back, or double-rail, are

graceful furniture. The double-rail settee had rectangular arms, also with double rails. The number of legs depended on the length of the settee—a 6- to 7-foot one had eight legs. Settees, like all good Windsor chairs, had a shaped seat.

The number of spindles that make the back of a side chair or armchair is one indication of the quality, though not the antiquity, of a Windsor chair. Other points contributing to the quality are the shaping of the seat, the turning of the legs, stretchers, and spindles, and the rake of the legs. The sharper the rake, the finer the chair. Proportion and scale also must be considered. On a really old Windsor, several spindles may be loose or broken off at the seat (spindles were socketed in place). These can be replaced easily, but the value of the piece is reduced in proportion to the number of broken ones.

Not only many Windsors but also many slat- and banister-back chairs had rockers added later. True rockers also were made during the 1700's, but it was about 1810 before rockers achieved their immense popularity in this country. The majority of the rockers that are found nowadays were made between about 1830 and 1890.

The legends that have sprung up about rockers are not true, for the most part. For generations, many people have believed that the rocker was an American origination, that Benjamin Franklin was the first person to put rockers on a chair, or that rocking chairs came from Boston. Putting rockers on a chair, admittedly, is the sort of thing Benjamin Franklin might have thought of doing. However, according to the Chester County Historical Society, the first record of a rocking chair in this country is a sale made in 1766 in Middletown, Pennsylvania. This was a true rocking chair, not an old side chair or armchair with rockers added.

Rocking chairs always have been more popular in America than anywhere else, yet the earliest-known rocker was not American but English and was unearthed in London in 1948. This is a seventeenth-century rocker in the older Tudor style.

Rockers, converted from existing chairs and brand-new, were fairly well established here by 1810. The transformation to a rocking chair is easily spotted, for the wood of the rockers is usually different from that of the rest of the chair. Furthermore, the legs were usually shortened in order to add rockers, and this brought the rungs too low. These rockers often looked awkward although they work perfectly well.

Most popular of all styles was the Boston rocker, its vogue extending from about 1825 to 1890. The true Boston rocker had a high, bent-spindle back with a wide headpiece, arms ending in a downcurve to fit the hands, a rolling shaped seat, and turned legs

on rockers that projected at the back. Most Boston rockers were painted and had a stenciled decoration of flowers, fruit, or landscape on the headpiece.

Boston rockers were made in many places other than the city of their name. There were many variations too. Certainly the so-called Salem rocker was one, and it's hard at first glance to see any difference between the two. The Salem rocker had a lower seat and a higher back and possibly a narrower crest rail, with its shaping somewhat different from the Boston rocker.

*A painted rocking chair (circa 1850) has a stenciled headpiece and the shaped seat of the Boston rocker. The true Boston rocker has downward curving arms and a higher back.*

*An unpainted maple rocker with hickory arms, made in New England before 1850. The wide, carved back splat is unusual. The seat consists of three pieces of maple, two wide ones side by side and a narrow piece pegged across the back.*

Another variation was almost an exact copy down to the paint and stenciling, except that this chair did not have arms.

Not all rocking chairs were as comfortable as the Boston rocker. Undoubtedly the Pennsylvania Dutch rocker, which had a splat instead of spindles in its back, and downcurved arms, was. This style was painted with typical decoration of the region on headpiece and splat. On the other hand, the slat-back Shaker rocker was far from comfortable. This high, unpainted rocker was a traditional style that is literally almost worth its weight in gold today. Big, slouchy country rockers may not even have had paint,

let alone the decoration of Boston rockers, yet they followed the lines and parts almost exactly and are very comfortable.

Country furniture, as a matter of fact, abounded in rockers. There were large ones and small ones, some of the latter with quite low seats. Many of the small rockers were armless but nonetheless comfortable. Some had only one or two horizontal splats, and these might be curved or shaped for comfort. Seats were caned or rushed if not solid wood. A mid-nineteenth-century style had an oval back and round seat frame, usually of maple, enclosing cane

*Rocking chairs with maple frames and cane seats and backs were made all over the United States in the years between 1840 and 1870. This one has been refinished and recaned.*

back and seat. About 1870, the back of this style became rectangular with a curved crest rail, and the seat square. Both the oval- and rectangular-backed ones were made in large and small rockers with and without arms.

As distinct a style as the Boston rocker, and appearing about the same time was the Hitchcock chair. This is the most famous and best-known of the painted chairs. It is more than just another chair, however, because it marked the beginning of a drastic change in furniture-making. Hitchcock chairs were made by hand, but were cut, turned, assembled, painted, and decorated in more or less assembly-line fashion at Lambert Hitchcock's factory in Hitchcocksville, Connecticut. When a group was completed, they would be taken out and sold. The little factory also shipped chairs to various parts of the country.

The Hitchcock chair was a side chair with a rectangular back which had one or more horizontal splats and a wide crest rail, legs and stretchers with simple turnings, and a square rush seat. All wood parts were painted a red-brown to simulate rosewood and mahogany, or black. Stencil decoration in gold was applied to the splat and crest rail, and the turnings of legs and stretchers were emphasized with gilt lines. A few chairs with downcurved arms also were made.

All chairs produced in the Hitchcock factory had a stencil across the back

stating: "L. Hitchcock, Warranted," or "L. Hitchcock, Hitchcocksville, Ct.," or "Hitchcock, Alford & Co." The factory was in business from about 1826 into the 1840's. Chairs with any of these stamps and particularly with the original stencil decoration still fairly clear are most valuable.

Next in value would be similar chairs made during the same period in other shops. This was such a popular style of chair that there were many imitators, even while Hitchcock's factory was busy. In other places, from New

*This small chair circa 1850 (seat 14 inches and over-all height 29 inches), with rush seat, painted black frame, and gold stenciling, is a Hitchcock type made in West Winsted, Connecticut.*

England to New York and Pennsylvania, details of the chair differed. The back and seat were usually rectilinear, as were mahogany side chairs of the same years. Backs often were outcurved as were the backs of Sheraton side chairs. Instead of simple stencil decoration of flower, fruit, and geometric motif, the middle splat might be carved, perhaps with an eagle, and then stenciled with gilt. In short, the term Hitchcock or Hitchcock-type is now applied to almost any light, painted and stenciled chair made between 1825 or 1850 or a few years later.

Painted chairs of all kinds were immensely popular from 1820 into the 1890's, and many that were rated as kitchen chairs 100 and more years ago are given more status nowadays. The painted side chair without arms was a staple all over the country in villages and cities, mansions, farmhouses, and taverns.

One of the most prized of these side chairs is the one known as an arrow-back because of the shape of its back splats. Most chairs have three, some have five, splats. The arrow-back was undoubtedly an offshoot of the Windsor chair, although the splats were flat and tapering rather than rounded spindles. Arrow-backs were made in all degrees of refinement, from handsome enough for the parlor to gay ones for the kitchen. However simple the construction, when the arrow-back was painted black and given a stencil decoration across the crest rail and gilded lines to mark the arrow splats and the

*These painted or fancy chairs (1820-40) have rush seats and stencil decoration as do Hitchcock chairs, but otherwise are quite different. About twenty-five years ago, a cabinetmaker added arms to one of the six side chairs.*

*An arrow-back chair at least 100 years old. The chair is painted black, but the stencil decoration on the crest rail and the lines on the splats and turnings are in metallic gilt and color.—Ted Eastwood*

turnings of the legs and stretchers, it was good-looking enough for any room. When it was painted green and floral decoration added in bright colors, it almost certainly was made in Pennsylvania Dutch country and intended for kitchen use. The back splats varied from flat pieces of wood tapering at either end, to those with an obvious arrow cut into the center section.

Although the arrow-back is easiest to recognize, these painted side chairs were made with an almost infinite variety of backs. Another of the most common types had a wide back splat from which three to five fairly heavy, turned spindles extended down to the seat. Then again the crest rail or headpiece was wide and spindles or narrow splats extended from it to the seat. The arrangement of horizontal and vertical pieces in the back of a chair of this type varied widely.

The seats of these innumerable side chairs were shaped and usually were made of thick wood, sometimes of two or three pieces fastened together. On the whole, the turnings of the legs and stretchers were simple, but the workmanship ranged from fine to coarse, according to the skill of the workman.

One reason for painting the finished chair was that it generally was made of two or three kinds of wood. Pine, whitewood, or maple might be used for the seat, hickory or ash for the splats, maple, birch, or oak for the

turned legs and stretchers. Kitchen chairs were painted green, brown, blue, or red. For use elsewhere in the house black paint or a red-brown paint was usual, and these chairs often had stencil decoration in gilt.

Fewer armchairs than side chairs were made. Low-back ones were fairly common after 1840 and not unknown before that. Some people call them firehouse chairs because they were used in firehouses, but they probably were as general in offices and, in lesser number, in homes. The arms and back

*A maple side chair (1880-1910) that was restored by removing three coats of dark paint, waxing the natural wood, then caning the broken seat.*

formed a horseshoe, with a rail added to the center section. The seat was a broad horseshoe of one or several pieces of thick wood. These late-nineteenth-century chairs were usually painted.

They were undoubtedly copied from the early-nineteenth-century "captain's chair," which has been called the "Windsor that went to sea." This was a polished wood chair with the same horseshoe-shaped back and arms, but with more and finer turnings on the spindles. The legs had the distinct rake of a good Windsor chair and, preferably, crossed stretchers. The seat was saddle-shaped and carved from a solid block of wood.

Settees following most of the styles of painted chairs are attractive and good finds. They ranged from love-seat length (about 34 inches) to 6 or 7 feet. Some of them had arrow backs, others had plain or turned spindles. Sometimes the spindles extended from the crest rail to the seat, again only from a horizontal splat under the crest rail. The stretchers were either three or four in number and, like the legs, simply turned. Most of these settees—even the longest—had seats shaped from a single solid piece of wood. Some followed Hitchcock chairs in having rush seats.

A very few of these wood settees are to be found with rockers nowadays. Even more of a find would be a settee with one end fenced off at the front edge of the seat to form a cradle. The idea was that a woman could sit unencumbered and knit or sew while the baby lay safe behind the fenced-in area. (If you find such a settee with a fence at both ends of the seat, you'll know that the original owner had twins.) A settee of this sort is known as a settee-cradle, but separate cradles in various Windsor styles also were made.

All of the settees were painted, and the fancier ones, like fancy chairs, had stencil decoration on the crest rail and the turnings of legs and stretchers marked in gilt, metallic green, or bronze. Flowers and fruit were the usual motifs for stencils. In some areas, brighter base paint and decorations were customary.

*Wooden bench 90 inches long from a meeting hall upstairs over the general store in Guilford, Connecticut. The bench has been painted. Most unusual are the metal arms that permit the back to be flipped from one side to the other, somewhat as the seats in the old-fashioned open trolley car were. Only two of these benches, first used in the hall in the late 1800's, survive.*—Ted Eastwood

*Between 1800 and 1850, a low, slat-back two-seater of maple, pine, or hickory was often made to fit in the bed of a farm wagon. Occasionally rockers were added.*

Much plainer than these attractive settees were the so-called town-meeting or deacon's benches. These also were 4 to 7 feet long, with a curved piece topping the spindles of the arm, and a spindle back beneath a wide rail. Sometimes they were unfinished, occasionally painted. Deacon's benches are considered New England in origin, but are found elsewhere in the country as far west as Ohio and Illinois.

A low, two-seat settee may seem at first glance to have been made for children. It wasn't. Instead,. it was a portable seat to be carried out and placed in the bed of a wagon for a comfortable ride to town. It is properly called a wagon seat. Actually, the seat was 14 or 15 inches from the floor, which is not much lower than the average chair. Wagon seats had two outer arms. Three uprights, each tipped with a

57

finial and with slats, were used for two-seaters. The uprights and legs were sturdy and round with simple turnings; the stretchers were more slender. The wood was maple, hickory, or other hard varieties, and often two or more kinds were used. It was either painted or left its natural color. Seats were rush or woven splint. Believe it or not, some of these wagon seats had attached rockers.

Children were not forgotten when country furniture was made. For them Windsor, slat-back, Hitchcock, and everyday side-chairs were turned out in small sizes. So were Boston and other styles of rockers, decorated in the same manner as their elders' chairs.

If it is possible that any category of furniture was more important than chairs, chests and cupboards were. After all, no matter when or where a person lived, he had some possessions that needed to be kept safe. Not only were chests and cupboards generally functional; many of them were cleverly built for particular types of storage. Of course both these storage pieces and hutches can be pretty battered if they've been used since 1840 or even 1870 or 1880. Nevertheless, their like will not be made again—and fresh paint works wonders.

Oldest, of course, was the ordinary chest with a lid. This was made in all lengths and depths, chiefly of pine and maple. Some were so precisely joined that it's a pleasure to look at them,

**58**

*The cupboard with its two drawers beneath can be lifted off the table so that each can be used separately. These matching cherry pieces were made in Ohio between 1820 and 1840.*

however worn their corners. Many of these plain ones were made as late as the 1870's.

Individual styles of chests have been made in this country since before 1700. The chest with a lid that lifts up and two drawers beneath it was for blankets. One of the most famous of this kind was the Hadley chest. It was deep and three-paneled, and there was all-over carving of tulips, stems, and foliage. Only about 100 real Hadley chests were made in Hadley, Massachusetts. Many similar ones appeared in the Connecticut River Valley, farther south. These Connecticut ones were usually called sunflower or sunflower and tulip chests because of the type of carving on the three panels.

Chests with one divided drawer were made in Pennsylvania. These, the dower chest, which had no drawers, and later chests of four drawers were painted and decorated in vivid colors in the Pennsylvania Dutch region. The dower chest had varicolored designs painted on the three panels. Incidentally, the motifs of the decoration differed typically from one county to an-

*Every Victorian bedroom had a washstand or commode with its pottery wash set. This small pine commode has a hinged top that can be raised, a small drawer, and a cupboard at the bottom. It stands 31½ inches high, is 20½ inches long and 18 inches deep. (A full washstand set, like the one shown here, consisted of six to eight pieces; a chamber set was made up of three pieces—bowl, ewer, and chamber pot, usually with a cover.)—Ted Eastwood*

*A small pine chest, 24 by 12 by 10 inches, that was cut and fitted with great care some 100 years ago.*—Ted Eastwood

other in this farmland area. Both dower and everyday chests often had the owner's name or initial carved or inlaid in the center panel.

Chests of drawers made from about 1730 onward were from three to six or eight drawers in height. They varied somewhat from state to state, but the highest ones are said to have been made in New Hampshire and Vermont, where the men were taller than average. A six-drawer chest also sometimes might consist of two three-drawer ones set side by side. Most of these plain chests were painted.

Cupboards range from milk and pie safes to even smaller spice cupboards and boxes to hang on the wall. Drug cupboards and some spice cupboards were made up of tiny drawers, each generally with a small wooden knob. Cupboards of this kind were placed atop either a slant-top desk or a wide

chest of drawers, usually set well back from the edge on a chest of drawers.

The hutch and the dresser were primarily country styles. They were the forerunners of the twentieth-century kitchen cabinet, but much more attractive than the latter. Many styles of hutch and dresser were made, with the details and the arrangement of closed and open spaces changing with the locality. Although they were made in quantity into the 1870's, these pieces are worthwhile today.

A hutch consisted of two pieces. The bottom was an arrangement of either, or both, cupboards and drawers. The

*A pine cupboard made in Vermont, which is said to have been a pie cupboard, though it may have been used for storing preserves. It is 42 inches high, 39 inches long, and 18½ inches deep. The single door consists of two wood panels with a strip of wood fitted rather loosely between. (The cat is a real live one. The old copper teakettle at the right is oval and has a fixed handle.)*—Ted Eastwood

hutch top was removable and consisted of two or more railed shelves for the display of pewter or china, with either a cornice or an open top. A dresser, which was a cupboard to hold dishes and cooking utensils, also usually had two parts: a bottom of drawers and cabinets, and a top with either open or closed shelves. The top section normally was recessed to provide counter space. A kitchen cupboard also sometimes consisted of two deep cabinets under a row of drawers, but it had no upper section. A rail along the sides and back of the top kept objects from falling off the work surface.

The water bench was about as high as the hutch. The cupboards below were for storing water buckets; the counter provided a surface on which to place them when filled. Instead of having two or three shelves like the hutch, it had a row of shallow drawers attached near the top of the back, well above the counter. Dry sinks with part of the top depressed were smaller than water benches.

Cupboards, hutches, dressers, and sinks were painted, more often than not. However, when the wood—maple, cherry, pine, or birch—had been carefully chosen, the piece was sometimes only waxed and polished to display its natural wood color. These pieces make up probably the most sought-after and salable group to be found today.

Beds were less affected by changing styles or individual whims than any other country furniture. There were no towering four-posters in rural homes. Instead, throughout the 1700's and most of the 1800's, the low-post bed was made everywhere in single and small-double widths. It was often called the "under-eave" bed. The two low head-posts, which were slightly higher than the foot-posts, usually supported a low headboard. The headboards were plain and the posts simply turned and almost stubby. These bedsteads included two side and two end rails with either holes or knobs for holding the bed ropes (there were no springs), which had to be drawn taut. An important accessory was the wooden bed wrench used to tighten the ropes.

After 1825, beds were made occasionally with a sort of footboard between the foot-posts — two rails framing stock spindles—but the posts themselves and the headboard were no fancier than those of the under-eave bed. Hitchcock's fame rests on his chairs, but he or one of his imitators also made very plain headboards painted and decorated with stenciling in gilt.

Only one style of desk rounded out country furniture. The little desk known as the schoolmaster's desk may be found from the East Coast throughout the Midwest and the Plains states. It had no pigeonholes or drawers in the interior of the body. It did have one drawer under the slant top which formed its writing surface. The top had to be lifted to get at the materials

A *cherry schoolmaster's desk with a slant-top writing surface that can be lifted to get at the materials stored inside. It was made in Ohio before 1850.*

stored underneath. This type of desk was small and set on comparatively high legs. It was made of maple, pine, perhaps cherry, or two woods, and was usually painted.

Native woods always were used for country furniture. Pine and maple predominated, but oak was an early choice and in the nineteenth century cherry was not uncommon. Hickory, walnut, butternut, ash, poplar, chestnut, and whatever wood the region offered came in handy too. Two or more kinds of wood were common in even the smallest object, and that—as has been pointed out—was why so many pieces were painted. Not only were several colors of paint employed, but in the 1800's paint was often applied to represent the grain of wood.

Restoring country furniture does not necessarily consist of scraping off all the various coats of paint down to the original pine, maple, or hickory. Of course some pieces entirely of pine, maple, or cherry will gleam beautifully if reduced to the wood, polished, and waxed, but a thorough cleaning and the application of a coat of paint in a suitable color and texture are frequently the most appropriate treatment.

Country furniture is bound to show signs of hard usage. Judge its quality on the basis of how good its proportions and scale are, how well joined it is, and how good the turnings are.

The most likely finds in country furniture are such pieces as hutches, dressers, and painted chairs of the kitchen variety. However weary you may be from cleaning out an old house, never neglect to look in the cellar, the shed, or what was formerly the barn. It's in such spots that you may unearth a chest appealing for its small size, or a schoolmaster's desk discarded long ago because it was starting to come apart. Amazingly, all country furniture, no matter what its condition, has marketable value. A piece in good condition can be sold for a surprising amount of cash. A bona fide early-eighteenth-century chest is worth anything up to $1,000, depending on the amount of its carving and decoration and state of preservation. The plainest nineteenth-century pine or maple chest with no more decoration than a molding around its lid can bring $35 to $50. Cupboards have an equally wide price range, and painted hutches and dressers are worth almost as much as current, unpainted but polished, wood reproductions.

Among chairs, the Windsors are the best gamble. Depending on its age and quality, a Windsor chair can be sold for from $10 to $1,000. A signed Hitchcock chair is worth more than Hitchcock-type chairs. The latter may bring no more than $20 or so each, even though they were made more than 100 years ago. A set of six, including one armchair, to use around a dining table can be sold for a tidy sum.

A slat-back rocker, uncomfortable as it is to sit in, may be worth $50 to $250. A Boston rocker, depending on how true to type it is and how good its condition, sells for perhaps $10 to $150.

An arrow-back kitchen· chair, painted and faded to a dingy gray, is bound to be worth a few dollars to someone. If you find one with a crest rail stenciled as well as painted, its selling price can be anything from $10 to $150. Just one wagon seat—not the complete set of two or three in which they were usually made—will bring not less than $25 and, depending on its workmanship and condition, perhaps $50 or more. Occasionally, a wagon seat is sold for $100 to $125.

No one can argue about a Hitchcock chair because it was signed. Some other makers of this sort of chair between 1830 and 1860 also stamped their name and town on the back, so it's possible to trace the date of origin. However, Hitchcock chairs are being made at the present time in New England. Although Lambert Hitchcock's original patterns are used and his stamp placed on the back, they are not antique chairs. A nineteenth-century Hitchcock may be worth only about $25 or it may be good enough to bring $150. The twentieth-century Hitchcock chairs with rush seats sell for $50 and up, in their gleaming newness.

Windsor chairs, slat- or ladder-back chairs, captain's chairs and other low-back armchairs, Boston and other types of rockers, are reproduced too. Not as many types of Windsor chairs are being manufactured, but it can be difficult to tell one made in 1850 from a similar one made in 1950. All styles include sizes for both adults and children. Many of the current reproductions are copied faithfully from eighteenth- and nineteenth-century examples in museums and restorations. The excellence of the reproductions and the continuing manufacture of long-popular pieces are all the more reason for authenticating the approximate date when a more worn-looking counterpart was made.

# 4
## Victorian Furniture

VICTORIAN FURNITURE is unquestionably plentiful. Every state from Maine to California, Alaska, and even Hawaii has its quota of odd pieces as well as parlor and bedroom sets. Not all of the furnishings that were fashionable during the long Victorian era are entitled to be called antiques at this time, yet restorations of gingerbread mansions already are under way in, for example, Connecticut and California.

Every year brings more Victorian furniture and the bric-a-brac so dear to Victorian housewives closer to the status of antiques. After all, the sofas and chairs of the first phase, which extended from 1840 into the 1860's, are a minimum of 100 years old. They are quite different from the American Empire style that preceded the Victorian era. Each decade of this twentieth century certainly will bring greater recognition to even late Victorian styles and foibles. With so little authentic eighteenth-century furniture likely to be found, that of the nineteenth century becomes more and more worth looking for.

Victorian furniture has made a more substantial return to favor in some parts of the country than in others. For example, starting in the 1950's, there was such a demand for sofas, chairs, and tables in Texas and many of the southern states that antique dealers bought heavily in the New England states and shipped their Victorian finds southward. Southerners prefer very dark woods and white marble because it is cool-looking. Many of the towering pieces fit nicely into large houses where the rooms have high ceilings (this is as true in any state as it is in southern ones). In New England and the Atlantic states where homeowners feel space is more restricted, sofas and other small pieces are preferred. Whatever market exists in the vicinity of New York City shows a preference for pieces topped with marble that has pink and chocolate variegations.

Everywhere, people have begun to learn that some pieces of Victorian furniture are highly adaptable. Used in moderation and chosen carefully, pieces in the Victorian style add a note of elegance and blend with the most contemporary furnishings. The marble-topped commode, indispensable to every Victorian bedroom set, makes a serving table or side table as charming as it is useful in a dining room. A pair can be used

effectively along a long wall in a living room. A marble-topped bureau, with the large mirror detached and hung on the wall above, makes a good sideboard.

Victorian side chairs more often than not are treasures. Miscellaneous ones are snapped up by ones and twos. In one Connecticut dining room, the six chairs for the table all have naturalistic carving of flowers or fruit and foliage on the crest rail, but only two chairs have identical carving. All were made within a twenty-five-year period in the mid-1800's.

*This side chair of mahogany with scrolled contours and a bold carving of grapes with foliage belongs to the early Victorian Rococo period (1840-60's). The strong-looking legs are curved. (The crest rail has been repaired.)*

*A sturdy, comfortable side chair of solid mahogany with the seat covered with modern needlepoint. The carving on the crest rail is simple and the back typical of the Victorian Classic period. After 1865.*

Much of the Victorian furniture actually is extremely comfortable. The sofas of the old parlor sets that were covered with shiny, slippery, prickly horsehair in the 1880's, and later, are comfortable after they have been reupholstered with a softer fabric. Admittedly, a Victorian bed with its wide sideboards into which spring and mattress sink is the most inconvenient one to make, but that does not mean it is not comfortable for sleeping.

*A spool or Jenny Lind bed (1850-65) can be recognized by the turnings of the headboard and footboard, which are the same height. Sometimes the posts were spool-turned too.*

The Victorian era was a long one, coinciding with the reign of Queen Victoria of England. She was crowned in 1837 and died in 1901, but for convenience the period in this country is usually dated from 1840 to 1900. These were years when living for many people was elegant and leisurely: years when fortunes were being made in America, when many industries were being developed, when the shoe factory reduced the number of shoemakers but not cobblers, when the metal factory put the village brazier and itinerant tinsmith out of work. These also were the years of mass emigration to America.

More people, more homes, and more money led to a greater demand for furniture during the 1800's than the 1700's. A natural outgrowth of this need was furniture factories.

Lambert Hitchcock with his inexpensive painted and stenciled chairs had blazed the trail for mass production of furniture. The next, and an equally successful, attempt at mass production and assembly-line manufacturing came about 1850, with spool-turned pieces. They were much less expensive than the same pieces of furniture from cabinetmakers of the time, which were made of exotic woods, had more elegant lines and hand-worked details.

Factory-made spool furniture was produced chiefly between 1850 and 1865, and in smaller quantity to 1880. It was also called "Jenny Lind" because it first appeared in the years when that famous and popular singer was touring the United States. The term "spool" is descriptive of the turning done on the straight members of each piece (spindles, railings, and the towel bars on a washstand), which resembles a string of wooden spools. Beds, tables, chairs, whatnots, and washstands were made in greatest quantity, although probably some other miscellaneous pieces were also spool-turned. This furniture was usually made of maple, birch, or other native hardwoods. Often it was painted or stained a dark tone in imitation of the cabinetmaker's rosewood and black walnut pieces. Today, frankly, spool-turned pieces are cherished, and since less spool furniture was produced, scarcity has increased its value. It's impossible not to recognize spool-turned pieces. For one thing, they are lighter-looking and in smaller scale than most of the more elegant Victorian furniture.

The success of Hitchcock chairs and spool-turned furniture led to more and more factories' being established after 1850 in New England and the Midwest. The first factory in Grand Rapids, Michigan, was opened in 1847, and long before 1900 this city had become known as the furniture capital of America. It was not until the 1870's, however, that more funiture for general household use was produced in factories than in cabinetmakers' shops. Probably large-scale manufacturing, whereby furniture was produced faster and in greater quantity, to sell less expensively, led to the popularity of sets for various rooms. A parlor set, for example, consisted of a sofa, an armchair, and two side chairs, plus a marble-topped table. Because it was used only on special occasions, parlor furniture has survived in better condition than sets for other rooms. A bedroom set was highlighted by a ponderous bed with towering headboard, a commode, a bureau and possibly a dressing table, a chest, or in late years a chiffonier, a side chair and possibly

a small rocking chair, and a small round or bedside table. The dining room set included a large table with undistinguished lines, a sideboard that at certain times during the Victorian era was quite fearful and wonderful, a serving or side table, six chairs with one usually a little larger than the others and having wood arms, and, in late years, a china closet or cabinet.

Most famous of the new pieces of furniture originated by the Victorians was the whatnot, made to fit in a corner or to stand parallel to the wall. This consisted of many open shelves, often with low railings, on which to display Canton china, art glass, dried flowers or wreaths under glass, daguerreotypes, Staffordshire dogs and figurines, and whatever appealed to the Victorian lady's fancy. A vase holding peacock feathers was a triumphant acquision for a whatnot.

The china closet or cabinet also was for the display and safekeeping of the finest tea set in the house, a set of dessert or cake plates, and cut glass, which became increasingly popular as the Victorian period progressed. China closets appeared toward the end of the Victorian period, and although they were an improvement on the whatnot, they displaced the lovely cupboards made during the eighteenth century and the open dressers found in rural homes of the nineteenth century. China closets were case pieces on short legs, with front and sides of glass framed in wood, and a wood back. The shelves inside also were wood. The chiffonier, another late-nineteenth-century piece, was not nearly so handsome as the previous century's highboy, high chest, or chest-on-chest.

The one new style of chair originated during the long Victorian era was the Morris chair, named for the English poet William Morris. This was a low, deep-seated chair with flat, almost straight, wood arms and a hinged back that could be adjusted to any angle and kept in position by a movable crossbar or rod that rested in notches. Separate, thick, soft cushions covered seat and back. The old Morris chair was far from handsome, but it was—and still is—mighty comfortable for reading, dozing, and, with its broad, flat arms, convenient for a writing pad or sewing equipment.

If it seems odd that a chair should be named after a poet, then let it be remembered that William Morris led a group of artists and writers in deploring the stifling of craftsmen and the repetitive, cheapened output from factories for home furnishings. Morris did more than deplore this state of affairs, for he became interested in decoration and started a business that concerned itself with furniture, tapestries, carpets, chintzes, and the like that emphasized natural decoration and pure color. The basic principle of this "Art Nouveau" movement, as it was sometimes called, was combining beauty and utility, and it soon became lost in the frills of the late Victorian years.

The rocking chair continued to be a great favorite and many changes were wrought in it. These chairs had a tendency to travel across the floor as a person rocked, and to correct this the platform and the stationary rocker were patented. Both types usually had upholstered backs, seats, and arms. The platform rocker, patented in the 1840's, had no legs, but the frame of the seat was bowed and it both rested and rocked on a stationary rectangular platform-base of wood. Another type of stationary rocker known as a "track" rocker was introduced in the 1880's. This had four, comparatively short, canted legs usually on casters, and the chair rocked by means of a mechanism under its deep seat. These chairs often were covered with plush tufted on back and seat, and had fringe hanging from the edge of the seat.

Rockers without platforms or other devices to keep them stationary took on new lines. One popular one was known as the "Sleepy Hollow," with its long, S-curved back and scrolled arms. The Lincoln rocker was so called because President Lincoln was sitting in one when he was assassinated. It had the scrolled lines of frame and arms popular in Victorian furniture from 1840 into the 1860's, and an upholstered back, seat, and arms. Often the wooden framework of the arms was elaborately scrolled and the crest of the back was carved.

Much simpler rockers also were made throughout the Victorian era. One of the nicest was the "lady" rocker, with either an oval or rectilinear back and seat. This was a low, armless, upholstered chair. Similar small upholstered rockers or small wood ones with cane seat and back were made as part of bedroom sets. Toward the end of the nineteenth century, mahogany rockers were made for downstairs rooms. These were usually comfortable but were of no particular style and bore no relation to the rockers that were popular much earlier. They might be fairly highbacked with turned spindles or lowbacked with a wide splat, a curved crest rail, and narrow, scrolled, downcurved wood arms.

As for furniture in general, the Victorian era was such a long one that not one but several distinct styles were developed. Interestingly enough, each of these styles borrowed from some period of the past, starting with Medieval days and progressing to Renaissance and eighteenth-century Louis XVI. However, the Victorians managed to embellish everything made for their houses. The chief influences are summarized briefly as follows:

| | |
|---|---|
| 1830's–1850: | Early or Transitional Victorian |
| 1840 –1865: | Gothic |
| 1845 –1860's: | Victorian Rococo or Louis XV |
| 1850 –1880: | Spool-turned (factory made) |
| 1855 –1875: | Renaissance Victorian |
| 1865 –1875: | Victorian Louis XVI |
| 1870's——: | Victorian Jacobean |
| 1870 –1880: | Oriental, also Turkish |

Although it is possible to confine some of these influences to a span of years, many of them continued to be followed to some degree long after furniture-makers had gone on to a fresh style. Also, American Empire pieces and details continued to be produced long after the first Victorian fashions were in full sway.

Then there was Biedermeier's furniture, which had appeared first in Germany about 1825 and had been imported and also copied in America in the 1830's. The Biedermeier style was a comfortable, rather provincial one that was made in reaction to the classic Empire style so popular in France and elsewhere in Europe. Biedermeier's furniture was imposing and, above all, luxuriously cushioned and padded. As a matter of fact, Biedermeier contributed a good deal that lasted throughout the Victorian era—thick curtains, festooned draperies, covers on all kinds of tables including the smallest ones, antimacassars, tassels and fringes everywhere and on everything.

What is now called Victorian Gothic actually had begun to appear in the 1830's. Victorian Gothic furniture was far less bulky than either Medieval Gothic or nineteenth-century Biedermeier. The name came from details such as the pointed arch shape of the chair backs. Instead of splats or spindles, the supports in a chair back were carved so that they copied (although they were less intricate) the tracery of Gothic windows. On large pieces of furniture, the carving followed the lines and details of Gothic architecture.

A Victorian Gothic bed, like the Empire sleigh and low-post beds, had headboard and footboard of the same height. It usually had posts that were solid, carved, octagonal columns attached to the headboard and footboard. These also were solid wood and displayed arched and carved panels. The wide sideboards were more simply carved to show Gothic arches. A Victorian Gothic table recalled the lines of a classic Empire table—rectangular top with ogee-molded drawer in the skirt and supports at either end that consisted of carved columns mounted on bracket feet.

If you chance upon a Victorian Gothic cupboard, you will see how the compulsion for frills showed up. The lower section will be a cupboard but probably will follow the lines of a several-sided Gothic column. The open shelves topping the cupboard will offer a minimum of display space but will be framed and backed with wood elaborately carved in more or less intricate Gothic tracery, and perhaps embellished with finials and railings—in short, a superstructure so fussy that nothing can be displayed advantageously on it.

By 1845, a lighter and more graceful

style that is now known as Victorian Rococo or Victorian Louis XV came into favor. It lasted longer than any other single influence during the era. Most of the furniture of this period was the product of cabinetmakers. The carvings and scrolled lines usually were not overdone, and as a result the furniture was as attractive as it was comfortable.

This period was characterized by curved but not cabriole legs, scrolled and rounded contours forming a cartouche back, and naturalistic carvings of roses, other flowers, grapes, leaves, and birds. The wood was bent, shaped, and carved into good lines and designs. Mahogany or rosewood sofas and chairs displayed a boldly sculptured bunch of grapes with a leaf, or a rose surrounded by leaves.

Side chairs of this period were comfortable as well as handsome and, as a gen-

*Sofas with carved frames were popular throughout the Victorian era. This one of rosewood carved with foliage and scrolls is about five feet long and has sides and arms that curve into the back.*—Ted Eastwood

eral rule, are better liked today than chairs of any other Victorian style. Sofas in various lengths and love seats with upholstered wood frames were graceful. The frame often was serpentine and always displayed some carving, usually on the arms and back. One form of sofa had an oval or round medallion framed in wood in the center of the back. The carving topping the medallion was repeated farther along the frame on either side. In the 1860's, some sofas had rounded upholstered arms with carved wood fronts. Occasionally, these arms could be let down by means of chains to lengthen the sofa so that a person could stretch out and take a nap—or sleep there when the house was crammed with overnight guests.

Look also among the furniture of this period for a pair of husband and wife, or lady and gentleman, chairs. These were upholstered. One had a high back and arms; the matching chair was a little lower and did not have arms. The armless one was the wife's chair, convenient to sit in while doing needlework, crocheting, or knitting. These pairs of chairs were made well into the 1870's, possibly the 1880's, but those that followed the rounded lines of Victorian Rococo between 1845 and 1860 are most attractive and least dated.

The Victorian Rococo period claims one of the few American cabinetmakers whose name still lives. John Henry Belter, who worked in New York City between 1844 and 1867, produced furniture a little different from the average. Belter became famous for his rosewood furniture, which was more richly

*The pair of chairs known as husband and wife, or lady and gentleman, chairs was made throughout the Victorian era. The mahogany pair with scrolled and rounded contours shown here came from a Massachusetts cabinetmaker between 1840 and 1860. The husband's armchair has a seat about two inches wider than the wife's, which is proportionately more slender.*

and ornately carved than the general run. Instead of confining himself to carving the crest of a chair, Belter continued the carving down the sides of the back. Foliage, flowers, and fruits were worked into involved designs held together with scrolled and pierced framing.

John Belter was uncommonly skilled at shaping and bending wood, too. As a result, his beds and other large pieces have fascinating serpentine and rounded contours. He was, perhaps, the leader in the 1840's in making beds with headboards much higher than the footboards. His headboards and footboards, curved, bent, and variously shaped, and displaying the elaborate carving of which he was capable, were joined to high shaped boards along the sides of the beds.

Whether Belter or some other cabinet-maker produced the first high-headboard bed, this style of the 1840's was new, different from the four-posters that had been made for almost a hundred years and the more recently popular bed with headboard and footboard of equal height. The new style endured throughout the Victorian era, although it was not always carried out in as good proportions or as good taste.

Although the John Belter bed is famous, comparatively few were made. This craftsman turned out an astounding number of Victorian Rococo tables, chairs, and sofas in his New York City shop. Furthermore, these were shipped

to fill orders from all parts of the country, so it's quite possible to find in a midwestern or southern state a sofa, chair, or table that undoubtedly came from Belter's hands.

About 1855 or a couple of years later, reminders of the Renaissance began to show up in furniture. It is easy to distinguish a Victorian Renaissance chair or sofa from a Rococo one, for the Renaissance piece will look much heavier, be more solid, and lack curves. Chairs for every purpose were made with rectangular or square seats and rectangular backs, in contrast to the scrolled Rococo lines. The carving on Renaissance chairs was heavier and more elaborate. It was based less on flowers, fruits, and foliage and more on classic scrolls, knots, and the like. Whatever the motifs, the carving was generous. Some piercing appeared in the carved areas. Wide moldings also were applied.

A Victorian Renaissance sideboard was an imposing conglomeration of wood, carving, and molding. The doors of the cupboards had carving that was framed with molding. The ends were likely to be flanked with carved columns or wide applied molding. All Victorian sideboards had a high backboard towering over the top surface. In addition to being carved in all possible places, this back had small shelves, railings, and columns attached to it and was often finished off with a fussy pediment. During the last couple of decades of the Victorian era, sideboards often had a framed mirror along their full length. These late sideboards, fortunately, did not have as much carving.

Marble, one of the great Victorian loves, became firmly established with this Renaissance revival. The tops of tables of all sizes, of commodes, bureaus, and many sideboards, were made of it. Somehow marble suited these heavy wood pieces. Marble in all color combinations was used, with predominately white, white and gray, and pink and chocolate the prime favorites.

Long before Victorian Renaissance had run its course, a simpler style began to appear. This is called Victorian Louis XVI or Victorian Classic. It too is easy to identify, if only because it was so much simpler and less heavily ornamented, and hence lighter in appearance. Lines became curved again rather than rectilinear. Scrolling was not as strong nor cartouche backs as common as they had been twenty years earlier. Actually, elements of Victorian Classic and Renaissance and perhaps Victorian Rococo often were combined in one piece.

In the 1870's, furniture-makers turned to Jacobean for inspiration. This trend combined with the trend toward increased amounts of factory-made furniture led to a loss of elegance. A typical Jacobean detail was wide, flat, ornamental molding twisted into designs. This, of course, was an adaptation of the seventeenth-century Jacobean strap-

work. Small turned spindles, not at all like the spool-turned ones, were used as railings on sideboards, cupboards, whatnots, tables, and everywhere else possible.

Carving was not forsaken, but it no longer was done in the high relief of the early years. Because so much furniture now was mass-produced instead of handmade, carving was replaced by shallow, incised ornamentation. Sprays of flowers and leaves were cut in outline instead of being rounded. Dots, dashes, and other simple motifs were repeated monotonously, sometimes in combination with outlined flowers. Beveled edges became a substitute for beautiful modeling and scrolling of wood.

The small table made in the 1870's and 1880's displayed a wood skirt cut gingerbread-fashion with incised ornamentation. This was joined to either a marble or a wood top and also to the one or two shelves of wood underneath. These tables with shelves were higher than the small tables which have been favorites in all furniture periods before or after Victorian Jacobean. The shelves were convenient for displaying some of the bric-a-brac without which no house was complete, and were a natural development in view of the popularity of whatnots.

Probably the most easily recognized piece of this Jacobean period was the whatnot. Its several shelves often were supported wholly by spindles. But shelves backed with wood also might be separated by spindles or have spindle railings. Many whatnots were fussy in construction.

Commodes were as indispensable as whatnots. Every bedroom had to have one. This small piece, approximately 16 inches wide and 34 inches long, was a case piece with one long drawer and the space beneath divided into a cupboard on one side, narrow drawers on

The whatnot (1850-65) was one of the few new pieces of furniture originated by the Victorians. The spacers between the tiered, open shelves of this one are spool-turned, but that was not always the case; sometimes they were round, rectangular, or free-standing. The china shown is Canton.

*A small parlor table 30 inches in height, made after 1870. The pink and chocolate marble top (16 by 19½ inches) rests on a black walnut base with incised decoration. (The china matchbox holds wooden matches, which can be lit by striking them on the corrugated inner surface of the cover; it is a typical Victorian accessory. The china group is a covered inkwell.)*

the other. More often than not, the top was marble. The splash or splatter rail (4 or 5 inches high) that fit behind the top was marble too. On the whole, after 1870 all furniture became rectilinear, rigid, and solid-looking. The grace of the Victorian Rococo and Classic and the distinction of Victorian Renaissance were lost in the pieces, however similar, made in the last years of the era. Chairs and sofas became more angular and were laden with strapwork or molding, sometimes with the addition of gingerbread.

*A walnut commode made in the 1880's. It has burl veneer on the drawer fronts and a pink and chocolate marble top; the matching splash rail has been removed from the back. The metal hardware and the arrangement of cupboard and narrow drawers are typical of late-Victorian commodes.*

*A cylinder-top desk of black walnut has beveled edges, incised decoration, panels of veneer, and applied moldings. Yet it is more restrained than much of the furniture made after 1870. Cylinder-top secretaries were also popular.*

Frames were ornamentally incised. These sofas and chairs appeared to be far less comfortable than earlier ones of basically the same size and shape.

The quarter-round cylinder-front desk and secretary were prized. These were quite handsome, if bulky, pieces. Occasionally the glass doors of the secretary had flower sprays painted on in various colors, although this decoration may have been specifically Pennsylvanian even if less stylized than the better-known Pennsylvania-German type of decoration. The rolltop cylinder desk was a workaday piece that invaded the home.

Bedsteads continued to have wide sideboards and very high headboards. A bed was a bed, and fairly undistinguished. Probably to make them higher, headboards often had two or more rows of wood paneling separated by boards with incised decoration. Generally, these beds are too high to look right in present-day bedrooms with lower ceilings. Better scale and proportion are achieved by having a woodworker remove one row of panels, thus reducing the height of the bed and making it not only more usable but also more attractive-looking.

By the 1870's, two other influences became noticeable in the Victorian grab bag of styles. These were oriental, chiefly Chinese, and Turkish. The oriental trend in a way was natural, for Americans had a long-standing acquaintance with blue and white china, teakwood chests, Kashmir shawls, and tables with fretwork carving and mother-of-pearl inlay brought by sea captains and sailors from China and India. Late-Victorian furniture made in the United States, however, displayed pseudo-oriental touches. Fretwork and Chinese-type carving did replace some of the earlier, heavier carving. Lacquer and bamboo were popular. The Turkish influence also was purely American in interpretation. Another style of the 1870's was known as American Eastlake because it was derived from the published writings of an Englishman of that name. Furniture took on a still different look because dark wood was used as decoration on naturally light-colored wood. To accomplish this, greater use was made of walnut, ash, cherry, maple, chestnut, and particularly oak than of the long-popular rosewood, mahogany, and black walnut.

Wood in itself is not necessarily indicative of any one Victorian style. Rosewood and mahogany were preferred, especially by the cabinetmakers, and were used from beginning to end. About 1855 black walnut came into favor, and continued to be used fully as much as rosewood.

Veneer, particularly of burl or with an unusual grain, was used a great deal after 1870. Panels in the doors and drawers of cupboards, sideboards, and commodes frequently were veneered. Similar panels fancied-up the cylinder-top desk or secretary. This cylinder

*This maple commode, 16½ by 34 inches, with a white marble top was made in the Midwest after 1850. The carved drawer handles are wood.*

was supported by brackets when raised. From 1840 into the 1860's, cabinetmakers used rosewood and some satinwood veneer and moldings on mahogany and rosewood pieces. Belter, of course, made extensive use of laminated rosewood, which is not technically veneer, in shaping his pieces.

Between 1840 and the 1860's, drawer

*A close-up of the drawer pulls on the maple commode shows the naturalistic carving of leaves, with fruits like pears in the center. These pulls can be gripped under the lower edge with the fingers.*

pulls were made from rosewood, mahogany, or black walnut to match the wood of the piece. These drawer pulls, 4 inches or more wide, were beautifully carved to represent leaves or leaves centered with fruit. Rarely, as on a commode, they were the only carved decoration. After 1870, metal drawer pulls became the thing. These consisted of a large plate, embossed with elaborate, rather meaningless designs, from which hung proportionately large, rectangular bails.

Upholstery on Victorian furniture was almost as typical as marble tops. Satins and velvets were used on the elegant Rococo sofas and chairs. Flower-sprigged fabrics and some brocades were well-liked. Velvet was used to some extent throughout the Victorian years, but by the 1870's plush was well established. Thereafter, plush, shiny horsehair, and tapestry weaves were popular. All pieces in a set of furniture were upholstered to match, but the extra rocking chair in the room quite likely was plush-covered and edged with deep fringe. It is interesting to peel off the upholstery on an armchair made in the 1840's and note the various materials with which it has been covered. In the process of reupholstering one pair of husband and wife chairs during the 1950's, remnants of seven other fabrics were found.

Throughout its span, the Victorian era produced a good many oddities. One of these, the ottoman or stuffed and upholstered footstool, was a sensible piece of furniture. It was outsized and overstuffed, on variously shaped and often carved, wood legs. This large footstool was common during the early and middle years, but had disappeared by the time the so-called Turkish influence flowered. The Morris chair had its forerunner in fancier reclining chairs with a high adjustable back and a leg-rest that could be pulled out from under the seat to which it was attached. Couches with a headrest like a bolster appeared late, competed with Morris chairs, and were equally undistinguished.

Belonging chiefly to the early years but never entirely out of fashion were small tables and stands made with mother-of pearl inlay and gilt. Similar pieces were made of papier-mâché with mother-of-pearl inlay. The hatrack and combination hatrack and umbrella stand were as indispensable as whatnots and far more imposing. Usually a mirror was worked in someplace in the framework, which was always tall and loaded with some kind of hook or spindle on which to hang outerwear. Hatracks took on strange shapes and outlines.

While first the elegant, then the indifferent, furniture was being produced for urban areas, country adaptations were being made. Instead of rosewood, mahogany, or black walnut, the country pieces were produced from maple, ash, hickory, birch, some cherry, and, of course, pine. Many country pieces made of light wood trimmed with dark are still to be found, and many that were stained or painted. Drawers continued to have plain wood knobs. Turnip feet became common on chests and bureaus, although bracket feet were not forgotten.

Instead of commodes with marble tops and marble splash rails, country bedrooms relied on the washstand of all wood, even including the splash rail. This washstand often had two cupboard doors under the top drawer, and behind one of the doors would be shelves. This was easier construction than one cupboard and three narrow drawers with pulls. One of the popular and common bureaus consisted of a chest of four drawers with two shallow, narrow drawers attached to the top on either side. Recessed between these two drawers was an attached mirror. Tables were more likely to have wood than marble tops, and skirts were scalloped or jigsawed. Rocking chairs and side chairs with frames of walnut or lighter-colored wood such as maple, and with cane seats and backs, were made in quantity during the 1860's and 1870's.

The quality of Victorian furniture must be judged according to the standards by which eighteenth-century furniture is. The kind of wood and its patina, normal signs of wear and general condition, and the amount and kind of restoration required must be noted shrewdly in order to set a valuation and selling price.

Since Victorian furniture was pro-

duced both by cabinetmakers and factories, the origin is an important part of identification. Sound workmanship predominated. Still, the products of cabinetmakers are bound to be valued more highly, for many reasons, than those from factories. Not that all cabinetmakers worked with the same degree of skill. Some of them were less adept at carving and veneering, and some of them handled proportions poorly, such as shaping too delicate a leg for an upholstered chair or adding one shelf too many to a whatnot.

The fact that many factories were

*A corner shelf of black walnut carved to resemble leaves and branches. The side pieces, which measure 17 inches along the center spine, are hinged; the shelf, 16 inches at its widest point, has to be hooked to the left-hand side piece to keep it in place. (The vase is early twentieth-century Royal Worcester.)*

flourishing by the 1870's did not put all of the cabinetmakers out of business. Remember that furniture with scrolled and shaped parts and bold carving came from the cabinetmaker. Later, he also used moldings. However, the flat applied molding and the shallow decorative cutting were typical factory work.

A pair of husband and wife chairs, factory-made in the 1870's or 1880's, with rather angular lines, flat molding, and incising, have been sold at auctions recently for as little as $35 to $50. A pair with Victorian Rococo lines, however tattered the upholstery, start at $50 and may bring as much as $150.

Spool-turned furniture, for which there is a demand, brings higher prices than the later nineteenth-century factory pieces. A small spool bed in only fair condition can be sold for $50 and one in excellent condition may bring $70 to $85 in some areas, $100 or more in others. A washstand with only two spool-turned members—the rods on which towels are hung—will bring $10 even if it's rickety, and one in good condition may sell for as much as $35.

A Belter bed ranges between $200 and $500; other beds of the same period (1840–60), between $100 and $300. On the other hand, it may not be possible to sell a three-piece bedroom set in Victorian Jacobean for more than $75 to $100 in many parts of the country, even though the bureau and commode have marble tops. It is sometimes possible to obtain more money

by selling a bureau and a commode separately.

A commode, incidentally, should be downgraded in price if the splash rail has been removed or lost.

Some pieces of Victorian furniture are disposed of more readily· than others. Sofas, particularly those made between 1840 and 1870, find a ready market. Side chairs and armchairs that are not too heavy sell whether they are early or late Victorian. Prices begin at about $15 per side chair and go on up to $50 or higher, according to condition, kind of wood, and the amount and kind of carving and scrolling. One possible weak point should be examined in side chairs: the crest rail topped with carving and shaped to carry out the curved lines of the uprights. This may break off during current use if the wood is excessively dried out or if someone leans back too heavily, or even in carrying the chair. The break usually will be a clean one, but since the crest rail was originally doweled into the uprights, successful and long-lasting repair is tricky.

A market exists for anything with a marble top. Granted, some people who buy marble-topped furniture do so only for the marble, which they remove and use in some contemporary fashion. Commodes and small tables, even some round center-tables, are sold and bought on their own merits.

It's the cumbersome beds, the heavy bureaus, the undistinguished dining tables and large living-room tables, the peculiarly decorated sideboards that are hard to sell. This is well known to anyone who has had to clear out the furnishings of an old house during the last ten years. Even desks and secretaries, however handsome the wood, are not easy to sell. The chief disadvantage of these pieces is their size. However, I consider it a mistake to strip off excess ornament and curlicues in the hope of making a quick sale. Let the buyer do the stripping if he wants to. After all, Victorian styles are not likely to be repeated in the forseeable future. The patience to wait for an interested buyer and then to agree on a modest price will free a person of any Victorian monstrosity eventually.

The hobbies and interests with which leisure time is now filled inspire a certain number of sales. China closets and bookcase-cupboards have been bought with the intention of converting them to gun cases or racks. The transformation is not complicated, and because these pieces have glass doors which can be locked, they display their contents with safety. These bookcase-cupboards are space-consuming, late-Victorian pieces. A typical example is a case piece, 5 to 6 feet tall, on short legs. One half is shelves behind a glass

*This mahogany melodeon or parlor organ can still be played although it is more than a century old and some of its ivory keys are battered. It came from a Midwestern home. The metal eagles have been stained to match the wood. The needlepoint on the stool is contemporary work.*

door, the other side consists of a chest of three or four drawers topped with a multitude of shelves and small cupboards.

On the other hand, some of the most unlikely Victoriana predictably finds buyers. The towering and usually ugly hatrack sells more often than not. Some people claim they buy it as a whimsey. Actually, even if no one wants to admit it, a hatrack can be most convenient in spite of its size. Parlor organs or melodeons, which became popular after 1850, are having something of a vogue again. These probably vary more in the wood and workmanship of the case than in musical quality. The selling price may have to be much less than the appraised value, depending on how much interest there is in your part of the country. Whether you charge extra or throw in the plush-covered and fringed stool or bench is your decision.

The prices that can be obtained for Victorian furniture, even the oldest and finest pieces, are comparatively modest, but they will undoubtedly increase a little with every passing decade. If you are unwilling to wait for better prices, however, you still will not have to pay to have nineteenth-century furniture carted away. Sooner or later, someone will give you something for even the most tasteless piece.

Reproductions of Victorian Rococo sofas, chairs, and tables, from the size that displayed the Boston fern to the large round center one, already are being sold in furniture and department stores. The scrolled lines and contours ape those of authentic Victorian origin but seldom are in as good proportion to the whole. The carving of any piece and the wood details of table supports are not comparable either, nor is the wood usually rosewood or mahogany. These twentieth-century reproductions are priced higher in most cases than the selling prices that can be obtained for Victorian originals in good condition.

## GLOSSARY

*Antimacassar:* a decorative cover, or tidy, pinned to the back of a chair to prevent its upholstery from being soiled; also matching pieces to protect the arms. The name comes from oil of Macassar, which was used in a dressing for men's hair.

*Beveled:* cut away at an angle or slant, as the edge of a wood tabletop or chest, for instance.

*Cartouche:* a scroll-like design; the term is used particularly to refer to the backs of chairs and sofas.

*Chiffonier:* a chest of drawers resembling a bureau but higher in proportion to its width and less often equipped with a mirror.

*China cabinet:* a case piece with glass sides and front, a wood back, and shelves for displaying good china.

*Commode:* a small, low chest with drawers and one cupboard, specifically for a bedroom, to display and store the various pieces of a china or pottery washstand set.

*Incising:* decoration cut shallowly into the surface of wood, unlike carving, which stands out in relief.

*Melodeon:* a type of small reed organ in which a suction pump draws air inward through the reeds. Also called a parlor organ. Another type of reed organ called a harmonium has a bellows that forces air outward through free metallic reeds.

*Molding:* strips of wood, flat or variously curved, rounded, or cut, and applied usually as projecting decoration.

*Patent rocker:* any of various styles of rocking chair, such as the platform rocker and the track rocker, that did not travel when in motion. Mechanism was patented.

*Spool furniture:* common household pieces in which the straight members were turned to resemble a string of spools.

*Whatnot:* an open flight of shelves, usually quite tall and sometimes tapering toward the top; used to display bric-a-brac.

# 5

## Mirrors and Frames

IN THESE DAYS of picture windows and glass walls, as well as mirrors that can be cut in any size or shape homeowners desire, it is hard to realize how highly prized a framed looking glass was 250 years ago. Although it hung on the wall, it was fully as important as the gateleg table and the wing chair. Not every household could boast of owning a mirror, for glass backed with metal so that it would reflect images was scarce and costly.

Unlike window glass, which was a product of the first glass factories in America, mirror glass was imported until almost 1800. As a matter of fact, England herself had imported it from Venice until 1673, when a glassworks was established at Vauxhall near London. This became a source of mirror glass for England and America for a good many years.

Framed mirrors too—or looking glasses, as they were usually called in America—were imported through the 1700's. The specific term "looking glass" was in general use here until at least 1800. In earlier centuries and other countries, mirrors had not been made of glass but were any polished surface, such as ivory or metal, that reflected.

During the early 1700's, silvered or mirror glass was imported, too, so that framing could be done by workmen in this country. But framed mirrors continued to be imported, for the eighteenth century brought an increasing demand for them in this country as well as in Europe and England.

Many a housewife in Philadelphia, during the years when it was the first capital of the United States, must have made her husband's life miserable until he commissioned a local cabinetmaker to copy for her the latest style mirror of Mr. George Hepplewhite, recently sent over from England. And many another housewife, after she was fairly well settled in Ohio or Kentucky, must have nagged until a carpenter was permitted to make a frame for her precious bit of looking glass.

To a greater extent than any other accessory, mirrors kept pace with the changes of style in important pieces of furniture. The woods fashionable for chairs and tables were used to make frames for mirrors, and decorative motifs and finishes also were repeated. The several distinct styles of frames that became established during the 1700's and early 1800's are all easy to recognize, in antiques or present-day reproductions, because their characteristics are so different.

Mirror glass was made in small sheets, even in England, through the 1700's. Thus, the looking glass itself was small and the frame important. When scrollwork or other trim was added to the top of the frame, as it often was, this part was called a crest. Similar decoration along the bottom of the frame became known as the skirt.

In America, the shape of the looking glass and the type of frame around it followed the style current in England and Europe. However strong the influence of English designers on American craftsmen, they managed to produce mirrors with a distinctly American look. This became more pronounced toward the end of the eighteenth century, when the elaborately decorated crest often displayed a gilded or painted eagle instead of the phoenix favored in England. When medallions became a fashionable ornament, George and Martha Washington were likely to be represented in them here. A good many of the frames that were made in this country after about 1740 were as elegant as any that were turned out in Chippendale's own workshop in England.

During the William and Mary period (1688-1702), mirrors made in England and hung in homes there and in America were comparatively small, square or rectangular pieces of glass with beveled edges held in a wide frame of walnut or pine that was carved or inlaid. During this period, some mirror frames had a high, arched crest that was carved or had a design inlaid in lighter-colored wood. Early mirrors of this style are rare and seldom seen except in museums or restorations. Furthermore, they are unfamiliar because they are not reproduced.

As the more comfortable Queen Anne furniture began to take over after 1702 in England and about 1725 in America, some cabinetmaker hit on the idea of using two panels of glass together to make a more imposing mirror. The two-panel mirror continued to be popular in this country until about 1840.

It became extremely American in character.

As it was made in this country, the Queen Anne style mirror had no strip of wood to conceal the line where the two pieces of beveled glass met. Perhaps because these mirrors were larger, frames were narrower. They usually were arched at the top, with each side showing the simple cyma or S-curve. Some frames had a crest four inches or more high, which generally had a scrolled edge and frequently an ornament carved in relief or, if it was a shell, incised and gilded. Some of the finest ones made in either New England or Philadelphia eventually came to have, along the sides, ornaments carved from wood and gilded. The inside edge of the molding nearest the glass also was often gilded.

Throughout the 1700's, the majority of the mirrors made in this country were rectangular. Only rarely was an oval looking glass framed to hang on the wall, and when it was, the frame followed the style of the rectangular ones. This became the century of the fretwork frame. It began with a minimum amount of scrolling on the crest of the Queen Anne mirror. It increased under the influence of Chippendale, with fretwork on the top and bottom of the mirror and sometimes along the sides, too. Later mirrors had a crest with a broken pediment, a fretwork apron, and carved ornaments along the sides. Top ornaments, carving, and gilding were common.

Fretwork mirrors varied in size, the intricacy of the scrollwork surrounding the frames, and the decoration. Some were quite small, with glass no larger than 8 by 13 inches. The frame itself was solid wood, but the scrollwork usually was veneer. Many fretwork mirrors were undecorated and depended on the wood for their beauty.

After 1740, the scrollwork and the broken pediment of the crest were likely to be emphasized with gold leaf. Then, too, carved garlands or other

*The fretwork mirror has been popular in this country since about 1750. The one shown here still has its old looking-glass in a veneer frame with solid-wood crest and apron. Both the frame and the scrollwork have been repaired.*

side ornaments also were covered with gold leaf. Any decoration on the crest or any top ornament also was covered with gold leaf. The phoenix was popular as a top ornament until it was superseded by the eagle in the 1790's. The three feathers of the Prince of Wales were used as an ornament on the crest of fretwork mirrors made in this country as well as in England, and this motif too was covered with gold leaf.

One style of Chippendale frame is generally called a "Constitution" mirror. (A similar style also was made in England.) It was popular by 1750 here, which was a long time before the Colonies had adopted a constitution and become the United States. This rectangular mirror had a frame with a broken pediment crest surmounted by a phoenix or an eagle. Moldings beneath the pediment were sometimes carved and were always gilded, as were the cyma curves of the pediment and the bird. Not all Constitution mirrors had gilded side ornaments, but they all had an apron that was either scrolled or outrounded. The mirror glass—in one piece—also was accented with a narrow gilded molding.

When Hepplewhite and Sheraton furniture began to displace Chippendale's styles in England, mirrors as well as furniture in this country reflected the changes too. It is interesting that both Chippendale and Hepplewhite mirrors usually held only one piece of glass, whereas the Sheraton styles in

this country were based on two panels. There was considerable variation in the height of the rectangular mirrors framed in the fretwork and Constitution styles derived from Chippendale and the frames with typical Hepplewhite ornament. Some were only 13 to 18 inches high; others were 45 inches or more.

Hepplewhite mirrors displayed less fretwork but were usually elaborately decorated; many had scrolled or fretwork aprons. One distinctive characteristic was the carved draperies, garlands, or sprays of foliage and flowers that hung partway down on either side. The crest was almost invariably a broken pediment surmounted by an

*A mahogany mirror (circa 1815) distinguished for its broken pediment and garlands covered with gold leaf.*

urn that held graceful flowers and foliage on wirework stems, or occasionally sheaves of wheat. The side ornaments, the urn, and its contents always were gilded. With its delicate details, a mirror framed in the style of Hepplewhite was something to be proud of.

Few Hepplewhite mirrors had two panels of glass like the Sheraton style of mirrors that became general around 1800. Those that did, usually had painted decoration on the small upper panel. However, a Hepplewhite mirror of this sort can be distinguished readily from a Sheraton mirror because of the details of the frame. The Sheraton styles on the whole were simpler

*Mirrors with two panels were common until about 1840 because glass was made in small sheets. The upper panel invariably was painted.*

than the Hepplewhite, although those with Sheraton influence often were completely gilded.

Mirrors consisting of two panels of glass must have been extremely popular between 1800 and 1840—otherwise, so many of them would not be around still. The lower piece, more than twice as long as the upper one, was looking glass. The smaller panel (it gradually displaced the elaborate scrolled crest as ornament) was painted—or, later, stenciled—with a landscape, a seascape featuring a sailing vessel, a vase of flowers or a basket of fruit, or an eagle with garlands or medallions. These subjects, which seem to have been about equal in popularity, were done in colors or in gold leaf and black. The more stylized painting of an eagle was sometimes done against a white background. The *Constitution*, a ship that gained fame in the War of 1812, was a popular theme for a good many years. Other mirrors displayed a painted seascape with a vessel that could not possibly be the *Constitution*. Although painted landscapes were usually attractive, there were many that could be classed only as folk art.

Two architectural details help to identify a Sheraton mirror or one made during the years his style was dominant in this country. Both emphasize the rectilinear lines that distinguished his furniture. Most Sheraton mirrors had a flat cornice. On some rather elaborate frames, the cornice was topped by a good-sized eagle with urns or fini-

The Sheraton gilt mirror (1800-1820) with cornice and balls and spiral molding was a popular style in this country. The mottled glass is old but may not be the original, since the upper panel is not painted.

A two-panel mirror (circa 1820) with the original painted panel, looking glass, backboard, and unretouched frame. The corner blocks and the strip between the glass panels are veneer; the half-round pilasters are painted black and decorated with metallic gold paint.

als at the outer ends. These exceptions, as well as the majority of the flat-topped, undecorated ones were set off by a row of small wooden balls under the cornice. The balls, like the frame, were gilded.

The second, easily recognizable characteristic was the superimposing of pilasters or half-columns, first along either side of the frame, then on all four sides. These were often simple rounded half-columns, but just as often they were spirally or vertically reeded. They were gilded to match the rest of the frame, painted, or painted and then burnished with gilt or metallic paints to contrast with the frame.

The walnut frame of this mirror with a painted upper panel borrows its cornice from Sheraton, the three turned pilasters from the Empire style. (1815-30)

A distinct style that owed nothing to Sheraton and was perhaps the first to be called a "mirror" in this country appeared around 1800. This was the round, convex mirror with a heavy, circular gold frame. It is often called a Duncan Phyfe mirror, although cabinetmakers in other parts of the country turned out this style too. The convex mirror was usually small, about 24 inches in diameter, but the frame was wide and often deep and repeated the circular lines.

When candleholders were fastened on either side of the base of the frame of this circular mirror, it was known as a girandole. Some mirrors had brackets for four candles. With or without the

*Girandole mirrors made in this country were ornate, but usually had only attached candle arms. However, this one, made in England about 1740, also has a head of Apollo, gilded as is the frame.* Courtesy Colonial Williamsburg

candleholders, there was plenty of other ornament on these circular frames. They were deeply carved and usually displayed a row of small balls, rope, or other ornamental trim. An eagle usually surmounted the frame. In addition, many of these frames had a pendent finial of carved foliage at the base. These circular frames for convex mirrors were invariably gilded. They were made until about 1820 and frequently are copied today.

Perhaps even rarer than the round convex mirror is the courting mirror. The first ones were imported from China about 1800 and others were made in this country. The name came from the fact that these unusual mirrors were given to young women by their suitors. The courting mirror was small, 8 to 12 inches high by 6 to 8 inches wide. Between the finely molded edges of the wood frame were inserted small pieces or bands of glass with flowers painted on them. Often such a mirror was hung on the wall in the box into which it fitted—with the lid removed, of course.

The turn of the century also brought into wider use the shaving stand or dressing glass. This was an oval or rectangular mirror mounted on a shallow chest of two or three little drawers in which shaving articles could be stored. When the shaving stand was placed on a bureau or high chest, the mirror was at the right height for a gentleman to see himself while shaving. These stands had been made in the

A *Tabernacle mirror (1820-40), especially when its frame is covered with gold leaf, is an imposing piece. The pilasters on the four sides of the mirror shown here are both turned and carved with acanthus leaves; the corner blocks are centered with rosettes. Probably the original upper panel was painted.*

A *shaving stand or dressing glass was made to stand on a bureau. This mahogany one was built in the workshop of a Virginia plantation between 1830 and 1850.*

early 1700's, but they were little seen in this country until about 1790. Most of those that are found have an oval or shield-shaped glass indicative of the Hepplewhite influence and, after 1800, a rectangular glass typical of Sheraton. Many shaving stands or dressing glasses were made of mahogany. Other choices were walnut, cherry, maple, and pine, the pine sometimes faced with veneer.

The massive gold frame of the convex mirror, so popular in the early 1800's, indicated a trend. Rectangular frames soon lost their delicate lines and decoration. The half-round pilasters that first appeared on Sheraton mirrors became the most important part of the frame in the 1820's and 1830's. These pilasters were the basis of a style known as the Tabernacle mirror, which was made in several versions during the American Empire period (1815–40).

This strictly American style lacked the cornice of Sheraton-type mirrors. It was a rectangular mirror consisting of two pieces of glass, with the joining covered by a narrow piece of framing. The half-round columns on the four sides were spirally reeded, vase-and-ring, vase-and-cylinder, or spool turned, or carved with acanthus leaves. In some examples, carving and turning were combined. Square blocks or rosettes were mounted on the four corners. A country version of this mirror had turned columns and plain, square corner-blocks of wood, neither painted nor decorated. A handsome mirror in this style might well be made of cheaper wood, but this would not matter because every inch of the frame would be covered with gold leaf. Such a mirror would have rosette blocks and probably some carving.

However fashionable the Tabernacle mirror was between 1815 and 1840, more of the simple ogee-molded, or American Empire, frames probably were made. This plain style, usually rectangular and consisting of one piece of glass, was made in many sizes. These mirrors could be hung either vertically or horizontally. The frame, about 5 inches wide, had an inch-wide flat banding on the inner and outer edges, with a 3-inch ogee molding in be-

*During the American Empire period (1815-40), mahogany frames as much as 5 inches wide made small looking-glasses appear more important. The example pictured was made in Massachusetts, but the style was common throughout the country.*

tween. The corners were mitered. Mahogany or mahogany veneer was most often used, for it was the fashionable wood of the Empire period. A few of these wide-framed mirrors were painted to look like either mahogany or rosewood. The fact that this still is probably the easiest style of mirror to find does not detract from its simple good looks.

The early 1800's brought two other types of mirror to the attention of Americans. Both the pier glass and the mantel mirror gained in popularity during the American Empire period and have been made in some form ever since. Not only were they larger than the mirrors popular during the 1700's, but also each one was made for a specific location.

The pier glass was a large, vertical mirror considerably higher than it was wide, and narrow enough to be hung on the wall between two windows. The frames of the first ones were likely to be either mahogany or a cheaper wood covered with gold leaf.

The mantel mirror was a horizontal one consisting of three panels of looking glass. The center panel was the largest and was flanked by smaller panels. Four columns usually framed the sections of glass. The earliest mantel mirrors often had upper panels of glass on which garlands or baskets of flowers were painted. By 1820, the frames displayed Sheraton and American Empire details. They were likely to be made of pine and covered with gold leaf. Mantel mirrors continued to be made during the Victorian era, and the later frames sometimes were mahogany or rosewood. The mantel mirror always has been more popular in the United States than elsewhere.

The Victorian era (1840–1900) itself made no outstanding contributions to mirror styles. Looking glass of better quality and in larger sheets became more readily available with each decade. As furniture began to be turned out in sets for different rooms, it became customary to attach sizable mirrors to sideboards, bureaus, and other appropriate pieces, thus tending somewhat to decrease the use of mirrors separately on the wall.

*Another late-Victorian style of frame for a photograph or mirror was made of pine, painted black, and decorated with raised clusters of flowers and fruit covered with gold leaf. The oval mahogany or walnut frames from family photographs of the late 1800's also make attractive mirror frames.*—Ted Eastwood

*Fresh gold leaf strengthens the naturalistic ornament of a 3½-inch-wide frame that was used for a looking glass before 1860.*

Before the Victorian period was too old, the cheval glass began to be popular in the United States. This took up almost as much room as some pieces of furniture, since it was large enough to reflect the whole figure. The usually narrow and simple frame was mounted in a wooden support so that the mirror could be tilted, the support itself being equipped with wheels or casters that made it possible to move the cheval glass about.

Attaching mirrors to pieces of furniture did away also with the need for mirror knobs or mounts. Few people nowadays recognize them, but it was fashionable throughout the 1700's and in the early 1800's to support a looking glass or mirror on small ornamental rosettes or disks attached to long screws or spikes, which were inserted into the wall. They were used in pairs below the mirror and helped to tilt the glass forward (an advantage when looking glasses were small). They seem especially appropriate with fretwork mirrors but were used under other rectangular ones too. The ornamental disk might be glass, pottery, or metal. Many were brass. Metal mounts sometimes framed a painted or enameled medallion or a simple pottery or glass button. Pressed glass rosettes were made in different patterns, and slipped onto spikes of pewter or other metal, where they were held in place by a screw knob. These pressed glass mounts were made in various sizes and in clear as well as colored glass. Between 1830 and 1850, matching rosettes were made in a small size for a mirror and in a larger size to hold curtain tiebacks.

All styles of mirrors during the eighteenth and nineteenth centuries were made by skilled cabinetmakers and frame-makers in prosperous cities.

*Mirror knobs like these brass ones with china rosettes were screwed into the wall to tilt the small looking-glass forward. Ornamental mounts were customary throughout the 1700's; pressed glass ones were popular in the 1830's.*—Ted Eastwood

They also were copied by traveling craftsmen and rural cabinetmakers and carpenters, who frequently erred in proportion, finish, and decoration. The style may be easy to recognize, but the skill with which the frame has been made and the proportions of the various parts differentiate between an excellent and a mediocre example. The amount of ornament and the skill with which it was applied are other factors in arriving at a current monetary value.

An antique mirror authentic in every detail is certain to have glass that is cloudy, mottled, and blackened in spots. Replacing this with modern, clear glass reduces the value of the old mirror. So would resilvering the old glass, which is a hazardous job even when done by experts. Old glass is brittle. There is no reason why a person should not put new glass in an old mirror, if the substitution seems desirable, before hanging it on a wall. If the substitution is made, then the old glass should be packed away carefully and saved, to be restored in the event that the mirror is to be sold.

The glass in the oldest mirrors had beveled edges. If a frame belonged to either the William and Mary or Queen Anne styles, which were fashionable in America until about 1750, one proof of its authenticity will be the beveled edges of the glass. The original glass itself certainly will not be clear now and the beveled edges will be uneven and wavy to the touch. On modern mirror glass, the bevel is smooth as well as wider. The edges of mirrors made after 1750 with fretwork frames or two panels of glass—as made up to about 1840—seem not to have been beveled. Incidentally, it is not uncommon today to find an old two-panel mirror with plain glass in the upper section, for the painted upper panel was sometimes removed by a late-nineteenth-century owner.

The looking glass in mirrors made in the eighteenth and early years of the nineteenth centuries was protected by thin backboards, usually pine and unfinished. In other words, the backs were not closed in neatly as are those of modern mirrors.

The golden color of trim and frames always was gold leaf, not metallic paint. Gold leaf is an extremely thin sheet of real gold, and applying it is an expert art. It does wear thin and come off in patches eventually. Excessive humidity for weeks during summer is, in my opinion, hard on gold-leaf frames. If frames are to be refinished, it should be done with gold leaf rather than by gilding or painting. Retouching is not advisable, for it will always show. To have a frame recovered with gold leaf is expensive. Whether or not you decide to have such a frame, which is in bad condition, done over before selling will depend somewhat on the possible market for the mirror.

The kind of wood from which a frame was made is not always a factor in its valuation. All mirrors that were cov-

ered with gold leaf or veneer—and there were a great many of them— were made of pine. If a veneer frame had a crest and possibly a skirt, these parts were made of thin wood that matched the veneer. Small strips of pine glued on the back were placed there by the original maker, not added later.

Many of the fretwork mirrors made between 1750 and 1780 were solid mahogany. Mahogany was popular again during the American Empire period, and rosewood might have been used then as well as during the Victorian days. Walnut, cherry, and maple were frames. Veneers frequently showed other fine hardwoods used for mirror burl or cross-grain markings.

Almost all of the eighteenth-century styles are still being made in some quantity. The Queen Anne with graceful arched top, the Chippendale or fretwork mirror, the Hepplewhite with classical urn and flowers, the convex glass in a round frame, and the rectangular mirror with upper panel of painted glass are part of the usual stock in most furniture stores. The finest examples of these styles made during the 1700's and early 1800's are certain either to be in a museum or restoration or else to be cherished antiques hanging on a wall in the homes of the persons who have inherited them.

There seems to be a ready market for almost all styles of old mirrors except those with the wide mahogany frames made during the American Empire period. These may have the original glass still in quite good condition, but in spite of the fine mahogany frame and the over-all simplicity of the mirror, they can seldom be sold for their appraised value, which may be less than $50 or as much as $150. In fact, at country auctions, I have seen a fine American Empire mirror go for as little as $5. The Tabernacle mirror, made at about the same time, is easier to sell, perhaps because it seems more unusual. One in this style refinished with gold leaf or with the original gold leaf in good condition might sell for $50 to $150; a plain wood one with turnings instead of carving, for $15 to perhaps $35.

The skill with which the frame was made, its present condition, and the glass in it help to determine a fair selling price for the popular styles of eighteenth- and early-nineteenth-century mirrors. An excellent and authenticated example of Queen Anne, fretwork, or a Sheraton mirror with balls under the cornice might be appraised and sell for several hundred dollars. On the other hand, there are many in all of these styles which sell for less. A small fretwork mirror with some of the scrollwork broken off and veneer chipped from the frame is worth $5 if all the pieces can be found. With care, it can be repaired to look quite good.

Not yet scarce but always popular are

the early-nineteenth-century mirrors with two panels of glass, the upper one painted. Almost all of them are attractive, even if the painting is quite primitive. A small one with a mediocre painting might bring $15 or less. Many of these from 12 to 15 inches wide and 24 to 27 inches long sell for $35 to $50 or perhaps a little more, depending on workmanship and condition.

A shaving stand or dressing glass made between 1800 and 1850 can be valued at $150 to $300, depending on the wood from which it was made and its condition. At any time, it should be possible to sell one in almost any part of the country for $150.

There is no doubt but that mirrors are more popular today than they ever were. In fact, some kind is likely to be found in every room of a house. This helps the sale of old mirrors, although many people buy one chiefly for the frame and scorn the dingy-looking glass. Here, then, is an outlet for some of the picture frames stacked in many an attic.

Although the Victorian period may not have originated any styles of mirrors, it did see pictures used abundantly on walls. Frames, whether for oil paintings, prints, and, in the late years of the century, photographs of relatives, were either heavy or fancy enough so that no one could help but notice them. Styles ranged from rococo with infinite curlicues to simple wood moldings.

The large rococo gilded frames that were customary for oil paintings actually make handsome mirrors. Most of them framed a rectangular painting, but occasionally an oval one is found. By all means, look carefully at the painting or print within the frame to be sure that it has no particular value. Quite often these frames with their still life or floral paintings darkened but intact are seen at auctions. If you come across a half-dozen of these wide, scrolled and gilded frames, a dealer or interior decorator may take them off your hands for a nominal sum.

Two common styles of small, oval Victorian picture frames are especially adaptable for conversion to mirrors. One of these is the painted wood frame with applied clusters of flowers or fruit covered with gold leaf. The other is the simple, wide frame in a molded curve of mahogany or walnut. Both of these oval styles are easiest to find in frames that are about 13½ inches long and 12 inches wide with openings 8 to 9 inches long and 6½ to 7½ inches wide. After mirror glass has been cut and fitted into these frames, they will need new backing, for the original ones usually were rough wood. These new mirrors can be hung on the wall or fitted with an easel back for use on a dressing table or other surface.

In the late Victorian years, oval mirrors of about the same size were often golden. The finest ones had frames about 2½ inches wide with raised decoration twining around the outer edge in the form of clusters of grapes and leaves or perhaps flowers and foliage. These should be recovered entirely with gold leaf. Another style of picture frame, which can be converted to a mirror if it is large enough, had a narrow frame, plain or molded, which was gilded. The latest and narrowest were metal.

Frames of wood in natural color decorated with shallow carving or incising were commonly used for family pictures toward the end of the Victorian era, the larger sizes for the lithographs that were so popular. The carving in some cases was no more than reeding in two widths. Many of these frames crisscrossed at the corners, where there usually was some kind of ornament. A china button ringed with brass was sometimes attached at each corner. If a carved leaf decorated each corner, the wood frame was often carved or incised to resemble bark.

These frames, some of which had slender wooden easels inserted in their backs, were made in a range of sizes. Some had openings only 3½ by 2¼ inches; others were 6 by 4⅛ inches, and some were as large as 11 or 12 by 8 inches. The smallest ones have no particular value except as picture frames. The larger sizes are possibilities worth considering for mirrors, particularly since they may already have easels.

Narrow, light wood frames that need repairs on the molding, a refitting of joints, or refinishing of the wood are likely to be worth the time and effort, since the resulting mirror will be distinctive. With patience, the broken curl of scrollwork on a rococo frame can be built up and will not be noticeable if the frame is to be gilded or painted before the new mirror glass is inserted.

An oval frame of walnut or mahogany with an opening 8½ by 6¾ inches probably can be sold for $5 or so. A pair is often appealing and may perhaps bring $12.50, instead of only $5 each. Larger sizes with the wood in good condition are worth $10 with an opening 8½ by 11 inches, $12.50 with an opening of 14 by 12 inches. A crisscross wood frame (an opening 6 by 4½ inches) with carved leaves at the corners would not be overpriced at $3.50 to $4, and a larger one (12 by 8 inches) at $7.50.

The oval gold-leaf frame will be worth more than a gilded metal one. A simple molded gold-leaf frame with an opening 8 by 5¾ inches should bring $5 or more, depending on where you are trying to sell it. Similar frames with larger openings, perhaps 7½ by 20 inches, start at $10 or so. The smaller gold-leaf frame with relief decoration should sell for a higher price, to be determined by the amount of the decoration and the condition of it and of the gold leaf. If it is in excellent condition, certainly even a small frame of this sort should be worth $10 to $14.

If the market seems sluggish for old picture frames to be transformed into mirrors, look them over for other possible uses that may help to dispose of them. If they are sturdy as well as good-looking, a shallow box could be attached to the back so they could be hung on the wall to display many things that are better preserved under glass. Certainly many frames can be found that will hold one or more opened fans more appropriately than the rather cumbersome glass fan boxes that can be bought for the purpose. Shells, bits of fine old needlework or lace, butterflies, dried flowers, and many other treasures arranged against an effective background (fabric offers many choices) in a Victorian picture frame can be a stunning wall decoration in homes with either contemporary or traditional furnishings. If you resort to this method, it may be necessary to line up cooperation, perhaps first from a carpenter who can prepare the frames for their special contents, and then from an antique shop, gift shop, or interior decorator, who will take the finished ones on consignment. Or one of the latter outlets may see the advantage of taking the frames and having them prepared by their own workmen for display purposes.

The assortment of picture frames that clutters the attic and often the walls of an old house is bound to include some that deserve no more than being turned over to a rummage sale or second-hand store. The most likely ones for conversion into mirrors or other purposes may be sold individually. The sum total brought by the choicest frames will probably compensate for those that must be given away and for the in-between ones that go to make up the miscellaneous lot sold to a dealer for a small amount or sent to an auction, from which the return is likely to be the minimum.

You will probably want to destroy the photographs of grim-looking relatives and friends—and somehow in the early photographs people always did look grim—before the frames are disposed of in one way or another. It is worth the time to investigate the possible value of paintings, however crudely done, or prints. In any case, anyone you approach who knows something about selling old picture frames will be able to advise on whether the contents should be destroyed or left in place.

# 6
## Clocks and Watches

THE SUN, MOON, AND STARS were the
chief means by which man judged the
passing of time before clocks and
watches were invented. Some people
still claim to recognize the time of
day by the opening of certain flowers,
earliest of all being dandelions about
4:00 A.M., and the latest moonflowers
and cereus that unfurl after dark.

Flowers open according to the sun and
never adjust themselves to Daylight
Saving Time. Nor can sundials, which
were mentioned in the Old Testament,
be adjusted to Daylight Saving Time
without a great deal more trouble than
is needed to set clocks and watches.
The principle of the sundial is simple.
Most sundials are made of metal with
a style or gnomon whose shadow falls
on a marked dial in such a way as to
indicate the time of the day. Since
there must be sun in order to have
shadows, sundials are of little use on
cloudy days.

The water clock, or clepsydra, was invented by at least the second century
B.C. as a means of measuring time. It
was used by both the Egyptians and
the Greeks. The sandglass and the
hourglass, which may contain water or
mercury instead of sand, work on the
same principle as the water clock. Such
a glass can be made in smaller sizes to
measure shorter intervals of time than
an hour, but of course does not indicate the time of day.

The mechanical clock probably was invented by the tenth century, perhaps
earlier. It came into use in Europe during the thirteenth century. The early
ones functioned chiefly by a system
of weights and counterweights. Both
clocks and watches are known as timepieces; a watch, however, is a timepiece to be carried on the person. It,
like the clock, was invented in Europe, but not until several centuries
later. Generally a clock has a mecha-

nism by which it strikes the hours and sometimes lesser units of time on a bell or gong; a watch merely shows the time (periodically, they have been made to chime, strike the hour, or perform various services).

The earliest clockmakers certainly had some scientific bent, if they were not actually astronomers. Jewelers, locksmiths, blacksmiths, carpenters, and cabinetmakers also contributed to clockmaking. Many of the clockmakers in this country and elsewhere were also watchmakers, but the man who could repair a clock was not necessarily a clockmaker as well. During Colonial days in America—even later, perhaps—a boy served a long and arduous apprenticeship in order to become a clockmaker.

Among the hundreds, if not thousands, of men who aided in the development of mechanical timepieces, three were outstanding: Christiaan Huygens, a Dutch scientist, who was the first (1656) to employ the pendulum to regulate the movement of clocks; Robert Hooke, an Englishman, who invented the anchor escapement for clocks in the 1670's; and Peter Henlein, a locksmith in Germany, who about 1500 figured out and used a mainspring, thus making it possible to produce small timepieces or watches. Both Huygens and Hooke have been credited with the invention of spiral springs and the balance wheel for watches.

American clockmakers, however, were

the ones who worked out methods of manufacture and interchangeable parts, so that the price of clocks was reduced so fantastically that any family could afford to buy one. This was chiefly during the 1830's. As a result, there are many interesting nineteenth-century clocks to be found in this country. They are not limited to any one region or state, for peddlers carried and sold them far from the places where they were manufactured. Furthermore, many clockmakers who had served apprenticeships in New England and Pennsylvania in the late 1700's moved southward and westward. Most of the clocks made during the 1800's are still telling time, or can be repaired so that they do. So are many that were made during the 1700's. Some of them, inevitably, have had electric works substituted for their old wood or brass ones.

America has added great names to the history of clockmaking too. The list includes not only enterprising Eli Terry and Chauncey Jerome of Connecticut, who revolutionized the industry, and Seth Thomas, who also helped to establish it so firmly that it is still a leading one in that state. Their equally great predecessors during the 1700's included the Willard family in Roxbury, Massachusetts, David Rittenhouse, perhaps most famous of the many tall-case clockmakers in and around Philadelphia, Pennsylvania, and Levi Hutchins, who is credited with making the first alarm clock—in Concord, New Hampshire, in 1787 (this was a pine shelf clock with a glass door 29 inches high and 12 inches wide).

Clockmaking was a highly honorable profession, although the average clockmaker produced only four or five tall-case clocks per year and David Rittenhouse probably turned out no more than two a year. Pennsylvania was as important as New England during the late 1600's and the 1700's. Skilled clockmakers who trained many younger men were attracted there, and as a result, Philadelphia and Lancaster became centers noted for fine tall-case clocks as well as excellent watches. Not that good tall-case clocks were not produced in New England, but it was not until the 1830's that New England took the undisputed lead in clockmaking.

Still considered one of the best devices for accurate timekeeping and timetelling is the weight-and-pendulum clock whose cumbersome mechanism gave rise to the tall- or long-case clock. This is more familiarly known as a grandfather's clock, although this nickname did not become common until a songwriter, Henry Clay Work, in 1875 wrote the song entitled "Grandfather's Clock." The earliest-known surviving tall-case clock is one in England dated 1681, but this style had been made earlier in both England and Holland. It also was made in France. In this country, it was made along the East Coast, notably in New England and Pennsylvania throughout the eighteenth century and at least in the early

years of the nineteenth.

Occasionally an uncased weight-and-pendulum clock is seen. The dial, usually a fairly simple one, was mounted on a square block and the weights and the pendulum hung free against a backboard.

The tall cases that housed the works —they often were nine feet tall and averaged two feet in width—were examples of fine cabinetwork. Details of style changed with the period, as did those of other pieces of furniture, but not the over-all outlines and proportions. Seventeenth-century cases were rectangular and heavily ornamented, and had flat tops, sometimes with a cornice. The arched top appeared in the early 1700's, the scrolled top about 1750. The broken-arch top was much in evidence on' Pennsylvania tall-case clocks between 1760 and 1800. Some were more heavily carved than others. About 1790, the fretwork top with three finials became fashionable.

Oak was used for the cases of the earliest tall-case clocks made in England. Walnut and mahogany were used throughout the eighteenth century in both England and America, and here also cherry made many handsome cases. Satinwood and other costly exotics were preferred for inlay.

Some of the famous eighteenth-century cabinetmakers produced the tall cases. John Goddard and John Townsend, who made such beautiful furni-

*The tall-case clock was made from the 1600's to about 1850. The painted dial, the cartouche with a rocking ship, and the fretwork top with its three finials indicate that the one pictured here may have been made between 1780 and 1800.*

during the 1700's, are to be treasured —or sold for a good price today. Some of the oldest clocks have been repaired or worked on by later clockmakers, not always to the advantage of the clocks.

The dials are sometimes more interesting than the wooden cases. Originally, dials were brass with numerals engraved on a silver ring. After 1770, these were gradually supplanted by painted or enameled dials. The dials of the early tall-case clocks with flat tops were square. When the arched top began to be made soon after 1700, the dial also was arched, with a cartouche or semicircle above the dial proper. The four spandrels, or pie-shaped corner pieces, that filled out the round face were sometimes decorated with floral sprays or figures, or with ornamental metalwork.

Clockmakers often signed their names and perhaps places of business on the dial. This signature frequently was on the cartouche. Then, about 1720, motion was carried to the cartouche. Within it might be a ship that rocked in the sea, a deer that pranced, Father Time with his scythe, or some other animated figure that seemed appropriate. Soon afterward, some clockmaker thought of making a moon wheel that would progress through the moon's monthly phases, and the cartouche became the obvious place for this. The two hemispheres that obscured the moon for certain of its phases became part of the cartouche too. The moon wheel, which usually had a "Man in

ture in Newport, Rhode Island, built fine clock cases with a block-and-shell motif in the long panel. Probably many of the skilled cabinetmakers who turned out the Philadelphia Chippendale furniture made some clock cases too. There is no question of the grace and beauty of the cases that were made by master cabinetmakers, but it should go without saying that some tall cases were finer than others. However, even the crudest ones, if they can be authenticated as having been made the Moon" face—some of the moon cartouches also had painted sky and gold stars—had to be set independently of the clock, but it could be quite accurate. A variation, not as widely made as the moon wheel, was the planetarium, which showed the motion of several planets, including Uranus, Jupiter, Saturn, and Earth.

Tall-case clocks struck the hour, of course, and most of them the half- and quarter-hours too. On the hour, the number was struck. The quarters and half-hour usually were differentiated by different notes or combinations of notes. Some tall-case clocks had chimes —that is, a set of five to twelve bells tuned to a musical scale. Chimes usually played a recognizable tune on the hour, and some, during the late 1700's, were adjusted to play more than one tune.

A tall-case clock was as much a symbol of a family's wealth and community standing as silverware. Even during the 1700's, such a clock could cost several hundred dollars, and so anyone who owned one was—understandably—quite likely to mention it in his will. In fact, these cherished tall-case clocks were almost always handed down carefully from generation to generation.

Of all the clockmakers who were busy in and around Philadelphia during the 1700's and up until about 1850, the greatest one was David Rittenhouse. At the age of seventeen, he had estab-

lished himself as a maker of accurate clocks. Actually, Rittenhouse was as much a scientist as he was a clockmaker. He was an associate of Benjamin Franklin in the American Philosophical Society and succeeded Franklin as the Society's president.

No one is likely to stumble on a Rittenhouse tall-case clock (he probably made no more than 100 in his 47 years of work at this trade). Nor is there much possibility of finding a clock made by Matthias W. Baldwin, who was a maker of tall-case clocks in Philadelphia in the early 1800's, before he turned to locomotives. Samuel Bispham was working in Philadelphia as early as 1696.

Many clockmakers who had served their apprenticeship in Philadelphia moved on to other parts of the country. Lancaster and various towns south and west of Philadelphia also produced some fine clockmakers. Martin Shreiner, who conducted his business from 1790 to 1830, was one of the best of Lancaster's many excellent clockmakers.

John Wright in New York City and James Jacks in Charleston, South Carolina, were other noted clockmakers of the 1700's. The Willard family of Roxbury, Massachusetts, made their name one of the most honored in early clockmaking in New England, as we have already mentioned. There were four Willard brothers — Benjamin, Aaron, Ephraim, and Simon — who

*The style of clock that required a long case to house its weights and pendulum was also known as a grandfather's clock. Aaron Willard, an expert Massachusetts clockmaker, signed the dial of this one.*

engaged in clockmaking from the 1760's to the early 1800's. Simon became the most famous, not only for his magnificent tall-case clocks but also as the originator of two new styles of clocks—the lighthouse and the banjo.

Simon Willard probably was the foremost clockmaker of his time in New England. However, there were other notable ones. Thomas Harland was almost as influential in Connecticut as Simon Willard was in Massachusetts. Joshua Wilder in Hingham, Massachusetts, David Wood in Newburyport, James Dakin and Daniel Munroe in Boston, and B. C. Gilman in Exeter, New Hampshire, were only a few who

were active around 1800 and who left splendid examples of clocks that still keep accurate time.

Half-high or grandmother's clocks were small ones, about 4 feet tall, made along the lines of the tall-case clock. These smaller versions appeared in the late 1700's and were made to about 1820. They are much rarer now than tall-case clocks.

In many respects, the hanging wall clock was a miniature of the tall-case clock. It, as well as the bracket, or shelf or mantel, clock, was made in America from about 1780. In England, bracket clocks had been made almost as early as tall-case clocks. There, as well as in this country, a wooden support or bracket to attach to the wall often was made especially to display this good-sized clock.

The first bracket or shelf clocks were not only large but also owed a great deal to the tall-case clock. They were more squat in their proportions, but were much larger than the shelf or mantel clock that became popular after 1830. Two feet or a little more was probably the average height. Most of the early ones had a cupboard underneath with a door that could be opened to get at the works. Fine cabinetwork was evident in most of the cases, and the faces on the whole were simpler than those of the tall-case clocks.

Probably Simon Willard's famous

*The hanging wall clock shown here, made in New England between 1810 and 1830, has been electrified. The smudged dial was washed carefully, new hands similar to the original ones were added, and the broken case was restored by a cabinetmaker.*

lighthouse clock, which he patented and made between 1810 and 1820, could be classed as a bracket clock. The works were encased in a graduated two-section base of wood, and the clock face was covered with a large glass dome. The clock did indeed resemble a miniature lighthouse. Lighthouse clocks are rare.

The earliest of the hanging wall clocks also were close to two feet long. Although they, too, had some resemblance to the tall-case clock, they were

not nearly so handsome. Most famous of the hanging wall clocks—and much easier to find than older styles—is the banjo clock. As made by Simon Willard, who patented it in 1802, the case called to mind the musical instrument of that name. It averaged three feet or a little less in length. The round face at the top was surmounted by an eagle or simpler finial. The tapering case ended in a rectangular box (the length was needed to house the pendulum). The banjo clock was copied widely by other clockmakers. Many of them followed Willard's style quite closely, but banjo clocks made in Connecticut had a square top enclosing the face.

The dials of banjo clocks were quite simple and very clear, as a rule. Some few had plain all-wood cases. More of them had glass panels on the two lower sections, and these were painted. The lowest rectangular part often displayed a scene or perhaps an eagle framed with a garland.

From the banjo clock came the girandole. This was an ornate case design based on the shape of the banjo clock. The frame of a girandole clock was not only elaborately decorated but also usually covered with gold leaf. The girandole was perhaps the most elegant of all American clocks; certainly it was the fanciest.

Whether or not New England produced more tall-case clocks than Pennsylvania or any other state may be questionable. However, there is no doubt but that New England became the leader in shelf and mantel clocks. Clockmaking is not only one of New England's oldest industries but, because of Yankee ingenuity, remains a leading one to the present day.

Until about 1830, any kind of clock continued to be made by hand in New England. Eli Terry, a Connecticut Yankee, gets credit for introducing assembly-line methods for the manufacture of clocks. He began making clocks in Waterbury, Connecticut, in 1793,

*The banjo clock was patented by Simon Willard in 1802. This example, made by a New Haven clockmaker between 1810 and 1820, has its original case, face, pendulum, and works, and still keeps time accurately. The finial was carved to match the original one, which was broken, and the glass over the middle section is also new.*

and in 1797 was granted a patent for an equation clock. At first Terry and his helpers would make a few dozen clocks by hand, and then Terry would set out with clocks hanging from his saddle, and sell them. As orders began to increase, Terry installed machinery, and became the first clockmaker to do so. One of his mechanics was Seth Thomas, who soon went into business for himself and made a name that is still honored.

Another Connecticut Yankee, Chauncey Jerome, figured out the advantages of brass over wooden parts. Dampness could halt wooden parts, the teeth of gears broke easily, and skilled hands were needed to put the wooden movements together. If pieces were brass, they could be made by machine, assembled more easily, and also be interchangeable from one clock to another. At first, in 1837, Jerome is said to have produced 200 brass clocks a day. This number grew in a short time to 600 per day.

Although there was an economic depression throughout this country in 1837, Jerome's ideas kept the clock industry humming. Furthermore, he helped allied industries such as brass stamping and woodworking. Terry's revolutionary assembly-line methods had produced a shelf clock that could be sold for as little as $40, but Jerome's innovations brought the price of similar clocks down to about $12. Later, a fairly reliable brass-movement clock could be bought for $6 or less.

Both Terry and Jerome produced clocks that were smaller and less cumbersome than heretofore. In addition, they kept accurate time yet had interchangeable parts. Because they were smaller and could be carried in greater numbers by the omnipresent nineteenth-century peddlers, distribution multiplied. Shelf clocks with brass movements also could be carried more safely than those with wooden works. So successful were they in this country that Jerome began exporting his inexpensive clocks to England.

The cases for Chauncey Jerome's first inexpensive clocks with brass works

*Mantel or shelf clocks were made in quantity after 1837 and sold at prices everyone could afford. The maker's paper was usually pasted inside the case. When this clock was repaired and restored fifteen years ago, the paper was removed and as a result the value of the clock was reduced.*

were quite simple, although decorative, wooden ones. After 1837, mantel or shelf clocks were produced not only in quantity but also in a great diversity of cases. Many of them were roughly 11 to 19 inches high by 7 to 10 inches wide. By the 1870's, much taller and heavier-looking cases were being made. All of these mantel clocks struck the hours, and a few of them had alarms that could be set. More rarely, at least when they first became generally available, did they chime.

The dials of shelf or mantel clocks were simple, with Roman or Arabic numerals. Only an occasional dial had painted decoration. The cases were made of good woods such as walnut, mahogany, rosewood, cherry, and maple. The glass door, more often than not, had the lower panel painted so that the pendulum was not visible. This custom of painting the lower part of the glass door was, in fact, popular for many styles of clocks throughout the 1800's. It had started early, with the pillar-and-scroll case, but was not necessarily characteristic of that or any other later styles. Scenes, ships, horses, and birds were common subjects. Often a medallion would be painted in colors or in metallic paints against a black background.

The pillar-and-scroll shelf clock got its name from the woodworking of its case. This was an Eli Terry style of the early 1800's. In a way, it was an adaptation of a tall clock case to a mantel clock. The top was scrolled and had

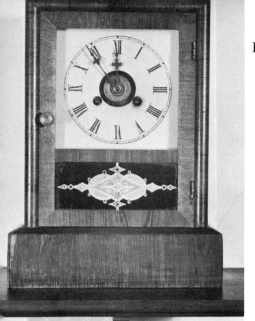

*Pasted inside the painted door panel of this shelf clock is the paper of the New Haven Clock Company, New Haven, Connecticut, which reads: "1 Day Ex. Cottage Time Piece Alarm." Although the clock does not strike the hours, it has an alarm that is set by means of the small brass dial with numbers, under the hands. The clock dimensions are 11 by 7 by 4 inches.*

Sometimes these columns were burnished or stenciled with metallic paint. After 1850, Doric columns sometimes set off a rosewood or mahogany case.

The first two really different cases were the steeple and the beehive, both of which appeared in the 1840's and remained popular for more than twenty years. They were made probably by almost all New England clockmakers. The steeple clock had a comparatively simple and elegant case, although its proportions and hence its beauty, depended on the skill of the woodworker. The case followed the outline of a Gothic point with steeple finials on either side. When a steeple clock was made of mahogany, with a brass knob on the door and brass frames around

*The steeple clock was a new style in the 1840's. This mahogany one, 19 inches from base to point, was made by Gilbert B. Owen of Winsted, Connecticut, in 1870.*

three finials; the skirt was also scrolled, and usually there were columns along the sides, and bracket feet. This style of case was used by other clockmakers too. Some of the pillar-and-scroll clocks that still tick have wood movements.

Many of Jerome's first inexpensive clocks had simple rectangular cases. Up until about 1845, some of them were enhanced with ogee molding. The half-round pilasters on clock cases were copied, of course, from those on American Empire chests and bureaus.

the dial glass and the smaller oblong glass in front of the pendulum, it could be a handsome mantel piece. Not all steeple clocks were as simply elegant. Some had finials with more turnings, and some had the lower part of the glass door painted.

The beehive clock was a little taller than most steeple clocks and the case looked heavier. The case was true to its name, coming to a softly rounded point at the top, like an old-fashioned beehive. Simple molding usually outlined the case.

After 1860, cases for mantel and shelf clocks became larger, heavier-looking, and sometimes almost fantastic. The names by which they were known described their shapes—acorn, hourglass, lyre, etc. Finally, by the 1890's, some could only be described as "gingerbread," so elaborate and complicated were the swirls, scrolls, moldings, and the like combined on a single case.

Other materials beside wood contributed to the fanciful and odd shapes. A few clocks had pressed glass cases, some from Sandwich, some from other factories. The popular Daisy and Button pattern, introduced in the 1880's, was used in both clear and colored glass. Some milk glass was used for clocks too. The glass cases usually were made for small clocks, possibly to hang on the wall or place on a table. China cases were popular for mantel clocks. Many of these were attractive, though

some seem almost too ornate now. Probably more clock cases were made of Delft and Dresden than anything else, but Haviland, Royal Bonn, and possibly other porcelain factories also turned to clock cases in the late 1800's. Cast iron, bronze, marble and bronze, and papier-mâché with mother-of-pearl insets were other Victorian favorites.

Cases for mantel and shelf clocks usually were not made by the factory that made the clock works. Instead, the cases were ordered by contract. Then, too, many clockmakers, including Eli Terry, supplied movements to firms

*Clocks with china cases were prized between 1870 and 1900. This one, 10 inches high and 6 to 7¾ inches wide, has a Royal Bonn porcelain case with hand-painted sprays of flowers and turquoise scrolls outlined with gold. The clock works have been electrified.*—Ted Eastwood

that made cases. This was particularly true of odd clocks such as the Victorian china ones.

In the 1880's and 1890's, the Victorians became fond of mantel clocks with cases that combined marble and bronze or ormolu trim. Many of these resembled French clocks of an earlier era, with a lion, elephant, or rhinoceros in dark bronze as part of the decoration.

Somewhat later but still widely admired today are the small table clocks with glass sides. The four glass panels (one acted as a door) were mounted in brass frames and there was a small brass carrying handle on top. These clocks were made in several sizes, but all were quite small; probably the largest was no more than 6 inches tall.

Clocks made for specific places and purposes during the last century are goals for many collectors, particularly since so many of these have now been replaced by electric models. For instance, a large, plain but distinctive wall clock with an exceptionally clear face used to be mounted on the wall in every railroad station. The old schoolroom clock has now become another collecting specialty, as have striking clocks combining a chronometer with the traditional ship's bell, which were manufactured for ships by a Connecticut clockmaker in the 1870's. In later ship's clocks, a softer chime was substituted for the bell. A ship's clock divided the day

into six periods of four hours each, starting with one bell at 12:30, 4:30, and 8:30 and progressing to eight bells at 4, 8, and 12 o'clock. Then, between 1850 and 1875, brass carriage clocks became fashionable.

Interest in old clocks is so strong that there is a National Association of Watch and Clock Collectors with several thousand members. Then, too, many persons who are not members like to get hold of an old clock because they enjoy tinkering with it and getting it to run again. In fact, more than one man has built up a hobby and small business on the side by scouring near-by places for nineteenth-century shelf clocks, putting them in running order and restoring their cases if necessary, and then selling them.

Any clock made during the 1800's and some of those from the early years of the twentieth century are salable. There is a ready market not just for special-purpose clocks but for fairly ordinary mantel or shelf clocks. The fact that a clock does not run is not necessarily a drawback—all it may need is oiling.

Many a 75- to 200-year-old clock still ticks off the minutes, strikes or chimes the hours, and keeps remarkably accurate time. Even if a clock has not run for years, it can be made to do so again by a skilled repairman. However, no one should attempt to repair the works or restore the finish on the case unless he knows how to handle a clock. An unskilled repairman can do more harm than good. To begin, there is a right way to remove a clock from its case. Cleaning it can be tricky, and the restoration of a dial, particularly one from a tall-case clock, is not a job for an amateur. Sometimes a dial needs no more attention than a careful washing to remove accumulated dust. If restoration is necessary, it should be done by an artist who confines the work as much as possible to retouching.

A clock that still tells time may need to be regulated for accuracy. Directions for starting and adjusting a clock usually were printed on a paper that was glued to the inside of the case.

The age of a clock does not necessarily have too much bearing on the price for which it can be sold now. The clockmaker's signature may, just as does the condition of the clock and its case.

Three things increase the value of a clock. Most important is the printed sheet of paper pasted inside the case. This paper identifies the maker and the period or approximate age of the clock. Next in importance is knowing whether or not the movement and the case are from the original maker. When a case made in the 1840's has had a more recent movement installed, it will not interest collectors, although it might be sold to a noncollector who simply likes the clock. The value of many an old clock has been reduced

by the fact that the original movement has been replaced by a later and less valuable one. Equally important is the presence of the original tablet—that is, the painted glass panel on the door. If the original tablet is still intact and has not been replaced by a recent artistic effort, the value is enhanced.

Occasionally an expert clock repairer may suggest substituting electrical works. This happened when a Virginia couple who owned a hanging wall clock decided they wanted to have it tell time again. The clock was in poor shape, with the case and many parts of the works broken. An expert clock repairman in Norfolk suggested that, instead of the time-consuming and perhaps not completely successful search for authentic replacement parts, a small electrical movement, which would not be visible, should be installed. The dial needed only washing and a slight retouching of its decoration. The hands were missing, so a search was made to find some in the right style. A cabinetmaker repaired and restored the original mahogany case. The finished job is shown in one of this book's illustrations.

Any old clock, even a banjo wall clock, has had its sale value as an antique reduced if it has been electrified. Any tampering with movement, dial, or case, or replacement of any original parts, means some reduction in the sale price. The clock that needs a great deal of repair and refinishing is not going to sell for nearly as much as a similar clock in fairly good condition. There is no basic standard price to be placed on any clock, not even those made entirely by hand before the 1830's. The price range for any style can be a broad one, as broad at an auction or an antique shop as in a person-to-person sale. By the way, if you're *buying* a clock, be sure the key to wind it is tucked away in the case.

Gongs, bells, or chimes, metal decoration around the face, painted dials like the Pennsylvania German *Fraktur* style, little figures—all these are individual touches that may add to the monetary value of a clock. So may any unusual decoration or attachment.

If a local jeweler, clockmaker, or repairer cannot help you to place your clock historically, there are other possibilities. A horological group or a branch of a clock and watch society may be active locally or nearby. A visit to a museum or restoration also may be helpful. There is a Clock Museum (with library) in Bristol, Connecticut. Other notable exhibits of clocks are to be seen in the Springfield, Illinois, State Museum of Natural History and Art; Old Sturbridge Village in Sturbridge, Massachusetts; the Henry Ford Museum in Dearborn, Michigan; and the New York University Gould Memorial Library in New York City.

Since tall-case or grandfather's clocks were handed down from one generation of a family to another, sometimes a reliable history of a clock is available from the time the clockmaker sold it to its first owner. This, naturally, would be influential in its sale today. A tall-case clock may be sold for any amount from $50 to several thousand dollars. Where a particular clock fits in this scale depends upon its condition, the presence of replaced parts, the amount of restoration needed, the maker, and the clock's history. An uncased weight-and-pendulum clock would probably be toward the bottom of the price scale. An early-nineteenth century grandfather's clock in a pine case might bring no more than $150 to $300. Even one with a mahogany case and a dial topped by a cartouche with a painted landscape or seascape might bring no more than $200.

The tall-case clock that can be authenticated as having been made by one of the Willards, David Rittenhouse or Edward Duffield of Philadelphia, or Martin Shreiner of Lancaster is the one whose sale price starts in the hundreds of dollars and may go into the thousands. Any Rittenhouse clock, if one were to be found, probably would sell for no less than $2,000 and perhaps much more than that. If a New England clock has a case that was made by a cabinetmaker such as John Goddard, that fact is enough to raise its selling price.

The condition, the existence of the maker's paper, the original painting on the glass door, original parts, and the various other requirements of collectors determine the price of a mantel or shelf clock. This may be anywhere from a few dollars to $50 or $75. A steeple clock, for example, made by Gilbert B. Owen in Winsted, Connecticut, in 1870 may sell for no more than $20 even if the case is well-proportioned and not overornamented. On the other hand, a steeple clock with a mahogany or rosewood case made in New England in 1850 may be priced fairly at $50.

A mantel or shelf clock that still has a paper identifying it as having come from the shop of Seth Thomas, Eli Terry, or Chauncey Jerome usually can be priced higher than one from a less famous maker. A Terry pillar-and-scroll mantel clock from the early 1800's might be valued at $200 or more. But a Terry clock with the half-round pilasters or ogee molding of the American Empire period may sell for no more than $100 or as little as $50 (Empire currently is not fashionable).

The late Victorian clocks with china or glass cases sell for $10 to $50 or so, more if the glass is authenticated Sandwich glass. A clock of Haviland china with gold trim and an American movement is probably priced fairly at $65 or thereabouts. Oddities may appeal to some people, but are not likely to sell for much money. Frankly, it's hard even to give away some of the Victorian marble and bronze clocks, and probably no one except an enthusiastic collector would pay more than a couple of dollars for a wall clock in a cast-iron frame.

The owning of a watch was as much a sign that a man was prosperous in business as was the tall-case clock in his house. George Washington, Benjamin Franklin, and many others who helped to establish the United States owned watches. In fact, in 1683, only one year after William Penn founded Philadelphia, a watchmaker and repairer was working there.

Watches or portable timepieces date from about 1500. They were made first in Germany and originally were small clocks with mainsprings enclosed in boxes. These were much too large to carry in a pocket, and may have hung from the girdle around the waist. Many of the earliest watches were encased in odd shapes, and all of them were handsomely decorated and jeweled.

Many problems had to be overcome in the making of a satisfactory watch. The invention of the chronometer in the early years of the nineteenth century ended the search for a watch that would keep accurate time yet withstand the rocking motion of a ship. In fact, improvements in watches had been stimulated by the need of a timepiece for finding longitudes at sea.

Like clocks, watches were made by hand for centuries. It was 1838 before the first factory for watchmaking was opened in Hartford, Connecticut, and approximately 1850 before watches were being made in quantity and brought within the price range of any but well-to-do people.

There are many important dates in watchmaking. Keyless watches appeared about 1700. Watches with a second hand were new about 1780. During the seventeenth and eighteenth centuries watches usually had a double case; that is, they were set in a protective case attached to an outer, decorative one. Open-face watches did not appear until about 1890. However, the radium dial is far from modern, for it was seen first about 1896. Wristwatches, first worn generally by men, did not become popular until the time of World War I or about 1918 in this country.

Long before wristwatches became fashionable, ladies wore either chatelaine or pin-on watches. Both styles became a vogue in late Victorian days. A watch was only one of the things that might be suspended from the group of short chains known as a chatelaine. From other chains might hang keys, a needle-case, small scissors, penknife, or the like. Around 1900, a lady might wear her gold watch, about 1⅜ inches in diameter, on a long gold chain with a jeweled slide and either tuck the watch into her belt or fasten it to her bodice with a pin to which the watch could be hooked. This, technically, was not a chatelaine watch, and it was only a step to the pin-on watch that was worn without a chain.

Pins designed to be fastened to a lady's shirtwaist had hooks on which a watch could be suspended. These pins were plain gold bowknots or twists or some other simple form set modestly with stones. Pin-on watches usually had a closed case, one side of which could be snapped open to see the face of the watch; the other side was either monogrammed or had a design, carried out with precious stones, depicting, perhaps, a butterfly. After 1900, fewer lady's watches had closed cases.

Most men's watches during the seventeenth and eighteenth centuries were silver, and silver pocket watches were commonly carried through the nineteenth century too, at least for everyday and to work. The double case that was common throughout the eighteenth century covered a watch that was round and thick and usually required a key for winding. But before 1800, watches in Europe, if not here, became thinner and often were made in fancy shapes such as a cross or a seashell.

Stopwatches are not a recent invention. And novelties of the past included also calendar, chiming, and repeater watches. A calendar watch was one that could record the day of the week, the month, and the year by somewhat the same means as a moon progressed through its phases on a tall-case clock. Calendar watches have never been rated as the most accurate sort. Some watches in the past chimed the hours, the half- and quarter-hours, and some occasionally contained a small music box. Repeater watches were prized before the days of friction matches, for they enabled the owner to learn the time after dark. A repeater watch could be made to strike the hours and either the quarters or the minutes by pressing a handle to wind up a striking mechanism.

Grandpa's or Great-grandpa's "turnip" pocket watch was not inexpensive. The name, of course, was descriptive of the fat, round shape of the watch. Equally unmistakable with its clear face was the pocket watch railroad trainmen used to carry.

Mass production of cheap pocket watches began in Waterbury, Connecticut, in 1897, and these first ones were often called "Waterbury watches." Although a great many were manufactured, the venture was comparatively short-lived and it was not until Robert Ingersoll came along that enormous production and vast merchandising brought the heyday of the "dollar watch."

Watches, even cheap ones, have steadily become smaller and thinner. For the most part, their cases are plainer too. The single-case and open-case watches of the 1880's and 1890's often had elaborately engraved designs or insignia on the back. A deer, a horse, or a detailed locomotive with smoke trailing over the train of cars behind it were among the popular decorations on men's pocket watches. Or an initial or a monogram might be engraved at the center of an elabo-

rately scrolled design almost covering the back of the watch.

Watches have been owned so generally for 75 to 100 years that old ones are quite plentiful. But, fortunately, there are collectors who are interested in buying a watch merely because of its double case, because of the engraved decoration, because of the person who originally owned it, or simply because their own collection lacks one of the type offered for sale. Hence, it is usually possible to sell one or more old watches, if you are willing to do so for a modest price.

A stem-winding pocket watch with a closed case of silver made in the 1880's probably cannot be sold for more than $20, and perhaps for less. Most of the men's watches carried after 1880 sell for $10 to $20 or $25. A lady's gold watch may sell simply for the value of its old gold, or for $20 to $50 if the watch runs and the case is extremely ornamental. However, if you want to keep an old watch, you can make effective and decorative use of it by hooking it under a glass dome that fits on a wooden stand. It will make an unusual small table clock.

The value of a late-eighteenth- or early-nineteenth-century watch may increase if the ownership is known. If its history has been interesting or the original owner was a famous person, the selling price goes up automatically. Ownership can do more for the selling price of a watch than the maker or firm name.

The price of a double-case watch goes up, too, if one or more watch papers are still in place. These were small circles of paper, silk, muslin, or other fabric that were set between the two cases to keep the outer case closed firmly and to protect the works from gathering dust. The first ones were homemade by the ladies, often as gifts for relatives or friends. Some were cut in elaborate designs; others were hand-painted or, if made of fabric, embroidered with silk or with human hair. If the watch papers were a Valentine gift, this was apparent in their decoration.

Watchmakers saw an advantage to themselves in watch papers, as well as to the watches. Soon these papers were being printed, engraved, and lithographed. Some stated simply the name and address of the watchmaker or repairer. Others in addition had a decorative design, the head of a public character, or a motto. Watchmakers inserted their own papers whenever a watch was brought in to be cleaned, regulated, or repaired. Some of them wrote the date the work was done and the charge for it on the back of the paper. Old watches with double cases have been found with as many as three or four watch papers. There are collectors who specialize in these papers, and if you fall heir to a collection of them, it can undoubtedly be sold as such. Probably the most sensible way to go about this would be to write to

the National Association of Watch and Clock Collectors (whose most recent address can be obtained from your local library) and to advertise in publications aimed specifically at such collectors as well as those of more general hobby interests.

Devices for marking rather than telling time, such as sandglasses and sundials, have a much longer history than clocks and watches. Any sandglass or hourglass made of unusual materials or with an interesting history certainly is salable.

Most of the sundials being made today are simple copies of quite old ones. Since the eighteenth century, when the clock and watch began to supplant it, the sundial has been chiefly a garden ornament. In this case, it is a fixed dial carefully attached to a pedestal or set on a low wall. At one time sundials were put on the side of the church tower or the wall of a house so that all who passed could note the approximate time on a sunny day. A number of these are known to have marked the sun's passage over old houses in this country. More common, even into the days when most houses had clocks, were the windowsills that had numbers cut into them to act as a sundial.

Pocket dials were small, portable sundials. One type, which became popular during the seventeenth century, was made in the shape of a ring with a hook so that it could be held in the hand to tell the approximate time.

Other pocket dials were flat. If you find and recognize a pocket sundial, you may be able to sell it for $25 to $75, depending on the materials of which it was made, the maker, and its age. Before trying to sell a fixed sundial that has stood in a garden for years, it is advisable to check in all possible ways to determine its age and history. It may not be as old as you think it is.

*Horology* is a word seldom heard any more. It means the science of measuring time and the art of constructing, regulating, and testing sundials, clocks, watches, and other instruments for indicating the divisions of time. A maker or vendor of clocks and watches once was known as a horologer, and any sort of timepiece as a horologe.

## GLOSSARY

*Chatelaine:* a group of short chains, worn by a lady, from which she suspended her watch, keys, needlecase, etc. Also, the watch worn on such a chain.

*Chronograph:* an instrument for recording the exact instant at which an event occurs, or for measuring a small interval of time, such as a stopwatch.

*Chronometer:* a watch or timepiece of great accuracy, designed to be used for determining the longitude at sea or for any other purpose where an exact measurement of time is required.

*Clepsydra:* a device for measuring time by the graduated flow of a liquid; a water clock.

*Clock:* a device for measuring and indicating time by the motion of its parts and by striking the hour and sometimes lesser divisions of time.

*Clock-watch:* a watch that strikes the hours like a clock.

*Dial:* (1) an instrument for indicating the hour of the day by means of a shadow thrown upon a graduated surface. Both sun and moon dials, fixed and portable dials, were made. (2) the face of a clock or watch on which the time is shown.

*Gnomon:* the triangular projecting piece, or style, that casts a shadow to show the hour of the day on a sundial.

*Hourglass:* an instrument for measuring, but not indicating, time—specifically, the interval of an hour—by how long it takes a certain quantity of sand, mercury, or water to flow from one compartment to another.

*Sandglass:* an instrument which measures time by the movement of a quantity of sand.

*Timepiece:* a clock, watch, or other device that measures and indicates the passage of time.

*Watch:* a timepiece with a spring-driven movement, to be carried in the pocket or on the person.

## SPECIAL CLOCK TERMS

*Cartouche:* a semicircle above the dial, particularly of a tall-case clock.

*Case:* the structure that houses the works of a clock.

*Dial:* the face of a clock or watch upon which the hours and minutes are marked and over which the hands move.

*Hands:* the two pointers on the face of a clock.

*Original tablet:* the painted glass panel on the door or front of many old clocks.

*Spandrel:* the pie-shaped corner pieces on the dials of tall-case clocks.

## FOR FURTHER INFORMATION:

AMERICAN CLOCKS AND CLOCKMAKERS by Carl W. Dreppard. New York: Doubleday and Company.

PENNSYLVANIA CLOCKS AND CLOCKMAKERS by George H. Eckhardt. New York: Bonanza Books.

# 7

## Lamps and Lighting Fixtures

ONLY DURING THE EARLIEST, most primitive days of a community was light from the hearth fire considered sufficient illumination indoors after dark. If candles were in good supply, a household would have all sorts of candleholders from wall sconces to chambersticks. If some kind of oil was available, then one or more lamps would be in sight. After all, lamps had been known in this country since the earliest Colonial days, but the first ones were so inefficient that candles were preferred when they were obtainable.

A lamp in its crudest form consists of a vessel to hold oil and a wick. By 1800, a lamp consisted of an oil font, possibly on a standard, a wick and a burner, a chimney, and possibly a reflector. Hanging lamps had smoke bells just under the ceiling, to protect it. After 1860, shades became common for all kinds of lamps.

Experiments in Europe and America, after 1750, helped to improve the lamp, and when whale oil became plentiful in the early 1800's, lamps became as common as candles. Actually, lamps have been used for interior lighting for almost as many centuries as candles, yet only since about 1860 have they generally replaced candles. The nineteenth century also saw lamps being made in as many diverse forms as candleholders. Hanging lamps, bracket lamps, chandeliers, and probably girandoles, too, were made to illuminate either by candles or oil, as were lanterns for outdoor as well as indoor use. Most oil-burning lamps were of modest size and portable, designed to be set on a table, chest, or bureau.

Portable lamps, particularly those made and used from the early 1800's on, generally are as adaptable to present-day use as are mirrors and picture frames. Almost all styles of lamps used

*This magnificent chandelier (circa 1760-70) of English or Irish cut glass has shades for the candles and is embellished with crystal drops. It hangs in the Governor's Palace at Williamsburg.* Courtesy Colonial Williamsburg

during the nineteenth century, regardless of the fuel they burned originally, can be converted to electricity.

Some styles of the late-Victorian lamps are still being manufactured, but mostly to illuminate by means of electricity (a few are still made for kerosene). However, lamps made between 1850 and 1900 are not scarce, and a surprising number of people prefer them to reproductions. They may be dusty and lack chimneys, but this is not a serious drawback because chimneys are being made now to fit the old lamps. So are glass shades.

Anyone who finds a peg lamp nowadays has a rarity. This was a lamp made to burn whale oil, and it fit into the socket of a candlestick. The round

globe that held the oil had a metal burner at the top. A projecting end or round "peg" of glass on the bottom of the font permitted it to be placed securely in a candlestick. Some peg lamps were made of tin and were hooked into a block of wood. Peg lamps were quite common in the early 1800's, but have been lost track of in the multitude of oil-burning lamps made after 1850.

Like candlesticks, lamps were made of many materials—metals such as pewter, britannia, brass, tin, and cast iron; pottery, china, and all kinds of glass. Glass and metal lamps were made in greatest quantity, if availability today is any clue.

*The chandelier in the family dining room of the Governor's Palace, Williamsburg, is a sterling silver one made in England about 1710.* Courtesy Colonial Williamsburg

*This tin chandelier with sockets for six candles, which now hangs in Colonial Williamsburg's Printing Office, was probably made in England in the early 1700's and exported to Virginia. Courtesy Colonial Williamsburg*

Lanterns also were made of all available metals, and occasionally even of wood, and burned either candles or the oil in use at the time. A lantern differed from a lamp by being entirely enclosed so that its light was protected from wind, rain, or drafts. Small ones were made to be carried out-of-doors and also could be hung up on a nail or a peg for a fixed light. Handsome, large ones of brass, pewter, or sometimes copper or bronze were made to hang in entrance halls, an English custom that was brought to this country in the late 1700's. Well-to-do families illuminated their halls and some rooms with more than one hanging lantern. Several styles can be seen hanging in the buildings at Colonial Williamsburg. The lantern itself, seldom less than 18 inches long, hung from the ceiling by

means of chains. It had glass panels, sometimes richly colored; both clear and colored glass occasionally were etched or engraved instead of plain.

Simpler than the indoor lantern with a metal frame was the type that consisted of a glass dome suspended from brass chains, with a smoke bell above to prevent the ceiling from being darkened. This was about the same size as other indoor lanterns. In the 1700's, when hanging lanterns first became fashionable, they were fitted with candles; now candle-type electric bulbs are substituted.

*Lanterns to hang from the ceiling by chains were brought from England to America during the 1700's. This one with brass frame and clear glass panels, 21 inches high and 9 inches wide, now hangs in the hall of the Brush-Everard House, Williamsburg. Courtesy Colonial Williamsburg*

Lanterns made to light specific places (ships, taverns, railroad and Pullman coaches, for example), as well as those for carriages and the early automobile and miner's lamps, are of special interest to collectors. And don't throw away a policeman's lantern or any farm lantern you may happen to find. Some of these lanterns are almost as old as lamps and originally held candles. Incidentally, many lanterns for special purposes were made to fit into brackets or holders (the miner's lamp could be fixed to his cap).

Ship lanterns were even more varied than those used on trains. Starboard and port lights with heavy, hinged tops that could be turned back to insert candles are easier to find than those used in other parts of a vessel. Some were copper, some were glass cylinders; others, combinations of metal and glass in odd shapes. Because such countless numbers of boats plied the many rivers in states from Connecticut and New York to California during the nineteenth century, the chance of finding an old ship's lantern is greater than most people realize.

Railroad lanterns included styles that illuminated the exterior and also the interior of trains, as well as those used by conductors. The conductor's lantern was similar to those still in use today, but many of the old ones had the initials of the railroad ground into the glass. Some of the first railroad lanterns burned whale oil. Both these and ship lanterns often had reflectors.

By far the greatest number of lanterns was made to be carried by watchmen at night and by individuals when they went out after dark. Many of these are much older than railroad lanterns. A triangular tin lantern probably was older than the one commonly, but incorrectly, called a Paul Revere lantern. This type was not made until fifty years or so after Paul Revere's famous ride. Still, it was one of the most individual of American-made lanterns. The metal cylinder of tin or iron had a pointed top and pierced sides.

Square, octagonal, or hexagonal lanterns with glass sides gave a great deal more light. They were carried by means of metal bails or leather handles. Some were quite elaborate, many of them no more than functional. They had sockets to hold from one to several candles. Mica instead of glass panes were not uncommon in purely utilitarian lanterns in the early years of the twentieth century and horn was used in some very early lanterns.

Lamps and many lanterns made early in the nineteenth century burned whale oil. In fact, whale oil was not immediately displaced by camphene, introduced between 1830 and 1840, or by kerosene about 1860. However, because of its availability, abundance, and its perfection as a fuel for illumination, kerosene eventually replaced other fuel oils and also was a factor in bringing lamps into general use. Almost as influential were the experiments with wicks and burners that enabled lamps to give brighter light. (Double wicks had been tried even before 1800.) Camphene, an explosive fuel, necessitated a longer burner than whale oil. Actually each fuel required its own special kind of wick and burner for satisfactory illumination, but these fixtures on a lamp could be changed to suit whatever kind of oil was available.

Glass lamps with burners and chimneys and, later, shades were made continually after 1800. Early in the century, lamps were made of blown and blown-molded glass. Etched, frosted, and cut glass lamps were not uncommon. The invention of pressed glass about 1825 reduced the price and increased the number and diversity of

*A pewter lamp with a pierced, rococo design, probably made not later than the 1840's. It has been converted to electricity but may have burned camphene originally. The lamp is 7 inches high including the feet, and 8 inches in diameter at its widest part.*—Ted Eastwood

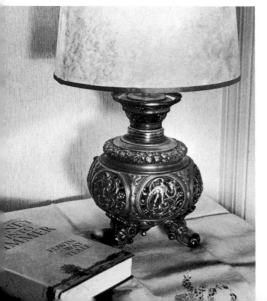

lamps. The famous Boston and Sandwich Glass Company is given much credit for popularizing glass lamps. It made small ones and large ones, hand lamps with handles and standard lamps with bases and fonts of various shapes. One was appropriately called a "squat" lamp. Often several techniques were combined in the making and decoration of a single glass lamp. Some of the whale oil lamps made by the Boston and Sandwich Glass Company had cut glass bases and fonts and frosted glass shades. One oil lamp of the 1850's with a colored glass font was a combination of free-blown, cut, and pressed glass.

Pressed glass lamps were made in many patterns, most of them clear glass, some of them colored. Peacock Feather, an early and quite lacy pattern, and Harp, a pattern of the 1850's, included squat lamps with handles. The early, simple Argus pattern boasted two styles: a footed lamp and another with a 4-inch colored base. Table or standard lamps, between 7¾ and 8½ inches high, appeared in many patterns, from Block with Thumbprint (first made *circa* 1840) to Actress (in the 1880's).

Glassmakers everywhere seemed to delight in finding different shapes for the oil fonts. In addition to round, oval, octagonal, square, waisted, and flaring fonts, other favorite variations were urn and pear shapes. Lamps with colored glass fonts were produced in innumerable combinations and varia-

A *pressed glass lamp in Block with Thumbprint pattern, made to burn whale oil but now converted to electricity. The smooth edge of the opaque white, hand-painted shade is one indication that it was made during the 1800's.*

tions. The font might be simple cranberry glass, an overlay colored glass with etched or faceted decoration, or two colors with one cut out in designs to show the other color beneath. Blue, amethyst, apple-green and rich deep green, reds, and shades of amber were the popular colors.

The base under a colored glass lamp could be opaque white glass, cut glass, or marble. The fittings were metal, and sometimes there was a metal standard or shaft between a marble base and a cut glass font.

Miniature lamps, which were turned out in great diversity, were made in some of the pressed glass patterns. They were widely used as night lights

and in sick rooms and nurseries. These small replicas are also—and quite logically—believed to have been used as courting or "sparking" lamps. They held only a small supply of fuel and, presumably, when this was exhausted it was time for the suitor to leave. Some miniature lamps certainly were salesmen's samples, for many of them were reproductions of the parlor lamps so popular in the 1880's and 1890's.

These little lamps ranged from 4½ to 8 inches tall. They burned kerosene and consequently were made in greatest quantity after 1870. One earlier

A *pressed glass kerosene lamp in Three Face pattern, made between 1870 and 1885 by a Pittsburgh glass company. The style with ornamented font shown here was made in three sizes, as was a style with a clear, round font.*

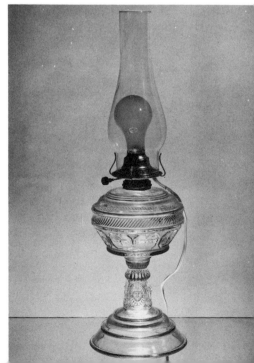

style of clear and colored pressed glass was called "acorn," not for the pattern of that name but because of the shape of the lamp. The base, often covered with hobnails, resembled a deep sauce dish. Into this fitted a dome of ribbed or swirled glass with a hole in the top. This style was patented by the famous Hobbs firm in Wheeling, West Virginia.

Fairy lamps, first made in the 1840's, burned candles and consisted of two parts similar to those of the acorn lamp. The name "Fairy Light" was patented by an English firm that manufactured candles. Rival firms soon were producing fairy lamps, but the most valuable ones today are those with the fairy trademark of George and Samuel Clarke, the originators. Fairy lamps were miniatures, of course. They were made of delicate blown glass, clear and colored pressed glass, and all kinds of art glass. All the types of glass for which England, France, and the United States have become famous were used to make bases and shades. A certain number had glass shades and metal bases.

Many of the fairy lamps were delightful confections of exquisite coloring and decoration. Later in the nineteenth century fairy lamps became gaudy combinations of colored glass. A good many reproduced animal or bird heads—owl, pussycat, dog, etc. These are probably scarcer today than simpler forms.

Miniature lamps made in this country after 1870 often copied the larger lamps used about the house. These miniatures, bigger than most fairy lamps, were commonly made of satin, Amberina, and other kinds of art glass, clear and colored pressed glass, and opaque and decorated types such as the Mary Gregory. Some also were made in the shape of animals (the owl was a favorite), street lights, even a schoolhouse (the building held the oil; the wick and chimney were attached to the roof). Novelty miniatures were popular in the 1890's.

However, miniature lamps were only a by-product of the wider use of lamps to illuminate a house. As fuel became more plentiful and less costly, larger

*The miniature lamp at the left has an opaque white font, with flowers around the base painted green. The taller kerosene lamp has a handle for carrying it, and a large chimney or shade with a colorful garland against a wide band of frosted glass. The knob at the side of each lamp is for adjusting the wick to regulate the amount of light.*

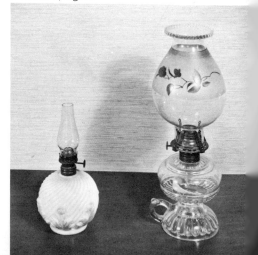

and larger lamps were made. Ornament increased too, so much so that an Argus or lacy Peacock Feather pressed glass lamp seems the height of simplicity. Many lamps of the late nineteenth century are much too gaudy and overornamented for present-day taste.

One example is the parlor lamp without which no home was complete during the 1880's and 1890's. This type, also now called a Gone-with-the-Wind lamp, consisted of a large globular base and matching globular shade of the same size. These were made of glass and china, singly or together, and usually were painted or otherwise heavily ornamented. Some charming examples are to be found. A white china lamp of Dresden or Meissen type with decoration of small raised and painted pastel blossoms is delightful, but many parlor lamps were pretty awful. More common than the Meissen type—and more widely reproduced —is the style with bold floral painting on the base and shade.

The glass prisms or drops that had long been hung from candlesticks were also used with both glass and metal lamps. Their purpose in both cases was to increase the illusion, if not the actual amount, of light. Prisms were not generally used with pressed glass oil lamps. However, they were hung from solar, astral, and Argand lamps, as well as from parlor and other decorative styles.

Lusters, a specific type of glittering fixture hung with prisms, were popular throughout the Victorian era. They were made of glass, with a round base, a tall hollow stem, and a cuplike top from which the prisms were suspended. By inserting a metal candleholder, a luster could be used for illumination. Without this holder, a luster might hold fresh flowers. Lusters, which were used in pairs on the mantel usually, were highly decorative. Various kinds of glass, including colors and overlay, were favored and the holders themselves often were enameled or gilded. The prisms were cut glass. They probably were made in greater quantity in England and Europe than in this country, but they were displayed in many homes here. Nowadays lusters often are converted to electricity.

Also prism-hung were girandoles. At one time the term girandole meant a branched and ornamented lightholder for candles or lamps, but today generally refers to a three-piece set for the mantel. The girandole or mantel garniture consisted of a candelabrum, usually three-branched, plus two single holders to stand on either side. The fixtures were likely to be made of brass or perhaps bronze, and to have marble or alabaster bases. Prisms for all three pieces were cut in whatever manner was currently stylish.

In short, the Victorians loved their prisms. Most of their prism lamps can be converted to electricity without damage; in fact, prisms were combined with the early (around 1900) electrically lighted lamps and chandeliers. One particularly nice example of a Victorian prism lamp, first made to burn oil, has an etched or frosted glass chimney or shade, a glass base, and prisms hanging from the cup around the burner. Like candlesticks, prism lamps usually were made in pairs.

The various art glasses so plentiful in the 1880's and 1890's are responsible for a mixed legacy of exquisite lamps and shades and many horrors. With natural gas and electricity beginning to compete with kerosene in the 1890's, small glass shades were commonly made for wall lights and large shades for center lights or chandeliers.

A tremendous number of lampshades can be found among the various kinds of art glass. The iridescent Tiffany glass with its glowing colors, perhaps the finest of all the art glass made in this country, was used for lamps with matching shades as well as for shades for lighting fixtures. The first Tiffany lamps burned kerosene, but after 1900 both lamps and shades of Tiffany glass were made for illumination by gas and electricity. Between 1900 and the 1920's, a good many shades in various sizes were made of carnival or Quezal glass, both of which are sometimes referred to as "imitation Tiffany."

The demand for satin glass also has increased. This lovely art glass with the mat finish was used not only for minia-ture and fairy lamps but also to some extent for standard ones, as well as for shades on lamps of other materials. So were Amberina, Peachblow, Burmese, mercury, and probably other kinds of art glass. A Crown Milano oil lamp in the Henry Ford Museum in Dearborn, Michigan, is a lovely thing, for this glass has a mat finish that makes the glass look like fine white porcelain.

Few pressed glass oil lamps are found with shades, yet this part of a lamp was borrowed and adapted from candlesticks. The first glass shades were tall cylinders slipped over candlesticks, to rest on the table or other surface beneath and shield the light from drafts. Similar shades for whale oil lamps were made in New England as early as 1820.

Lamp chimneys, however, were not an adaptation of hurricane shades. In the 1780's, Aimé Argand, a Swiss, invented the central draft burner that so greatly improved illumination from oil lamps, and one of his workmen is credited by some sources with having accidentally discovered the glass lamp chimney. It is said that the workman held a bottle too near the flame of a lamp with the result that the bottom came out, and since the bottle had become too hot to hold, the workman let it slide down over the flame. Not only did the bottle not break but also the flame seemed to become steadier and brighter. Thereafter chimneys were used on all lamps. They were seldom decorated, although the top edge might be crimped or beaded.

Astral and solar lamps were variations of the Argand lamp burner, the latter patented in 1787. They were popular at least through the 1870's. Early ones burned whale oil, later ones kerosene. All three types were combinations of a metal and glass and were equipped with chimneys. After 1830, shades of cut and colored glass were made in this country for Argand lamps. The solar and astral lamps were likely to have etched, or engraved, or cut glass shades.

*Floral decoration was popular for many late-Victorian lamps, like this one of glass with a brass base and fittings, which has been converted to electricity without damage. Similar Victorian lamps were made of pottery and porcelain.*

Oddly enough, kerosene, which became plentiful for illumination after 1860, made shades as common as chimneys for lamps. The kerosene flame was so much brighter than that from the fuels used previously that globe shades were considered a necessity to reduce the brilliance. Still, lamps with globe shades were hung with prisms. Since shades became even more desirable with the advent of natural gas and electricity, a great many different kinds were made between 1860 and 1900. With each decade, more shades were produced in plain and fancy colored glass and, finally, art glass.

The large globular shades were most popular until the 1880's, when metal lamps required a flaring glass shade. However, some shades were shaped like enlargements of chimneys, others like vases. Etching, engraving, frosting, and cutting decorated shades of clear and colored glass. After 1890 many shades, including the flaring ones, were hand-painted in floral designs.

In the 1880's kerosene lamps with metal bases appeared in two styles that retain their appeal today. One was the student lamp; the other was a metal lamp known as a Rayo, which was vase-shaped with a globular or almost elliptical font supported by a filigreed or plain metal base. Its burner was confined by a glass chimney, and the flaring or circular glass shade was supported on three metal arms. The amount of light could be adjusted by means of one or more knobs (depending on the number of wicks) below the chimney. Shades were white glass with a yellow or green outer surface that was sometimes fluted.

These Rayo lamps were brass. A good many, however, were brass covered with nickel. The silver-colored nickel can be stripped off, if you prefer a brass lamp. A few antique dealers and lamp collectors specialize in this job.

If you find one of these Rayo lamps with a shade, you can tell whether the shade was made in the nineteenth century or just a few years ago. The test is no more than rubbing your finger along the bottom edge of the shade. Glass shades made in the nineteenth century feel smooth, but this century's reproductions are invariably rough to the touch, however perfect the copies are in other respects.

*A Rayo lamp. These metal lamps appeared in the 1880's. The brass base and the smooth-edged fluted shade are typical of early examples; later ones were nickel-plated. Two knobs at the side indicate a double wick.*

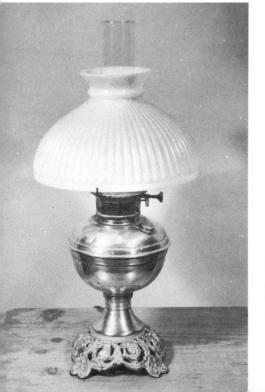

Student lamps that burned kerosene were made from about 1875 until after 1900. They can be converted to electricity, but most of them will not give as bright a light as when kerosene was the fuel, since only a bulb of the size used for Christmas tree lights will fit. Perhaps they were called student lamps because their round wicks gave such a soft, even light. Currently, the style has become popular again, and a modern electric version is now being made.

The basis of the old student lamp was a metal standard with a simple base. The standard supported one or two burners on arms, which could be adjusted at different heights, and an oil font, which was attached to the stand so that it was higher than the burners. The chimneys were narrower, taller, and straighter glass cylinders than the chimneys for other types of oil lamps. Sometimes a brass reflector shade was fastened to the standard by a slender arm so that it rested a little above the burner. Or the shade might be a porcelain one.

All parts of a student lamp except the chimney and perhaps the shade were made of metal. Certainly the brass ones are the most beautiful. One owner of a two-armed nineteenth-century student lamp has had the burners removed but the brass oil fonts left in place; she uses the hollow spaces for cut flowers. When this oil lamp was purchased in northern New York State in the 1930's, it had its original etched glass chimneys. The burners and chimneys can be put back in place at any time, and so the lamp still can be used for illumination in the old style.

Metal lamps, the majority of glass lamps, and some china ones are most readily converted to electricity without damaging the originals. Units or adapters come in two different styles, either of which can be fastened to the neck of the lamp. One has three metal arms to support the shade and a metal rack onto which the chimney fits after it is slipped over the light bulb. The other type holds upright an oval metal

*The brass student lamp, popular since 1875, had a round wick that gave a soft, even light. When electrified, the old student lamp gives less light than when kerosene was the fuel because only a small light bulb will fit. The reflector is spun brass.*

ring on which a shade is dropped and secured with a finial; no chimney is needed.

Even if no boring of holes for electric wiring is involved, it is advisable to have any lamp-conversion done by a skilled workman in either a glass or electrical shop. Such shops stock adapters, and it is a comparatively inexpensive job to have an old whale oil or kerosene burner removed and a suitable adapter put in place.

There is at least one exception to the craze for converting old lamps to electricity: On Block Island is a man who own three early whale oil lamps and who is determined not to electrify them. In 1962 he succeeded in obtaining sperm oil, considered, in the days when whale oil was burned, to give the best light; his most difficult problem has been locating burners and satis-

*Tiffany glass boudoir lamps, over-all height 11 inches, made to burn kerosene. The lamps and shades are primarily green and gold and iridescent. The tiny chimneys are also opalescent but more delicately tinted than the shades.*

factory wicks. Fortunately, he depends on electricity for illumination and wants to use the whale oil lamps for "atmosphere and interest."

At the other extreme are the people who make lamps out of almost any so-called "antique"—drums, salt boxes, and other farfetched objects that never had anything to do with the illumination of a house. There is, however, a precedent for wagon-wheel chandeliers, for they or something similar were often hung from chains in the common room of a tavern, with candles affixed to the rim. Stoneware jars and jugs sometimes can be converted into electric lamps without damage. But an antique china vase or a cut glass vase of the Brilliant Period through which a hole has been bored for electric wiring is damaged and, therefore, less valuable.

Furthermore, many of the china, earthenware, and cut glass lamps of the nineteenth century that burned oil can be converted to electricity—in most cases without harm. Glass oil lamps are not scarce, but pressed glass ones in certain patterns have considerable value and sell for premium prices. Even the plain glass, standard lamps made to burn kerosene as late as the turn of the century will have some value before the twentieth century ends, in addition to their present convenience when a severe storm causes a failure of electric power. There is always a market for a metal lamp in good condition, particularly a brass one,

even though good copies of the two chief kerosene-burning styles are currently being manufactured.

Portable or table lamps, regardless of material, do not have to beg for buyers. They seem to sell with or without chimneys and shades, and whether or not they have been converted to electricity. It certainly is not necessary to go to the trouble and expense of having an oil lamp changed so that it can illuminate by means of electricity. In certain cases, such as a brass student lamp, one that has been converted skillfully can be sold for more money to most people. On the other hand, some buyers would prefer to have the original student lamp untouched. This is particularly true of those who collect nineteenth-century lamps.

Certain kinds of lamps can be sold for higher prices to collectors than to the average person. This applies especially to fairy and miniature lamps, colored glass and cut glass ones, and such oddities as peg lamps and lanterns made for various special purposes. Certain patterns of pressed glass also will be of more interest to collectors and hence probably can be sold to them for a higher price than to the person who is shopping only for an attractive lamp.

Since a peg lamp does not lend itself to electricity, it is likely to be of interest only to a collector or a museum. At that, a peg will not bring a high price. A metal one to be attached to a wooden block sells now in the neighborhood of about $7, a glass peg lamp probably for a little more if it is complete and in good condition.

Pressed glass lamps, whether they originally burned whale oil or kerosene, have a market value ranging from a low of $2 to about $100. A squat pressed glass lamp without pattern decoration can be purchased almost anywhere for about $2 (with oil burner but possibly no wick and undoubtedly without a chimney). Pattern glass lamps vary in price, chiefly according to the pattern and collectors' interest in it. In rural areas, the selling price is bound to be less than in a city antique shop.

If the lamp itself is in good condition, one in the early Ashburton pattern might bring $15, a Beaded Tulip or a Block and Fan about $6.50. A lamp in the popular Bellflower pattern can be sold for as much as $25, a bracket lamp in the same pattern for a little less. Blackberry, another one of the most popular patterns among pressed glass collectors, also brings a good price. A Blackberry lamp with a milk glass base and clear glass font should bring at least $25. Daisy and Button, a late pattern, which is still very popular but which was made in quantity after 1880, is not as rare as Bellflower and Blackberry. A clear glass lamp in Daisy and Button may not sell for more than $5, but a colored glass one commands a higher price—$10 or so for an amber or blue one, perhaps $15 or a little more for an apple-green one.

A footed lamp in the early Argus pattern should sell for not less than $15, and one with a colored base should bring somewhat more.

The colored and art glass oil lamps and those with fine decoration such as cutting, etching, or overlay start at higher prices than the majority of pattern glass lamps. A nineteenth-century cranberry glass lamp—and many were made in the late years, in numerous different styles—in the right market will have a selling price that starts at not less than $30. The price can rise according to the condition, style, the other materials used, and the workmanship. A hanging lamp with cranberry glass panels in a brass frame may sell for as much as $50; if it is etched or otherwise decorated, for considerably more. A portable or table lamp with cranberry glass font may be priced fairly between $30 and $35. Any lamp that can be certified as having been made by the Boston and Sandwich Glass Company brings a premium price. For example, one of their lamps with an apple-green font and an alabaster base, made to burn whale oil, is worth about $150. A similar lamp not necessarily made by the Boston and Sandwich Glass Company is not worth as much, but still can be sold for a good price. For instance, a lamp of unidentified origin with a clear glass base and blue font is certainly well priced at about $25.

Before asking such a price for a lamp that can't be used for illumination after dark in its present state, it is important to be absolutely certain that it is a nineteenth-century one. Not many of the pressed glass patterns are being reproduced, although hobnail glass is used for shades of many contemporary reproductions of lamps. A good many modern electric table lamps are being made currently with glass fonts in the popular cranberry, blue, and amber glass. Some of these lamps have pseudo-milk glass or alabaster bases, too. Electrified reproductions of various styles of metal lamps also are being made.

On the other hand, some genuine late-nineteenth-century lamps are appraised at a value that is far higher than the price for which they can be sold. A cut glass lamp with prisms, for example, if it was made between 1876 and 1900 (the Brilliant Period), can be valued at $100 or more. Few people are willing to pay that much for cut glass now when there are so many attractive pressed glass lamps to be had. Tiffany glass lamps are another example, for they probably cost much more originally than they can be sold for today. Because of the great interest in and increasing demand for satin glass today, it may be possible to sell a lamp with a satin glass shade for closer to its appraised value. A large hall lamp with pastel satin glass shade and brass frame might be priced reasonably at $100 to $125, if it is in perfect condition. It probably also will be possible to sell the odd-shaped shade of satin or other art glass that was made for a newel-post lamp in the hall, although goodness knows what the buyer will do with it.

Authentic globular parlor lamps sell for $35 to $75. China lamps, even the Meissen type with raised floral decoration, range from about $35 to as much as $100. First, however, you must find an interested buyer.

Prices for both fairy and miniature lamps have skyrocketed, more or less, in recent years because collectors have shown so much enthusiasm. A complete one in good condition is almost certain to sell for at least $10. Many appealing ones can be sold for $15 to $20. Unusual and rare ones may bring considerably higher prices, well over $100 and in some cases close to $200.

A pewter whale oil lamp made before 1850 may be sold for $20 to $25. The Rayco lamps of the late 1800's sell for $5 to $10. A nickel-plated one without a shade is hardly like to sell for more than $5 to $7.50, though a brass one without shade may perhaps bring $10. Student lamps have more than doubled in price since the 1930's. A single-arm brass one complete with shade is likely to sell now for as much as $50 to $75; a double-arm one with its shades intact, and electrified, may bring as much as $150.

Lanterns not only do not begin to bring the prices that lamps do, but sell a little more slowly. Find a collectors' market and you can get rid of any sort, from a small brass oil one from an early automobile (perhaps $20 or a little more) to a carriage lantern ($15 and up, or slightly more than double for a matched pair). A Baltimore and Ohio

Railroad lantern with handle should sell for not less than $5, possibly a little more. The pierced tin lantern appeals to many people, so even if it's rusty try to sell it. One in reasonably good condition should sell for about $10; the so-called Paul Revere style for a little more, possibly as much as $17.50.

It's not unusual to come across a part of a nineteenth-century lamp and not recognize what it is. For example, a blue glass bowl about the shape and size of an oriole's nest puzzled the person who found it, along with a couple of smooth-edged glass lampshades of the nineteenth century, in the corner of a Pennsylvania cellar. Finally, it proved to be part of a hanging lantern from which the metal candle socket had been removed or lost. Originally, it had been hung with brass chains. A smoke bell is almost as difficult to recognize if it's found by itself. So, too, would be the tiny pewter shade on the burner of a small and very old glass and pewter oil lamp.

Shades alone are valuable finds, and if they cannot be used on lamps in your home, are sure to be salable. Shades for ceiling lights, table lamps, and wall or bracket lamps are likely to be unearthed in cellars and attics, for they were made in greater quantity than lamps as the use of natural gas and electricity spread. When such shades have been cleaned or washed gently, they may prove to be things of beauty, in color if not entirely so in form. A Burmese glass lampshade with a 2-inch opening at the top flaring to 6 inches

is worth any amount from $24 to $50 that you can get for it. A small Tiffany glass shade made for a gas lamp can be appraised for $25 and sold to a knowledgeable collector for that price too.

Large shades consisting of pieces of colored glass fitted together with lead seams to form a strong pattern or design were popular for table and piano lamps as well as ceiling lights during the early 1900's. Although these are not yet more than semiantiques, some interest is being shown in them again. So far, this interest is chiefly on the part of decorators. However, whether a decorator uses this type of shade in a department store window, a model room, or a stage setting, it's bound to recall them to the average person's mind and spark some small revival of interest. A large lead and glass shade for a ceiling fixture has some small cash value at present, but as the market grows for these late-nineteenth- and early twentieth-century shades, so too will the prices that can be obtained for them.

Few families, if any, will have stored away anywhere a gas-burning street light. Baltimore was the first city in the United States to install gas fixtures along some of its streets—in 1817. Philadelphia did so in 1835, and still maintains gaslights around Independence Square. All gaslights, starting with those that illuminated the streets of Baltimore and Philadelphia, became a collector's item in 1957 when some with authentic old Welsbach burners were offered for public sale by a New York City department store. They were snapped up quickly to light driveways and entrances of homes in the suburbs. Although at their peak, about 1915, gaslights illuminated the streets of many cities from coast to coast, it is believed that a larger number now are installed in America's suburbs.

Authentic replicas with the white dome, the cast-iron pole, and the cross-bar against which the lamplighter rested his ladder· every evening are being made in several places. The contemporary ones burn either gas or electricity (gas illuminates with a soft radiance and without glare) and may even have an electronic control to dim the light at dawn and turn it up at dusk. These reproductions sell for worthwhile prices, so it goes without saying that a gaslight that actually gave service along the street of any city or town can be sold for somewhat more.

In these days, streets and highways are well-lighted and indoor illumination is planned carefully not only to avoid eyestrain during any activity after dark but also to create decorative effects. It is hard to imagine getting along with a tiny, smelly lamp that burns some kind of fat. The development of lamps and lighting fixtures has been phenomenal during the last 200 years, yet many people enjoy the old styles adapted to the modern flood of electric light.

## GLOSSARY

*Burner:* the part of the lamp that holds the wick, from which the flame issues.

*Candelabrum:* a large ornamental candlestick, and later a lamp, with two or more branches each tipped with a light.

*Chandelier:* a branched cluster of lights suspended from the ceiling.

*Chimney:* a glass cylinder surrounding the flame of a lamp, to promote combustion and keep the flame steady.

*Font:* the part of the lamp that holds the oil. A font may be variously shaped — globular, elliptical, pear, etc.

*Girandole:* a highly ornamental, branched holder for candles or lamps, usually embellished with prisms. It may rest on a standard or project from the wall. Also, a mirror with candleholders attached; an ornate wall clock.

*Hurricane lamp:* a tall, broad glass chimney placed over a lighted candle or lamp to protect it from wind. The earliest ones rested on the table and covered both light and holder. Also known as a hurricane shade.

*Lamp:* originally, a vessel that held oil or other inflammable liquid and had a wick that could be ignited to produce a flame for artificial light. Now, any fixture whereby illumination is provided after dark.

*Lantern:* a light entirely enclosed by a transparent or translucent case to protect it from wind and rain. Lanterns were made for indoor and outdoor use for various purposes, and to be carried, hung, or placed on a bracket.

*Prism:* a glass pendant faceted and cut in any of various shapes (pear, spear-pointed, rectangular, etc.); several were attached by small metal hooks at regular intervals around the socket of a candleholder or lamp. Also called crystal drops.

*Reflector:* a polished surface attached behind the flame of a lamp to reinforce the light by reflection.

*Rush light:* a kind of candle made by dipping a hollow-stemmed rush in grease and lighting it at one end.

*Shade:* an ornamental cover placed over a lamp to reduce the intensity of light. Common here after 1860.

*Smoke bell:* a glass disk or cup suspended over the chains of a hanging lamp to prevent the ceiling from being darkened by smoke.

*Standard:* the base or support for a lamp.

*Wick:* a bundle of fibers or a loosely twisted cord or tube of spun cotton threads which by capillary action steadily draws up the oil from the font to the burner in which the wick is fastened.

### SPECIAL KINDS OF LAMPS

*Betty or Phoebe:* a small open vessel to hold oil or fat, shaped at one point into a groove or slot for a wick.

*Argand:* a style of lamp patented by Swiss engineer Aimé Argand in 1787, which greatly improved illumination. It had a round wick, fed upward over a hollow metal tube that was perforated to admit air, which circulated through the tube and aided combustion. The oil font was large. This style of lamp is rarely found now.

*Astral:* an improvement on the Argand lamp, invented by Benjamin Thompson of Woburn, Massachusetts, and made in this country from the early 1800's until after 1860. The font was

at the side, and oil was fed by gravity into a small cylinder below the wick burner. May be single- or double-arm.

*Camphene:* a lamp made to burn the explosive as well as inflammable liquid, camphene, and hence requiring a wick tube that projected well above the collar of the burner. If there were two tubes, they slanted away from each other and usually were capped with metal when not in use. These usually were small lamps.

*Solar:* an adaptation of the Argand lamp, developed in Philadelphia, in 1843. It had the oil font under the burner, a round wick, a bulblike chimney, and an ornamental shade.

# 8

# All Kinds of Glass

GLASS HAS BEEN KNOWN and valued in all of the great civilizations that have dominated the world. However, few if any other countries besides the United States can claim that glassmaking was the first established industry. Two glasshouses existed in the Jamestown Colony in Virginia, one started in 1608 and the second in 1621. Both attempts failed, probably because even skilled glassmakers who emigrated to America found there were more essential tasks for survival than making so fragile a product as glass—even for such everyday purposes as windowpanes for new dwellings and beads to trade with the Indians.

Many other glasshouses were started in other colonies along the East Coast, but the industry had its ups and downs until firms turned to making pressed glass shortly after 1825. Yet even after pressed glass became popular, other, more ancient techniques of glassmak-

ing were pursued. As a result, the United States has an interesting and individual heritage in spite of all the glass that was imported during the 1700's, 1800's, and even most of the 1900's.

Although so many who attempted to establish a glass business during Colonial days failed, the names of three men of that time are still essential to any knowledge of glass: Caspar Wistar, who started the glass industry in southern New Jersey in 1738; Henry William Stiegel, often called Baron Stiegel, who established his glasshouses in Manheim, Pennsylvania, in 1763; and John Frederick Amelung, in New Bremen, Maryland, in 1784. All three came to this country from Germany.

Any pieces of Wistar or other Colonial "South Jersey" glass, Stiegel, or Amelung glass that are known unquestionably to have been produced in these eighteenth-century glasshouses are almost certainly in museums now. Often a piece of glass is identified tentatively as "probably Stiegel" or "South Jersey type," but that is as close as anyone who comes across a piece of undocumented glass today can be expected to go. The fact that a small wineglass has a clear bell-like ring is no more proof that it was made at the Stiegel works in Manheim, Pennsylvania, than that a pressed glass plate is Sandwich glass.

The products of these early glassmakers

and Midwest. Since most of this nineteenth-century glass was for household use, a considerable amount can be found even at the present time. Of course, there is more pressed glass (Chapter IX) and cut glass than blown-molded or blown-three-mold still to be discovered. First, however, you must know what to look for.

Caspar Wistar's glasshouses flourished for forty years or so in the eighteenth century, but, more important, led to other men's producing glass in south-

| TYPE | METHOD | IDENTIFICATION | COLOR | DECORATION |
|---|---|---|---|---|
| *Blown* Offhand or Free-blown | By blowing and manipulation | Scar or pontil mark, but this was polished off on many pieces. | Clear, colors, also green or brown tinge in cheap glass | Applied, painted, etched, engraved, cut |
| *Blown-* or *Pattern-Molded* | Blown into a small mold, then removed and expanded by blowing | Pattern within the glass; handles and feet applied. | Brilliant colors and clear | Pattern of ribs, swirls, quilting, etc., within the glass |
| *Blown-Three-Mold* | Glass blown into full-size molds of 2 or more parts hinged together | Seam marks where mold sections met. Design in reverse can be felt on the inside. | Clear and colors | All-over pattern of swirls and scrolls, geometric lines, arches |
| *Pressed* | Machine-pressed into molds | Designs shallow and smooth to the touch. | Clear, opaque, and some colors in both types | *Lacy:* intricate design against stippled background *Pattern:* motifs, including stippling, forming a recognizable design |

were hand-blown or blown-molded. Their techniques, colors, and styles were copied and used throughout the nineteenth century, even after the advent of pressed glass, by glasshouses that flourished throughout the East

ern New Jersey. "South Jersey" is a term for glass made not only in that state but also in Pennsylvania, New York, New England, and, later, Ohio. The pieces are free-blown yet sturdy and usually quite thick glass. Whether it was a pitcher or a vase, Wistar's pieces and other South Jersey glass, too, were likely to be broad at the base, with curving sides. Ornament was applied as trails or threads of glass that often formed a leaflike pattern (lily pad), loops, waves, ribbons, or a crumpled ribbon effect known as crimping. Colored or opaque glass was often worked into the clear glass.

Baron Stiegel was the first to produce cut glass on this continent, but he is better remembered for his pieces decorated with colored enamels. Stiegel's glasshouses in their comparatively few years of operation turned out not only free-blown but also blown-molded glass.

John Frederick Amelung was noted chiefly for the marvelous engraving on his blown glass. Although his factory in New Bremen was sold in 1795 after only eleven years of production, many of his workmen drifted to other glasshouses in Maryland and Pennsylvania, where they continued to do the sort of work they had done under Amelung himself.

Glassmaking moved westward as settlers did. First western Pennsylvania, later Ohio, West Virginia, Indiana, and Oklahoma became busy centers. There was always a demand for window glass, bottles and flasks, and bowls. Actually Wistar, if not Stiegel and Amelung, produced more window glass and bottles than anything else, although it is their decorative glass which has made their names famous.

Glass can be made anywhere that sand and an alkali are available. These two classes of ingredients have to be melted together. In its liquid form glass is referred to as "metal." A distinction must be made between metal to which chemicals have been added to color it a rich blue, amethyst, green, red, or some shade of yellow, and glass which just naturally turns out to have a slight tinge of color because of its formula. Green glass, incidentally, is still made for soft-drink bottles and the like. Much of the early window and bottle glass made in this country had a green tint or looked almost brown or yellow. The famous purple windowpanes in houses on Beacon Street in Boston are very old; they became tinted through the action of sun on the glass, which probably came from a batch of metal that contained an excess amount of some chemical.

Master glassmakers in Europe, England, and America experimented to produce a clear—that is, a colorless—glass. The first clear glass was lead glass, also known as English flint, which had lead as an essential ingredient. Crystal is used sometimes as a synonym for glass of high lead content, but the designation white or clear glass is technically correct. It refers to a clear or transparent glass in which no coloring agent has been used. It is as different from milk-white glass as it is from ordinary bottle glass.

The oldest method of making articles from glass was blowing. A blob of metal was blown and manipulated by

*Old and varied techniques were used for wineglasses . The two at the left, are hand-blown with clear glass stems and colored bowls. The wineglass at the right is also hand-blown, but it has cutting below the red rim. The goblet at the rear has a flashed red bowl with a grape design etched through to the clear glass.*

Blown-molded glass is an inheritance from Stiegel. The technique was widely used during the nineteenth century. The workman blew the glass slightly into a small mold of wood or iron, which gave it a pattern, and then removed it, and continued to blow and rotate the glass until the article achieved the desired shape and size. The finished piece had sparkle as well as a pattern of swirls, ribbing, quilting, or the like, which appeared to be within the glass. Blown-molded pieces are often referred to as expanded glass. Handles, feet, and other added por-

*The small pitchers or creamers shown here are* (left to right) *blown-molded in blue, and clear pressed glass in the Lacy Daisy, Cameo, and Cardinal Bird patterns.*

a workman using a blowpipe, a pontil or punty, and such shaping tools as tongs and shears. The pontil or punty rod was used to hold the object while it was still hot, and when it was broken off it left a scar, which is known as the pontil mark, on the bottom of the article. Lack of a pontil mark does not necessarily discredit old blown glass, for the rough mark was sometimes polished off. Glass made by blowing and manipulation is known as offhand or free-blown glass.

tions on the blown-molded pieces usually were hand-blown.

After 1812, blown-three-mold glass was made in this country by adapting an ancient technique. Glass was blown into full-sized molds consisting of two, three, or more parts hinged together. One way of detecting blown-three-mold glass is the seam marks left where the sections of the mold met. Blown-three-mold glass, which really was an attempt to imitate expensive cut glass

Pitchers have been made of all sorts of materials. The two here are (left) clear, blown-molded glass, made between 1815 and 1825, and (right) opaque blue, pressed glass, 4½ inches tall, made some time after 1850.

at modest price, had an all-over pattern. However, the motifs were more limited than those of cut glass, which were made entirely by hand. Patterns were based on one of three general types — swirls and scrolls known as baroque, combinations of geometric lines, and arches.

These hand-blown sweetmeat jars show pontil scars on the bottom. The larger jar is 12 inches tall and 5¼ in diameter; the smaller one is 10 inches tall and 4¼ in diameter. Rings of clear glass, applied after a piece had cooled, were widely used as decoration after 1820.

Most of the various kinds of decoration brought here from England and European countries during the seventeenth and eighteenth centuries continued to be used during the nineteenth, although not always in such detail or with such skill as in the Wistar, Stiegel, and Amelung factories. Threads or trails of glass applied to blown glass can be traced back to Caspar Wistar. Sometimes the thread was wound spirally, then again to outline lily pads or other leaves or flowers, or drawn around the outside to form a wave. Crimping was a ribbon design. Applied rings around the body and threads or finer rings around the neck of a bottle or jar were used everywhere for more than a century after Wistar's glasshouse closed.

The use of colorful painted decoration stemmed from Stiegel. Enamels in color were applied to the outer surface and fused with the glass by heat. Gilding was used with colored enamels as well as on engraved pieces.

Engraved decoration was common on Stiegel glass and brought to a high degree of skill on Amelung glass. Whether the design was a simple or intricate floral, or was based on classic motifs or an elaborate fantasy, the engraving was done on the outer surface of the glass by means of a series of small copper wheels. Engraving is a very old type of decoration and rarely was polished.

Etching, a somewhat similar type of

applied decoration that was done by the application of acid, is newer. It was much used during the nineteenth century. The result is more frosty-looking than engraving, which of course is deeper.

Sometimes engraving was combined with the cutting of glass. Cutting a pattern also was done by a moving wheel, and when completed the piece was polished. Glass has been ornamented by cutting for hundreds of years; in the United States, since about 1770.

William Henry Stiegel little dreamed that, by 1870, few towns in Pennsylvania would be too small to have their own glass factory. In the Lackawanna Valley of northeastern Pennsylvania from Wilkes Barre north to Honesdale, few of the twenty-two towns lacked a glass factory. Between 1890 and 1910, one of the smallest of these towns, Jermyn, with a population of about 3,000, had two glass factories. Neither of the Jermyn factories turned out as notable pieces as those of T. B. Clark and Company in Honesdale, and C. Dorflinger and Sons, Inc., in White Mills, a few miles farther north.

England and, for a period, Ireland also were known for cut glass. Ireland's great period of glassmaking extended from about 1780 to 1825, and although Waterford is the best-known name now, Belfast, Dublin, and Cork were other glass centers. The designs even from this great period of Irish cut glass

were relatively simple in comparison to the finest made in the United States later. Diamonds, swags, prisms, the thumbprint, a round lozenge, and sawtooth were used in various combinations. The edges of Waterford glass pieces were usually scalloped and rims were likely to flare and possibly be turned over or lipped.

By 1800, cut glass was being made in Pittsburgh, Pennsylvania, at the Pittsburgh Glass Works founded by Col. John O'Hara, and in the early years of the new century by other firms in western Pennsylvania. The New England Glass Company in Cambridge, Massachusetts, and the Boston and Sandwich Glass Company in Sandwich also were producing some excellent cut glass.

What is now set aside as the Middle Period of cut glass manufacture in the United States covered the years from 1830 to 1880. Many new glasshouses were built during that time. They turned out a considerable amount of engraved glass as well as cut glass, which generally was a clear, lead glass. Cutting motifs were fairly simple, with the flute probably the most popular. Decanters that were blown, then decorated with flute cuttings and given a steeple stopper, are now perhaps the best-known pieces of this period.

The peak period of cut glass production in this country extended from about 1880 to 1905, and then tapered off gradually to next to nothing by

1915. Experts in the field call the years from 1880 to 1905 the Brilliant Period. During these years, glass of exceptionally fine quality was made, cutting was deep and designs often elaborate, for the wheels now were powered by electricity. In fact, the cut glass of the Brilliant Period was as fine as, if not finer than, the very best quality made anywhere at any time.

Even during its greatest and most popular period, cut glass was never inexpensive. Furthermore, these pieces of the Brilliant Period are now irreplaceable, for no firm anywhere today could afford to make and sell glass of the quality of the Brilliant Period and with a comparable amount of cut decoration. Almost all glass of the Brilliant Period was heavy and all of it sparkled. Irreplaceable too are pieces from the Middle and Early Periods. Although the cuttings were much simpler during the Middle Period, the pieces compare favorably in value with those of the Brilliant Period, if only because they were made earlier.

Perhaps no other type of glass has been in and out of fashion as often as cut glass. Because it was beautiful as well as expensive, it was a status symbol of the nineteenth century. Between 1880 and 1910, no bride felt officially married unless her presents included cut glass. It also was the correct present for anniversaries and special events. Then suddenly, after World War I, cut glass was out of fashion and started gathering dust in cupboards and attics. Often it was given away to anyone

who would take it, and replaced by modern or contemporary "crystal."

The last few years, fortunately, have seen a new appreciation develop for American cut glass of the Brilliant Period. It's acceptable, if not fashionable, to display and use it. Some people are collecting it and if you have pieces you want to sell, it's possible sooner or later to find a buyer. Prices for cut glass depend on the eagerness of the buyer as well as the quality and the cutting. It is safe to say, though, that a great deal of fine cut glass can be purchased now not only for much less than it would cost if it could be made at this time, but also for less than it cost when it was made and first sold.

The appraised value of cut glass is much higher in most parts of the country than the actual price for which a piece can be sold. Certainly some of the large cities have more prospective buyers and it brings better prices there. In northeastern Pennsylvania, where so much cut glass was made, it may not be possible to sell a dozen sauce dishes for more than $15 or a 10-inch-high vase of good workmanship for more than $10—and both originally cost much more. Almost anywhere, a person who owns a sugar and creamer in Pinwheel pattern (certainly worth $20 now, if it isn't nicked or cracked) is likely to give up and sell the pair for $10. Tumblers, even in a common or simple pattern, are worth not less than $4.

Of all the cut glass pieces, decanters

are probably easiest to sell. Few, if any, of those that are in good condition and have their original stoppers should be sold for less than $25, and many of them will be worth $35 to $50. Cruets, perfume bottles, candlesticks, inkwells, and paperweights also are easier to sell for a decent price than most of the tableware. A paperweight, depending on the intricacy of its cutting, should bring from $10 to $20. A knife rest, which is as sensible an article today as it was seventy years ago, can be priced at not less than $5 and perhaps $7.50. As a matter of fact, knife rests, like any kind of glass salts, are an item that attracts collectors.

If you can find a collector who is interested primarily in cut glass, such a person will appreciate whatever pieces you have and be prepared to pay a worthwhile price for any that would round out her collection. So far, cut glass has not attracted the amount of interest and the number of collectors that its imitation, pressed glass, has acquired. But it is entirely possible that cut glass will reach this peak of popularity. When it does, it will be easier to sell for prices at or near the appraised values. At least the cut glass market will not be cluttered with reproductions.

All cut glass is good glass, heavy and sparkling. Some pieces, naturally, are better than others. According to Dorothy Daniel, an expert on American cut glass, the four tests to determine whether glass has been entirely cut, partly cut, or not cut at all are

based on ring, sparkle, sharpness, and weight. All pieces of cut glass ring like a bell when struck lightly with a pencil or the fingers. Not all pieces ring with the same tone, and closed pieces such as carafes, decanters, and bottles sometimes smother the ring.

When a piece of fine cut class is held to the light, there is refraction. According to Miss Daniel, glass made during the Brilliant Period has the greatest refraction because of the purity of the ingredients and the quick fusion made possible by use of natural gas as the fuel. The deep cuttings of the Brilliant Period also increased refraction.

When you run your fingers over the cutting, the edges should feel sharp. A motif such as a nailhead may have been polished so that its sides are smooth, but the points still feel sharp. The edges of any motif will be sharply defined. Cut glass, as we have already mentioned, always is heavy because of the high lead content of the glass.

Cut glass was made in sets for table use, chiefly for desserts and liquids. Corinthian, a pattern of which almost every glasshouse had its own version, was made in at least the following pieces:

Berry bowls—round, oblong, and square, in sizes from 6 to 10 inches
Bonbon or olive dishes—round and square, in two sizes
Butter patties

Celery dish
Cheese dish with cover
Cologne bottles
Compotes, high and low
Cruets
Decanters, pint and quart
Finger bowls
Goblets
Honey jar
Jelly tray
Mustard pot
Nappies—low, shallow serving dishes
—in various sizes
Pitchers, in various sizes
Plates—round, oblong, and square, from 6 to 12 inches
Punch bowl
Rose bowl
Salts—individual and table
Sauce dishes to match nappies
Sherbet cups on stems
Spoonholder
Sugar bowl
Tumblers
Vases
Wineglasses: champagne, claret, cordial, sherry and wine

Tumblers often came with both a carafe and a water pitcher in the same pattern. A knife rest, toothpick-holder, jam jar, syrup pitcher, and punch cups were other possible pieces that might be included in a set. Condiment sets and candlesticks as well as vases and bowls for flowers also often were made to match tableware. Ice-cream sets, although a small part of many patterns, could be purchased as a group. In some patterns, tableware could be accumulated for a luncheon set and other pieces added to this nucleus to make a more elaborate setting for dinner parties. In fact, it was never necessary to buy a complete set at one time. A gift of a half-dozen tumblers might be the beginning. Then, a few months later, a water pitcher in the same pattern might be another gift or a purchase. Any number of pieces could be added singly or by the dozen or half-dozen over a period of years.

Decanters and perfume and cologne bottles could be bought individually or in pairs. Some gemels or twin perfume bottles that fit into one base also were cut. Candlesticks, lamps, lampshades, and chandeliers were available separately or in pairs too. Miscellaneous items were made in many patterns, some of them to match tableware. Vases were made in all sizes and shapes, in addition to rose bowls and rose jars. Cut glass baskets with handles were an important acquisition. These also were made in all shapes and sizes: taller ones with flaring tops were intended for flowers, the shallow, flat ones to display fruit. Boxes were made in varied shapes to hold jewels, gloves, handkerchiefs, hairpins, powder, puff, and salves. Many of the boxes are charming. Some of the boxes had silver, usually sterling, covers or mountings; others had cut glass covers. There were pin trays too.

Doorknobs, tiebacks for curtains, knobs for mirrors or furniture, napkin rings, inkwells, and paperweights were not uncommon but are likely to be passed over by present-day owners or finders. They shouldn't be, though the cutting on these smaller items was always much simpler than on table and ornamental pieces. The usual four tests will prove whether or not a doorknob or paperweight actually is cut glass. Incidentally, the glass panel in the entrance doors of some of the houses in Pennsylvania glass-factory towns is made of cut glass.

All of these various cut glass items were made in hundreds of patterns. In the Brilliant Period at least, the different glasshouses gave the patterns names or numbers to distinguish them. A named or numbered pattern generally was composed of two or more basic motifs arranged together artistically.

Flutings and other facetings and prism cutting—the latter either straight, broken, or notched—were important earlier, but were overshadowed by the more elaborate motifs and patterns of the Brilliant Period. Carried over into this period were such old motifs as English hobnail and English strawberry diamond, bull's-eye, and block. The hobnail motif was six-sided and flat-topped and resembled the hob-

nail of a shoe. Strawberry diamond was widely used with larger motifs. It was a diamond-shaped unit of small, deeply cut, equal-sided diamonds. American strawberry diamond with one cross cut into the flat, top surface of each small diamond was coarser-looking but fully as sparkling as the finer-cut English strawberry diamond. Hatching is the term for the fine crossed or parallel lines that often filled in between other motifs.

Fan, palm leaf, bowknot, and chair bottom or cane were much used during the Brilliant Period. During this time the hob-star, which had so many points that the intersection of their lines formed a motif resembling the hobnail, came to full flower. Some hob-stars or rosettes were large enough to fill the base, 3¼ inches wide, of a flaring 7-inch berry bowl. Stars with 6, 8, 10, 12, and 18 or more points as well as simple stars were made time and again.

The pinwheel or buzz, cut around 1900 and later, was a many-pointed,

*Hob-stars with 6, 8, 10, 12, 18, and more points were an important motif for glass cut during the Brilliant Period (1880-1905). Both the berry bowl and the vase have hob-stars as the dominant motif.*

The cut glass tumbler at the left is in the Pinwheel or Buzz pattern made around 1900. The smaller one at the right is in the older Strawberry Diamond and Fan pattern.

swirling star with fan cuts following the direction of the points. It was an elaboration of the hob-star. The Pinwheel pattern probably was first made by the American Glass Company of Chicago, Illinois. Variations of this pattern included Cut Buzz, made by the United States Glass Company in Pittsburgh; Marvel, from the Maple City Glass Company in Honesdale, Pennsylvania; Pinwheel and Star, from J. Hoare and Company in Corning, New York; and Twenty-two, by Pairpoint Corporation, New Bedford, Massachusetts.

Like the pinwheel motif and patterns, floral patterns belong to the last years of the nineteenth century and, more plentifully, to the twentieth century. The later the piece was cut, the more realistic the flowers looked and the shallower were the cuttings. Bristol Rose, patented by a New Bedford glass-cutter in 1893, does not display the flower but takes its name from the cutting of 32-point stars with raised rosette centers.

One of the first floral patterns was Lily of the Valley, made by the H. C. Fry Glass Company in Rochester, Pennsylvania. Most realistic stems of these dainty blossoms and their leaves were finely cut in a panel arrangement alternating with traditional cut glass motifs. This early floral pattern as made by Fry was not only well done but also on glass of extremely fine quality, two characteristics not always applicable to floral patterns made after 1900.

T. B. Clark and Company of Honesdale, Pennsylvania, produced several floral patterns after 1905. This was the only glass factory to reproduce a poinsettia and make a pattern of it. Cornflower, another of this firm's patterns, used none of the old motifs, no stars or rosettes, but a realistic line-cutting of leaves and natural though conventional blossoms. Floral patterns often were based on recognizable flowers such as poppies and roses, then again were simply flowers. Some, like Cornflower, are quite modern in appearance; many are attractive but some are rather clumsy-looking.

Probably the most famous pattern of the Brilliant Period was Russian, which was patented in 1882 by a cutter who worked for Thomas G. Hawkes Company in Corning, New York. It was derived from the older Star and Hobnail pattern and was based on a 24-point star. Eventually, the Russian pattern was cut by many glasshouses, including such well-known and good-quality ones as C. Dorflinger and Sons

*The cut glass bowl at the left combines star and bull's-eye, two old motifs, with flower sprays. It probably was not cut until· after 1905. The 10-inch-high footed dish, with intricate hob-star cutting on the bowl, a notched-prism stem, and the base in Fan and Strawberry Diamond pattern, is older.*

in White Mills, Pennsylvania. A half-dozen or so variations also were cut, including Spiderweb, which combined Russian with Strawberry Diamond and Fan, and Polar Star, in which the size of the larger star motif was increased in proportion to the hobnail. Russian probably was cut in more pieces than any other pattern, and by most glass-houses.

Russian pattern with the addition of an engraved eagle crest had the distinction of being ordered in 1886 for use at the White House in Washington. Additions and replacements were ordered over a period of about twenty years, and the cut glass was still being used at state dinners through the

1930's. There also was a pattern called White House that made use of lines of notched prisms with a simple star.

Corinthian was another well-known pattern because practically every glass-house cut some version of it. Basically, the pattern had a 16-point hob-star,

*At the left, the shallow cut glass nappy (9 inches in diameter) is a good illustration of a florid version of the Corinthian pattern made after 1900. The square candy dish at the right is sparkling Venetian pattern.*

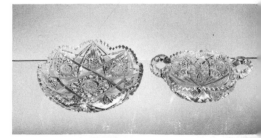

boxed, as the central motif. From each corner rose a triangle of strawberry diamond with smaller, boxed 16-point hob-stars in between. Intervening spaces were filled with triangles of crosshatching. A fine example of Corinthian pattern was made by the Libbey Glass Company, Toledo, Ohio, and smaller firms in other states often made more florid variations.

Harvard, which was based on chair bottom or cane cutting, was another pattern made by almost all glasshouses, both in its original design and in such variations as Corning Harvard, Quilt Block, and Trellis. Simpler but fully as popular was Strawberry Diamond and Fan.

Cut glass is thought of as being clear or white glass which sparkles like diamonds in sun or light. By far the greatest amount of cut glass was clear, but in its heyday colored cut glass was by no means uncommon. However, although the popular Russian pattern was cut in green, ruby, amber, amethyst, blue, and yellow as well as clear, Strawberry Diamond and Fan in red, green, and yellow, these colored pieces are rare nowadays. Corinthian and White House presumably were made only in clear glass and Harvard was chiefly clear glass too. Many other patterns had wine or cordial glasses in color, or combining clear with a color such as rich green or red. Knife rests were made in color to some extent.

Not all colored cut glass was one color all the way through. More common was glass flashed with another color. Flashing differs technically from overlay, but the results are similar. A flashed piece has a thin coating of glass in a contrasting color, and when the design is cut, the two colors show. Another method of adding color, used on cut glass of poorer quality, was applying a luster stain after the piece was finished. It was then heated to fix the stain. It is far more difficult for a novice to identify colored cut glass of whatever technique as having been made during the nineteenth century. One reason is because of the reproductions made in Europe during the twentieth century.

Colored cut glass lamps are perhaps recognized more readily than colored cut glass tableware, decanters, and bottles. A vast array of lamps was cut from the time whale oil was burned early in the nineteenth century to gas and electric ones of the early 1900's. The fonts of the whale oil lamps were the portion that was likely to be colored and decorated by cutting.

Toward the end of the Brilliant Period, some glassmakers started to patent their designs. The first patent was taken out by Henry C. Fry of the H. C. Fry Glass Company in Rochester, Pennsylvania, in 1886. However, not all of this firm's patterns after 1886 were patented. Even after 1895 not all patterns were patented, and for those that were, a patent wasn't always protection against copying by another glasshouse. Even so, several hundred patent marks were registered between

1886 and 1914. Some companies etched their mark into the glass, others pressed them into the blanks before cutting started. C. Dorflinger and Sons simply pasted a paper showing their mark onto finished pieces and this, of course, did not stick on for long. If you detect a trademark, it is proof of origin and the company who cut the glass. However, lack of a mark has no bearing on the quality of cut glass.

Many of the glasshouses exhibited at the Centennial Exposition staged in Philadelphia, Pennsylvania, in 1876. The Boston and Sandwich Glass Company of Sandwich and the New England Glass Company of Cambridge, Massachusetts, C. Dorflinger and Sons of White Mills, a little town in northeastern Pennsylvania, and Hobbs Brockunier Company of Wheeling, West Virginia, were among those who arranged notable displays. However, they were outdone by James Gillinder and Sons of Philadelphia, who did more than anyone else to popularize cut glass, for they set up a glassworks on the Centennial's grounds. Visitors not only took souvenirs but also bought cut glass to take back home with them.

Cutting was only one type of decoration and of glass made at many glasshouses. This was particularly true of such firms as Boston and Sandwich Glass Company, New England Glass Company in Massachusetts; Bakewell, Pears & Company, Adams and Company, Bryce Brothers and others of Pittsburgh, Pennsylvania, Challinor,

Taylor Company and Richards and Hartley Company of nearby Tarentum, Pennsylvania; A. J. Beatty and Sons in Tiffin, Ohio, Bellaire Goblet Company in Findlay, and others in that state.

Outstanding names in fine cut glass included Gillinder and Sons in Philadelphia, C. Dorflinger and Sons in White Mills, T. B. Clark and Company in Honesdale, and H. C. Fry Company in Rochester, Pennsylvania; Adams and Company and the O'Hara Glass Company of Pittsburgh; A. H. Heisey and Company in Newark, Ohio, Libbey Glass Company in Toledo; Pairpoint Corporation in New Bedford and Union Glass Company in Somerville, Massachusetts; T. G. Hawkes Glass Company, and Corning Glass Works, both in Corning, New York.

New York City had several glasshouses led by Bloomingdale Flint Glass Works. So did Brooklyn, with Brooklyn Glass Works, Williamsburg Flint Glass Works, Long Island Flint Glass Works, and Greenpoint Flint Glass Works. However, cut glass was produced from the Vermont Glass Factory in Salisbury, Vermont, and the New Hampshire Glass Factory in Keene, New Hampshire, to the Maryland Glass Works in Baltimore; the American Flint Glass Company and Hobbs Glass Company in Wheeling, West Virginia to the St. Louis Flint Glass Works in St. Louis, Missouri, Richard Murr in San Francisco, California, and the Seattle Cut Glass Company in Seattle, Washington.

Cut glass continued to earn money for the glass firms and to wrap its buyers in prestige until 1910 and perhaps a few years longer. Its superiority was never challenged by imitations such as blown-three-mold and pressed glass. Neither of the latter are regarded now as imitations of cut glass, but are valued for their own distinct qualities. Nor did any of the various kinds of art glass made in such profusion after 1880 challenge cut glass.

Art glass was different from anything made before in this country. All of the many kinds were highly colorful. Often they resembled something other than glass. Few if any kinds involved new techniques. In fact, glassmakers for the most part fell back on or revived old techniques, some of them used in Europe many years earlier. Among others were attempts to produce a contemporary glass that imitated the iridescence developed by antique glass.

The lead in producing and introducing art glass was taken by New England and other East Coast glasshouses. Their reasoning was sound, for art glass was their answer to the threatening competition of midwestern glasshouses, which were well established and producing in quantity by the 1870's. Eventually, of course, Ohio, West Virginia, and other midwestern glasshouses joined in the production of art glass.

With its fancy names, high coloring, and unusual finishes, art glass appealed to late-Victorians with their love of ornament and bric-a-brac. New interest has arisen recently in late-nineteenth- and early-twentieth-century art glass. A few kinds are lovely enough to impress the most modern homeowners, but even the gaudier and less attractive sorts find buyers. The almost two-dozen kinds of art glass can be subdivided into four groups—those that based their appeal on cased or overlay glass, metallic glass, painted glass, and iridescent glass.

| ART GLASS | CHARACTERISTICS | COLORS | PIECES |
|---|---|---|---|
| Agata | glossy surface | mottled rose with white | bowls, pitchers, cruets, tumblers, vases |
| Amberina | transparent, pattern-molded or pressed | vivid shading from yellow or straw to rose or red | many serving and ornamental pieces |
| American Bristol | frosted, with painted or gold decoration | white and pastels | vases, some lamps |
| Aurene | true iridescence | rich, with notable range of blues to purple | vases, baskets, compotes, goblets, liqueur glasses, decanters, bottles |
| Burmese | opaque, mat or glossy finish | delicate shading from yellow to pink and rose | tableware in variety, vases and lamps |

| ART GLASS | CHARACTERISTICS | COLORS | PIECES |
|---|---|---|---|
| Cameo | cased glass carved to show color underneath | strong colors, especially cranberry and rose, also white | vases, lamps, bottles, jars, plaques, brooches |
| Carnival or Taffeta | iridescence, chiefly on pressed glass, in imitation of Tiffany | marigold or pumpkin, blue-green, purple | tableware, vases, lamps and shades |
| Crackle or Ice | smooth inner surface, rough outer one | clear and pastels | vases, pitchers |
| Crown Milano | mat finish, texture similar to porcelain | white and pastels, often with dainty gold, silver, and colored garlands | lamps, vases, cookie jars, syrup jugs, rose jars, bowls |
| Kew Blas | opaque, somewhat iridescent, coated with clear glass | deep blue, green, rose, gold, bronze | vases, candlesticks, creamers, pitchers |
| Lutz | striped, also threaded | stripings or loopings in various colors; threading spiral or lacy bands of white, gold, or color | vases, bottles, creamers, pitchers, cruets |
| Mary Gregory | glass painted with Kate Greenaway-type figures | clear and colored glass, white decoration | vases, lamps, pitchers, cruets, bottles, some serving dishes, toilet sets, etc. |
| Mercury or Silvered | two layers of thin glass with mercury or nitrate of silver sealed within | silvery appearance | candlesticks, vases, spooners, paperweights, knobs, lamps and reflectors |
| Peachblow or Wild Rose | opaque, mat finish | red-rose shading to yellow at base | serving dishes, tumblers, water bottles, decanters, pitchers, lamps, vases |
| Pomona | contrasting textures, sometimes pattern-molded or etched | clear with pale amber band at top, tinted decoration against stippled background | bowls, creamers, pitchers, vases, lamps |
| Quezal | iridescent, design in outer layer | mostly gold and green, some blue, rose, purple | vases, light shades, bonbon dishes |
| Rubena Crystal | transparent | clear at base shading into red | vases, bowls, pitchers, bottles, etc. |
| Rubena Verde | transparent | yellow at base, red above | |
| Satin or Mother-of-pearl | cased glass, mat finish, satiny texture | pastels and beige | rose bowls, vases, lamps, shades, ewers, tumblers, cracker jars, salt and pepper shakers, various dishes |
| Spangled | cased glass, sparkling flecks | flakes of metal against a dark or pastel background | vases, baskets |
| Spatter or Splash | smooth | over-all blending from melting of small pieces of colored glass | vases |

| ART GLASS | CHARACTERISTICS | COLORS | PIECES |
|---|---|---|---|
| *Tiffany* or *Favrile* | true iridescence | rich blendings of gold, greens, and blues | lamps and shades, vases, compotes, other ornamental pieces, some tableware |
| *Tortoiseshell* | resembles material of its name | amber with dark areas | small quantity of ornamental ware |
| *Vasa murrhina* | heavy; clear glass coating; some blown or pattern-molded | variegated appearance from flecks of metal particles in various colors | baskets, vases, pitchers, ewers, footed tumblers, bowls |

Several kinds of art glass are basically a cased or overlay glass. This is an old European type which consists of a core of glass encased within a thin layer of glass of another color or several layers in different colors. Cased glass can be decorated in many ways. Best known of the European cased or overlay is Bohemian glass, usually with a color layer on top, which is engraved in a design. Cased or overlay glass had been made in the United States to some extent before 1876. It was particularly common on whale oil lamps, and many fine examples are still to be found.

Cameo glass, a form of overlay, was made to a greater extent in England than in this country. Here it was sometimes used to make lamps. Frederick Carder, later to become noted for his iridescent Aurene glass, also made excellent cameo glass. True cameo glass consisted of layers of glass carved through to expose colors underneath and presented almost a sculptured effect. A combination of etching and cutting techniques was used in this country during the 1880's and 1890's, chiefly for vases, plaques, scent and cologne bottles, and brooches.

Satin glass is the most coveted of cased glasses nowadays. It is sometimes called mother-of-pearl glass. The white core usually has a pastel overlay in solid color or shaded. The texture of satin glass is as appealing as its color. The outer surface has a mat finish with a satiny texture. One test of good satin glass is holding it up to sunlight or other bright light to see "fire"—a sort of opal sparkle at the base.

Satin glass is said to have been perfected by glasshouses in eastern and western Pennsylvania but by 1885 was

*This fruit bowl (10 by 7¼ by 4½ inches) is a perfect as well as an unusual example of satin glass. The inner core is shaded rose, deeper toward the crimped edge; the outer layer is white. The garland of red raspberries and blue-black blackberries is enameled, the stems and leaves gilded.*

being made by many scattered factories, in some cases achieving similar products by different methods. There are differences in the quality of satin glass, for some pieces have a better and more typical mat finish than others. Colors are clearer and more attractive in some pieces too, and decoration varies from excellent to poor. A piece of satin glass of exquisite coloring and good finish sells at many times its original price nowadays, and those of indifferent quality never fail to sell.

*Satin glass rose bowls, from 2 to about 5 inches in diameter, can be recognized by their crimped edges. Some satin glass bowls had painted decoration, some applied decoration of clear and colored glass.*

Best known of all pieces of satin glass are the round bowls with crimped edges called rose bowls. These were made from about 2 inches in diameter to 6 inches or more, each size increasing by 1 inch. The colors were chiefly pastel—rose, pink, blue, turquoise, yellow, mauve, and occasionally chartreuse. In other ornamental pieces, a beige shading into brown was sometimes seen. Colors shaded from top to bottom, were striped or perhaps multi-colored.

Unornamented rose bowls were most common. However, some had applied decoration such as a garland of leaves and flowers in clear and colored glass. Occasionally, a piece of satin glass would have enameled or painted decoration, but this was more rare.

Vases of all sizes and shapes, lamps, ewers, mustard pots, footed bowls, were made in quantity, but that does not mean that a piece in good condition is not well priced today. Tumblers

are not rare nowadays but they are expensive, and a person is lucky to stumble on one or two tumblers out of the full water set of tumblers and pitcher made in the 1880's. Lamps, especially miniature ones, and lamp shades of satin glass are charming.

*Satin glass vases, shading from white at the base to blush pink into deep rose, have a diamond quilted design molded into the core. Other molded designs were swirls, rib, herringbone, polka dot, and the like. The two matching vases are 8 inches tall; the smaller one is 5 inches high.*

Tumblers and unembellished vases frequently displayed a swirl, diamond, rib, herringbone, quilted, moire, or polka dot pattern that was molded into the core and shone faintly through the outer layer of soft satiny glass. Flecks of mica are said to enhance some pieces.

One kind of satin glass was so distinctive that it was given its own name— Coralene. The satin glass piece was more often shaded than solid color. Tiny glass beads were the applied decoration on the outer surface. A favorite design for the beads was the natural branching of coral, hence the name. On some pieces, the beads were applied in a seaweed, leaf, or wheat pattern. The beads had a decided sparkle that contrasted strongly with the mat finish of the satin glass. Coralene vases from 4 to 10 or 11 inches high are most likely to be found (the satin glass may have gathered so much dust that it is hardly recognizable in spite of the delicate beading). Bottles and some other pieces, chiefly ornamental, also were made.

Burmese, another opaque shaded glass, was made with either dull or glossy finish. The shading ranged from a tint of yellow or orange to pink or rose. Pieces often were painted or enameled. Both tableware and ornamental ware were turned out, some of it highly decorated.

*Art glass vases* (left to right): *a footed vase of clear and opaque vaseline glass; a Coralene vase of shaded pink satin glass with iridescent yellow bead trimming; a 2½-inch satin glass rose bowl; a slender vase of milk-white glass; a vase of amethyst and clear glass with an engraved design touched with gold.*

Three different kinds of art glass that imitated something else were Peachblow, Crown Milano, and Tortoiseshell. Crown Milano with its satin finish resembled porcelain. Beautiful lamps and vases, cracker jars, and bowls were made in white and pastel colors, often embellished with flower garlands and perhaps scrolls of gold. Tortoiseshell, never made in any quantity, looked like its name, for it was an amber glass with darker areas.

Peachblow, copied from Chinese porcelain of that name, was opaque glass that shaded from white or ivory to rose, red, or yellow. The Peachblow that was made by Hobbs, Brockunier and Company in Wheeling, West Virginia, had a white lining and outer finish of dull satin. The pieces made by the New England Glass Company in Cambridge, Massachusetts, did not have the white lining but did have the same sort of finish. Some of the New England Peachblow was called Wild Rose, a name fully as appropriate. The West Virginia firm really capitalized on the popularity of the name Peachblow by making a wide range of useful and ornamental pieces—salt and pepper shakers, mustard pots, custard cups, butter dishes, celery vases, pitchers, tumblers, water bottles and decanters, vases, and shades for lamps. Fewer pieces—and those chiefly ornamental—were made in New England.

Pomona, a delicate-looking glass, was as lovely as it was expensive. Its overall appearance was dainty, both because of its coloring and decoration. Pomona, which was either blown or pattern-molded, was clear glass but always had a border about an inch wide of pale amber around the top. The background was etched in such a manner that it looked finely stippled. Usually a simple and graceful design of flowers, berries, or leaves was etched and colored against the background. Exquisite coloring and contrasting textures gave the pieces a more fragile appearance than that of most art glass.

The strikingly shaded Amberina, introduced by the New England Glass Company, was one of the first kinds of art glass. It was a transparent glass that shaded always from a yellow or amber or straw to rose or red, either from top to bottom or vice versa, and was vivid in comparison to satin glass and Peachblow. Pattern-molding in diamond, quilting, and the like was common, and both serving and ornamental pieces were made. Pressed glass in the Inverted Thumbprint pattern also was made in Amberina.

Agata, also from the New England Glass Company, was made for a much briefer period than Peachblow and satin glass. It was really a variation of Peachblow. After the glass had been blown, it was treated to produce a mottled effect in shades of rose with white. Agata ware was glossy.

Incidentally, Amberina, Agata, and Pomona glass are said to have been developed and introduced by one workman, Joseph Locke, at the New England Glass Company. Even though all three kinds proved popular and were copied by other companies, the New England Glass Company operated with a deficit. In 1888 the owner, E. D. Libbey, whose father had bought the New England Glass Company in 1878, moved the firm to Toledo, Ohio, in order to make use of cheaper fuel. Libbey is still a well-known name in the production of various kinds of glass.

Rubena, another transparent, shaded ware is not as well known. Rubena Crystal was clear glass at the base shading into red toward the upper part. Rubena Verde was yellow below and started at the center to shade into a good red above. George Duncan and Sons in Pittsburgh made a good deal of Rubena in pressed glass in a pattern they listed as Polka Dot. Rubena vases, pitchers, and cruets also were made.

Silver or mercury blown glass revived another long-known technique. It's said that Deming Jarves, founder of the Boston and Sandwich Glass Company, had doorknobs using real silver made for the home of his son. However, silver was too precious to be used for making art glass, so mercury (quicksilver) or nitrate of silver solution usually was placed between two layers of blown glass and sealed tightly. Nitrate of silver did not tarnish unless the seal was broken and it became exposed to air. An old piece in which mercury was placed may have been jarred or knocked so that the material no longer spreads evenly throughout the piece. Knobs for doors, furniture, and curtains, paperweights, candlesticks, lamps and reflectors, vases, and ornamental pieces were and still are to be cherished. Vases, candlesticks, and doorknobs probably are the most plentiful pieces today.

Spangled glass was achieved by adding flakes of lustrous metal, usually mica but sometimes gold or silver, and gaycolored bits of glass to the batch. They added bright color and sparkle to a dark background glass. Some pastel pieces were made, in which case mica flakes usually were used (mica was most effective in pale green, for example). Again, methods of manufacture differed in New England and the Midwest. Hobbs, Brockunier and Company in Wheeling, West Virginia, made a cased glass lined with opaque white, and usually added mica flakes for spangling. Boston and Sandwich Glass Company made spangled glass without a white lining. The body of their pieces was a solid, and often a dark, color that was covered with a layer of thin glass to which metal flakes and bright-colored glass were added. Some spangled glass pieces had clear glass handles or an applied decoration such as a bunch of cherries with the fruits in red glass, stems and leaves in clear glass.

Spatter glass usually displayed less contrast than spangled glass, although the

*The pieces shown here represent three of the many kinds of art glass popular in the 1880's (from left to right): a clear, fluted vaseline glass vase, a rubena vase, and a crackle glass cruet with a pewter top and an applied handle of clear glass.*

background also might be fairly dark. Colored glass broken into small pieces was incorporated for this art glass.

Vasa murrhina, which was first made by the Boston and Sandwich Glass Company, generally was dark although it was flecked with gold, silver, mica flakes, or metallic particles in various colors, which gave a variegated effect. Usually the background glass was so dark that it appeared to be almost opaque, although the whole outer surface was covered with clear glass. Vasa murrhina pieces were likely to be heavy. Some of them were blown, some pattern-molded.

The striped glass that was produced in the late nineteenth century by the Boston and Sandwich Glass Company copied a style of old Venetian glass. It is sometimes called Lutz glass because it was made by Nicholas Lutz (earlier he worked for C. Dorflinger and Sons in Pennsylvania). Striped or Lutz glass is thin, with colored and twisted stripes in it.

Mary Gregory, who worked for the Boston and Sandwich Glass Company in the 1870's or 1880's, was another artist who gave her name to an art glass. Her specialty was painted decoration, always in white on transparent glass, both clear and colored. Her style was distinctly individual. Her children are reminiscent of Kate Greenaway's. A pair of vases might have a girl on one piece, a boy on the other, in harmonious but not identical compositions. She also reputedly did miniature

*Mary Gregory glass is named for the artist, who worked for the Boston and Sandwich Glass Company. She used white paint or enamel for scenes in which children predominated. The pitcher and decanter are clear glass; the 5-inch-high vase is yellow glass.*—Ted Eastwood

landscapes in a similar style. Vases, lamps, toilet sets, and knickknacks such as match-holders were the chief pieces ornamented with Mary Gregory decoration, as well as a few water sets. A good many firms produced painted glass, but Mary Gregory's style of painting was the most distinctive.

Black glass vases with enameled decoration in white and color, artist unknown, can be handsome. On the whole, the black vases are more distinguished than the white or light-colored glass that was painted with fairly naturalistic flowers and fruits. Considerable foliage often was used in these painted or enameled decora-

tions, and often sprays or garlands of foliage were touched with gold. Painted vases were made in all imaginable shapes—cylinder and footed cylinder, square, vase, and some that can only be described as bulgy.

One of the most sought-after types of decorated glass is the Bristol-type which was made briefly in this country. Bristol, England, had been a glass-making center from the seventeenth century, and from the middle of the eighteenth century became known for an opaque white glass and a dark blue glass. An opaque white glass with blue decoration based on florals and birds was perhaps the best-known of the Bristol glass. So-called American Bristol, how-ever, was neither opaque nor blue and white but a frosted glass, either white or pastel colors, with decoration in colored paint or enamel and gold. Flowers and foliage, often quite natur-alistic, were popular and sometimes they were worked into an over-all de-sign that included scrolls and geometric tracings. Vases are most often found nowadays, and some of them are lovely. Miniature hats, potpourri jars, some lamps, and miscellaneous pieces also were made of American Bristol glass.

Colored glass with painted decoration and sometimes frilled edges was dear to the hearts of Victorians, but much of it is undistinguished and has little appeal today, even for collectors. Vases, pitchers, and cruets were common ex-amples and are not at all rare now. An exception is bride's baskets, which were a specialty of midwestern fac-tories. The name came from the fact that they were so widely given as wed-ding presents between 1880 and 1900. These bride's baskets, usually round and of good size, were colored glass with heavily frilled and rippled edges. Some of them had glass handles in a contrasting color; others came with a silver-plated stand or holder into which the base of the glass basket fitted. In the latter case, the handle also was plated silver and attached to the stand. A ruffled bowl without a handle that is found now may well have been a bride's basket that fitted into a stand. With or without stand, they are sal-able.

*A cologne bottle made in Bristol, Eng-land, 1762-87. The glass is opaque white; the decoration, blue enamel.*

Bride's baskets averaged 6 to 7 inches high and were at least 4 inches in diameter. Most of them were pastel colors, although they also were made in cranberry, amber, and occasionally an art glass. Many had white linings. Ruffles often were clear glass, applied.

Crackle or ice glass was originally pro-duced by the Venetians in their early days of glassmaking fame. It was nat-ural that this old process should be copied during the art glass decades. The Boston and Sandwich Glass Com-pany produced, for a short period, a crackle glass that is better known as overshot glass. It had a smooth inner surface and a sharply rough, outer one that had almost a crystalline look. This Sandwich overshot glass is recognizable almost instantly by its surface. There was no real pattern to it although the

Boston and Sandwich Glass Company made it in a full line of tableware, in addition to a few ornamental pieces.

A considerable amount of crackle glass was made by glasshouses in Pennsylvania and the Midwest. It is interesting, but its quality is not comparable either to the old Venetian and later European crackle glass, or probably even to the crystalline overshot of the Boston and Sandwich Glass Company. Other firms made crackle glass in colors, mostly attractive pastels such as green and shades of pink. Sometimes applied decoration in clear and colored glass was added to pitchers and vases.

Iridescent glass was a natural goal for late-Victorian glassmakers. The lovely and priceless iridescence on ancient glass was not originally a color or an intrinsic attribute of the glass. It was the result of corrosion after centuries of being buried in the earth, and showed up on these old pieces when they were displayed in museums. But iridescence added so much beauty to the simplest pieces of glass that its achievement was irresistible to Victorian glassmakers. There were many unsuccessful attempts to produce even a passably iridescent art glass. Kew Blas, made at Union Glass Works, in Somerville, Massachusetts, obtained its name by a scrambled spelling of the name of the factory manager (W. S. Blake). It was a sort of iridescent, opaque, colored glass that depended more on staining of color for effect than sparkling iridescence. The effect

is more opalescent than iridescent. Kew Blas, which is often so marked on the base, did have a smooth finish similar to satin or milk glass.

It was not until almost 1900 that a truly iridescent glass was produced. The best pieces were made for some years thereafter. Louis Comfort Tiffany produced after much experimenting his glowing Tiffany or Favrile glass. By 1904, Frederick Carder had perfected Aurene, another iridescent glass, for the Steuben Glass Works in Corning, New York.

Tiffany and Aurene both were of exceptionally fine quality, magnificent shadings of color and unmatched iridescence. Both were expensive glass to produce and to sell. Aurene was made for a much shorter period and in smaller quantity than Tiffany glass. Most of the pieces of Aurene were ornamental. The range of blues from peacock to purple was notable.

Louis Comfort Tiffany had established his own factory on Long Island in 1878. He would have gained honors for his stained glass windows, in which he endeavoured to reproduce Medieval-quality stained glass. But he is remembered chiefly for his ornamental iridescent pieces, which resulted from his experiments with leftover lots of his wonderfully colored glass for windows.

Tiffany or Favrile glass was smooth and characterized by a magnificent blending of colors plus true iridescence.

Blues, greens, and golds were particularly fine. His gold shades and cobalt-blue are probably the most famous. Favrile, which means simply "hand-wrought," is used as often as the name Tiffany for this glass. All pieces, incidentally, were signed either with Louis Comfort Tiffany or with his three initials.

Tiffany produced an enormous and varied number of ornamental pieces from the 1890's until about 1918. Lamps that burned oil and lampshades for gas and electric fixtures became immensely popular. So did his vases, some of which were in the shape of flowers. Realistic flowers, leaves, and vines were incorporated in many of Tiffany's ornamental pieces.

Many bowls and vases, compotes of various sizes, smaller footed dishes, and other ornamental pieces were as varied as they were glowing. His factory also produced a limited amount of tableware such as plates, dessert dishes, and drinking vessels. Tiffany was not above making colored glass panels for screens and windows. In addition to his glass windows for churches, he also made some other religious pieces.

Reaction to Tiffany and Aurene glass is always definite. A person either likes and admires it, or can't stand the sight of it. Like cut glass, Tiffany glass was consigned to cupboards, cellars, and attics in the late 1920's and disappeared from sight for many years. Now, although it's not genuinely antique, it is arousing collectors' interest.

An excellent, well-rounded exhibit of Louis Comfort Tiffany's work as a painter and glass craftsman was shown at the Museum of Contemporary Art in New York City during 1958. How much this exhibit did to arouse new interest in and appreciation of Tiffany glass cannot be estimated, but the fact of the matter remains that interest has mounted steadily ever since. A piece of Tiffany glass is decidedly salable and will probably gain in value with each coming decade.

Like cut glass of the Brilliant Period, Tiffany glass will never be made again. The two very different kinds of glass were expensive in their own time. Anyone who wishes to get rid of Tiffany and Aurene glass may not obtain as much for it in the 1960's as it cost originally, but prices are certain to increase in the future.

Anything as unusual as good iridescent glass was bound to inspire imitations. Inexpensive imitations, that is. And an imitation made about 1915 is likely to sell for considerably more in the 1960's than it originally cost.

One of the first imitations of Tiffany glass was called Quezal, after the national bird of Guatemala, the quetzal, which is noted for its golden green iridescent coloring. Quezal glass was made in Brooklyn, presumably by former workmen at the Tiffany factory, for only about two years. It has gained status and is now ranked with art glass. Quezal glass was iridescent and opaque and often in shades of gold. Lampshades and vases probably were its chief products.

Another imitation was carnival or taffeta glass and this, like Tiffany glass, is currently having a revival of interest and is in considerable demand. Since the production of carnival glass started about 1910 and continued into the 1930's, it may have had something to do with the fall from grace and favor of Tiffany glass. For carnival or taffeta glass also is iridescent, though more harshly iridescent and harshly colored than Tiffany and Aurene.

Carnival or taffeta glass was made in vast quantities in shades of gold to red. It also was made in a blue-green, a deep purple, and a blue and a green, all with iridescence. These last colors, however, were less common, at least in the East, than the golden shades. This unmistakable color sometimes is described as a marigold luster or as a little darker than pumpkin color. Some pieces verged into almost a red-gold.

Much of the carnival glass was made in western Pennsylvania, West Virginia, and Ohio. Probably the most aggressive manufacturer of carnival glass was Harry Northwood of Northwood, Ohio. Pieces from his factory have an "N" impressed at the middle of the plate or piece, usually on the underside but sometimes on the top as well. Sometimes the letter was circled.

Other companies seem not to have marked their carnival glass, but it is easily recognizable as such.

Carnival glass was not as expensive in its day as other kinds of art glass had been. Certainly it was far below the price of Tiffany and Aurene. In fact, the name "carnival" came from the fact that it was often given as prizes at fairs, carnivals, and the like. Butchershops and other shops also gave pieces as premiums. It could be purchased, too, and whether it was bought or won has no bearing on its sale prices today, which are much higher than between 1910 and the 1930's.

It is easy to see why this glass was given the name "taffeta," for its iridescence was not so much that as a sheen, more comparable to that of some taffeta fabrics.

Most carnival or taffeta glass was pressed. Occasionally a piece looked like a golden reproduction of cut glass. The notched edges and strawberry diamond and pseudo hob-stars were not sharp as they would be in cut glass. The acanthus leaf, a classic motif, often was worked into the pattern. Foliage, fruit, and flower patterns of all kinds were worked out, but they lacked the originality and imagination given to pressed glass patterns. The grape designs, which were popular for carnival glass, were much more routine than those on nineteenth-century pressed glass. The Peacock was another favorite motif.

All kinds of ornamental pieces were made in quantity, Vases were large and small, classic and tortured in shape. Lamps, some lampshades, compotes, candy, pickle, and other serving dishes were and are plentiful. Berry sets consisting of a serving bowl and small dishes, drinking mugs, lemonade glasses, and pitchers were probably given individually as premiums until a person had completed a set. Plates were common in sizes suitable for serving cake and the like, and for dessert and salad.

Art glass on the whole can always be disposed of, and almost certainly at higher prices than were paid for it between 1880 and 1910. There is a very great deal of painted, with the possible exception of the Mary Gregory type. A pair of blue glass vases, 8 inches high, with a boy painted on one by Mary Gregory and a girl on the other, is fairly priced now at $65; a pair 14 inches tall is worth about $125. A plaque painted by Mary Gregory probably will sell in the neighborhood of $50, a pin tray for about $15. Of other painted glass, American Bristol is probably one of the better-selling types to collectors and flower-arrangers. It also is more likely to be cherished by owners and finders.

Certainly plenty of Tiffany glass remains to be found wherever it was packed away forty years or so ago. It is true that Tiffany glass has been included in the auctions of reputable art and auction galleries in New York City, and anyone with a small but representative collection might consider this method of sale. Otherwise, the problem at the present time is to find buyers. A Tiffany shade for a gas

*Carnival glass copied the more expensive iridescent art glass. These pieces (1910-30) are common marigold luster. The vase with orange trees and acanthus feet and the plate garlanded with strawberries imitate pressed glass. The berry bowl has the motifs of cut glass.*

lamp ought to bring at least $25, a lamp correspondingly more, and a pair of candlesticks about 7 inches high $50. A small Quezal glass lampshade of about the same size as the Tiffany one really should not sell for more than $10.

Some pieces of carnival or taffeta glass are selling for prices that compare favorably with Quezal glass. Certainly the prices nowadays are much higher than the original ones for carnival glass. Furthermore, there seems to be a ready market. A marigold berry set can be sold in some parts of the country for $25, in others for $35 or so. A water set with pitcher and six tumblers that are not nicked brings fully as much. A 5-inch-high vase will sell for $5 to $10. Grandparents who won pieces of carnival glass should be gratified with present-day prices.

Of all the art glass, none at the present time is in greater demand than satin glass. There always seems to be some available, yet it brings excellent prices. Even satin glass not of the best quality or with the finest sort of decoration finds buyers willing to spend good money. As an example of how satin glass prices have skyrocketed: a turquoise rose bowl 5 inches in diameter that was purchased for 25 cents in the 1880's now could be sold for $30, and it is a plain rose bowl without decoration or molded pattern. A plain 4-inch bowl in any pastel color brings $25. A pair of salt and pepper shakers with flower decoration also sells for about $25; a tumbler with a diamond quilted pattern may sell for anything from $12.50 to $35, depending on the area where you are trying to sell. Large vases and pitchers may be priced at more than $100.

Amberina, almost as plentiful as satin glass, sells quickly and well too. A covered butter dish with glass insert is considered fairly priced at $75. A milk pitcher in the Inverted Thumbprint pattern of pressed glass has been sold recently for $75, and a taller water pitcher in the same pattern and coloring is waiting for a buyer at $100. A toothpick-holder with a molded pattern can be priced at $25; vases start at about $40 for one 4½-inches high.

Cameo, Burmese, Agata, crackle, Crown Milano, and other types of art glass that were made in smaller quantities have great allure for collectors and consequently bring worthwhile prices. Unless you are a collector of that particular glass, it's hard to believe the prices for which Agata now sells. It's ironical that hardly a piece now sells for less than $200—and that price is for a tumbler; and many of them sell for considerably more — when you stop to think that Agata was not a success with the public in the 1880's. It was not made for long, and as a result much less is available now than of satin glass. Genuine Burmese sells for prices very much higher than comparable pieces of satin glass. A

Crown Milano syrup jar with metal top is worth about $75 now, as is a garlanded vase about 8 inches high.

Bride's baskets, made in such quantity, average from $15 to $25 if they lack a holder, and with holder from $25 to $50. In the latter case, the price will be influenced by whether or not the holder needs resilvering. A Vasa murrhina basket in a plated holder is unusual, and so it might be priced at about $50. Vasa murrhina vases 6 inches or so high may sell for only a few dollars at a country auction, for perhaps $35 closer to a metropolitan area. A syrup jug of the same type of glass with a pewter top cannot be sold for more than $25 to $35.

The truth is that there undoubtedly is a buyer for any piece of art glass. The lovelier ones like satin, Peachblow, Pomona, and Burmese bring premium prices, as do the scarce ones like Agata. Furthermore, the colorful art glass sells much more readily than cut glass, even though much of the art glass was not of as good quality or as expensive in its heyday.

Chips and cracks reduce the value of a piece of any kind of glass, and if cracked, a piece may be unusable. A chip can be polished off. However, if a chip is removed by polishing, the value of both American and Waterford cut glass is lessened, as is that of other types of old glass.

## GLOSSARY

*Annealing:* the process of cooling glass slowly from extraordinarily high heat.

*Baluster:* an upright support, as in wine and champagne glasses and the like, which at some point between base and top swells outward in some manner.

*Batch:* the quantity of materials melted at one time to make glass.

*Blown-molded:* formed by blowing into a small mold, which gives the glass a pattern such as swirls, ribbing, or the like, then removing and rotating until the desired shape and size are achieved. Also referred to as pattern-molded and expanded glass.

*Blown-three-mold:* blown into full-sized molds consisting often of three pieces, sometimes two, or sometimes more than three pieces.

*Cased glass:* also known as overlay glass; a piece in which a core of glass is encased in one or several layers of glass, usually in more than one color.

*Clear glass:* transparent glass to which no color has been added. Clear glass may be colorless, or in cheaper batches may show a green, yellow, or brown tint, which comes from the ingredients.

*Crimping:* glass decoration applied in folds or waves so that it looks like crushed ribbon.

*Crizzling:* a roughness that develops on

the surface of glass and clouds its transparency, making it look almost crackled.

*Crystal:* natural crystalline quartz; also used in reference to fine glass of high lead content.

*Cutting:* the decoration of glass with various motifs in a pattern, accomplished by application of a moving wheel to the surface of the glass. Usually followed by polishing.

*Engraving:* the decoration of the outer surface of glass by the use of a series of small copper wheels. The design is impressed, though not as deeply as by cutting, and is usually left unpolished.

*Etching:* the decoration of glass by means of the corroding action of an acid. Effect is similar to engraving but the design is frosty and not as deep.

*Flashing:* the coating of clear or one-color glass with a thin layer of another color.

*Flint glass:* glass in which flint-bearing sand is an essential ingredient. Flint glass is heavy, brilliant, and colorless.

*Gather:* the small amount of metal taken on the end of a blowpipe for blowing. It is held on a pontil while being worked.

*Lead glass:* glass of high lead content, usually from an oxide of lead.

*Lime glass:* a glass of which lime is the principal ingredient, along with silica (sand).

*Metal:* glass in its liquid or molten state of fusion.

*Muddy:* descriptive term for clear glass with a yellow or brown tint caused by the ingredients.

*Overlay glass:* specifically, cased glass on which a design has been cut through the outer surface to show the clear or colored glass underneath.

*Pattern-molded:* formed by blowing into a mold, then removing and expanding by more blowing. Same as blown-molded.

*Pontil:* the metal rod used to hold glass while it is hot and being worked. Also known as pontil rod or punty.

*Sick glass:* glass which becomes cloudy and loses its luster or transparency because of too high alkaline content or some other error in formula. Common in non-lead glass.

*Staining:* the process of applying a color to the inside or outside of glass, which is usually clear, and then heating to fix the color.

*Threading:* fine filaments of glass, clear or colored, applied on the outside as decoration, sometimes worked into lacy bands.

FOR FURTHER INFORMATION:

AMERICAN GLASS by Helen and George S. McKearin. New York: Crown Publishers, Inc.

CUT AND ENGRAVED GLASS by Dorothy Daniel. New York: M. Barrows and Company, Inc.

NINETEENTH-CENTURY ART GLASS by Ruth Webb Lee. New York: M. Barrows and Company, Inc.

# 9

# Pressed Glass Collectors Mania

THIS COUNTRY'S BIG CONTRIBUTION to the glass industry was the development of a new method of making articles from this prized material early in the nineteenth century. The result was pressed glass. The new product was perfected here about 1825, and each succeeding decade of the 1800's saw it produced in greater quantity, just as each decade of the 1900's has found more people discovering—and collecting—it. Thus, there is a ready-made market all over the country.

Because pressed glass was made in such quantity by so many firms throughout New England and in the Middle Atlantic and Midwest states, miscellaneous and perhaps surprising pieces are ignored every day in many households. It is important to recognize pressed glass for what it is and to identify it.

Because so many people now collect pressed glass, any piece made during the nineteenth century is salable today. Indeed, a pressed glass sugar and creamer, plate, pitcher, or any other piece probably will sell now for more than the price paid for it 100 years ago, more or less. But once you've identified and learned something about the piece of pressed glass you find—or buy because you could make use of the pickle jar, or the pressed glass match-holder is pretty—you too may become a collector.

What is pressed glass, and how can it be distinguished from other types? Actually, pressed glass is an imitation of cut glass, but it soon developed a character of its own. The reason for developing the technique of making glassware by pressing was to achieve an ornamental and attractive product that would not be as expensive as cut glass.

Some of the early pressed glass copied patterns and motifs from cut glass. Even so, the two types are impossible to confuse, for the motifs are deep and sharp to touch on cut glass. Straw-

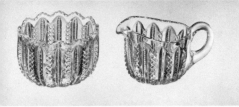

*This sugar and creamer, 2¼ inches high, are in a pattern seen only infrequently. It is called either Paneled English Hobnail with Prisms, or Hairpin.*

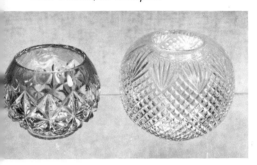

*The typical globular rose bowl was made in pressed glass too. The clear glass example at the left, 5½ inches, is no recognizable pattern. The other one, 7 inches, also clear glass, is in a variant of the Diamond Point and Fan pattern.*

berry diamond, bull's-eye, and block, copied exactly from cut glass, were reproduced shallowly and feel almost smooth on pressed glass. The use of traditional cut glass motifs continued

throughout the nineteenth century, but was especially important to the decorating of pressed glass from the 1830's to the 1870's.

In general, pressed glass falls into one of two main groups. The first pieces were known as lacy glass. Most of the pressed glass made from 1825 to 1840 and, to a lesser extent, until about 1850 was this type. From 1850 onward, pressed glass was generally referred to as pattern glass.

All of the early pressed glass characterized as lacy was made with intricate designs, but, more important, always had an all-over finely stippled background. It is this background of finely raised dots on the underside of a glass plate, for example, that earned the name "lacy glass." As a consequence, lacy glass although often quite thick sparkles almost as brightly as cut glass when the sun strikes it.

The stippling also set off the pattern, which shone forth in clear glass. Al-

*These clear lacy glass cup plates show* (left to right): *the side-wheeler* Benjamin Franklin; *one of the many Bunker Hill patterns, this one with a draped border; and one of the numerous eagle designs, here dated 1831. Cup plates were fashionable during the first half of the nineteenth century.*

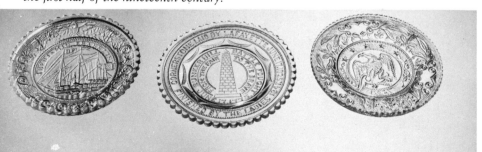

though patterns of lacy glass were inclined to be intricate, yet always delicate, they are recognizable. Lacy glass patterns, however, are not as familiar or as well-known as the innumerable ones made after 1850, which in some cases made use of stippling, but not as a complete background. Hearts, leaves, and especially the acanthus, simple flowers, the butterfly, and geometric motifs formed the patterns on lacy glass.

Tulip and Acanthus pattern, for example, showed a motif shaped like a tulip bud against a stippled background in the center, acanthus leaves against the stippled background of the rim. Fleur-de-lis had four of these classic motifs in the center, and a fleur-de-lis alternating with a basket and scroll design in the border; again both center and border had stippled backgrounds. Bull's-eye, Acanthus, and Oak Leaf patterns are among the more easily recognizable patterns in lacy glass.

All kinds of objects were made of lacy

glass—plates, cup plates, salts, candlesticks, oil lamps, curtain tiebacks or rosettes, pitchers, sugar and creamers, and so on. Some small windowpanes also were made at both East Coast and midwestern glasshouses. Lacy glass was not made in complete sets of tableware as was the later pattern glass.

A very great deal of the pressed glass output was clear or "white" glass. However, considerable lacy and much pattern glass also was made in colors. The lacy Butterfly and Flower pattern was made in a rich blue as well as clear glass. Amethyst, amber, and green also are stunning finds in lacy glass.

Pressed glass also was made in opaque white, commonly known as milk glass, and opaque colors, in opaque white and a color, known as marble glass, and in opalescent. Patterns that combined a color with clear glass became fashionable in the 1880's and 1890's, and many of these pieces are still around. If the color was painted on the clear, it may be worn off somewhat by

*The lacy glass cup plates at left and right are a Sandwich pattern known as Heart. They are 3½ inches in diameter and have thirteen stippled hearts in the rim; the design sometimes differed. The 6-inch plate (center) is dominated by a design of acanthus leaves against a stippled background.*

this time. Vaseline glass, either clear or opaque, was a special type of yellow pressed glass.

Almost all of these several styles of pressed glass were made to some extent by the Boston and Sandwich Glass Company in Sandwich, Massachusetts. Its founder, Deming Jarves, while he was a partner in the New England Glass Company in Cambridge, Massachusetts, had been one of the people most active in developing the process of pressed glass. The Boston and Sandwich Glass Company, in business from 1825 until about 1888, was the source of Sandwich glass, one of the two or three most famous names in the history of the glass industry in the United States.

The term "Sandwich glass" applies to any glass made at this factory. It is not a synonym for all pressed glass, for only a small percentage of the pressed glass made between 1825 and 1900 came from this factory. The fact that a piece of glass rings like a bell when struck lightly is no proof that it's Sandwich glass. Some known pieces of Sandwich give a dull sound, not at all musical.

Nor was pressed glass the only product of the Boston and Sandwich Glass Company. Cut glass, both clear and colored, blown and blown-three-mold, engraved glass, and, late in the century, some art glass came from the famous factory. Whatever type of glass was made at Sandwich, it was of the finest quality.

Although they were not wholly responsible for discovering how to press glass, the Boston and Sandwich Glass Company set certain styles in the new product. Sandwich is almost a synonym for lacy glass, which was made first by the Boston and Sandwich Glass Company. Another first for this glasshouse was the dolphin candlestick. However, both lacy glass and dolphin candlesticks

*The dolphin candlestick was a famous pressed glass style. Made by the Boston and Sandwich Glass Company in the 1830's, it was thereafter made by many glasshouses in other states. This one, known as a "petticoat dolphin" because of its base, was made after 1850 in Pittsburgh. The socket is opalescent, the dolphin standard and the base are clear glass.*

were made later in the century by firms as far west as Pittsburgh, Pennsylvania, and Wheeling, West Virginia. The Boston and Sandwich Glass Company also made innumerable patterns without stippling after 1850, a few such as Petal and Loop, Peacock Feather, Peacock Eye, and New England Pineapple before midcentury. Because they made such beautiful glass, it is not strange that other glass factories followed their lead.

*Jewel with Dewdrop is a late pattern made in Pittsburgh. Dewdrops outline the alternating clear and stippled panels and the relief ornaments on the latter. Similar oval plates were lettered "Cake Plate."*

Factories for making glass items were successful in all the eastern and many midwestern states. The New England states, Pennsylvania, New York, Ohio, and West Virginia supported innumerable glasshouses whose names stood for quality and interesting products.

The New England Glass Company, Cambridge, Massachusetts, was almost as versatile as the nearby Boston and Sandwich Glass Company. Although such fine glass was produced in Massachusetts, this state did not have a monopoly, by any manner of means. Portland Glass Company in Portland, Maine, was another distinguished New England firm.

James Gillinder and Sons of Philadelphia and Greensburg, Pennsylvania, was one of the notable firms of that state. The western part of Pennsylvania became fully as important a glass center as Massachusetts. Glass was made so by such firms as McKee and Brothers, Bryce Brothers, George Dun-

can and Sons, Doyle and Company, Adams and Company, Ripley and Company, King Glass Company, and Bakewell, Pears and Company. The last firm, during its many years of business, was known under several names —Bakewell, Page and Bakewell, and B. Bakewell and Company. Tarentum, east of Pittsburgh, supported two companies active in pressed glass: Richards and Hartley, and Challinor, Taylor and Company. The second was especially noted for opal and marble glass.

Wheeling, West Virginia, had probably the best-known firms of that state. Hobbs, Barnes and Company, which in 1863 became Hobbs, Brockunier and Company, and Central Glass Company were two of the leading ones.

Many small cities in Ohio had their glass firms. Bellaire Goblet Company in Findlay, A. J. Beatty and Company, Tiffin and Steubenville, Lancaster Glass

A *Cabbage Rose compote, minus its cover, which had a rosebud-and-leaves knob. This oldest of four rose patterns in pressed glass was made during the 1860's in Wheeling, West Virginia—in clear glass only.*

Company, Lancaster, Nickel Plate Glass Company, Fostoria, and Crystal Glass Company in Bridgeport were only a few. Many of these Ohio firms as well as some in Pennsylvania were absorbed when the United States Glass Company was formed in Pittsburgh in 1891.

The pattern called Baltimore Pear was not made by a firm in Maryland but by Adams and Company in Pittsburgh. There were some commercial glasshouses in Maryland as in other East Coast states.

Makers' marks, trademarks, or other means of identifying the firm were not usually indicated on pressed glass.

The exceptions to this are few. A person learns to know the various firms noted for pressed glass by the patterns that they made and the quality of the glass used.

Styles and designs that caught the public's fancy were soon copied by factories other than the one that originated them. Sometimes patterns were altered in one or two details and became known as variants. These patterns were described in the catalogues of glasshouses either by name or number, and specialists in pressed glass have written books about their findings.

Petal and Loop pattern, which appeared in the 1830's, was made by the Boston and Sandwich Glass Company, Sandwich, Massachusetts, by the Central Glass Company in Wheeling, West Virginia, and by two or more glasshouses in Pittsburgh, Pennsylvania. The number of firms probably accounts for its having been made in clear, various colors, opalescent, and opaque glass, and covered dishes combining any two of these variations. The shape of the loop motif varied somewhat in products of different glasshouses.

Huber, another simple early pattern, was made by the New England Glass Company in Cambridge, Massachusetts, and Bakewell, Pears and Company in Pittsburgh. Sawtooth was even more popular, for it was produced by the Cambridge Glass Company and the Boston and Sandwich Glass Company as well as by Bryce Brothers, Rip-

*Beaded Grape, made in a tableware set by the United States Glass Company of Pittsburgh, is one of the handsomest grape patterns. The square dish and celery vase are distinctive; oblong ones also were made.*

ley and Company, and probably others in Pittsburgh. Slightly different patterns featuring cherries were made in the 1870's by Bakewell, Pears and Company in Pittsburgh, Pennsylvania, and the Lancaster Glass Company, Lancaster, Ohio.

Because so many of the Boston and Sandwich Glass Company's designs and

*This Ribbed Palm goblet, footed salt, and creamer belong to an appropriately named table set in heavy glass. Although the pattern was made in Pittsburgh in the 1860's, the rayed bases are typical of earlier table-glass.*

*Spoonholders, or spooners, were included in most pressed glass table sets. Sawtooth (left) is an early pattern (1850's), with typical rayed base. The Nailhead variant (right) looks like a pattern that could have been made before the 1880's.*

pieces, such as the famous dolphin candlesticks, were copied by numerous other glasshouses, about the best an expert can do today is to identify a piece as "probably Sandwich." Lacy glass or a piece in Petal and Loop pattern well may be. It's nice to own a piece of pressed glass that you are convinced is Sandwich, but many other factories turned out equally fine things.

The majority of pressed glass after 1850, as already explained, falls under the designation of pattern glass. The term refers specifically to the complete and matching sets for the table. A table set consisted of four matching pieces: sugar bowl, creamer, butter dish, and spoonholder. All large sets included these, but in some patterns a set consisted of twenty to thirty or more different pieces.

The simple but distinguished Sawtooth pattern was one that included a water bottle and tumbler set. This pattern

was made from the 1860's to the 1890's in Massachusetts and Pennsylvania. The pattern consisted of coarse, short points covering the outside. In a covered dish such as a compote, the sawtooth edges of dish and cover fit together precisely. Early Sawtooth pieces were heavy and good-quality glass; later ones usually were lighter and sometimes were not quite as fine glass. Because so many factories made Sawtooth, there were some variants. Basically, the pattern had the teeth covering the body of the piece. A complete set of Sawtooth would have to have these pieces, according to glass expert Ruth Webb Lee:

Bowls—covered and with a low foot in 4 sizes, without a foot in 2 sizes
    fruit bowls footed in 7 sizes, on a low foot in 3 sizes, open and without a foot in 5 sizes
Butter dish
Cake plate on standard in 6 sizes from 7 to 12 inches in diameter
Candlesticks
Celery vase
Champagne
Compotes—covered and on high standard 2 sizes, on low standard 2 sizes, and on standard 4 sizes, open on high foot in 4 sizes, on low foot 2 sizes
    nappies in 4 sizes
Cordials
Creamer
Cruet
Decanter
Egg cups
Goblets

Honey dish
Lamps
Pomade jar
Salts—covered, footed, and open
Sauce dishes—round in 3 sizes
Serving dishes—round in 3 sizes, and
　　oval
Spoonholder
Sugar bowl — covered, also footed
　　and open
Trays—4 sizes
Tumbler—more than one style
Water pitcher—2 sizes
Wineglasses

The early Petal and Loop pattern included goblets in three styles, cordial and champagne glasses, wineglasses, and footed tumblers. Other special drinking glasses were made for ale, lemonade, and, rarely, claret. Then there might be jelly glasses with matching lids and mugs with handles.

Few patterns included all of the various kinds of glasses, but most of them had three or four. Tumblers and goblets, wines and cordials, were most common. The low broad tumblers known as bar glasses were made in different sizes, to hold ⅓ or ½ pint or as much as ⅓ quart. So varied were bar tumblers that one page of a glassmaker's catalogue during the 1870's pictured 54 bar glasses, each one in a different pattern or size. Jiggers were not always miniature tumblers. For example, a jigger pressed into the shape of a man's boot was only one of the many uses to which Victorians put glass boots and slippers. Decanters and a bitters bottle were natural accom-

*Drinking accessories: The low, broad tumbler known as a bar glass was made in various sizes and simple patterns. A decanter was included in many pressed glass patterns, but not jiggers. The boot-shaped one shown here has toe and heel covered with silver. On one side, above a bird, are the words "Just a Swallow."*

*Water pitchers in perfect condition are not common. This one at left in Beaded Tulip pattern, 7 inches high, the other, Wildflower pattern, 11 inches high.*

*Water pitcher in Cottage pattern* (left), *Feather* (right), *both made in Midwest.*

paniments to the drinking glasses in some patterns.

Water sets could be purchased separately in some patterns. Painted Hobnail, Thousand Eye, Shell and Jewel, Daisy and Button, as well as its variants Daisy and Button with Thumbprint and Daisy and Button with Crossbar, were some of the better-known patterns that included water sets. Other late patterns, less popular probably, were Festoon, Crown Jewel, Star and Oval, and Moon and Star. The water set consisted of the large water pitcher, a matching glass tray, and water tumblers, lemonade tumblers, or goblets, or — in some patterns — all three. A carafe or water bottle and matching tumbler were sold separately and were referred to in some old catalogues as "water bottle and tumble up."

Plates 6 inches in diameter were important in most patterns. Some had plates in two or three sizes up to 10 inches in diameter. The more sizes plates were made in, the greater the popularity of the pattern, experts say. Platters seem not to have been as essential as serving dishes with or without covers. A syrup jug and pickle dishes were made in many patterns. Sauce bottles and caster bottles, a berry bowl, and, more rarely, an ice tub were other possibilities. Candy dishes became more general in patterns of the 1880's and 1890's.

Most sauce dishes were round, but occasionally a pattern would have oval or square ones. Bleeding Heart, for example, had both round and oval sauce dishes, Shell and Tassel had round and square ones. To complicate

A *Shell and Tassel platter and sauce dish, part of a table set with square pieces. The frosted shell-shaped ends and corners alternate with panels of stippled drapery ending in a tassel. A less decorative variant of this pattern is known as Round Shell and Tassel.*

matters further, Shell and Tassel sauce dishes were made both flat with a handle and footed. Two and occasionally three styles of goblets and water tumblers were not unusual in any one pattern.

The earliest patterns were made of excellent-quality glass. By the 1880's and especially in the 1890's, some of the patterns were interesting and at-

tractive, but the glass itself might be of poor quality, heavy and dull.

Tableware was made in hundreds of patterns between 1850 and 1900. Such motifs as hobnail and bull's-eye became as important in pressed glass as they had been in cut glass. The bull's-eye or some adaptation of it was the chief motif on a group of handsome patterns made of brilliant, heavy glass of good quality in the 1860's. The bull's-eye, which is a concave, round ball, predominated on the pattern of that name, as well as on such variants as Bull's-Eye with Fleur-de-Lis, Bull's-Eye with Diamond Point, and Pillar and Bull's-Eye. Other 1860 patterns in this series were Horn of Plenty, Comet, Tulip and its variants, and New England Pineapple.

The New England Pineapple pattern was first made at the Boston and Sandwich Glass Company. Later, the very same pattern was made in other places as far west as Ohio. Outside of New

*Sauce dishes in the Swan pattern might be either footed or flat like the one shown at the left, but all of them had a scalloped collar. The sauce dish in the Marquisette pattern is shallower. This pattern is based on panels resembling frosted mesh, outlined with clear glass. Swan was made in clear, yellow, amber, and blue; Marquisette, only in clear.*

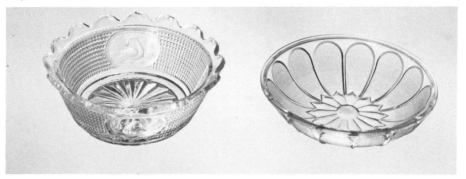

**178**

*Egg cups, a standard item in early table-ware sets, are now often used for other purposes. This one in New England Pine-apple pattern, 3½ inches high by 2 inches in diameter, was made by the Boston and Sandwich Glass Company.*

England, this pattern frequently was called Loop and Jewel.

Diamond, Sawtooth, and Waffle patterns during the 1860's also copied their motifs from cut glass. Thumbprint and ribbing were other classic forms used in many combinations and variations for patterns in the 1850's and 1860's.

The tiny pointed hobnail called a dewdrop distinguished more than a dozen patterns that were produced by glasshouses in New England, including those in Sandwich and Cambridge, Massachusetts, the United States Glass Company and other smaller firms in western Pennsylvania, Bellaire Goblet Company of Findlay, Ohio, and others in this state and Indiana, from the

*The shallow oval dish at the left, about 8 inches long, was probably a pickle dish; it was made in Ohio in the 1870's. The sparkling pattern, based on dewdrops or tiny hobnails, was known as "101." The 8-inch Fleur-de-Lis and Drape plate at the right is clear glass of excellent quality, probably made in the 1850's. There was also a Bull's-Eye with Fleur-de-Lis pattern.*

1860's through the 1880's. There was a plain Dewdrop pattern, but the most popular ones used dewdrops to set off another motif. Beaded Dewdrop, Paneled Dewdrop, Dew and Raindrop, Dewdrop and Fan, Dewdrop with Star, and 101 are some of the better-known. Of them all, Dewdrop with Star is as popular today among collectors as it was with buyers when it was made— in clear glass, several colors, and opaque white.

By the 1870's, stippling and frosting set off many patterns that became popular. These techniques gave the pieces a light and airy appearance that called to mind the early lacy pressed glass. However, these late sets displayed very definite patterns.

Three of the most popular frosted patterns, Westward Ho, Lion, and Three Face, were made first in the 1870's by Pennsylvania factories. James Gillinder and Sons of Philadelphia and Greens-

*Lion, one of the popular clear-and-frosted pressed glass patterns made between 1870 and 1895, included oval and round covered dishes and compotes.*

burg, Pennsylvania, who originated the popular Westward Ho pattern, which had a kneeling Indian as the knob on covered pieces, seems to have been expert in the technique of frosting. The Indian and the cover on which he crouched were frosted; so also was the band encircling the body of all pieces,

*Dewdrop with Star was one of several patterns formed by tiny pointed hobnails or dewdrops. This footed salt dish is 3⅛ inches across and 1½ inches high. The pattern was made in clear glass, milk-white glass, light and dark blue, amber, and yellow.*

which displayed a log cabin, a bison running across the plains, and running deer. Lion pattern or a variant of it was made by Richards and Hartley in Tarentum, Pennsylvania, James Gillinder and Sons, and probably other firms. Three Face, conceived by George Duncan and Sons of Pittsburgh, showed a woman's face full-view, profile, and halfway between the two. This was also known as Three Sisters and perhaps Three Graces.

These as well as other patterns that combined frosted with clear glass are sometimes called camphor glass. This was not a descriptive term used in the catalogues of nineteenth-century glasshouses. It has been coined by twentieth-century antique dealers. Certainly it arose because the frosting of the glass, which had a smooth surface, called to mind the look of a bottle of spirits of camphor after the camphor had crystallized. When frosting embellished patterns prior to 1850, it was accomplished by another method than that used on these patterns of the 1870's, and was rough to the touch.

Stippling was done on many flower and fruit patterns. It was the same sort of stippling as was done to produce lacy glass, but on these later flower and fruit patterns the stippling did not form an all-over background, but perhaps was confined to leaves with the fruit standing out in clear and perhaps raised glass, or to ovals or medallions around the fruit or flower. In any case, the effect was quite different from that

*The spoonholder at the left is a Grape Band variant because of the narrow strips of stippling above and below. The goblet is Currier & Ives pattern made up of a star pressed into a square, alternating with a round thumbprint. The only piece with a Currier & Ives comic print is a large round tray.*

of the stippling on lacy glass. Notable were the coveted Rose in Snow and such grape patterns as Paneled Grape and Magnet and Grape. Magnet and Grape was made in one pattern with a frosted leaf and in another with a stippled leaf.

Many delightful flower and fruit patterns were in demand during the 1870's and 1880's. The blossoms generally were easily recognizable whether they were fuchsias, clematis, thistles, morning glories, roses, or many others. There were fewer bird patterns—the four definite ones were Swan, Cardinal Bird, Hummingbird and Fern, and Frosted Stork. Several with unidentifiable birds such as Flying Bird and Strawberry (sometimes called Bluebird) or Bird and Fountain were made in the 1890's, and were poorer-quality glass.

These flower and fruit.patterns include some of the most popular ones with present-day collectors. Wildflower, Bellflower, Rose in Snow, and Blackberry (this one particularly in opaque white) are getting scarce. If a genuine nineteenth-century piece of Bellflower or Blackberry can be found, it can be sold quickly for a good price.

That flower and fruit patterns were also popular when they were first produced is proved by the large number of variants that were made. Fully a dozen patterns had grapes as the dominant motif, a half-dozen used tulips, at least four had roses, and three had cherry designs. Bleeding hearts appeared on several patterns, each one slightly different from any of the others. This repeated use of a motif to produce a variant pattern usually meant that, having noted the popular reception

*Some compotes were made without covers. This one in Paneled Thistle had scalloped edges; it came in several sizes. Thistles alternate in the panels with a conventional ornament. Thistle pattern appeared in the 1870's; Paneled Thistle, later.*

*Cardinal Bird, a pattern of the 1870's, is one of the few with birds. The footed sauce dish shows the bird on a berried branch. On one side, the creamer does too; on the other side of the creamer, the bird appears in a different position on a leafy branch.*

*This Flying Bird and Strawberry dish, 1½ inches high, belongs to a pattern made in the 1890's. One of the motifs in the border of the heart-shaped dish is the old strawberry diamond, which was copied from cut glass.*

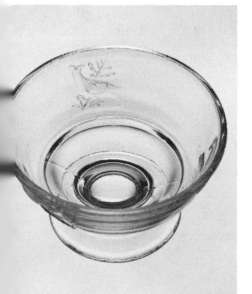

given a pattern, other firms adapted it to designs of their own.

Bellflower and Daisy and Button were patterns in a class by themselves. Vast quantities of both were made in the 1800's and reproduced in the 1900's. Bellflower, with its tendrils of delicate blossoms standing out against a ribbed background, was made by many glass firms from 1840, or possibly earlier, until the last years of the century. It was made in all sorts of decorative pieces, such as lamps, cologne bottles, and decanters, as well as tableware sets.

Daisy and Button was not made before the 1880's, some glass experts believe. Even at this late date, pressed glass was imitating cut glass, for pressed Daisy and Button was an adaptation of the popular Russian pattern in cut glass. Daisy and Button may have been introduced by the Sandwich factory, but does not compare in quality with their pieces made 50 years earlier. The daisy may be combined with a smooth, round button or with a starred button. Other variants included either of these two basic motifs worked in with a V ornament, thumbprint, crossbar, or panel.

Probably all patterns were made in clear glass. Just as some of the early lacy glass was made in rich colors, so also were many of the later patterns. Many were made in two or more colors as well as in clear glass, and as the century wore on, colored glass seemed to become more popular. Bellflower was made to some extent in deep blue, amber, opaque white, and clear glass. By the 1880's when Daisy and Button appeared, it was made in two shades of blue, two shades of yellow, as well as light and dark amber, apple-green, dark green, and amethyst.

Patterns in all one color and in a combination of clear glass and a color were made in greatest quantity during the 1880's and 1890's. This also was the period when cranberry glass, that soft rosy red that has been so popular among collectors in the mid-1900's, was first popular. Inverted Thumbprint, a pattern with round marks that stood out on the inside of the glass, was widely made in cranberry as well as other colors. A deep ruby-red and a pigeon blood also were in some demand. Thousand Eye, encircled on the

*The Bleeding Heart goblet at the left is one of the three goblet designs in this pattern. The Bellflower pattern of the other goblet has always been a popular one, for it was made from 1830 on, by many glasshouses.*

*Daisy and Button* (left) *and* Thousand Eye (right) *were two of the most popular patterns when they were originally made and are just as well-liked by present-day collectors. Thousand Eye was introduced in the 1870's, Daisy and Button in the 1880's. Both were made in several colors as well as clear glass, and both are currently being reproduced.*

outside with rows of raised buttons in graduated sizes, was made in true red and other colors but not in cranberry, as far as I know.

A distinction must be made between colors achieved by adding chemicals to the liquid glass and color that was only on the surface. Red and white patterns made during the 1890's usually had the red painted on the outer surfaces (in the appropriate places) of the pressed glass piece. Red Block was one of the patterns on which the color was painted. Nowadays, some of these pieces are in excellent condition; others such as creamers have the red worn off. Pink, yellow, or blue with white or clear glass and Amberina (shaded yellow to red) were other combinations offered to tempt customers.

Vaseline glass is a variation that is highly prized now. The name is a perfect description, for the pieces were a clean, light yellow with an underlying tint of blue that gave the oily look of the salve known as vaseline. The yel-

low had no trace of muddiness. Vaseline glass was made in both clear and opaque yellow, and sometimes the two were combined in one piece. Occasionally, too, vaseline was combined with clear glass.

Opaque glass, whether white or colored, was not transparent. There were both a caramel opaque pressed glass and a creamy opaque one nicknamed "custard glass" (this last also a product of the 1890's).

Of all the opaque glass, none is more popular now than the sort usually

*A* Red Block *sugar and creamer—the pattern was popular in the 1890's—are clear glass with red painted on the appropriate places.*

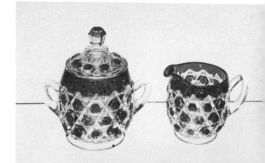

*Pressed glass with color throughout was made from 1825 to 1840, and to some extent until 1900. The match-holder has alternating panels of smooth, rich red glass and clear Daisy and Button. The candy or relish dish has a scalloped red border topping off panels filled with cane and daisy-and-button motifs and enclosed in prism loopings. There is a star in the base.*

*Vaseline glass, transparent or opaque, is the color of the product after which it was named. It differs in color from ordinary yellow or amber pressed glass. The pieces shown—a Cube hat and a footed candy dish with cane motif in the corners—are transparent, light yellow, vaseline glass.*

called milk glass. Glass with this appearance had been blown in Europe and England for many years, so it was natural that it would be tried in pressed glass here. The pressed opaque white glass acquired several names during the

last century, when it was variously known as opaque white, white enamel, and alabaster. Opaque glass also was made in colors, particularly in shades of blue and green. When it is colored, "opaque glass" is the correct name, not "milk glass."

Opaque white or milk glass was pressed in quantity between 1870 and 1900 and is copied currently in equal abundance. It's not always easy to tell whether a piece of milk glass is 10 or 100 years old. However, if certain characteristics are kept firmly in mind, it should be possible to do so. Nineteenth-century milk glass had a translucent quality, and was white but the white had a blue tinge. The translucency and the blueness can be noted when a piece is held up to the light. The color, if it can be called that, has a skim-milk cast. Modern milk glass is much whiter, so much so that it is almost a dead-white; it is also a denser and often thicker glass.

After 1870, tableware sets in a few patterns were made in opaque white or milk glass. Sawtooth and Waffle, which had been made much earlier in clear glass, at this time appeared in milk glass. Princess Feather, Icicle, and Wheat, as well as several of the fruit patterns, including Blackberry, Strawberry, Cherry, Gooseberry, and a Grape pattern were especially handsome in milk glass.

Milk glass, however, is probably best known for the odd dishes, particularly plates and bowls with lacy openwork or lattice edges an inch or more wide, and the vegetable dishes with covers in animal forms. A veritable barnyard of covered dishes can be found. Sometimes the covered dishes were all white, all opaque blue or opaque green. Then again the base of the dish might be opaque blue, the lion or lamb cover opaque white, or the other way around. Platters, except for the small, shallow ones in the shape of one or two hands with palms upward, were simpler than plates and covered dishes. Lamps and candlesticks naturally were made in milk or opaque white glass, as well as some vases.

Occasionally, a piece of opaque white glass is more opal than milky. That is, when it is held toward the light, it shows "fire." Opalescent pressed glass, either clear or colored, is valued highly by collectors. Berry and water sets, curtain tiebacks, and novelties were outstanding in opalescent glass. So were such patterns of the 1880's as Ribbed Opal Glass, Swirled Opal Glass, and

Opal Hobnail. Pennsylvania glasshouses in Tarentum and Pittsburgh, and to some extent others in West Virginia and Ohio, became well known for their beautiful opalescent pieces.

The use of two colors of opaque glass did not stop with the dishes with animal covers. Opaque white and a color were combined or fused in one piece. The most common name for this two-color glass is marble, but other descriptive ones are slag, agate, Connecticut, and calico glass. Challinor, Taylor and Company of Tarentum, Pennsylvania, who manufactured this glass during the 1870's and 1880's, called the two-color opaque glass "mosaic." During these decades, other firms in Ohio, Pennsylvania, West Virginia, New York, and New England also made marble or agate glass.

Marble seems an appropriate name for the pieces that combined a shade of purple or rose with white. The color

*Opaque white or milk-white glass was made in quantity between 1870 and 1900. Lacy-edged bowls like this fruit bowl were popular. The tiny (4½ inches) bud vase is decorated with a gold line around the top. The footed salt dish at the right is in Dewdrop and Star pattern, one of the few made in opaque white glass.*

ran in streaks as it does in the stone called marble. A really deep purple, not amethyst, was one of the handsomest combinations. Opaque combined with yellow in various shades, some of them almost brown, also was not rare. Blue and white marble or agate glass was made in smaller quantity, so this is a real find.

*A barnyard assortment of opaque glass dishes with covers in the form of animals became popular in the 1870's.*
TOP ROW *(left to right): opaque blue dish with opaque blue and white cat cover; opaque white hen with glass eyes glued into place; opaque blue dish with opaque white lion cover.*
MIDDLE ROW *(left to right): opaque blue dish with opaque white lamb cover; opaque white, lacy-edged dish with opaque white fox cover; opaque white dish and duck cover.*
BOTTOM ROW *(left to right): opaque white dish and rooster cover; opaque white dish and cover representing a rabbit (with glass eyes glued into place) surrounded by eggs; opaque light blue dish and swan cover.*

The Pennsylvania firm made marble glass tableware in two patterns, one with fluting, the other a flower pattern. However, when a person looks at a piece of marble glass, the pattern seems secondary to the coloring.

Plates in two sizes, 8 and 10 inches, with a wide, open edge also were made in marble glass in quantity. Candlesticks, vases, match-holders, and various odd dishes are other possibilities.

Thousand Eye, another one of the most popular patterns among collectors, must have been equally popular among customers of the last century. Like Sawtooth and Bellflower patterns, it was made in a staggering number of different pieces. There was even a twine-holder. Thousand Eye was made in clear glass, in several colors, in opaque blue, and in opalescent. When patterns such as Thousand Eye were made in clear glass and colors, not all pieces of a set were made necessarily in all colors. A complete set was more likely to be made in clear glass.

Many of these fancier types of pressed glass as well as rainbow hues first made their appearance in the 1870's. For one thing, great impetus was given to the pressed glass industry by the Centennial Exposition staged in Philadelphia in 1876. For that event, historical motifs were the obvious sort of decoration.

A complete set of pressed glass tableware called Liberty Bell, or Centennial,

was made by James Gillinder and Sons of Philadelphia for the Centennial Exposition. A toy set also was made in this pattern. Both the table set and the toy set were made in clear glass and some of the pieces of tableware in opaque white as well, although these are rare now. In addition to a small open salt dish, salt shakers were made in the shape of the Liberty Bell, with pewter tops. Other little bells with metal hangers were evidently souvenirs.

The bread platter, an oval 9¼ by 13 inches, had a large Liberty Bell in the center with 1776 on one side, 1876 on the other, and the words "Declaration of Independence." The lower half of the wide border displayed the names of the signers of the Declaration of Independence; the upper half, in large letters, read "100 years ago."

Bread service plates or platters were a popular commemorative item. For the Centennial Exposition year, eagles,

*This Centennial with Eagle bread platter was given as a premium by a small-town Pennsylvania grocer. It was one of the commemorative designs made at the time of the Philadelphia Centennial Exposition in 1876.*

flags, and mottoes were popular motifs. Another popular style was the oval bread platter known as Centennial with Eagle, which had an eagle in the center and in the border the phrase "Give us this day Our Daily Bread."

Bread platters, of course, were part of many sets, particularly those produced during the 1870's and 1880's. Lion, Egyptian, Clear Ribbon, Jewel Band, and Paneled Forget-me-not were only a few. On commemorative platters, Washington, Garfield, Cleveland, and McKinley were favorite subjects, but more bread plates were designed to honor Ulysses S. Grant than any other president. Commemorative patterns were sometimes round instead of the oval usually favored for bread platters.

Because many glass firms outdid themselves to display new and unusual patterns and forms of pressed glass, people who visited the Centennial Exposition left with a keener appreciation of the versatility of pressed glass than they had ever had before. When the World's Columbian Exposition opened in Chicago in 1893, colored glass was the vogue. Pressed glass was not as highly regarded a century ago as it is today, and the Philadelphia and Chicago expositions helped to establish it. The years from 1876 to 1900 saw pressed glass produced in more patterns, variations, and colors than ever before. These same years also were those when the finest cut glass was being made in this country—cut glass that in quality and design was second to that of no other country. Cut glass was expensive even then, but pressed glass finally had become an accepted substitute.

Pressed glass bread trays with patriotic decoration were probably first exhibited at the Centennial Exposition. They also were given as premiums at grocery stores and bakeries. (The Centennial with Eagle bread tray that I own was prized by my grandmother all her life, and I remember her saying that it had been a premium from the general store in a small Pennsylvania town.) Other pieces of pressed glass and particularly some of the colored glass and novelty pieces were premiums too. The fact that they were, does not lessen their value today if they are authentic nineteenth-century pieces.

The ten most popular pressed glass patterns, according to a consensus of experts, are Bellflower, Wildflower, Rose in Snow, Daisy and Button, opaque or milk-white Blackberry, Horn of Plenty, Thousand Eye, Westward Ho, Lion, and Three Face. Authentic nineteenth-century pieces of any of these patterns sell for premium prices.

A Bellflower mug with a clear glass applied handle may bring $30; a Horn of Plenty mug $35, because this pattern was made for a shorter period and hence the mugs are fewer. Mugs were not included in the sets of all ten most popular patterns. Goblets were. At the present time, the least expensive goblet is Daisy and Button, which will bring not more than $5. Wildflower

and Bellflower goblets are worth about $8 each, and Thousand Eye at least that much. A Rose in Snow goblet is reasonably priced at $12, whereas a Horn of Plenty or Lion goblet can be sold for as much as $17.50. A milk-white Blackberry goblet is worth all of $20, and one in Westward Ho or Three Face may bring $25 or a little more. These prices, with the exception of Blackberry, refer to goblets in clear glass. Those in color bring somewhat higher prices.

One drawback to finding a piece in any of the ten most popular patterns is the fact that it may well be a reproduction made only last year or 25 to 35 years ago. Daisy and Button, Wildflower, Moon and Star, and any number of old patterns are being made today. In fact, goblets have been reproduced in nine of the ten most popular patterns, the only exception being Bellflower. Some of these current copies are produced from original molds—or so they are advertised; others are outright, cheap reproductions. The quality is not comparable to that of pieces made 100 years ago in the same pattern.

A ring, clear and musical as a bell, when glass is struck with a knife or the finger is no more proof of nineteenth-century glass than it is of Sandwich glass. The clear ring does mean that the glass is made of good quality metal. Thin blown glass has the clearest ring, but pressed glass of good quality gives a musical ring too. Goblets, tumblers, sauce dishes, and other round pieces

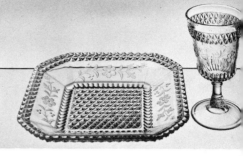

**189**

give a more musical ring than flat dishes. Colors usually will not ring quite as true as clear glass. The bell-like sound is most likely to be heard from old patterns such as Argus, Petal and Loop, and Huber.

It takes considerable knowledge and familiarity to tell the quality of glass and to recognize characteristics of authentic antique pressed glass. There is great variation among different patterns and different decades of the nineteenth century. Colored pressed glass often is not of quite as good quality but it does appeal to collectors. Not all nineteenth-century glass is of the finest quality and there is surely a difference between pressed glass made in the 1850's and that made in the 1950's.

Nineteenth-century pressed glass looks different and feels different. Run a finger over stippling on a known piece of old glass and note how sharply defined it is. On a reproduction, stippling is blurred. Molded or raised motifs such as faces or grapes and other fruits were in higher relief and more rounded in old glass. On reproductions, they can be almost flat.

Reproductions, more often than not, are made in more colors than the originals. Furthermore, the colors are not always true to the old ones. Clear glass in reproductions can be quite different —it may be dull, dead, or gray-looking or have a tint. The quality of the glass can be a giveaway even when old molds are used.

*A square plate and goblet in Wildflower pattern, one of the most popular among collectors; these pieces are being reproduced. The example shown is clear glass, but the pattern was made in light and dark amber, yellow, blue, and apple-green*

The dimensions of the goblet, sugar and creamer, or other pieces and the details of the pattern are the differences that are easiest to spot. The stem of a goblet may be shorter, compotes and covered dishes smaller, tumblers wider.

Patterns seldom display fine details in reproductions. For example, the veining of leaves, the hair on deer and lions, and similar delicate markings are likely to be indistinct. Some details may be missing entirely—a tendril on a reproduction of Paneled Grape, for example. Frosting may be more restricted on such frosted and clear patterns as Westward Ho and Lion. Designs often are altered or simplified in reproductions. In the popular Wildflower, a reproduction has fewer leaves and flowers than an original nineteenth-century piece in this pattern.

Few of the old patterns that are being reproduced at present are being manufactured in complete sets for the table. Copies usually are limited to the more

popular and currently useful pieces—goblets, salts, sugar and creamer, small plates in the sizes for dessert and salad, and small compotes are the most likely pieces. Lacy glass of a sort also is being made in salts, sugar and creamers, and candleholders.

The spoonholder or spooner, as it was called, was a part of most sets of pressed glass made during the 1800's. Since the piece is no longer indispensable on tables, it has not been reproduced. That was why one beginner who wanted to learn about pressed glass started thirty years ago to buy only spoonholders. Her collection has grown until it consists of more than 400 spooners. Most of them are clear glass, in an amazing range of well-known and generally unfamiliar patterns, although a few are custard glass and art glass.

*Spoonholders (5⅜ inches high) in two patterns of the 1870's: Ripple, at the left, is as simple as Egyptian is elaborate. Stippled bands divide Egyptian into three sections: one showing a temple, another a sphinx and palm trees, and the third a figure, a camel, and palm trees.*

Toy sets, incidentally, are not necessarily reproductions. These miniatures of the four pieces that made up a table set—butter dish, sugar bowl, creamer, and spooner—were made in some of the best-liked patterns and were first popular at the time of the Philadelphia Centennial Exposition.

When a person has found a piece of pressed glass and dusted or washed it carefully so that the design can be seen clearly, the first important step is identifying the pattern. A person in your town who collects pressed glass or an antique dealer who specializes in it may be willing to identify the piece

for you. If not, the library surely will have some books on the subject. When you are quite certain about the pattern, find out as much about it as possible and make all comparisons and tests to decide whether or not the piece was made during the 1800's. It is always helpful to compare a piece you have found with another authenticated piece in the same pattern to be sure that the general characteristics match.

Because so many patterns were made, chances are that you will not find pressed glass in one of the ten most popular patterns. This group does not necessarily include the best of all the hundreds, perhaps thousands, of pressed glass patterns. Each one of the ten simply has something a little extra in the combination of motifs, such as the stippled background for a clear glass, open rose in Rose in Snow, the classic form of Horn of Plenty, the quaintness of Daisy and Button, the simplicity of

**191**

Thousand Eye. Whatever it is, all of these patterns have an indefinable something that appeals to many people.

Horn of Plenty was an excellent glass that was made in quantity for many years, but it is still expensive because collectors are so interested in this pattern. The name came from the shape of the alternating panels combining sawtooth and a clear section with a bull's-eye. A person not too familiar with pressed glass might well confuse a later pattern, Dickinson, with Horn of Plenty. Actually, the two were quite different, and it's only at first glance that they could be confused. Pieces of Dickinson were circled with a curved panel of sawtooth and a similarly shaped clear panel with a thumbprint that was an elongated oval in comparison with the round bull's-eye of Horn

*A turkey in clear glass forms a dish that measures 9 inches from head to base and from breast to tail feathers. Outside width is 6 inches. The upper part is a removable cover.*

of Plenty. Dickinson sells for about a third as much as a comparable piece of Horn of Plenty.

The quality of glass appears to have nothing to do with popularity. Some of the top ten were made of excellent-quality glass. Some examples of Bellflower, which was made by many firms for so many years, are better-quality glass than others. Daisy and Button seldom was made in anything but average glass, and some of it was quite poor. In this century, all pieces of pressed glass are salable, regardless of quality or general popularity.

*The spoonholder and creamer are in the Dickinson pattern, which is sometimes confused with Horn of Plenty. Both these patterns have alternating panels of clear and sawtooth, but the clear panel on Dickinson has an elongated thumbprint, quite different from the round eyes of Horn of Plenty.*

Many of the simpler early patterns are fully as valuable as any pieces in the ten most popular patterns, although they do not sell for as much because the demand is not as great. Some of these early patterns are distinguished not only by their simplicity but also by the high quality of the glass. Ashburton and Argus, for example, are early enough to be flint glass. A person

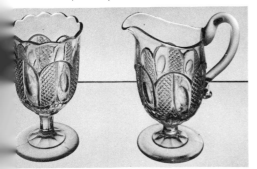

*These compotes show two of the several ribbon patterns made between 1850 and 1890. The covered one at the left, 10 inches high, is Clear Ribbon of the 1880's, with threaded bands alternating with clear panels. The low one, 3½ inches high, is Frosted Ribbon, made before 1876.*

need not be embarrassed to ask $7.50 for an Ashburton goblet and $10 for one in Argus pattern. Waffle, a pattern first made by the Sandwich factory, can be sold for as much as an Argus goblet, and one in Waffle and Thumbprint pattern, which is clear, brilliant glass and not as plentiful, for $10.50.

There is much less demand for Prism and Flute, which also is heavy, clear, and brilliant pressed glass, so it would be difficult to get $5 for a goblet in this pattern—probably $4 would be about right.

Any of the several Dewdrop patterns

*Feather pattern (not to be confused with Princess Feather, which is different), made in the Midwest, has also been called Doric, Indiana Swirl, Swirl and Feather, Feather and Quill. The spooner is footed; the covered butter dish has a medallion in the base, which is typical of the best-quality glass made in this pattern.*

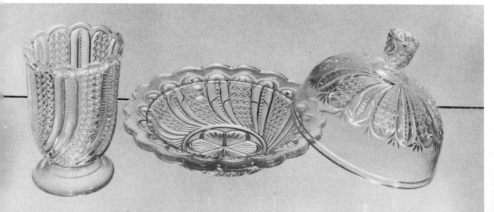

*Spooner, sugar bowl, and creamer in the Herringbone pattern (1880's), which combined diamonds and loops filled with dewdrops and also shield-shaped panels with its basic herringbone motif. Notice the pagoda-shaped cover.*

as well as the Ribbon ones made between 1860 and 1890 are not only attractive but also good quality. In clear glass, a goblet in Dewdrop with Star or one in sparkling 101 is worth about $6.50, a plain Dewdrop about $5. A goblet in Clear Ribbon might sell for a little more than $5, whereas one in Frosted Ribbon or Double Ribbon is worth $7.50. Of the frosted and clear group, Roman Key and Frosted Circle are as good quality as the much more popular Westward Ho, Lion, and Three Face. Again, demand rather than quality sets the selling price, and so probably it would be difficult to obtain more than $10 for a Roman Key goblet or quite that much for one in Frosted Circle. Yet a goblet in Lion, Westward Ho, or Three Face often is sold for $18 to $25 (Lion is least expensive).

Of the later conventional patterns, Marquisette, Herringbone, and Feather are more than run-of-the-mill. Yet $5 undoubtedly would be maximum price for a clear goblet of Marquisette or Herringbone. For a goblet in Feather pattern, which is somewhat better known, it might be possible to get $6.50 to $7.50. All of the fruit patterns are desirable ones, yet goblets in Cherry and Gooseberry sell for half to one-third as much as Blackberry. Flower patterns vary as much in quality as design, which extends from the naturalistic Bleeding Heart of not especially good-quality glass ($5 or so for a goblet) to the more formally arranged Paneled Daisy (goblet perhaps $10) and Paneled Thistle (goblet $7.50), both of them sparkling patterns.

A few pressed glass patterns are amusing. If you find a sauce dish in Cabbage Leaf, any youngster in the family will probably want to eat from it because the sides have been pressed to look like cabbage leaves and the base displays a rabbit's head. A butter dish in Cabbage Leaf—and other covered dishes—has as a knob a rabbit's head

*Paneled Daisy celery vase. The pattern was one of the attractive floral ones introduced in the 1870's. A set included round plates 7¼ inches in diameter, with scalloped edges, and also square ones with rounded corners.*

that emerges from the leaves that form the cover. A sauce dish has a market value of about $5, a covered butter dish between $20 and $25. It's easy to guess the name of the pattern, if you stumble on a large plate or round tray of Currier & Ives pattern, for the center supposedly reproduces a Currier & Ives comic print. Either piece would be worth about $10. Incidentally, Currier & Ives pattern originated with the Bellaire Glass Company, Findlay, Ohio.

The prices that have been quoted are for pressed glass in perfect condition. It's not uncommon to find a piece with a nick or a crack, or a compote or butter dish without its cover. Imperfect and incomplete pieces can be sold, in many cases almost as rapidly as a fine example. Of course, allowance should be made in setting the price.

No one should expect that pressed glass can be sold at a country auction for prices comparable to those in antique shops, particularly in city shops. And there is great variation in price for the same piece of glass in different parts of the country. A Cardinal Bird pitcher that is good, if not superior, glass sold at an auction in New Hampshire for $3 and was resold in Connecticut for $4.50. Another Cardinal Bird pitcher in a New York City antique shop that specializes in pressed glass was priced at $16. Admittedly, the New York City price seems high, and the New Hampshire auction price low, for a pitcher in excellent condition. A fair appraisal would probably set the price at about $10, for the pitcher is 5¼ inches high and 3 inches across, and shows a cardinal in two different poses. Obviously, there are a few locales where it would be possible to sell this pitcher for its appraised price or a little higher, but in most parts of the country it would have to be sold for less.

Where it is being sold is only one factor that influences variation in price in all kinds of pressed glass. This is as true of milk-white and colored glass as it is of clear. Both milk-white and colored pieces are more expensive than clear ones in the same pattern.

Colored glass is in great demand everywhere. However, interest is not quite as high in cranberry glass as it was fifteen years or so ago, and prices have dropped somewhat. Still, an authentic cranberry glass pitcher with painted or enamel decoration can be sold for about $25. It is especially important to be certain that cranberry glass is not of recent manufacture, either in this country or abroad, and that pieces in other colors are nineteenth-century examples and not reproductions.

In a pressed glass pattern that was made in one or more colors as well as clear, the latter is least expensive. In Pointed Hobnail pattern, for example, a clear goblet can be sold for $5 to $8.50, an amber one for $10 to $12.50, a blue one for about $15, and a green one for as much as $17.50. Green sells

for a higher price than any other color. Vaseline glass also can be priced a little higher than clear glass pieces of the same pattern. Usually vaseline can be sold for about the same amount as amber or yellow, which are quite different. (Daisy and Button, Thousand Eye, Maple Leaf, and Primrose are among the patterns made in vaseline glass.)

A few patterns, among which Blackberry, Strawberry, Gooseberry, Cherry, Waffle, Princess Feather, and Sawtooth probably are best known, were made in milk-white as well as clear glass. In each case, the milk-white piece usually sells for considerably more. In Icicle, a less-well-known pattern, a clear creamer may be sold for $5, the milk-white one for $12.50 to $15. A sauce dish of clear Icicle probably will not bring more than $3, one of milk-white glass more than $4.50.

Odd pieces of milk-white or opaque colored glass bring satisfactory prices. That is, if they obviously were made during the 1800's, are complete, and have no nicks or cracks. A milk-white glass dish, 5 inches long, with the cover pressed in the form of a duck, may be priced fairly at $20, one of the same size with a hen cover at about $12, and with a rabbit about $15. A compote with a lace edge and a high standard certainly should bring close to $35. Milk-white bowls with lacy or lattice edges sell now for much more than their original price. One 8½ inches wide with lattice edge is worth about

$20; plates with lattice edges, $5 to $10.

Collecting nineteenth-century pressed glass became a popular hobby in the 1920's. Certainly the people who started then or in the 1930's, aiming to get together a complete table set in one pattern, had a better chance of achieving their goal than those who start in the 1960's. Or, at least, of doing so for a modest cash expenditure. Collectors of the 1920's and 1930's bought pressed glass for much less than it can be purchased for now. Thus their pieces have proved to be a good investment, for they have increased greatly in market value. Even at to-day's prices, pressed glass is a good investment if the purchaser is careful to buy only pieces made during the 1800's. And collecting is not a hobby only for the wealthy. The collector who chooses his goal wisely and searches widely should find it possible to buy many pieces of some patterns of excellent pressed glass for a couple of dollars each. Many flower patterns, for example, are not only less expensive than Bellflower but easier to find.

Small pieces in both colored and clear glass appeal to collectors because a good many can be displayed in a limited space. Thus, if you find no more than one or two salt dishes, a mug, and a spooner in different patterns in an old cupboard or sideboard, this

From left to right: *10-inch Heart with Thumbprint vase, part of a late pattern made only in clear glass; Willow Oak tumbler, made in clear and colored glass in the 1870's, with stippled panels showing two kinds of leaves and a daisy-like flower; a shallow dish (7 by 4½ inches) in the Actress pattern of the last half of the nineteenth century that reproduced likenesses of stage figures (this one shows Maggie Mitchell; among others pictured were Lotta Crabtree and Kate Claxton).*

Salt dishes of various sizes and shapes were made in most pressed glass patterns. From left to right: Tulip, Harp, lacy glass Cathedral, a Broken Column shaker, English Hobnail and Prism saltcellar.

small haul of clear glass has a cash potential of not less than $10, and perhaps considerably more. To be sure of not cheating yourself or the buyer to whom you sell, it is desirable to identify the pattern of each piece. Clear glass salt dishes have a market value ranging from $1 to $9 each. Few spooners and mugs sell for less than $3.50 each, and some patterns bring two and three times as much.

If you are intent upon selling every old article in a house that must be cleared out, then it's a good idea not to become overly curious about any pressed glass that you find. Anyone who delves deeply enough may decide to keep rather than sell, and his finds may turn out to be the nucleus of a collection. Nineteenth-century pressed glass may have been looked down on by Victorians in the beginning as cheap stuff. That they soon changed their minds is evident from the quantities that were produced by 1900. Maybe the sparkling lacy glass first made by the Boston and Sandwich Glass Company was responsible, or perhaps it was the premiums given by stores, or the exhibits at the Centennial Exposition in 1876. In any case, the pressed glass made during the 1800's is fascinating to study, worthwhile to keep, and profitable to sell.

## GLOSSARY

### BASIC TYPES OF PRESSED GLASS

*Clear*: transparent glass to which no color has been added and which, therefore, is usually colorless. In the case of pressed glass, sometimes referred to as "white."

*Colored*: glass that is tinted by either of two methods: (1) adding chemicals to liquid glass, for color throughout, or (2) painting the outer surface of the glass.

*Lacy*: pressed glass with intricate patterns in smooth glass against an all-over background of stippling on the underside.

*Pattern:* pressed glass on which a combination of motifs forms a recognizable design. Stippling may be one of the motifs, but does not form a background as it does in lacy glass. After 1850, most pressed glass was pattern glass.

### SPECIAL COLORS

*Cranberry:* a soft rosy red throughout, made chiefly 1880 to 1900.

*Opalescent:* iridescent, like an opal. Clear, opaque white, and opaque colored glass, including opaque blue and opaque yellow, were made opalescent to some extent. Among opalescent patterns were Ribbed Opal, Swirled Opal, and Opalescent Hobnail.

*Vaseline:* light yellow, with an underlying tint of blue and a slightly oily look; made in both clear and opaque.

### OPAQUE TYPES OF PRESSED GLASS

*Caramel:* an opaque glass in a color typical of its name.

*Custard:* an opaque glass, creamy in color, sometimes with gold or painted decoration. (1890's)

*Marble:* opaque white glass combined with an opaque color; generally the white and some shade of rose or purple is called marble glass. Opaque white also was combined with various shades of opaque yellow and blue. Other names (synonyms) for marble glass are agate,

calico, Connecticut glass, onyx, and slag.

*Milk:* see Opaque White.

*Opaque white:* translucent, rather than opaque, white glass with a faintly blue tinge. Also called milk, milk-white, white enamel, and alabaster glass.

*Opaque colored:* glass similar to opaque white glass, but colored throughout and less translucent; made especially in shades of blue and green.

*Slag:* see Marble.

### GENERAL TERMS

*Camphor glass:* pressed glass with a smooth frosted surface, usually in a pattern that combines clear and frosted glass. Westward Ho, Lion, and Three Face are among those referred to as camphor glass.

*Frosted glass:* clear glass with a mat finish. Prior to 1850, the frosting on pressed glass was rough to the touch and was produced by grinding or sandblasting. After 1850, frosting was smooth, accomplished by the application of acid.

*Sandwich glass:* any glass produced by the Boston and Sandwich Glass Company in Sandwich, Massachusetts. The firm was a leader in developing pressed glass and made a great deal of lacy glass.

*Stippling:* tiny, fine, raised dots set close together.

*Variant:* a pattern adapted from another one, retaining the main motif but differing in some detail. The basic Daisy and Button pattern gave rise to these variants: Daisy and Button with V Ornament, Daisy and Button with Crossbar, Daisy and Button with Thumbprint, Daisy and Button Paneled, Daisy and Button with Single Panel, Daisy and Button with Narcissus.

FOR FURTHER INFORMATION:

EARLY AMERICAN PRESSED GLASS by Ruth Webb Lee. Wellesley Hills, Massachusetts: Lee Publications.

MILK GLASS by E. M. Belknap. New York: Crown Publishers, Inc.

SANDWICH GLASS by Ruth Webb Lee. Wellesley Hills, Massachusetts: Lee Publications.

VICTORIAN GLASS by Ruth Webb Lee. Wellesley Hills, Massachusetts: Lee Publications.

# 10
# Glass Treasures and Novelties

WHIMSICAL ITEMS HELPED to keep many glasshouses in all parts of the country in operation during the nineteenth century. Some of them were purely decorative, others were useful, and none of them were regarded as whimsical at the time they were made. Little cup plates, 3¼ to 3½ inches in diameter, seem so in the twentieth century now that it is highly unfashionable to drink tea out of a saucer, but they were an important segment of many a glassmaker's business for about fifty years. Toothpick- and match-holders also were indispensable in late-Victorian homes and many of these were made in whimsical forms.

After it was established in business, a glasshouse might go on to specialize in cup plates or preserving jars or to make cut glass or pressed glass. However, the foundation of any glass company was the production of bottles and window glass. The manufacture

of bottles always has been important, and those made in the United States were seldom just plain glass containers with narrow necks and without handles. They traced the history of public events and commemorated famous people and also revealed what the average person drank, what medicine he took, and what things every household needed.

Anyone who rummages around an old house will almost certainly find a few old empty bottles. It is foolish not to look closely at such finds before tossing them into the garbage can or wastebasket. The two or three dusty, cobwebby bottles discovered on a shelf or in a corner of a cellar probably are worth a good deal more in cash than you'd believe. They were purchased originally for their contents—pickles, preserves, patent medicine, vinegar, or any one of a dozen other things—and the bottles represented only a fraction of the cost. At the present time, all nineteenth-century bottles are valuable on their own account.

Most of the old bottles that a person is likely to find will be blown-molded or blown-three-mold. If a bottle is rough and irregular at the mouth and has no rim, chances are it was hand-blown and the mouth of the bottle was snipped with shears while the glass was still pliable. Very old hand-blown bottles, such as those made during the eighteenth century, also have a round scar on the base, left when the bottle was broken off the pontil on which it was held while the glassworker shaped the neck.

Unlike bottles for liquids, snuff bottles were often very plain. Stiegel made them in the eighteenth century, and they were made through much of the nineteenth century too. Snuff bottles are not rare, but few persons nowadays

recognize what they are. They were small, rectangular or square, narrow, and sloped gently to a short neck. Many were made of quite thin glass, clear or opaque and colored. Those of plain colored glass were evidently everyday snuff bottles, for handsome examples—some made of cameo glass —also have been found.

The earliest bottles hand-blown in this country for household use were commonly either slender and rather arched or squat and bulbous. Most difficult of all the hand-blown bottles to fashion was the large green carboy. It was made to hold vinegar, cider, and—it's been said—applejack. Carboys, strictly speaking, should come encased in wickerwork or a wooden box, and are still made in that way to transport corrosive chemicals. Vinegar was put up also in a demijohn, a large bottle with a narrow neck but smaller than most carboys. The demijohn was usu-

*Colored glass bottles: The oldest is the hand-blown square one, which was made for snuff. The tall pink bottle at the left was blown-molded late in the nineteenth century; the one next to it, somewhat older, was blown-three-mold, as was the perfume bottle at the right.*

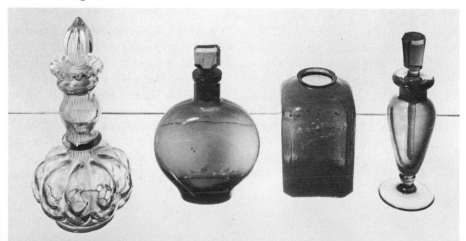

ally of green or brown glass and originally was enclosed in wickerwork or a wooden box like the carboy.

However they were made, old bottles were seldom colorless glass. Although the majority were clear, the formula and the cheap materials used resulted in a light green color at best and some verged on yellow or brown. Many of the utilitarian bottles of the 1800's and 1900's were deliberately made a deep blue, a deep green, or some shade of amber, brown, or amethyst.

Pattern-molded or expanded bottles had vertical ribbing, swirled ribbing, broken swirls, and—rarely—daisy in a diamond. After 1820, when blown-three-mold was used to a great extent for bottlemaking, the designs became more varied. However, bottles continued to be hand-blown and some made during the 1850's had smooth bases, others hollow ones. Neither color nor size is any clue to the date when a bottle was made, but the design may be.

The kind of bottle that it's fun to discover could have been made at any time from 1820 into the 1890's. This was the era when pickles came in "cathedral" bottles, which were green glass with an arch design on each of the four sides, or in smaller, more slender bottles with spiral ribbing. Glass jars for home preserving were small with rough mouths, or tall, somewhat like twentieth-century milk bottles. After 1860, preserves were some-

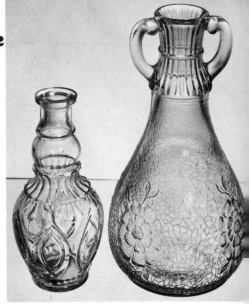

*Both the clear glass, blown-three-mold bottle at the left and the taller, patented pattern bottle held household supplies about a century ago.*

times sold in colored bottles of various sizes and shapes.

Essences and flavorings were put up in smaller bottles than pickles and preserves. Sometimes these bottles had special shapes according to the contents. Peppermint bottles usually were tall, slender, and cylindrical; lemon extract came in elliptical bottles.

Of course, many liquids were sold in plain bottles with nothing more than the seal stating the name of the company. An exception was Poland water in a bottle shaped like a figure to depict Moses smiting the rock—fancier than many a whisky bottle.

Certainly, early Americans drank considerable quantities of spirits, if one is to judge by the enormous number of whisky and other liquor bottles as well as bitters bottles that have been found. Wine bottles (but not decanters) were plain in comparison to whisky bottles, but bitters bottles were particularly unusual. One was made in the shape of a standing Indian, and Dr. Fisch's bitters came in a bottle shaped like a fish standing on its tail and holding the mouth of the bitters bottle in its mouth. Plantation brand bitters was put up in a square bottle molded in the shape of a slave cabin of exaggerated height, Suffolk bitters in a bottle shaped like a pig.

On both bitters and patent medicine bottles, the brand or firm name was often worked into the sides. A liquor distiller in Philadelphia by the name of E. C. Booz added a word to the dictionary because so many people

*The two amber nineteenth-century fish bottles were made to hold Dr. Fisch's bitters. The historical flask at the right is green and shows an eagle clutching arrows.*

asked for his brand by requesting "a bottle of Booz." His bottle, 8 inches high, was shaped like a log cabin to represent the birthplace of President William Henry Harrison, who had campaigned on the slogan of "log cabin and hard cider" in 1840. The distiller's name and address were imprinted on the narrow sides of the bottle, and the sloping roof also carried printing.

Flasks, which are large, flat-sided bottles, were made originally to carry gunpowder and various things other than whisky or hard liquor. But it is the half-pint, pint, and (after 1850) quart-size liquor flasks, decorated and in colors, that are the most unusual. The first ones are said to have been made by the Kensington Glass Works in Philadelphia, about 1833, but by 1840 every glass factory in the country was producing what are now called historical flasks. Their popularity continued until about 1870, and while it lasted, the demand led to all sorts of odd and unusual designs. Patriotic emblems with an eagle to signify liberty or with a bust of Columbia were fully as well liked as agricultural motifs such as sheaves of wheat or rye, grapes, or cornstalks, sometimes combined with a cornucopia to symbolize prosperity and plenty. Portrait flasks honoring presidents, war heroes, and celebrities were probably made in greater quantity than the simpler flasks with floral garlands, sunbursts, and the like. Mottoes ranged from one word, "Liberty," to "The Father of His Country" over a profile of George Washington, and from a simple identification over other portraits to "Use me but do not abuse me." Some flasks carried more advertising than ornamental decoration, and now and then a joke or comic flask appeared.

Most flasks were rounded toward the neck and base, but some tapered inward more at the neck. The violin flask was shaped accurately enough for the violin to be recognizable. This type was decorated with scrolls and perhaps stars or a similar conventional motif. The decorative designs for all of these flasks were cut into the molds, which were prepared by professional mold-cutters. The molds were the full size of the flask, and the glass was blown into them. Shades of green and amber probably were most common, but rich greens, blues, yellows, an aquamarine, and amethyst also were made. The color appeared deeper in the thicker sections of the flasks.

One of the most famous of the many portrait flasks depicted Jenny Lind, her head and shoulders framed in garlands, her name spelled out above, on a ribbed flask. Washington, Adams, Franklin, Lafayette, Henry Clay, Andrew Jackson, and William Henry Harrison were among the presidents and statesmen honored on portrait flasks. Heroes of the Mexican War such as Zachary Taylor, Major Samuel Ringgold, and Captain Braxton Bragg were other favorites. The War Between the States was memorialized in several de-

signs. Most important on one were clasped hands advocating friendship between the North and South.

Other flasks commemorated such matters of historical interest as railroad building, Mississippi steamboating, and the Colorado gold rush; the last showed a prospector with his tools and bore the legend "For Pike's Peak." After 1848, flasks were made with Masonic and other fraternal emblems, ships (including a classic man-of-war in full sail and some famous vessels), and also miscellaneous but more conventional designs.

Then, suddenly, after 1870 these portrait and historical flasks were made no more. They cannot be said to have been displaced by the character bottles that started to appear in the 1870's. These were made in the form of an animal such as a bear, or of a bird, fish, gourd, or the like, as well as some portraits, and were used to hold perfume, medicine, liquor, and other liquids in small amounts.

Apothecary bottles made before 1900 are also of interest to collectors. These were clear, blue, or amber glass and usually bore the drug label. Some apothecary jars with matching covers were cut glass. Barbershop bottles of the Victorian era, probably mostly from about 1870 to 1900, were often made of handsome glass. Those of colored cut glass or of colored glass with an overlay design are the most valuable.

Decanters, fancier spirits bottles for use in homes and taverns, held wines and hard liquors that had been decanted or poured gently to avoid roiling them, and hence were ready to be poured into glasses for individual servings. All three of the great eighteenth-century glassmakers—Wistar, Stiegel, and Amelung—made decanters in various sizes and in wonderful colors or with colored decoration, a few with simple cut motifs such as the flute. Wistar left some magnificent mulberry-colored decanters.

*Decanters of blown-molded glass with three rings applied around the neck were made prior to 1850.*

Nineteenth-century decanters are the ones found most frequently. Those made in the early 1800's were hand-blown, blown-molded, or blown-three-mold. Blown-glass decanters were decorated usually with applied threads or trails of clear and colored glass. Blown-three-mold decanters had geometric and swirled patterns. Some of them are most attractive and quite sparkling, and—until touched—likely to be mistaken for cut glass. Sunburst and quilted patterns are more rare; they were made in Stoddard, New Hampshire, if not other places.

In pressed glass, cruets are easier to find than decanters. Some patterns, particularly early ones, did include decanters—for example, Fine Rib, Diamond Point, and Waffle and Thumbprint made by the New England Glass Company, Sandwich Star and Waffle of the Boston and Sandwich Glass Company, and Excelsior made by McKee Brothers of Pittsburgh, Pennsylvania. Decanters were made also in such later patterns as Wedding Ring and Lee.

Peachblow and other kinds of art glass were used for decanters too, but the greatest number and greatest diversity of decanters can be found in cut glass. They were being cut by B. Bakewell and Company in Pittsburgh in the 1820's. From 1830 into the 1870's, decanters with simple flute cutting and steeple stoppers were made in such quantities that undoubtedly a good many are still to be found. Those with star-cut bottoms were made after 1830. During the Brilliant Period (1880–1905), decanters were cut in most of the popular patterns. Among the many shapes were cylinder, globe, barrel, and one resembling a champagne bottle. Some patterns included more than one decanter either because two sizes, pint and quart, or a different style of neck were made.

Decanters averaged 9¼ to 10¼ inches

in height, until elongated shapes became fashionable in the late 1800's and extended the height to approximately 13¼ inches. Blown and blown-three-mold examples were made of much thinner and lighterweight glass than the pressed and cut glass ones. Pressed glass decanters are likely to be interesting because of their patterns, but cut glass decanters were generally of much finer-quality glass.

The rings around the neck of a decanter are always noted by collectors. The triple rings that were used on Waterford cut glass decanters were copied in this country and can be seen on many free-blown and blown-molded as well as cut glass ones. The rings usually were plain glass. However, on cut glass decanters they too were likely to be cut—simply, perhaps in a feather or a diamond cutting. A single broad ring or two narrower rings also were common. Many decanters, of course, were ringless.

Unlike many bottles and flasks, which were plugged with corks, decanters and cruets were made with glass stoppers. For cut glass decanters, steeple-shaped stoppers were customary during the first half of the nineteenth century. Two other styles of the early years, used both in Ireland and this country, were an upright circle and what I call the mushroom. During the Brilliant Period, globular stoppers with faceted cutting were common. Square stoppers, octagonal ones with a flat top, and variously cut steeple

stoppers were also popular.

Glass stoppers were blown, blown-molded, and pressed as well as cut. It was not unusual for a pressed glass decanter or cologne or perfume bottle to have a cut glass stopper. If the stopper was pressed glass, it sometimes repeated a motif from the pattern of the bottle. A rectangular Daisy and Button cologne bottle, for example, had a square stopper also pressed in Daisy and Button pattern. Etched decoration was used on stoppers to match the decoration of decanters and fancy bottles. Occasionally, an interesting hand-blown stopper was made, perhaps resembling an open flower.

Stoppers are another thing not to discard. A miscellaneous group of them always finds a buyer at an auction, and they are sometimes sold individually or in small numbers in antique and second-hand shops. Don't be discouraged if you find a decanter or cruet without its stopper; sooner or later you'll be able to run down an appropriate one that will fit the neck and at no great expense. A decanter that lacks a stopper is salable, although at a reduced price.

Wine pitchers have gone out of fashion, but they were a conceit during Victorian days. These pitchers were tall in proportion to their diameter and usually were elaborately decorated. Some are known to have been made of colored glass, but the majority probably were clear glass. Many etched ones were produced by the New England Glass Company in Cambridge, Massachusetts, and some were cut by various firms. In any pattern, the cut glass wine pitcher was in addition to a shorter water pitcher. Claret jugs were as tall as quart decanters but usually more graceful; they had plain handles.

Still on the subject of drinking, some types of glasses that were in wide and general use are no longer made. One of these is the flip glass. Flip, incidentally, was a sweetened and spiced hot drink in which ale, beer, or cider was the chief ingredient. It was drunk either from a mug made of glass or other material or from a flip glass. The mug, basically, was a tumbler with a handle and was made in various capacities. The term "flip glass" is perhaps a collector's way of describing a tumbler usually a pint or more in capacity, and such a glass undoubtedly was used for other drinks. Probably because flip was a hot drink, the glasses sometimes had covers with a knob or a finial. Hand-blown flip glasses with delicate engraving were made by Amelung in Maryland, and with engraving or a painted decoration of flowers and garlands by Stiegel in Pennsylvania. Flip continued to be popular into the nineteenth century, but it was drunk from plainer glasses then.

Rummers were large, tall goblets with short stems. The smallest size held only four ounces, but others were ten to twelve inches or more in height. The bases were round or square, the

One side of this hand-blown, nineteenth-century flip glass is decorated with simple engraving. The hump in the base is the scar left when the glass was taken off the pontil.

bowls variously shaped. Rummers were either hand-blown or blown-molded and often were decorated, particularly with etching.

Syllabub, that frothy mixture of wine or cider and milk which turns into soft curds, was served in cups or glasses of various styles. Some were slender footed glasses, others cups with straight or rounded sides. The cups always had handles. Many were plain but probably just as many had cut, engraved, or etched decoration. Syllabub glasses were made in quantity until about 1860, or possibly a little later. Probably blown-three-mold as well as free-blown techniques were used.

The wineglasses of 100 to 150 years ago, like those of today, can be classed as stemware. The lines or shape of the stem and its decoration have changed from one period to another during the last 250 years. The shape of the bowl generally varied according to the type of wine to be served in the glass. Thus, champagne glasses were broad and saucerlike, the width equal to or greater than its depth. The bowls of glasses for other types of wine were narrower than their depth, and certain specific shapes were intended for specific wines, such as sherry, claret, port, hock (white Rhine wine), and Madeira. Wineglasses were made with a capacity of two to three ounces. Cordial glasses held only one ounce in comparatively small bowls on long or short stems. The cocktail glass did not appear until late in the nineteenth century.

The various kinds of wineglasses were made of hand-blown and blown-molded glass, plain or with etched or painted decoration. These are rare finds nowadays. However, all kinds of wineglasses were made in pressed and cut glass patterns and these are quite plentiful, although it might be difficult to get together a matching set of a dozen or even a half-dozen.

A great variety of tumblers to be used for water and whisky were made of all types of glass. Larger cut glass tumblers holding five ounces or more were meant for champagne or mineral water in late-Victorian days. Cut highball glasses also appeared before 1900.

Tumblers for water and whisky also were made in patterned pressed glass. Comparatively few commemorative tumblers were made, but there were some historical ones in water and whisky sizes. Some were linked to the Civil War, more of them to the Spanish-American War (one of these proclaimed "Remember the Maine" under crossed flags held by an eagle), and there was a Yankee Doodle design too.

Cologne, scent, and perfume bottles, and little ones for smelling salts are something else again. Bottles for these several purposes had always been made to some small extent, but the introduction of art glass about 1876 brought with it a fashion of fancy bottles. Not that bottles of these types were made only of art glass. Probably more of them were pressed and cut glass. Colored opaque glass also was popular.

Cologne bottles, the largest in this group, usually were made and sold in pairs. However, one cologne bottle, especially if it is in good condition, is a worthwhile find. Colognes were made in a variety of odd shapes as well as square, globular, and barrel-like. In pressed glass, Trilby pattern (a heart motif) cologne was a round bottle with a heart-shaped stopper. Cologne bottles in the Bellflower pattern were made in both clear and opaque glass, with a space for a label. These are probably as rare as the bottles in the frosted pressed glass pattern, Lion, with cut glass stoppers. Colored pressed glass included a good yellow bottle in Star and Punty pattern, again with a cut glass stopper. Sometimes cologne bottles were so labeled.

Cut glass cologne bottles were made in quantity after 1875 in various patterns —in fact, in even greater quantity than pressed glass ones. Some were cut quite simply, many were elaborate. Shapes and heights varied greatly, but these bottles are always heavy.

Perfume bottles were not only smaller than cologne bottles but often were prettier and daintier. Scent and smelling salts bottles were smallest of all, for they were meant to be carried in the purse. These attractive bottles ran the gamut of glass techniques and decoration. The double perfume bottle, or gemel, was made in hand-blown and cut glass, clear and colored.

More important than perfume and cologne bottles were cup plates. They were indispensable in every self-respecting household from about 1800 into the 1850's—the period when it

*Perfume or scent bottles were carried in the purse. The pointed one at the left is blue glass with painted decoration. The matching pair are cut glass, and the double bottle above is red glass. All have silver caps.*

was fashionable to drink from the deep saucer and set the cup to one side on a small cup plate. The first cup plates in this country were made of china, and some of the old blue china tableware had cups with two saucers or a saucer and a cup plate. After 1825, as pressed glass became known, cup plates were made almost solely of this. Like bottles, cup plates too were manufactured in endless variety, and like historical flasks, they related history in miniature.

Pressed glass cup plates were 3¼ to 3½ inches in diameter (a china cup plate could be 4 inches in diameter). The majority were round with plain edges or with daintily or deeply scalloped ones. A few were octagonal. The rim, approximately ¾ inch wide, sloped up from the flat, level center. Both rim and center were decorated. Many cup plate patterns were made in one or more colors as well as clear glass.

The Boston and Sandwich Glass Company led the way in the production of pressed glass cup plates. It was not long, however, before nearly every glasshouse in the country was producing them. Many cup plates were lacy glass with the all-over stippled background that gave so much sparkle to the pattern. By no means all of these were made by the Boston and Sandwich Company. Firms from the East Coast into the Midwest made them too.

The Thirteen Hearts, for instance, was a Sandwich pattern. Thirteen hearts filled in with stippling circled the rim; the center displayed one of several geometric designs against a stippled background. Other glasshouses had heart patterns showing single and double hearts, hearts pierced with arrows, and borders in which hearts alternated with flowers or the like. Such cup plates often were exchanged as Valentine gifts.

Another Sandwich pattern was Butterfly and Flower, made in deep blue and clear glass. The butterfly against a stippled background filled the center; the rim was garlanded with sprigs of blossoms and leaves and edged with a tiny scallop. Other floral patterns, not necessarily Sandwich, were based on the rose, pansy, narcissus, and butterfly. There were several grape patterns. Pattern glass designs that included cup plates were Roman Rosette, Waffle, Oak Leaf, Wheat and Rosette, and Peacock Feather.

Historical cup plates bore the eagle and stars as well as other patriotic emblems. Several were designed around the career of General William H. Harrison and his campaign for president: one displayed his portrait, several showed log cabins, and another featured a beehive, which was a motif related to Harrison. The cup plate with Fort Meigs in the center commemorated his defeat of the Indians at Tippecanoe.

There were cup plates to commemorate Bunker Hill, Fort Pitt (twenty-four stars and a peacock border), and various ships, among them the frigate *Constitution* and the steamboat *Robert Fulton*. Henry Clay, Lafayette, George Washington, and several other generals and heroes also provided inspiration for cup plate designs.

Their size makes cup plates unmistakable. Because they are small as well as interesting and can be displayed in limited space, collecting cup plates has become an intense hobby. There undoubtedly are still nineteenth-century examples to be found. The trouble is that some of the better-known patterns have been reproduced within the last thirty years. The tests suggested for differentiating between antique and current pressed glass apply to cup plates too. In the reproduction of the popular Thirteen Hearts pattern, the hearts are spaced farther apart, and the plate as a whole appears shiny and new-looking when compared with an old one. Excellent as is the color of the blue reproduction of Butterfly and Flower made in the 1930's, the flower sprigs around the border are not identical with those of the nineteenth-century cup plates in this pattern.

End-of-the-day glass is a term that covers a miscellaneous group of objects that were the result of glassworkers' thrifty habit of using up leftover odds and ends of glass at the end of the day. Glassworks managers evidently did not

*Multicolor vases were often end-of-the-day pieces made from leftover batches of glass. The one at the right has applied feet of clear glass.*

frown on this practice. Probably some of the end-of-the-day pieces were made on the workers' own time anyhow. In the offhand blowing of clear and colored glass and in cut glass, too, free rein was given to the imagination. Miniatures, novelties, and whimsies are the main classifications.

End-of-the-day work is believed to account for the first tentative steps toward making paperweights in this country. After 1850, paperweights were made in some quantity and several distinctive styles. Again the Boston and Sandwich Glass Company was a leader. Other important contributions were made by C. Dorflinger and Sons in White Mills, Pennsylvania; Gillinder and Sons, Philadelphia, Pennsylvania; several firms in Pittsburgh; Pairpoint Corporation, New Bedford, Massachusetts; and Millville Glass Works, Millville, New Jersey.

The first paperweights were cubes or ovals of clear or one-color glass. Simple cut glass paperweights also were made. Later, geometric blocks were decorated with enameling. From about 1850 on, paperweights in this country were modeled on styles originated in Europe, but several American types nevertheless achieved their own special beauty. Although various metals, stone, and other materials were used, the most fascinating paperweights are those made of glass.

Three styles of paperweights—the Sandwich Crown, Poinsettia, and various fruit ones—were extremely well made by the Boston and Sandwich Glass Company. The Crown was a dome of clear glass with twists of colored glass radiating through it from a central colored rosette. The flowers and fruits in many paperweights were fully modeled and then encased in

*Two paperweights made by eastern Pennsylvania glasshouses between 1850 and 1890: The geometric one is clear turquoise with white enameled decoration. The clear glass one is unusual in that the circles of beading are under the surface; the turtle embedded in the center, about an inch long, is made of pieces of real turtle shell.*

clear glass. In the Poinsettia, the red flower with its green leaves was set against a background of strips of white glass (called latticin o). This is perhaps the most famous, although Sandwich used several other flowers such as the rose, dahlia, pansy, morning glory, nasturtium, and clover. The third type, featuring fruit, consisted of individual apples, pears, plums, or the like, or a group of smaller fruits such as strawberries or small pears. Still another sort for which the Boston and Sandwich Glass Company became famous was made up of a fully modeled fruit such as a Gravenstein apple, or a pear, beautifully colored and fused to a round base of clear glass. These look luscious enough to eat.

Not as enchanting as flower and fruit weights, but probably more plentiful and still to be found, are the clear glass ovals or rounds in which a spider, snake, turtle, or something of the sort was embedded.

As famous as the finest of Sandwich paperweights are those called Millville Rose, made at Millville Glass Works in New Jersey. In these, a fully modeled flower nestled against green leaves; its petals were shaded in red, rose, green, or yellow (white roses also were made). The flower was encased in a ball of clear glass, which was supported by a matching footed base.

Probably all of the glass factories that made paperweights turned out some of what are called millefiori, a word derived from the Italian for "a thousand flowers." This is a style of colored decoration perfected by the Venetians and copied in other European countries, notably France, England, and after 1850 in this country.

Any one piece decorated with millefiori shows literally a thousand fascinating shapes and colors. A true millefiori was made from glass rods of various colors arranged so that their ends made a design, such as a bouquet of flowers with green leaves or a single blossom with petals, stamens, and pistil in appropriate colors. The rods were fused by heat and then drawn out to any desired length. As they were extended, the design remained the same but was reduced in size. Finally, the rods were sliced through. The same arrangement of rods produced a different design effect according to the way it was sliced —that is, either straight across or at any of various angles. This is one reason for the diversity of millefiori. Another reason is that the convex surface of clear glass covering the millefiori in paperweights magnified the design. A millefiori appears different as it is viewed from different angles.

Other popular paperweights displayed cameo portraits of famous persons, coins, less realistic flowers, and combinations of latticinio and millefiori. Bits of colored glass rather haphazardly arranged made "candy" paperweights. The 1890's also saw America making the monument-shaped weight, which consisted of a slender pyramid or obelisk of glass on a pedestal. This style was first made in France. Paperweights with symbols of holidays and

sentimental designs for Valentine and birthday gifts were popular in the late nineteenth century too.

A number of different objects were combined sometimes with paperweights. When the choice was an inkwell, candlestick, or penholder, the union can be a little baffling today. Some paperweights were combined with or shaped like a glass hat.

Victorian styles of paperweights continue to be made to this day except for the flower and fruit ones, which no one evidently has quite dared to attempt. A paperweight can be a century old and still have a perfectly smooth surface, for scars and nicks can be ground or polished away. One test for determining whether a millefiori paperweight is 100 or a mere 10 years old is to pick it up and heft it. Antique ones are much heavier in proportion to their size than newer ones. Look at the paperweight from all angles, too, to see how perfectly the design was made.

Paperweights were only one application of the fascinating millefiori. It was used also to make beautiful inkstands, letter seals, doorknobs, and buttons, as well as attractive perfume bottles, vases, and sweetmeat jars. Sometimes a simple bottle was dressed up with a millefiori stopper. It was even considered pretty enough for jewelry, specifically brooches and earrings.

Colorful as paperweights were, a person was limited in the number he could find a place for. There were apparently no such bounds for the equally colorful miscellany of end-of-the-day pieces. Some of these pieces were practical, others were nonsensical, and all of them catered to the Victorian love of bric-a-brac. Whatever fancy the glassworker followed at the end of the day, his novelty, whimsey, or miniature usually was colored glass, and often varicolored or mottled.

One novelty believed to have been an end-of-the-day piece was the glass rolling pin. Certainly it was too pretty to be put to practical use and, consequently, was hung on the wall or placed on the whatnot. Whether a rolling pin was clear or colored glass, it was likely to have painted decoration. Some rolling pins were varicolored, some were striped. End-of-the-day work also contributed canes in clear, colored, or opaque glass with colored stripes, which were hung on the wall with ribbon. Doorstops and darners, fully as colorful as rolling pins and canes, were more practical—if the owner could bear to use them.

One object whose use is still something of a question is the round glass ball called a witch ball. These balls were made in Caspar Wistar's glasshouse in the late 1700's and in many other places well into the 1800's. Some people say they were made as covers for milk dishes or to be placed in the mouths of pitchers. Witch balls were made from the size of a marble, which

could have covered the mouth of a creamer, to as much as a foot in diameter for bowls. If there was a hole in the bottom of the ball, it could be placed on the end of a stick and set on a windowsill to keep witches away, or hung from the rafters for the same purpose. These balls were blown in both clear and colored glass. A few were varicolored or striped.

Many of the pitchers and bowls in the South Jersey style, carried on after Wistar's place shut down, are believed to be end-of-the-day pieces. So also were the miniature pitchers, mugs, washbowls, and goblets that were made as toys for children. Real toys kept on the shelves of whatnots were amusing—and fearsome—blown glass animals.

A vast array of slippers, boots, shoes,

*Both the witch ball and the bowl that it covers are hand-blown blue glass. There is still some question as to the true purpose of witch balls.*

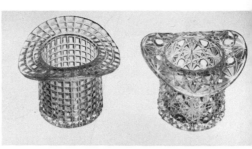

and hats also were end-of-the-day pieces. Some few of them, particularly slippers or shoes, ended up as perfume bottles or shakers; others held matches or toothpicks, and many were used purely as ornaments. Boots could be drinking glasses or jiggers. However, miniature slippers, high-buttoned shoes, and crumpled boots were not made only as end-of-the-day, free-blown glass. They became so popular that they were made for the trade. Many were blown-molded and thousands were done in pressed glass. The Daisy and Button pattern was probably used most frequently, but other patterns to look for are Sunburst, Diamond, and Cane. Lady's slippers in various heel heights, lady's high-buttoned shoes, baby shoes, and men's boots—probably every style worn by every age—were reproduced in glass. Even shoes and slippers on skates were not uncommon.

Pressed glass slippers probably were the most plentiful a century ago and hence the most likely still to be found. Both pressed and hand-blown slippers and shoes were made in clear and colors. Milk-white glass, Bristol, spatter, and marble were a few of the various kinds of art glass in which slippers were made. Frosted glass slippers decorated with cutting are attractive, if any can be found, but they are more rare than slippers with applied glass and painted decoration.

Glass hats were blown, blown-molded, blown-three-mold, and pressed. Many

*Pressed glass hats, 3 inches high: The one at the left is clear glass in the Cube pattern; the other, light yellow in Daisy and Button.*

more hats than slippers were engraved or cut. They were made in as wide an array of plain, art, opalescent, and opaque glass, and decorated in as many ways, as slippers and shoes. Some had silver hatbands or over-all decoration of silver deposit.

Top hats were made in greatest variety, but there were also the soft-crown and wide-brimmed types, as well as such popular shapes as caps, sailors or boaters, and derbies. A Quaker hat, a bandmaster's cap, and a fireman's helmet were among the more specific styles represented. The three-cornered hat or tricorne and the peaked hat are rarities, if they are to be found at all now. Ladies' bonnets were not overlooked, although they were not made in such quantity as the various men's styles.

Glass hats were almost as useful as they were decorative. The top hats were made in four sizes. The smallest size was an individual salt dish. The second size, about 3 inches tall, was a toothpick- or match-holder; it makes an excellent container for cigarettes today. The third size, between 4 and

6 inches tall, was a spoonholder, and the largest, 6 inches or more high, was used to hold celery at the table. The 3-inch size—or reproductions of it— are most likely to be found today.

Among the pressed glass patterns in which glass hats were made—mostly the 3-inch hats—were Thousand Eye, Raindrop, and Cube, in addition to the ubiquitous Daisy and Button. The latter was made in clear and various solid colors, and sometimes the buttons were decorated in color. In fact, hats seem to have been made in more colors than any other piece of glass. Two shades of yellow, light and dark amber, apple-green, emerald, and olive-green, light and deep blue, amethyst, cranberry, and russet are shades to watch for.

For twenty years or so, every glass factory produced hats. Striped and threaded glass ones from the Boston and Sandwich Glass Company were notable, as were colored blown glass hats from South Jersey and pressed glass ones from the area of Pittsburgh, Pennsylvania. So it was with slippers and shoes. Gillinder and Sons in Philadelphia turned out fine ones of frosted glass; the United States Glass Company in Pittsburgh was one of the firms that made slippers with attached skates. Of course the quality of the glass varied.

Most of the hats, shoes, and slippers were made for retail sale. A small percentage were imprinted as souvenirs or with advertising, the latter being given away. Many reproductions have

*The match-holder was a popular pressed glass novelty late in the nineteenth century. The two shown, dating from the 1880's, are the Cherub in clear glass and the famous Kitten on a Cushion in aquamarine with a Daisy and Button cup.*

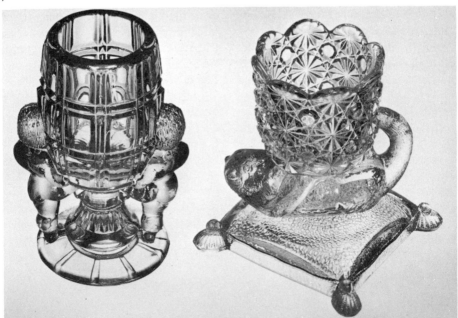

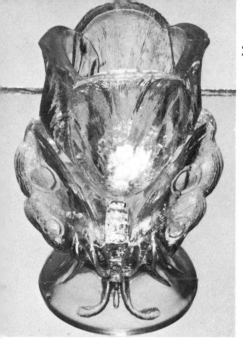

*Match-holder (or footed salt) made of pressed glass in the shape of a four-petal tulip cup clasped on either side of the base by a butterfly.*

been and are being made in this century, both in the United States and Europe, but their quality is not as good as that of the best nineteenth-century novelties and the colors are seldom identical.

In addition to the great quantities of hats and slippers, a good many other novelties were made between 1870 and 1900—and found customers waiting for them. Most plentiful were match-holders and toothpick-holders, the majority of which were pressed glass, either clear or colored. These were made in fanciful shapes, as well as more conventional ones such as an umbrella, kettle, basket, cornucopia, and hand.

It's hard to tell now whether a small glass novelty was meant to hold toothpicks or wooden matches, for there is little if any difference in size. The pressed glass wall pockets to be hung up were definitely intended for matches. Kitten on a Cushion is one famous match-holder. The kitten, lying on its back on a cushion, held with its paws and tail a cup in Daisy and Button pattern.

Animals often were the basis of a match-holder. Several holders featured a dog, others an elephant, frog, alligator, pig, dolphin, or rooster. One showed a rabbit standing on his hind legs.

Toothpick-holders in the shapes of small vases were made in cut glass to match the most popular patterns. Small pitchers, mustard pots, and salts were made in both art glass and pressed glass in novelty shapes. One example had a sitting bird holding a mustard pot on its back between its wings. Another mustard jar was a cow's head, and there was a creamer shaped like an owl.

Whimsies and many miniatures were end-of-the-day pieces, but numerous other miniatures and curiously shaped pieces were part of the day's work in glasshouses. Stores often gave away glass novelties as premiums. However, they could be sold too, for a real appetite for them was fostered by the Philadelphia Centennial Exposition.

The demand continued until about 1890 and a limited number were still made for a few years thereafter.

Two things that particularly attract collectors are miniature and small pitchers and various kinds of salt dishes. They're easy to display, sparkling and colorful, and they require little space. Many made during the nineteenth century are still around. Individual salts sell for as little as twenty-five cents and as much as several dollars. The price depends on the rarity, the quality of the glass, the way they were made, and the decoration.

Since salt always has been an important commodity and condiment, it is not surprising that containers in a wide range of styles, sizes, and materials have been made for centuries. Table containers for salt were of three types: the standing salt (more than 5 inches high, usually made of silver), shakers, and salt dishes (also known as salt dips or saltcellars). Shakers in pairs for salt and pepper began to be included in pressed glass patterns after 1875 (Paneled Daisy, Double Loop, Shell and Tassel, and many others). They also were part of cut glass sets in patterns of the Brilliant Period as well as in plain diamond cuts and faceting. Pairs of shakers also were made in satin glass, Peachblow, and other art glass.

The larger salt dishes, 3 to 3½ inches in diameter, also called salt dips, were used singly, in pairs, or at each place on the table. They sometimes had

covers but more often were open dishes. These are generally found in pressed glass patterns. Individual salts or saltcellars, footed or flat, are 1½ to 1¾ inches in diameter.

Salts have been made from the days of the Stiegel glasshouse to the present in every known technique. Colored, clear, opaque, and opalescent salts were turned out in vast quantity during the nineteenth century. The Boston and Sandwich Glass Company made many interesting colored glass ones. Those of clear pressed glass are probably most likely to be found nowadays, although many cut glass salts must be in hiding.

Salt dips and saltcellars were round, square, rectangular, or oval in shape. In pressed glass, the frosted Lion pattern had large oval salt dips. Crown and Jewel had a rectangular one, Loop and Jewel a footed one with handles, Harp a round and footed one. Salts were made constantly to match patterns, from the early Petal and Loop with its round, footed dish to the late Daisy and Button. Salt and pepper shakers as well as individual salts in various shapes, including a triangle, a boat, and a canoe, could all be purchased in Daisy and Button.

Many novelty salt dishes of pressed glass were popular, too, and these were likely to be colored glass. Boats and boots, hats and birds, were common. A greater find would be a wheelbarrow salt with long handles, or a covered salt shaped like a turtle. Birds were par-

*Salt dishes of pressed glass: opaque blue glass decorated with a lyre motif; clear glass with the strawberry diamond motif, which was more generally used for cut glass.*

*A pressed glass duck with every feather in place has a cavity 2½ inches long and ⅞ inch deep, to hold salt.*

*Square saltcellars (approximately 1½ inches across) with crosshatching on the base are an inexpensive type made as late as the early 1900's. The 120-year-old pewter pepper grinder at the left has a glass body shaped like a lamp chimney.*

ticular favorites. A small pressed glass duck with careful details of feathers and bill had a cavity in the back 2½ inches long and ⅞ inch deep for salt. Swans in colored, clear, or opaque glass were made in different poses. A famous pressed glass salt showed a sitting bird holding a cherry or seed in its upturned beak.

Simple round or square saltcellars of pressed glass were made through the early 1900's—some with diamond-point sides, or perhaps only crosshatching on the base of square ones, or a plain star on the base of round ones. These are bought and sold inexpensively now, for they are plentiful. Remember that they are just as useful as they ever were and a nice remembrance of earlier days.

Other niceties for the house were made in lesser quantity, for they were not as widely used as cup plates or as appealing as novelties. Bells were made in cut, engraved, and art glass, but not in pressed glass. Inkstands were likely to be decorative glass and fairly elaborate, although some were made of blown and some of cut glass. Glass jewel boxes and smaller trinket boxes were produced in various sizes and shapes. The cut glass ones are probably easiest to find now, but some were engraved glass, either clear or colored, and some were art glass. Painted glass jewel boxes were usually lined, especially if the glass was opaque, as it often was.

A household was much more likely to sport some of the several kinds of glass knobs. These were made in many designs and sizes, and in colors as well as clear, opaque, and opal glass, and were pressed, cut, or molded. Knobs for furniture were made in greatest quantity throughout the long Victorian era. Knobs and rosettes for supporting mirrors and pictures and holding back curtains were made from the 1830's to the 1850's—and reproduced in the 1930's.

The glass disks of curtain tiebacks were made in three diameters: 2 inches, 2½ inches, and 3 inches. These decorative supports had to be fastened permanently into the window frame. The glass disk, which was made with a hole in the center, slipped onto the end of a 3-inch metal rod and was held in place by a small knob that screwed onto the end of the rod. The rods were pewter, brass, or iron.

The famous Petal and Shell curtain tieback made by the Boston and Sandwich Glass Company had opalescent petals and clear glass shells of pressed glass. Like tiebacks in other patterns, it was made in colored glass also. Milk-white glass was another choice. A few tiebacks were made in cut glass during the 1880's and 1890's, long after pressed glass ones had been discontinued.

Doorknobs were made off and on, never in any great quantity at any one time, as were curtain tiebacks. Cut glass doorknobs were a fad between 1880 and 1910, mostly in plain lapidary cuttings, but some displayed a monogram. A few were made of silver or mercury glass and possibly other art glass.

It is as easy to ignore the doorknobs on the first floor of an old house as it is the bottles in the cellar. However, nothing is too small to be a possible antique. If a doorknob or curtain tiebacks are not appropriate for use in your own home, someone will be interested in buying them. A pair of mercury glass tiebacks are worth about $8, a pair of opalescent Petal and Shell ones considerably more.

Many people are avid collectors of all kinds of glass tumblers and salts, small pitchers, paperweights, hats, slippers

*A curtain tieback in the famous Sandwich Petal and Shell pattern in opalescent and clear glass. This pattern was reproduced in the 1930's.*

and shoes, and match- and toothpick-holders. Bottles also fascinate a good many collectors. Some specialize in patent medicine bottles, though cologne and perfume bottles and historical flasks probably have the greatest appeal. Occasionally, a noncollector will find an old pitcher or salt irresistible. Once you are certain that any particular glass item was actually made during the nineteenth century, you can sell it for a reasonable price.

Few bitters bottles, even those made in the late 1800's, sell for less than $3. A bottle in the shape of a log cabin that held Plantation bitters should bring at least $5 and perhaps a little more. So should a Tippecanoe or Travellers bitters bottle. An Indian Queen bitters bottle, particularly if it is dated 1868, is worth all of $20.

A cathedral bottle that held pickles is priced fairly at $5. The Moses bottle that held Poland water is worth about $15, if it is in good condition and was made during the 1800's (this form has been reproduced widely). A demijohn sells for $10 to $15, with the scarcer, smaller ones higher-priced than the large ones; carboys, old or new, are always expensive.

Flasks bring premium prices, probably because collectors are so keen about them. A basket of flowers on one side and a cornucopia of fruit on the other were common decoration, but if the color is a good green, you may find someone who will pay $35. A violin flask has been sold recently for $65 and is a rare-enough shape to be worth a minimum of $50 anywhere, however poor the market. Flasks with an eagle predominant range from $20 to more than $100, depending on the other motifs and the rarity. A Jenny Lind flask is worth $5 to $15, depending on its color and the factory that made it.

A clear glass apothecary bottle sells for about $3 if it is 7½ to 8½ inches high, for $5 to $7 if it is 11 or 12 inches high. A barber bottle in amethyst glass is worth at least $20, a little more if it has enamel decoration. A blown-glass one in a good shade of blue should bring $25, a plain amber one perhaps $15.

An early hand-blown decanter with triple rings around its neck and a mushroom stopper has a market price of about $25 at the present time. A cut glass decanter made before 1900, and in perfect condition, is worth not less than $20 regardless of its pattern. Some patterns can be appraised as high as $35. Since a decanter appeals to more people than many other pieces of cut glass, it usually is possible to sell one for a price close to its actual value. A pressed glass decanter in the early pattern Waffle and Thumbprint can be sold for $18.50, in Sawtooth with its original stopper for about $35.

Cruets with stoppers bring almost as good prices, even for a single one. Pairs for vinegar and oil are less commonly found. A small cut glass cruet, 6 inches or a little higher, is reasonable at $15, and a 9-inch-high cruet should bring $20. A pressed glass one in clear Peacock Feather sells for about $7.50, a blue in Inverted Thumbprint with clear glass handle and stopper for $25.

There is an extraordinarily wide range of prices for paperweights. Small ones, about 2 inches in diameter, that display a random pattern of colored glass sell for $2 or $3 at country auctions. Cut glass paperweights with a simple faceting sell for modest prices too— perhaps $5 or a little more. Slightly larger colored glass ones with delicate enamel decoration on the outside are worth at least $10. The glass domes that enclose flowers, fruits, millefiori, candy, and the like average 3 inches or a little more in diameter. Not size but workmanship makes them expensive now. Old millefiori, fruit, or flower paperweights bring high prices — perhaps $100 or more—and even higher ones (to $250) if they are known to have been made by the Boston and Sandwich Glass Company or Gillinder and Sons.

Small things sell for worthwhile prices. A cut glass knife rest, 5 inches long and with the ends cut simply, probably will bring $5; a longer and more elaborately cut one, $7.50 or more. Toothpick-holders in typical late-nineteenth-century glass sell for $5 to $10, with an occasional rare one bringing $20 or

more. A blue pressed glass hat, about 3 inches high, in Cube pattern sells nowadays for $6.50, a blue Daisy and Button with V Ornament for about the same price; a Daisy and Button hat in canary yellow should bring a little more — perhaps $8 or $9. An opaque white shoe about 2 inches high is worth $5 or $6. A slipper bottle, probably for perfume, is certainly worth $5. Open slippers and shoes that served as toothpick-, match-, or pin-holders range from $3 to about $10. Certain styles and certain patterns and colors in pressed glass or art glass bring the higher price. In the case of both hats and slippers, it is important to be sure that they were made in the nineteenth century.

Salt dishes vary greatly in price too. The small individual saltcellars made around 1900 may bring no more than $2.50 or $3 for a matching set of six or eight. A pair of cut glass shakers with glass caps should be worth $10 to $15 depending on the pattern. Individual cut glass salts, footed or flat, may be worth $2.50 each but probably will have to be sold for less—perhaps $10 for a half-dozen that match. Pressed glass salt dishes range from $2 to about $10 each, depending on the pattern and the color. Patterns that are not greatly in demand sell for the lowest prices (Banded Buckle for perhaps $3, Barberry for $5; both salts are footed). The footed salt dish from the early Waffle pattern probably can be sold for $7.50 or more, and the round, footed Harp salt for as much as $9 in an urban area, perhaps only $5 in the country. The salt in a popular fruit pattern such as Strawberry can be sold for $5 to $7.50 depending on where you live. The highest prices can be asked for the salt dishes made in fancy shapes such as a sleigh, crown, lyre, etc., of clear or colored lacy glass— that is, if you can authenticate one as having been made between 1825 and 1850.

A good many cup plates, even those of lacy glass, were bought for less than a dollar each—in fact, only a quarter or a tenth of that—in the 1830's. Now their prices start in dollars. Any that you find should be taken to someone who knows something about either pressed glass or cup plates for authentication and pricing. There are so many collectors that cup plates, like bottles, are no problem to sell.

## GLOSSARY

### TYPES OF BOTTLES

*Apothecary:* a clear, blue, or possibly amber bottle for drugs, labeled or with space for a label.

*Barber:* bottle used in barbershops for tonic and bay rum, often of colored cut or overlay glass.

*Carboy:* a very large globular bottle of green glass with a small neck; protected by either an outer covering of wickerwork or an open wooden frame.

*Character:* a bottle made in the form of an animal, bird, or the like, for holding small amounts of perfume, medicine, liquor, or other liquids.

*Claret jug:* a tall graceful bottle with glass stopper and one handle.

*Cruet:* a small glass bottle for vinegar or oil, usually made in pairs of the same size, sometimes with the oil bottle taller than the one for vinegar.

*Decanter:* a spirits bottle for table use; a vessel with stopper made in various capacities for decanting wines and

hard liquors and serving them at the table.

*Demijohn:* a large, narrow-necked bottle enclosed in wickerwork, especially for holding vinegar or rum.

*Flask:* a large, flat bottle with two sides and a narrow neck; many displayed historical subjects or portraits as decoration.

*Gemel:* twin bottles; there were two necks but bottles were fused together at the base or fitted into a single base.

*Snuff:* a small rectangular or square bottle, sloping gently to a short neck.

### MISCELLANEOUS PIECES OR TERMS

*Bobeche:* a disk that slips over a candle and rests on top of the candlestick to catch drippings from the candle. Made chiefly of blown, blown-molded, and simple cut glass.

*Cup plate:* a round plate, 3¼ to 3½

inches in diameter, on which the cup was set while tea was being drunk from the deep saucer. Chiefly in pressed glass.

*End-of-the-day glass:* Miscellaneous pieces of varicolored glass made from leftover lots at the end of the day's work in glass factories.

*Latticino:* strips of white glass arranged crisscross or in a pattern.

*Millefiori:* literally, "thousand flowers." Colored glass rods arranged to form a design in paperweights, inkstands, doorknobs, buttons, bottles, and vases; also in stoppers for bottles, letter seals, and jewelry.

*Novelties:* odd, often whimsical, pieces of glass both useful and ornamental. Many were made in pressed glass.

*Salts:* small dishes to hold salt at the table. Large ones are known as salt dips, smaller ones for individual use as saltcellers.

*Whimsey:* a glass miniature or other unusual piece made at the end of the day's work.

FOR FURTHER INFORMATION: (see also Chapters VIII and IX):

OLD GLASS PAPERWEIGHTS by Evangeline Bergstrom. New York: Crown Publishers, Inc.

# 11
## Pottery and Porcelain

SILVERSMITHS, BLACKSMITHS, and other metalworkers made many things of which no more could be said than that they were plain, practical, and necessary. But they also made bowls, candlesticks, and other household articles of unsurpassed beauty. This also was true of cabinetmakers and glassblowers. On the other hand, the first small potteries established in the Colonies made only the most utilitarian wares.

Clay suitable for making pottery and porcelain was found in many different areas. As a matter of fact, Indians all over the continent had long been producing their own pottery with their own style of decoration, however crude it might have seemed to the white settlers. Undeniably utilitarian as the Indian pottery was, it was more distinctive than that made by the colonists. The mugs, bowls, platters, and plates produced in their potteries were exceedingly plain and were not all-

important in the kitchen let alone the dining room. Woodenware and pewter were used fully as much, at least on the table for eating.

Throughout the eighteenth century and most of the nineteenth, both everyday earthenware dishes and company porcelain were largely imported, chiefly from England. It was not until 1825, when William Ellis Tucker opened his factory in Philadelphia, that the first porcelain was produced here. By 1850, a considerable variety of earthenware products was being manufactured in the United States, not only along the East Coast where suitable clays existed but also in Ohio and the Midwest.

No strictly new type of china ever has been originated in this country, but characteristic styles were developed in many kinds of pottery. The stoneware jugs, crocks, and bottles for which

Pennsylvania and New York State became famous are only one example.

Few people can bear to throw away old crockery or porcelain. Probably more houses have a half-dozen or so odds and ends of old china standing unused now in cupboards than any other kind of antique household furnishings. A platter, plate, or pitcher prized by grandmother or great-grandmother, who brought it with her from her homeland, may still be displayed proudly by her descendants. Old tableware and ornamental china almost always have an interesting history, whether a piece was brought to this country by its original owner or was purchased here from a merchant who had imported it from England or Europe or who bought his stock from local pottery factories.

Before deciding that grandmother's platter no longer blends with your dining-room decor, or that this spring the cupboard is really going to be cleared out thoroughly, you owe it to yourself to find out what kind of old pottery or porcelain you have. If it's possible to identify the maker from a potter's mark on the underside, or the span of years during which a dish was made by means of such clues as shape, coloring, and decoration, you may find that you have some fairly valuable pieces. There is general interest today in old china, and new uses have been found for pieces that are no longer made. Then, too, collectors always are searching for worthwhile or unusual pieces, and less valuable ones appeal to people who must run a household on a limited budget and, therefore, are willing to buy broken lots of tableware.

No other field of antiques seems to be quite so confusing as this one. Certainly anyone whose knowledge of pottery and porcelain has gone no further than shopping for kitchen and dining-room dishes can be excused for thinking that the remnants of her grandmother's creamware dinner set are porcelain instead of earthenware. (Creamware is a valuable earthenware to be prized as much as some porcelain.)

"China" has become a general term referring to all kinds of dishes used on the table and to ornamental and useful objects such as vases, doorknobs, lamps, and candlesticks. Specifically, it should be the common name for porcelain wares, for the word "china" was borrowed from the country of that name 300 years ago, to describe the

*Sprigged earthenware was popular for tea sets and tableware between 1850 and 1880. The pieces shown, probably made in England, have dainty green and pink sprigs.*

porcelain that was brought from there to Europe and England. This was the first porcelain Westerners had ever seen.

Porcelain is hard, white, thin, lightweight, and vitreous. Most important, it is translucent when held up to the light. The decoration is usually fine. Bone china, which was not made before 1800, is a type of porcelain with an admixture of bone ash from bones calcined in air.

The term "pottery" has a much broader meaning, for it refers to all articles made from clay and hardened by fire. Until Westerners saw the porcelain made by the Chinese and finally learned how to produce a similar ware, their products had been limited to earthenwares and stonewares, both of which are coarser than porcelain. Compared to porcelain, earthenware is opaque and soft. It has a porosity that stoneware lacks, but stoneware is much harder. "Crockery" refers to articles for domestic use, made of glazed earthenware or stoneware.

The basis of both porcelain and pottery is clay. Very little of the great amount of clay to be found around the world is unsuitable for making pottery of some kind. However, fine wares can be made only from certain types of clay that are prepared and mixed with the proper substances. Exposure to high temperatures of different degrees brings about physical changes (in color, hardness, etc.). Firing makes clay arti-

cles among the most durable in the world.

Glaze is a thin, glasslike substance that is poured molten over a clay vessel. It fuses at high temperature to make the clay impervious to liquids. Earthenware, for example, may be unglazed as in the case of bricks and flowerpots, or glazed as in creamware and Delft. The makeup of glaze varies and, according to the type used, so do the texture and appearance of the finished piece. Of the many different kinds of glaze, one is best suited to each major type of pottery. It was discovered long ago that the application of a glaze could change the color of clay when it was fired, and both clear and colored glazes have been used for centuries. Often more than one glaze was applied, each at a different stage of the firing.

Decoration, or at least color, has been common on pottery and porcelain ever since it was first made. The glaze itself is a decoration. This is particularly true on hard-paste porcelain, which does not require a glaze to prevent absorption of liquids, and on earthenwares, to which colored glazes were applied. Other decoration sometimes was done under the glaze, in which case it never wore off no matter how much a piece was handled and used. However, underglaze decoration was limited in colors. Overglaze decoration was not practical for everyday china, even though the resulting colors really were glasslike or vitreous enamels.

An early type of decoration, usually done under a glaze, was slip. This was potter's clay or paste reduced to a liquid (it could be white or colored). It was sometimes trailed on a piece in a quite elaborate, if crude, pattern. When a design was incised through the slip to show the contrasting color of the clay body, the decoration was called scratched or sgraffito.

Painting became the most widely employed decoration. Colored clays, an early method of decoration, are still applied as underglaze painting to some kinds of earthenware and stoneware. Enamels were used on porcelain, and both enameling and painting often were embellished with gold. The use of metallic pigments for luster decoration, which was so popular during the nineteenth century, can be traced back thousands of years to Persia.

About 1753, transfer-printing was originated in England. This process, developed by an engraver, made possible the mass production of a single design (it was fixed under a glaze). It was so much used by English potteries, particularly during the nineteenth century, that it is considered peculiarly English. It was not done to any extent in other countries.

Applied or modeled decoration was used at certain times, especially by German factories. Flowers and fruits are considered much more typical of Meissen than they actually are. The little pink roses and blue forget-me-nots belong to Dresden rather than only to Meissen, and are more often than not twentieth-century embellishments of ornaments.

Highly influential on the decoration of both the pottery and porcelain produced in Europe and England was the porcelain imported from China. This Chinese porcelain, a much finer clay product than any that had ever been made in Western countries, was so admired that both its coloring and its decoration were copied generally. This imitation of Chinese designs began about 1700, probably in France, since it is known as chinoiserie. The finest porcelain factories, and later potteries, in Europe and England deco-

*Scenic plates have been popular for more than 200 years. This small plate in rare mulberry color with Chinese-type decoration has the urn and bird mark of Podmore, Walker & Co., an old English pottery.*

rated their wares with chinoiserie patterns and modeled chinoiserie figures during the eighteenth century. Although a few artists are known to have worked from authentic Oriental pieces, little of the Western chinoiserie looks Chinese. Figures often had European faces, landscapes were fanciful, and often pagodas or latticework in the background merely suggested an Oriental atmosphere. Perhaps because chinoiserie was so imaginative and gay, eighteenth-century pieces are as appealing today as when they were made.

The nineteenth century found a great variety of pottery and porcelain available to Americans, and it is examples of these wares that are most likely to be found here today. Most of them were made in England, but all of the methods worked out during the eighteenth century for Western porcelain and different kinds of earthenware and stoneware were represented, for porcelain and pottery of fine quality were made on the Continent, too. In fact, England and the leading countries in Europe each are noted for more than one distinctive type of pottery and some kind of porcelain. A certain amount of authentic Oriental ware also is to be found in the United States.

EARTHENWARE is perhaps the most common kind of pottery. It is considered coarse in comparison to porcelain and most stoneware. Yet earthenware can be made almost as thin as porcelain and, when it is, usually is called china. However, earthenware is both opaque and porous under the glaze in contrast to porcelain, which is translucent and nonporous. Because many techniques were developed for making, glazing, and decorating earthenware, there are many different types that often are known under names that indicate their place of origin.

SLIPWARE, for example, is an old earthenware whose common name was derived from its decoration. It had been made generally in England as well as in this country wherever potteries were established throughout the 1700's and to about 1850. One of the most notable types is a coarse red earthenware made by the Pennsylvania Germans throughout that period. Slip was trickled over this red earthenware to make a decoration or pattern in low relief. Because tulips were a favorite motif, this is often called tulipware.

Neither tulipware nor much slipware of any kind is likely to be found now lying around unrecognized in cupboards. However, other kinds of porous and soft earthenware and the hard and nonporous stoneware may well be. Some few pieces were produced in this country, but most of them had been made in England or Europe. Although earthenware is not necessarily glazed, many kinds that are can be subdivided according to the kind of glaze and decoration.

Tin-glazed earthenware is called Delft, delft, majolica, or faïence, according to the country in which it was made. Each country developed its own colorings and decoration, although a good deal of both Delft from Holland and delft from England was blue and white.

DELFT, one of the best-known and most familiar of the tin-glazed earthenwares, is the ware for which Holland became famous. The making of tin-glazed earthenware started in that country before 1600. By 1640 the town of Delft was a thriving center, and the industry soon spread to other towns and cities. Delftware is still being made, but experts say the finest was produced between 1640 and about 1750.

Blue decoration against a white background is considered typical of Holland's Delftware (on contemporary pieces, the white is not considered to be as milky, the blue as soft, as on the finest antique ware). But Holland's Deltware was not always blue and white and the decorations were not always derived from the blue and white porcelain the Dutch East India Company brought from China. Nor were they based always on scenic Holland. Potters, however, were inclined toward blue. The second color they developed was purple. Other colors were used to some extent, including yellow, green, and brown during the eighteenth century. Pastels such as soft mauve, pink, orange, or salmon were attractive in floral designs.

In the nineteenth century, scenes based on the daily life of the Dutch became popular. Typical is a set of six plates, each 17 inches in diameter, made to hang on the wall. Each one shows a different village scene, and among them the four seasons are represented. The artist usually signed his name on the front of such plates and the potter's mark was on the back. Only display pieces such as these were signed by the artist.

*Two Delft wall plates, 17 inches in diameter, part of a set of six showing typical Dutch village scenes. The blue and white plates have holes in the back to facilitate hanging.*

Both ornamental and useful Delftware was produced in quantity. Plaques with scrolled edges were as common as outsize plates to hang on the wall. Tiles were made to face fireplaces and to serve as trivets. Large tiles, if they could be called that, were framed as pictures. Then there were vases, bottles, covered jars, figurines, slippers, and shoes. Plates to use on the table, serving plates, platters, and various bowls and dishes were indispensable. Tea caddies, spice boxes, caster sets, inkstands, and inkwells always are interesting. Of the many sizes and kinds of pitchers, one of the most appealing is shaped like a cow and known as a "cow creamer."

England also made a tin-glazed earthenware called delft, probably so named because the technique was introduced into England by Dutch and Flemish potters. A good deal of the English delft was also blue and white, but polychrome decoration was done more than in Holland. Blues, reds, greens, and yellow predominated in the polychrome pieces. English delft inclined more toward floral and fruit decoration instead of copying so much from the Chinese.

Mugs, jugs and plates, candleholders, and tableware of all kinds were made in England too, as well as wall pockets shaped like cornucopias, crocus pots to hang on the wall (they had holes through which the bulbs sprouted), flasks, teapots, punch bowls, and a wealth of decorative things. Many

jugs, mugs, plates, and other dishes still survive. English delft came from potteries established in Lambeth and elsewhere near London as well as in Bristol and Liverpool, good shipping points on the west coast. Liverpool was noted for its tiles, mugs, jugs, and wall pockets.

Delftware is unmistakable, but often it is impossible to know whether an old piece was made in Holland or England —that is, unless it was marked. The ware from Holland usually was. Delft is still being made in Holland. A small percentage of the output is faithful reproductions of eighteenth-century pieces originally made in Holland and England, which is sold chiefly through restorations in the United States.

Delftware from Holland was favored by the Dutch who settled in New York. Whether the English who followed them preferred Dutch or English wares is a question. The Quakers who came from England to Pennsylvania brought with them delft from Bristol or Liverpool, and probably imported some after they were settled in this country.

Tin-glazed earthenware had been made in Spain and Italy for some time before it was introduced into Holland. The Italians, who first saw tin-glazed ware in the fifteenth century, thought it came from the island of Majorca instead of Spain. As a result, their name for it was MAJOLICA. Soon Italy was producing its own quite distinct, tin-glazed majolica, in rich colors such as cobalt-blue, iron-red, copper, purple, orange, and various yellows and greens, and in many new forms and designs.

Americans are familiar, not with antique Italian majolica, but with majolica made in England and the United States in the 1800's. The distinguishing feature of this majolica is the naturalistic shapes that resemble leaves, flowers, vegetables, and fruits. Some pieces have applied decoration in naturalistic forms. Between 1880 and 1892, Griffin, Smith & Hill Co. in Phoenixville, Pennsylvania, marked their pottery "Etruscan Majolica" or "G.S.H." Their products and those of another pottery in Maryland were used as premiums by grocery stores, and housewives evidently enjoyed collecting in

this way. The premium market was a big one.

Highly coveted were large platters in leaf shapes colored more brilliantly than any autumn leaf. Serving dishes with covers were shaped and colored like cauliflower, cabbage, or corn, and looked almost real. An asparagus platter had stalks of asparagus in natural colors. Imagination even stretched to a bread platter displaying a folded white bread cloth bordered in lavender and fringed, with pierced brown handles. Although majolica is famous for its naturalistic forms and colors, many pieces were not shaped quite so realistically but were well covered with raised flowers and fruits.

Since Faenza in Italy was one of the

*The creamware platter with pierced border was probably made at Leeds in the north of England between 1800 and 1820. It is unbelievably light in weight. The squat teapot with luster decoration could have been made at almost any English pottery between 1800 and 1830.*

busiest centers for producing majolica, it was almost inevitable that when the French learned how to make this tin-glazed ware, they called it FAÏENCE. With the assistance of some Italians, they began production during the sixteenth century. Frankly, some faïence is fine enough to be mistaken for porcelain, and the French much preferred it to pewter for their tables. It was especially popular from the end of the seventeenth century to about 1850.

French faïence differed greatly in both form and decoration from Italian majolica and Holland's Delftware. Yellow and green glazes, for example, were used sometimes on faïence, and polychrome decoration was common. Chinese influence was strong at one time, classical motifs later. Attractive painted flowers and figures were also used.

Quimper, a seacoast town in the French department of Finistère, has produced a distinctive faïence identified by the place name since 1690. Best known to Americans, however, is the Quimperware decorated with colorful provincial scenes imported chiefly from about 1900 to 1939. This is fairly plentiful and hard to mistake, although it is not yet antique. Plates, platters, bowls, and butter dishes were almost as popular as the sugar and creamer that might accompany a small teapot. A chamberstick and an inkwell were other useful pieces.

CREAMWARE, a lead-glazed earthenware that made Delft, majolica, and other tin-glazed wares less important, was perfected by Josiah Wedgwood, one of England's most creative pot-ters. Wedgwood's experiments made creamware harder and more durable. In 1765, with the approval of Queen Charlotte, it was renamed Queen's ware. All creamware is lighter in weight than any other kind of earthenware. The surface lends itself to painting and transfer-printing, and the glaze, almost transparent, gives it a creamy color and texture

Creamware soon became immensely popular. Everyone liked it and it was exported to America too. Other potteries in England and on the Continent started to make it, but of them all, the Leeds factory in northern England became the greatest producer of creamware except for Wedgwood between 1780 and 1820.

Most experts agree that Leeds creamware is lighter in weight than that made by any other factory. The glazes also were quite different from Wedgwood's. A pale cream tint was used after 1780, which was harder and more brilliant than the glazes on Wedgwood's creamware. A great deal of the Leeds output was painted in patterns based on flowers, foliage, and birds, often with garlands worked into the designs. Outstanding and individual, however, were the many pieces with pierced borders. Some of these piercings were intricate designs of interlaced circles, ovals, and the like. Twisted handles on coffeepots and teapots were another characteristic.

Thomas Whieldon, who established his pottery in 1740, is especially remembered for his tortoiseshell creamware, which had a mottled brown glaze. It is extremely valuable today. Whieldon also made every kind of pottery that was being produced in the Staffordshire District during the eighteenth century. His china was lightweight and well-proportioned and his glazes were brilliant and varied. Incidentally, Aaron Wood and Josiah Spode, each of whom went on to become a famous potter in his own right, were apprentices to Whieldon, and Josiah Wedgwood was his partner for a time.

ROCKINGHAM was the name acquired by a quite different lead-glazed earthenware that began to be made in 1757. Its distinctive feature was the Rockingham glaze, mottled in shades of brown and buff. It was used first at a pottery in Swinton, Yorkshire, which was owned for a time by the Marquess of Rockingham. This glaze proved to be more distinctive than the earthenware to which it was applied. Before long, many other potteries in England were using a typical Rockingham glaze on a wide variety of practical and useful earthenware products, including teapots, tiles, and pudding molds.

In this country, a similar glaze became typical of pottery produced in Bennington, Vermont, after 1840. This also shaded from brown to buff. Some of the Bennington products had green or blue streaks added to the brown. The wares are sometimes called Bennington-Rockingham. Other potters in St. Johnsbury and Middlebury, Vermont, Baltimore, Maryland, and the Ohio Valley also used a sort of brown Rockingham glaze.

Cow creamers, hound-handled pitchers, and apostle pitchers are famous Bennington articles. Other styles of pitchers and jugs and a varied array of kitchen utensils also were produced. Nothing was too unimportant—or important—including even washboards and cuspidors.

STONEWARE was the traditional pottery of Germany, though it was made in England from at least 1675. It is fired at a much higher temperature than earthenware, is very hard and nonporous. The color ranges from gray to white and also includes some brown.

Some of the best-known pieces of the German stoneware are the beer steins or jugs and tankards formerly used in both homes and taverns. Most people think of them as being gray stoneware with blue decoration. Other colors, chiefly green, red, yellow, and white, also were used for decoration. Pitchers and vases are commonly found, and the vases often are of fine quality.

SALT GLAZE is one of the unusual stonewares. It had both a distinctive texture and color that were the result of table salt being thrown over the ware before the last firing (glaze in powder form was applied before the first firing). Because the salt vaporized, the surface of the finished piece became pitted or bumpy, rather like the skin of an orange. English potters duplicated the technique of salt-glazed stoneware before 1700, and a small amount was made in the United States after 1850.

Most of the salt-glaze ware a person might find now undoubtedly would have been made during the nineteenth century and probably had been imported from England. Staffordshire was the district where much of it was produced. A considerable amount of gray-white ware formed in molds was sold in the United States during the 1800's.

*Stoneware with a salt glaze has a pitted texture. This gray-white pitcher, made in Staffordshire in the early 1800's, has a molded pattern consisting of rope and calla lilies and their foliage.*

The molds produced a surface pattern —perhaps of rope in a geometrical arrangement, basketweave, naturalistic designs such as ferns and flowers, or callas with flower, leaves, and stems. This salt glaze seems not to have been made in sets, but such pieces as pitchers, syrup jugs, bowls, and serving dishes were produced in a variety of designs.

A good deal of the stoneware made in the United States since 1800 is likely to be found in houses in town as well as in the country. It probably will be thick with cobwebs and so dirty that it's impossible to tell what color it is, but it's well worth cleaning up and washing. It will turn out to be one of the utilitarian containers or storage vessels. Crocks of all sizes and shapes, jugs, quart containers for milk, and catsup bottles the size of pop bottles are the most likely pieces. These stoneware containers were invaluable for storing milk, molasses, cider, vinegar, and other liquids, as well as pickled foods, preserves, and butter.

Simply decorated stoneware of this sort was used for other kitchen articles too. Salt crocks to hang on the wall, for example, are charming and far more decorative than the storage utensils. Some kitchen stoneware displayed colored glazes, often in shades of blue, and molded designs in low relief such as butterflies. If you're lucky, you may come upon a batter jug, a modest-sized pitcher used to pour batter onto the griddle. Ring bottles, which were formed as rings two to three inches wide, are more unusual. Ink bottles, large and small, may seem almost unidentifiable until you stop to consider what purpose a rectangular piece without a stopper might have served.

The production of this practical stoneware started in New Jersey, and as proper clays were found or cheap transportation arranged, spread to southern Connecticut, other New England States, New York, and later Ohio. A good deal was made in potteries in the Ohio Valley. Until about 1800, most of this stoneware was given a salt glaze.

Albany slip, a type with tan or brown glaze inside, was made in the early 1800's. Stoneware with brown glaze inside and out, made later in the century, seems less attractive. After 1850, colored glazes gave stoneware an entirely different appearance and a completely different texture from that of salt glaze.

Most prized of this nineteenth-century stoneware are the gray or buff pieces with simple decoration. Between 1825 and 1880, the decoration was done mostly with slip, cobalt-blue in color. Some decorations were stenciled after 1850, and for this birds, chickens, flowers and foliage, and rural motifs were popular. For example, a bird perched on a leafy branch might be stenciled on each side of a jar or crock. On pieces that would be lifted and carried, handles were molded into shape on either side. Removable stoneware covers were made for pails and churns, but jugs and small bottles were stopped with corks.

STONE CHINA, another type of stoneware, was first introduced by the Spode pottery in England for tableware. It was cheaper and more durable than the new European and English porcelains.

IRONSTONE CHINA followed in 1813, when the Mason brothers in England applied for a patent on their process. This type of stoneware was extremely popular throughout the nineteenth century. It is hard, glossy, and white with a blue tint. It is sometimes called white granite, although the name ironstone originally was intended to indicate its hardness and durability. Many other English potters were soon making ironstone and it has been produced in America since about 1870. Currently, reproductions of popular nineteenth-century patterns are being made.

The usual mental picture conjured up by the word *ironstone* is of rather heavy-looking, opaque, and glossy white china with no colored glaze or decoration—the sort that was so popular from 1850 to about 1890. The tureens and other covered dishes were angular. Every possible piece from the tureen to the ladle that was kept in it was made of this ironstone, which might better be called graniteware or white granite. However, not all of this ironstone was plain. Some had molded decoration, such as a sheaf of wheat.

Actually, the first ironstone made by the Masons was beautifully decorated in colored enamels and often touched with gilding. This was done on the finest-quality ware. On the less expensive, transfer-printed designs were done in color. Designs in the manner of the Chinese were used to a great extent, especially those with flowers, birds, and butterflies. Some scenes that included figures also were used.

JASPER and BASALT are very special kinds of stoneware indeed. These fine-grained, smooth, unglazed wares were originated by Josiah Wedgwood and introduced by him in 1774. Both are still being made, the jasper in greater quantity than basalt. The latter is a black stoneware mainly used for decorative pieces. Candlesticks, ewers, plaques, and medallions are stunning when made of basalt, and pots for tea, coffee, and chocolate are handsome.

Jasper, a hard stoneware with a mat surface, is always decorated with cameo designs in relief. It combines two colors, one of which is the white decoration. If three or more colors appear in a piece, you can be sure it is very old and very rare. The best-known jasper has a medium blue (often called Wedgwood blue) ground with white relief ornament. However, a dark blue, lavender, sage-green, olive-green, lilac, and yellow were made in Josiah Wedgwood's days. The yellow is extremely rare now.

Jasperware was both ornamental and useful. Shoe buckles, beads, and jewelry were common during the eighteenth century. So were plaques and medallions to hang on the wall and cameos to be mounted in bracelets, lockets, and other jewelry. The medallions frequently displayed portraits of famous persons, including long-dead emperors, kings, and queens and current heroes—even Napoleon, who was so hated by the British. Candlesticks, inkstands, and vases of jasperware always have been popular and are extremely decorative.

Wedgwood himself considered the perfecting of jasper one of his most important achievements. That he was right is proved by its enduring popularity and the eagerness with which even contemporary jasper is purchased. However, his introduction of creamware was perhaps more important to many more people.

The eighteenth century would be notable in the field of pottery if only for the many types of earthenware and stoneware it added to commerce. Overshadowing that achievement, however, was the first successful attempt by a Westerner to produce porcelain, which had been unknown in Europe and England until pieces were brought back from China in the 1500's. Both European and English potters greatly admired the fine, white porcelain from China, and well they might, for the Chinese were the greatest potters the world has ever known. It took many years of struggle and experimenting before Western potters were able to produce a comparable porcelain. The first halfway successful attempt was made in Florence, Italy, between 1575 and 1588. However, it was about 1708 before a true hard-paste porcelain was produced by Johann Friedrich Böttger at the Meissen factory near Dresden, Germany. Perhaps because he was the first, Germany became as outstanding for porcelain as England always had been for the coarser kinds of pottery.

PORCELAIN is classified as either hard-paste or soft-paste. In either case it consists of the body, made of a mixture of clay and other ingredients (often referred to as the paste), and the glaze, which forms the vitreous surface and fuses with the body so that the two become indistinguishable. The principal ingredient of hard-paste porcelain is a clay known as kaolin, which is combined with a siliceous material (in China this was petuntse). The glaze is a similar material.

Soft-paste porcelain is not really soft. It too is hard, white, translucent, and vitreous, but both the materials and methods of production differ from those for hard-paste. It is almost impossible to tell offhand whether porcelain is soft-paste or hard-paste. However, if soft-paste porcelain becomes chipped, it usually shows a granular surface.

BONE CHINA falls between hard-paste and soft-paste porcelains. Some class it as soft-paste. There are con-flicting claims for the credit of introducing bone china. Experiments based on adding bone ash to known formulas for porcelain were undertaken before 1750 and continued at several potteries. One of the first to work with bone ash was William Cookworthy who was connected with three or more potteries. It was at least 1800 before bone china was marketed and perhaps the first potter to do so was Josiah Spode. Although the Wedgwood potteries never produced porcelain in an amount comparable to their other products, Josiah Wedgwood II introduced bone china in 1812. Excellent as Wedgwood's bone china was, the state of business after the years of war with Napoleon forced its discontinuance in 1815 and production was not revived until the 1870's.

Unlike earthenwares and stonewares, of which numerous kinds were made, there are only three basic types of porcelain—hard-paste, soft-paste, and bone china. Variations in these basic kinds have come about because such a great many factories were engaged in producing porcelain. Thus, the shape of a porcelain piece and the decoration help to establish where and approximately when it was made. From the time porcelain was originally produced in Germany, it was prized for tableware, figures and groups, and ornamental pieces.

The Meissen factory near Dresden, where hard-paste porcelain was first made in Europe, has continued to be important up to modern days. It is the best-known of the several potteries in and near Dresden, but all of them helped to make Dresden one of several notable centers in Germany for porcelain manufacture. During the eighteenth and nineteenth centuries other factories were located in Berlin, Nymphenburg, Frankenthal, Fürstenberg, Ludwigsburg, and Ansbach. Vienna was another important center. Many of the porcelain factories in Germany as well as in other European countries were under the patronage or protection of royalty.

The French, like the English, were making a soft-paste porcelain long before a hard-paste one. Sèvres is the name usually mentioned in a hushed voice, but it is not the oldest pottery in France nor was it the first to produce porcelain. Sèvres's first great accomplishment was modeled flowers, which were used to decorate clocks, candlesticks, vases, and the like. They are considered as fine as those made earlier by Meissen. Saint-Cloud and Chantilly are older names in French pottery and porcelain, and Strasbourg and Limoges are other important ones. All French porcelain is noted for its artistic painting and decoration.

Naples, Venice, and Florence were the important centers of porcelain manufacture in Italy. The most revered name is that of Capo-di-Monte, a factory established near Naples in 1743. Any pieces of Capo-di-Monte found today probably were made during the

nineteenth century at another factory that purchased the original Capo-di-Monte molds.

In England, porcelain was produced in factories established on the outskirts of London at Bow and Chelsea-Derby in the nineteenth century. The Spode pottery, which was producing earthenware during the 1700's, began to make porcelain about 1800, and various other potteries in Staffordshire, including Wedgwood, also added porcelain to their earthenware and stoneware lines. The Worcester Royal Porcelain Company in Worcestershire, which was established in 1748, has been making porcelain for more than 200 years. Leeds, at least briefly, became as famous for porcelain as for its creamware. Experts say the most perfect porcelain ever produced in England came from Swansea in Wales between 1814 and 1820. Later, the men responsible for it joined the Coalport potteries, where much fine china still is being manufactured.

By the early 1800's, pottery of all kinds, chiefly earthenware and porcelain, was being beautifully made not only in quantity but in diversity. Although factories became firmly established in the United States during the nineteenth century, most china was still imported. Almost all of it had something to recommend it, and tracing its origin can be a fascinating game. Besides, unless you know where and approximately when pottery or porcelain was made, it will be impossible to decide whether or not you are selling it advantageously.

After the War of 1812, English potters actually studied the American market, and an amazing percentage of their output was decorated with scenes, portraits, and themes based on places, events, and people in this country. Almost as important was the china brought to America from China. More than a dozen different kinds that were popular during the Victorian era are likely to be found anywhere in this country today.

CANTON is one of the most coveted wares. It was brought to the United States continuously from the 1780's on, after this country commenced trade with China, and between 1800 and 1860 clipper ships carried a great deal of it to East Coast seaports. Canton China was unmarked at first, but after 1890 the United States tariff laws required that all ware intended for sale in this country be stamped with its place of origin.

Canton china is primarily blue and white, although the shade of the blue used for decoration varied considerably. Motifs, typically Chinese, included a teahouse, a bridge, willow trees, a flight of birds, and a landscape background (the popular Willow pattern, which includes some of these motifs, is the creation of English potters).

Cantonware approaches stoneware, since it is heavier and thicker than fine Chinese porcelain. Therefore it became the everyday china of families who owned it, but the twentieth century has brought it out of the kitchen. It was made in dinner sets, tea sets, and serving dishes for the table, as well as water bottles, ginger jars, and other pieces that were chiefly ornamental here. The finest-quality Canton is found in old pieces that have clear, sharp decoration against a blue-gray background. After 1850, the designs were likely to be blurred and the blue not so attractive. There is a lot of Cantonware in the United States, some of it undoubtedly not recognized for what it is. Although not really scarce, Canton is prized and many persons who have inherited a few pieces of it search for others to fill out their sets.

*Cantonware, a heavy pottery with blue decoration consisting of typical Chinese motifs, was brought to this country from China between 1800 and 1860.*

Thus, there is a market for both early and late pieces.

LOWESTOFT is another ware that came directly from China—not from the town in England of that name. It was neither made nor décorated at Lowestoft, in spite of books that have claimed either one or the other for it. As a matter of fact, Lowestoft was a porcelain-making town, but the so-called Lowestoft dishes made in China are quite different from any made in Lowestoft, England. The Chinese ware is a hard-paste porcelain with a white to gray background color. Unlike Cantonware, Lowestoft was painted to order in China for English and American customers. The decoration was Occidental rather than Oriental, and included armorial designs as well as such typically Western motifs as a horn of plenty. The coloring of the decoration often contained some blue but was not confined to it; pink, yellow, and a bright green were fully as common.

FLOWING BLUE, also known as Flow Blue, Flowering Blue, and Old Blue, is not a product of China any more than Willowware is. English and later some American potters, inspired by Chinese ware, also made a good deal of earthenware and porcelain that was decorated in blue against a white background. Whatever you call this china, the name is derived honestly. Flowering Blue is a logical name for it because of the repeated use of flowers in the designs. Equally fitting is Flowing Blue because of the tendency of the good strong blue to flow beyond the outlines of the decorative design

*The Flowing Blue earthenware plate at the left dates from the 1810-30 period. The design, which combines a cowry and other shells with flowers and aquatic foliage, is known as Shell. The platter at the right is decorated only with flowers and foliage, and the little sauce dish employs Chinese motifs. All were made in England.*

and tint the cream or white base. Yet the design stood out distinctly enough and the flowing tendency of the blue enriched the base color.

Although flowering and foliage patterns always were popular for Flowing Blue china, the trend of the designs changed from time to time. Between 1800 and the 1820's, shells were important; they were often combined with flowers. Much later, concentric circles, medallions, and scrolls were used effectively.

A *Staffordshire teapot with a capacity of 1½ quarts, part of a tea set in a blue and white pattern called Carleton.* (Circa 1830-50.)

Flowing Blue is earthenware, and almost all of it was made in the county of Staffordshire in England. Staffordshire has been a center of pottery-making since the days of the Romans. Many of England's most famous potteries—Wedgwood, Spode, Davenport, Enoch Wood & Sons, James Edwards, J. & W. Ridgway, Thomas Mayer, William Adams & Sons, and many others—had their factories in this district. Earthenware, ironstone, salt glaze, jasper, bone china, porcelain, and all kinds of ceramics have been produced in Staffordshire, and some of the most famous processes, such as those for making jasper, basalt, and bone china, were originated there.

STAFFORDSHIRE has come to be a generic term and a synonym for transfer-printed decoration. This method, which was worked out about 1755, has been used chiefly to decorate earthenware. It involves far less handwork than any other method of decorating

china because the design is engraved on a copper plate and thereafter can be reproduced over and over. Portions of the transfer-printed pattern sometimes were colored by hand, but this is by no means true of most of the ware. Before the discovery of transfer-printing, however, each piece was decorated wholly by hand.

Blue and red were the first colors used for transfer-printing, and blue continued to be a favorite throughout the 1800's. The deep, dark, strong blues belong to the late 1700's and up to about 1850; thereafter, the blues became lighter and sometimes almost faded. After 1830, other colors and sometimes a combination of colors were plentiful. Pink and rose, mulberry, lavender, green, light blue, sepia or brown, and also black were used by all potteries. Black transfer-printing was a specialty of Liverpool potters from 1790 to about 1815. Green and

*Teapots have been important since before 1700. The small one is salt glaze and was made in Ireland. The other is brown and white transfer-printed, and was made in Staffordshire, England, after 1850.*

pink is one of the popular combinations sought by collectors. A good mulberry is probably the rarest of Staffordshire ware nowadays, and green, lavender, and brown are much scarcer than blue, rose, and pink.

Scenes and landscapes were the basis of Staffordshire decoration. Castles, villas, and pastoral views often were

*An old and rare Staffordshire platter in blue and white in the so-called Elephant design. Animals were unusual as the basis for a pattern by English potters.*

quite romanticized. They formed the center pattern, and plates and other pieces were given a flower and foliage border. The name of the pattern was stamped on the underside even when no potter's mark was. A brown Staffordshire pattern called Alhambra featured very English-looking castles. Little imagination is needed to accept the building in Abbey Ruins by T. Mayer as just that; this pattern in light blue had two cows grazing among the flowers and foliage in the foreground. Arabesque was a dark blue pattern with Chinese-type buildings, a bridge leading from one of them to the river below, and tall trees overhanging and framing the design. Lausanne Villa, transfer-printed in lavender, owed much more to China than to Switzerland or England for its house and church, the boat and the figures in the latter. All of these patterns, typically, had predominantly floral borders ex-

China made in England after 1842 can be identified by the Registry mark required by the British Patent Office. The blue and white plate (left) bears two marks on the underside (right). The top one is that of the manufacturer in Staffordshire — his name, John Ridgway & Co., appears on the loop; the words "Doria Stone" on the ribbon ends refer to the type of pottery. The official Registry mark (below), deciphered by means of the key, gives the following information: the IV indicates that the plate is earthenware; the C that it was made in 1844; the I (left), in July; the 20 (right), on that day of the month; the 5 at the bottom, the name of the potter or firm.—Ted Eastwood

cept Arabesque, which featured small shells as much as blossoms.

The Flowing Blue earthenware made in Staffordshire was transfer-printed too, but it is so distinctive that it is classified with a group name of its own. Much of what is now called commemorative ware also was transfer-printed in blue, and it is amazing how many towns and cities in the United States served as themes for commemorative Staffordshire earthenware. The visit of Lafayette in 1824 was recorded from his landing through practically every stop of his triumphal tour.

Other colors besides blue were used on transfer-printed ware for the American market. Views, both current and historical in the United States, portraits of patriots and heroes, and patriotic emblems were made in quantity. In the late 1800's, the souvenir plates that became popular purchases at summer resorts and important cities were also made in Staffordshire, quite often in transfer-printed blue.

GAUDY DUTCH and SPATTER-WARE also were made in Staffordshire in the early 1800's, chiefly for export to the United States, where both were popular among the Pennsylvania Germans. Gaudy Dutch, as its name implies, was highly decorated in red, yellow, and blue. Patterns consisted of butterflies, carnations, dahlias, roses, grapes, and doves. Look in the cupboards for Gaudy Dutch if any of your family ever lived in or around Philadelphia, Lancaster, and York, Pennsylvania.

GAUDY IRONSTONE is heavier and thicker but almost as brightly decorated. It was not made for as long a time as Gaudy Dutch. Gaudy Welsh, with blue-purple decoration, is considered more crude.

Although spatterware was a favorite of the Pennsylvania Germans, it was sold as far west as Ohio and actually was not limited to one area, as was the Gaudy Dutch. Spatterware is easy to recognize and most attractive. Another name for it is spongeware, stemming from the fact that the border was colored by daubing color on the white clay body with a sponge. (Whieldon had used a sponge for his tortoiseshell ware in the previous century.) A deep bowl or a plate may have a colored border, often blue, that was applied with the sponge, but this border will be broken regularly to display a flower in natural colors against a white background. A ewer or teapot sometimes was spattered or sponged all over with color, but somewhere it also would display a design against the white background. Roses, tulips, and other flowers, peacocks, and eagles were popular motifs.

The creamware originated by Wedgwood continued to be made in Staf-

*Staffordshire pieces were transfer-printed in various colors. The dinner plate is a pattern known as Lausanne Villa, lavender on white. The tea plate has a pink border surrounding a design in green, a popular combination of colors.*

*The "Old Man of the Mountains" plate at the left is patterned after nineteenth-century souvenir plates, but was made in Staffordshire only fifteen years ago. The other souvenir plate displays scenes of Great Barrington, Massachusetts; it was probably made in Staffordshire about 60 years ago.*

fordshire throughout the nineteenth century. Today, some people are inclined to push aside a creamware plate or platter as "that old kitchen one." It is old, but too valuable to push aside. Many of these leftover pieces of nineteenth-century creamware are decorated simply with a colored edging along the border. In their day they were referred to as the "blue-edged" or "green-edged china."

MOCHA CREAMWARE more correctly should be called BANDED CREAMWARE. It is neither mocha-nor coffee-colored, although shades of cocoa and brown were used in the decoration. So were yellows, pale blue, and green. However, one of the several patterns made in England was called Mocha; it resembled seaweed and was a light brown in color. There were also a Plain Banded pattern with bands in alternating colors, Cat's Eye, which

had a round motif half dark and half light, and several marbleized patterns.

Mochaware, as all such patterns now are called in this country, was made in England before 1800 and throughout that century. Some small amount probably was made in this country too. Dinner sets were not made, but washstand sets were. Other Mocha creamware was used chiefly in kitchens—jugs, creamers, covered sugar bowls, open salts, mustard pots, eggcups, tumblers, coffeepots and teapots, cups and saucers, bowls, and vegetable dishes. Collectors began to discover Mocha in the 1960's, and it is now one of the fast-selling types of old china.

LUSTERWARE, much easier to recognize, was a great Victorian favorite, especially for tea and dessert sets and for odd pieces. This also is ranked as a collector's item. It was something new that ushered in the nineteenth century in England, although Josiah Wedgwood had started experimenting with lusters in the late 1700's. By the early 1800's, potters throughout the Staffordshire District were making lusterware. The idea of decorating china with metallic or luster pigments actually came from the Near East, where it had been used by the Persians as early as the ninth century. Lusters were probably the Persians' greatest contribution to ceramic decoration. The Moors introduced lusters to Spain, and from there they began a long and interesting history in Europe.

Old luster varies from a rather dull

*The plate, decorated with dots and border of copper luster, was made in England. The pitcher, solidly covered with copper luster on which pastel flowers were painted, was imported into Canada from France. (Circa 1850.)*

yellow to golden brown, and from olive-green to a metallic iridescence. The lusterware made in England and imported freely into America during the nineteenth century falls into several color groups. Real metals—gold, platinum, and copper—were used to make the metallic pigments.

Silver luster, achieved by the application of a pigment made from platinum, was made first as a less costly imitation of real silver pieces. Sugar bowls, creamers, and teapots were solidly covered with silver luster. Any such pieces found today will not gleam like silver but are likely to be darkened.

After 1820, copper luster became most common, although gold and "pink" luster were great favorites. Purple luster was much darker. A mottled pink and white luster, made about 1850, was called marbled or spotted. Copper luster, which was derived from copper, was sometimes used to cover an entire piece. Mugs and pitchers were often as completely covered with it as sugar bowls and creamers had formerly been with silver luster. Frequently, however, the copper-luster covering was broken up by a band of a transfer-printed or embossed design.

Gold pigment produced a range of shades, most often pink or rose but also orange and purple. The pink luster tea sets so greatly prized by Victorian ladies were basically a gold luster. In a tea set, the pieces were not covered

*A silver-colored luster made from platinum was used at first as an imitation of real silver, as on the creamer at the right. The pitcher is covered with copper luster and decorated with a band of leaves in a rosy copper color.*

with luster but decorated with it in designs that were mostly floral and foliage and not strongly naturalistic. Sometimes part of the pattern was hand-painted, as in the case of a strawberry luster pattern where the berries and a bit of green clinging to them were painted, and the three-parted leaves and the lines forming the wide border were a mulberry-colored luster. Green leaves frequently were painted on tea sets where the chief decoration was blossoms and lines or scrolls in shades of pink, rose, and perhaps orange.

Tea sets usually were some kind of porcelain, but most luster decoration was done on earthenware. Mugs, pitchers, bowls, and other useful tableware, as well as vases and ornamental pieces, were made in profusion.

Not to be confused with metallic luster decoration is the pearl luster or iridescence typical of Belleek and Brianchon. The nacreous luster that reflects light somewhat like mother-of-pearl was patented by a French potter, J. J. H. Brianchon, in 1857. It was at about this same time that porcelain manufacture began at Belleek, which is not far from Belfast, Ireland.

Belleek porcelain has become as synonymous with Ireland as Waterford glass and damask linen. Some tin-glazed ware and creamware had been made in Ireland during the eighteenth century. Suitable clay for porcelain was not found there until the 1850's—at Belleek. The factory is still in business.

Belleek is a soft-paste porcelain, ex-

*A plate from a set of Staffordshire transfer-printed in brown on white earthenware in a design known as Alhambra. (Circa 1830-42.)*

Lusters were used for decoration, as on the creamer, with shades of pink and orange. They were also used to cover entire pieces, as on the mug, which has rose-colored leaves on a band of light copper, and the mustard pot, which has bands of deep blue as decoration.

ceedingly thin and with an iridescence that is colorless or palest cream. The decoration was either painted or modeled, usually in pink or green. Baskets with a modeled handle and roses attached to the rim, an old Belleek specialty, are being reproduced now. Because of Belleek's proximity to the sea, shells, corals, and mermaids were also favorite shapes and decorations. These are not always as attractive as the contemporary shamrock decoration. Tea sets and vases are the pieces most likely to be found in the United States today.

The resemblance to Belleek of some contemporary pieces of Lenox porcelain made in Trenton, New Jersey, is not accidental. Walter Scott Lenox, an American born in Trenton of Scotch-Irish ancestry, became interested as a boy in the pottery factories in and around his home city. In 1889 he became a partner in the Ceramic Art Co.; later he became full owner, and

in 1906 changed the name of the factory to Lenox, Inc.

Walter Lenox's aim always was to make porcelain that would rank with the finest made anywhere in the world. In his early years, he worked at producing a creamy, iridescent ware like that

*"Pink" luster tea sets were extremely popular during Victorian days. The cup, saucer, and serving plate shown here might have been made at any time between 1820 and 1870.*

from Belleek, Ireland. Later he worked out his own formula for a porcelain that is creamy and extremely thin but lacks the iridescence of Belleek.

Since Lenox ware is still being made, much that is in homes today is far from being antique. A pitcher or a decorative fern dish in Lenox Belleek made during the 1890's is a valuable find. Doubtless the swans, salts, and other delicate pieces as well as the place settings presently being made by the Lenox factory will be exciting possessions 75 to 100 years from now. Six Lenox china marks have been used since 1890, and the word Belleek or Lenox appears on each one.

Preceding Lenox in the making of fine porcelain in the United States was the comparatively short-lived venture of William Ellis Tucker in Philadelphia, Pennsylvania. He founded his pottery in 1825. After his death in 1832, his brother Joseph and a partner managed the firm until about 1838, when it ceased manufacturing hard-paste porcelain. Tea and table services, jugs, vases, fruit baskets, cologne bottles, and figures were produced in quite some quantity in view of the short time the firm operated. The decoration, applied by hand, can be classified either as landscapes or sprigged patterns, and gilding was used with both. Tucker porcelain is very nice indeed.

As distinctive although an entirely different ware came from a famous American pottery at Dedham, Massachusetts.

The production of this pottery or crackleware began in 1860. The factory was founded in Chelsea, Massachusetts, by Alexander W. Robertson, and in 1895 was moved to Dedham and the name changed.

Dedham pottery is easy to recognize. The gray-white base has blue decoration, and in the glaze there is a cobwebby effect of blue; this, in fact, gave rise to the name crackleware. The designs look as though they were stenciled. The most popular pattern was one with a rabbit. Others were based on apples, the azalea, butterfly, chicken, clover, crab, duck, lion, owl, turtle, water lily, and horse chestnut. The age of a piece of Dedham pottery is easy to tell by the mark, which was changed every few years. The last one used, from 1929 to 1943, was a rabbit mark with the word *Registered*. Since Dedham is no longer being made, examples become more valuable each year.

From 1840 until well into the 1900's, Haviland porcelain was the "best" china in many an American household. Actually, a set of Haviland was as traditional for a bride (as a present from her family) as rice at her wedding. David Haviland, whose ancestors had come to America in 1640, settled at Limoges in France in 1839 to produce this fine china, expressly for export to the United States.

HAVILAND CHINA is porcelain, noted for its translucency and hardness, which are the result of the temperature at which it is fired. The temperature seals the pattern in color so that it never wears off. Delicate floral patterns in pastel colors with the handles and other small areas gilded are typical of Haviland in the late 1800's and early 1900's. Cornflowers, forget-me-nots, roses, mignonette, and other dainty blossoms were made in lovely colors. Not all patterns, of course, were floral, but all of them are delicate-looking.

The most prized Haviland china is stamped with the firm's mark curving over the word *Limoges*, and underneath this appears *Imported by* (name of American retail firm). Stamped above all this in another color is *Haviland France*. Since about 1940, Havi-

land china has been made in both France and the United States. The patterns are different in each country, and of course the potter's marks are different.

Limoges has long been one of the centers for porcelain-making in France. Both hard-paste and soft-paste porcelains have been made there since 1771 by many other firms in addition to Haviland, which currently is the most famous of the operating factories. Porcelain stamped *Limoges* never has been noted for its decoration and, consequently, dainty floral patterns are typical of most of the Limoges to be found now.

Royal Copenhagen, made in Denmark, also was imported into the United

*Haviland china has been imported from the French city of Limoges since 1840. Dainty floral patterns like this one are typical of the porcelain sets made in the 1890's and usually given to brides.*

*From about 1890 to 1910, china plates of various sizes and many serving and ornamental pieces were hand-painted with realistic flower designs.*

States in considerable quantity from 1875 to 1900. As a matter of fact, hard-paste porcelain has been made in Denmark since 1772. The famous Bing and Grøndahl, which makes the Christmas plates, was established in 1853. These plates, with a different design each year chosen by means of a competition among leading artists, have been made annually for more than sixty years. Blue with perhaps a little buff or gray decoration against a white background are typical not only of the Christmas plates but also of most Danish porcelain. It was made in dinner sets, of course, as well as in such notable items as chocolate pots and coffeepots, tureens, and plaques.

Between 1890 and 1915, HAND-PAINTED CHINA also was extremely popular as a bridal gift or a remembrance on some special occasion. China-painting was as important an accomplishment for young ladies at

that time as fancy embroidery, and many young girls took special lessons in the art; china-painting clubs even became quite widespread. The more gifted of these painters worked free-hand or copied their designs; others traced and followed a pattern. Many charming pieces much too pretty to throw away are still around.

Flowers were the basis for hand-painted designs. Each dessert plate in a set of a dozen would be decorated with a different flower. The violet, pansy, garden and wild rose, arbutus, apple blossom, lilac, and chrysanthemum were favorites. These were painted most realistically, with buds and foliage, in pastel colors. Three sizes of plates were common—dessert, bread-and-butter, and large ones for serving. Equally favored by the china-painters were salt and pepper shakers, creamer and sugar bowl sets, sauce bowls, candy and bonbon dishes, pin trays, and trinket boxes. Many hand-painted vases, large and small, seem just as attractive today, and are not to be compared with some of the other late-Victorian horrors.

Not do-it-yourself, but commercially produced, were Gibson Girl plates, also a turn-of-the-century fashion. The Royal Doulton pottery reproduced a series of twenty-four of Charles Dana Gibson's drawings. Other portrait plates were popular in the late 1800's too. And Kate Greenaway reproductions on mugs, salt shakers, and children's sets were favorites during the 1880's and 1890's. Rose O'Neill's kewpie dolls, featured in magazine illustrations, appeared on plates, cups and saucers, and tea sets made in Germany and sold here around 1900.

Calendar plates were made in this country, a different design each year from 1906 through 1929. Most of them had the months of the year imprinted around the rim, and a design in the center that might be timely — the Panama Canal or an airplane—or sentimental. Less often the calender was placed in the center of the plate. ABC plates were made also—both of pottery and of other materials such as glass and tin. These alphabet plates were meant for children.

Except for items specifically made elsewhere, such as Gibson Girl plates, a good many of these china oddities as well as a great deal of earthenware were being made in the United States by 1900. Quite a long time before this, the principal centers for white earthenware had been established along both banks of the Ohio River in West Virginia and in East Liverpool and other Ohio cities. New Jersey and New York State also had important pottery factories.

Nineteenth-century American factories used a variety of marks on their wares, but earlier pottery and porcelain from abroad are much harder to identify. More often than not, potters marked their wares. However, sometimes these marks are complete and descriptive and sometimes they mean next to nothing. A plate made 150 years ago that has no mark except a crescent on the underside, or a pitcher that has only a number, is baffling, to say the least. Occasionally, only the name of

*The salt crock of blue glazed stoneware was made in the Ohio Valley. The two earthenware jars were made originally for crackers but are now used for a plant and a potpourri. (Circa 1890-1910.)*

the pattern is on the underside. Later, both the pattern and firm names were given.

Marking was common in Europe. Porcelain made at Meissen in Germany, in France, and in England in the 1700's was usually marked. In fact, such firms as Meissen and Wedgwood have used a whole series of different marks between 1700 and the present time. On a good deal of tableware, mostly earthenwares made between 1825 and 1842, the trade name of the pattern was the only identification.

A plate made by T. Mayer, Longport, in the pattern Abbey Ruins could only have been made between 1820 and 1829 at Stoke-on-Trent, whereas another plate in a pattern called Arabesque was made during the 1830's at Henley because it bears not only the pattern name but also the firm name of T. J. & J. Mayer. There was also a Mayer Pottery Company established in Beaver Falls, Pennsylvania, in 1881, but its marks are quite different from those of the earlier Mayer brothers, potters in Staffordshire, England.

Starting in 1842 in England, a system of marking was required by the British Patent Office. This "Registry" mark not only indicated that the design was registered at the British Patent Office, but made it possible to decipher the exact year, month, and day any object was made, if a person had the key. Most potters used their own trademark in addition to the Registry mark. The

key for the years 1842 to 1867 was as follows:

TABLE 1

| I — metal | III — glass |
| II — wood | IV — earthenware |

TABLE 2

| | | |
|---|---|---|
| X — 1842 | P — 1851 | Z — 1860 |
| H — 1843 | D — 1852 | R — 1861 |
| C — 1844 | Y — 1853 | O — 1862 |
| A — 1845 | J — 1854 | G — 1863 |
| I — 1846 | E — 1855 | N — 1864 |
| F — 1847 | L — 1856 | W — 1865 |
| U — 1848 | K — 1857 | Q — 1866 |
| S — 1849 | B — 1858 | T — 1867 |
| V — 1850 | M — 1859 | |

TABLE 3

| | | |
|---|---|---|
| C — January | E — May | D — September |
| G — February | M — June | B — October |
| W — March | I — July | K — November |
| H — April | R — August | A — December |

The Registry mark was diamond-shaped, with circles or curved lines at the corners to set off the key letters and numerals. The class and year were shown at the apex of the diamond, the month at the left corner, the day opposite at the right, and the potter or parcel at the base.

A similar Registry mark with a different key was used from 1868 to 1883. In this, the Roman numeral at the top indicated the type of ware manufactured, as it did in the earlier mark. The number in the circle below the Roman numeral indicated the day of the month; the letter in the bottom of the mark, the month (these were the same as on the first key); the number in the left-hand corner, the manufacturer; and the letter in the right-hand corner, the year, as follows:

TABLE 4

| X — 1868 | U — 1874 | Y — 1879 |
|----------|----------|----------|
| H — 1869 | S — 1875 | J — 1880 |
| C — 1870 | V — 1876 | E — 1881 |
| A — 1871 | P — 1877 | L — 1882 |
| I — 1872 | D — 1878 | K — 1883 |
| F — 1873 | | |

Marks were scratched, impressed, painted, or printed—usually on the underside of a piece of china. If you can identify the mark of a firm that has been in business for many years, it will help to date the piece and hence give you a more accurate idea of its value. But, unfortunately, marks are not the most reliable method of dating and judging china, for sometimes they were changed deliberately. Thus, though it may be a satisfaction to interpret them, they are not always accurate. Other clues to the kind of china and its age are the type of body, the glaze, coloring, modeling, and decoration. Also, since 1890, the United States has required that the country of origin be stamped on the base of every piece of china.

Many types of pottery and porcelain that were invented during the 1700's are still being made. The Wedgwood firm, for example, is still making jasperware. Then there are reproductions of a similar ware with white decoration against a blue background that are being made in Japan. The great Wedgwood firm, of course, is the one founded by Josiah Wedgwood. But there is another Wedgwood firm that is not nearly so old, which was founded by Enoch Wedgwood and confined itself to making earthenware tableware.

Pottery, including as it does the various earthenwares and stonewares, is much more varied than porcelain. The distinction usually is made according to body and glaze rather than decoration. The various kinds made in quantity since about 1750 can be divided into three groups, as follows:

| EARTHENWARE | STONEWARE | PORCELAIN |
|-------------|-----------|-----------|
| Creamware | Basalt | Belleek |
| Delft | Cantonware | (pearly |
| Faïence | Crocks & jugs | iridescence) |
| Flowing Blue | (with slip or | Bone China |
| Gaudy Dutch | decoration)* | Chinese |
| Gaudy Welsh | Graniteware | (various) |
| *Lusterware | Ironstone | Lowestoft |
| Majolica | Jasper | *Lusterware |
| Mochaware | Salt Glaze | Soft-paste |
| Rockingham | Stone China | Hard-paste |
| Slipware | | |
| Spatterware | | |
| Staffordshire | | |
| Tulipware | | |

* named for decoration

China, whether it is pottery or porcelain, is valuable. It is a highly personal possession, so personal that in some civilizations people were buried with pieces of their own. Rarely does a set survive fifty years of use intact, and so people always are ready to buy odd pieces in order to fill in a set. Some pieces are of interest historically because of their patterns or design. Others are valuable because of the pottery where they were made or the type of pottery they are.

Condition affects the selling price, although perhaps not as much as the kind of pottery and its age. Tableware on which the decoration has been rubbed or worn off by use is less valuable than that on which it is still clear and brilliant. By the same token, Staffordshire transfer-printed ware that has clear and sharp transfer-printing and clear colors is more valuable than that with blurred decoration and muddied colors. This generalization can be nullified by the subject matter—for example, a historical or commemorative plate.

According to George Savage, a recognized expert on pottery and porcelain in England and America, a cracked piece with brilliant decoration in good condition is more valuable than a similar piece that is not cracked but has decoration in poor condition. Mr. Savage also considers that chips are not important if they are not too conspicuous. Actually, chips are almost inevitable.

Crazing may appear on both soft-paste porcelain and earthenware. This is a network of tiny cracks over the surface. Because it results from a manufacturing defect, it is quite different from the crackling induced as decoration by the Chinese and a few Western potteries.

Any mending or restoring should be done only by experienced and skillful experts. Very few of these are skillful enough to reconstruct a piece from fragments. A clumsy or botched job has next to no value, for a person could neither display nor use the piece.

China is never difficult to sell. In fact, it may sell speedily. Some pieces that obviously are not really old enough to be labeled as antiques sell for unexpectedly good prices as novelties. Calendar plates made in the early 1900's sell for $4.75 to $7.50. Hand-painted china moves more slowly, but a dessert plate with flowers in the center and gold on the rim is worth $7.50 or a little more.

Cantonware does not bring as high prices as you might think. Plates now sell for $8 and up, platters $15 and up. Transfer-printed Staffordshire in lavender, green, and brown brings better prices than other colors. There is a tremendous amount of Staffordshire around and it differs widely in quality and interest. In this large and varied group prices too have a wide range, depending on age, condition, color, clarity, and pattern. A blue plate from T. J. & J. Mayer with a crack and a chip will bring no more than $2.50 even if it was made in the 1830's. A similar plate in good condition will bring twice as much. A dark blue Ridgway plate in good condition is worth $15 and up.

Flowing Blue, like some shades of Staffordshire, is becoming quite scarce, so it can be sold for premium prices. Six Flowing Blue dinner plates made by James Edwards that were purchased in 1939 for $1 each could now be sold for many times that amount. A matching platter in as perfect condition as the plates was sold for $5 in 1939 and certainly could be resold now for $25, possibly more.

The price for a Toby jug made in Bennington, Vermont, depends on the subject, but most of them start at $75. A Bennington tobacco jar is worth at least $25. A cauliflower plate in American majolica currently sells for about $16.50 if it is in good condition.

Anyone fortunate enough to have any Tucker porcelain can dispose of single pieces at high prices. Plates start at $25, platters at about $50. A handleless cup with saucer is worth at least $45. Pitchers, urns, and covered dishes bring much higher prices.

Spatterware or spongeware also brings surprisingly high prices, probably because it was made in smaller quantity than the variously colored transfer-printed Staffordshire. A spatterware

plate in perfect condition may be sold for between $50 and $75. Sugar bowls and platters are worth more, for prices range from about $65 to $90. A teapot showing good color, without chips or cracks, brings not less than $100 and perhaps as much as $125.

With the current interest in Mochaware, it will be bringing prices as high as, if not higher than, Spatterware. Already, mugs are selling for $45, and a 6½-inch-high jug in Cat's Eye pattern for $85. Such prices, of course, doubtless will be easier to obtain in a metropolitan area where there are interior decorators than in smaller cities.

Whether you're trying to sell some pottery or porcelain or merely want to brag about it to your neighbors, it's important to call each type by its correct name. Earthenware is not porcelain, although it may be fully as attractive. The fact that a piece is stoneware does not mean that it's rough or crude.

## GLOSSARY

*Biscuit:* porcelain left in an unglazed state and used largely for figures; also known as bisque and Parian.

*Bone china:* china, or porcelain, made with an admixture of bone ash from bones calcined in air.

*Cachepot:* an ornamental pot in which to display indoors a plant in a plain flowerpot.

*Charger:* an old term for a large flat dish or platter, usually round, for carrying meat.

*China:* the common name for porcelain and porcelain wares, both for the table and ornaments. Originally, porcelain ware was brought from China.

*Chinoiserie:* articles with decorations in the Chinese style, designed and made in Europe and England.

*Clobbered china:* old porcelain on which the decoration has been freshened, usually by painting.

*Compote:* a plate on a standard for

serving or for displaying fruit.

*Crackle:* network of fine lines or cracks caused deliberately for decorative effect on some Chinese ware; also used by a few Western potters.

*Crazing:* network of tiny cracks that sometimes develops in the glaze of earthenware and soft-paste porcelain because of a manufacturing defect.

*Creamware:* a lead-glazed earthenware, first perfected by Josiah Wedgwood and later made by most potters, chiefly for the table. Also known as Queen's ware.

*Crockery:* earthenware or stoneware articles made for domestic use.

*Delft:* a tin-glazed earthenware made in Holland; similar ware made in England is called delft.

*Earthenware:* dishes, vessels, and ornamental objects made of clay and fired in a kiln. It is opaque, porous, fine-grained, and may be glazed or unglazed.

*Ewer:* a large pitcher with a wide spout and a handle, to carry and hold water; usually made in combination with a bowl for washing.

*Faïence:* tin-glazed earthenware made in France.

*Firing:* the exposure of a clay body to intense heat in a kiln in order to harden or glaze it.

*Glaze:* a thin or molten covering, consisting of or resembling glass, which is poured over clay.

*Hard-paste:* a type of porcelain, also known as natural porcelain, of which the principal material is a clay known as kaolin, which is combined with some siliceous material. The

glaze is similar.

*Ironstone:* a hard white pottery, also known as white granite or graniteware; its name is synonymous with hardness and durability. First made in England, where it was highly decorated; later also made in the United States.

*Jardiniere:* a large ornamental pot, receptacle, or stand for plants or flowers.

*Lusterware:* earthenware decorated by the application of metallic pigments (lusters).

*Majolica:* tin-glazed earthenware, usually richly colored, made in Italy.

*Parian:* a kind of biscuit or unglazed porcelain used during the nineteenth century for making statues and the like; so called because of its resemblance to Parian marble.

*Porcelain:* a specific kind of pottery that has a translucent body and, when glazed, a translucent glaze. Porcelain is thin, lightweight, white, and vitreous as well as translucent.

*Pottery:* any and all articles fashioned from clay and hardened by fire; the term generally refers to the coarser kinds, which are opaque.

*Queen's ware:* the name given to Josiah Wedgwood's creamware in 1765.

*Rockingham:* a brown glaze, usually mottled, applied to lead-glazed earthenware made in England and the United States.

*Salt glaze:* a stoneware with distinctive texture resulting from the addition of table salt before the last firing.

*Semi-porcelain:* pottery of a fine body, first made at the Royal China works at Worcester, England, about 1850. It is white and very hard and makes excellent tableware.

*Sgraffito:* a kind of pottery in which clay or slip is laid on top of a clay body of a different color and the design produced by cutting away or scratching the outer layer. Made in Europe, England, and Pennsylvania.

*Slip:* potter's clay or paste in a liquid state about the consistency of cream; sometimes used to cover the whole body of an earthenware vessel and sometimes used only for decoration.

*Slipware:* earthenware which is coated or decorated with slip.

*Soft-paste:* a type of European and English porcelain made in imitation of the fine ware from China and Japan. Soft-paste porcelains vary in formula.

*Staffordshire:* a county or district in England where pottery has been made since the days of the Romans; also, earthenware decorated with transfer-printed designs in various colors, first made in Staffordshire.

*Toby:* a small jug, mug, or pitcher made in the form of a stout man with a three-cornered hat, the angle of which forms the spout from which liquid can be poured, and colored appropriately. A Toby often portrays a traditional English character, including many famous ones from Dickens, or an important living person.

*Transfer-printing:* a method of decorating earthenware, introduced about 1755 in Staffordshire, which makes possible the reproduction of the same pattern with little or no handwork.

*Trembleuse:* a style of teacup and saucer, the saucer having a deep depression into which the cup fits so that it cannot slide.

*Vitreous:* glassy, also nonporous.

# 12
## *Everyday China*

AN EARTHENWARE JELLY MOLD is a rare thing to run across. But a syrup pitcher, cracker jar, or hatpin-holder is taking up space in many a cupboard. These and other odd pieces of china are not used any more, yet people hesitate to throw them away, perhaps because there is nothing wrong with them, possibly because they're rather pretty. They need not be left to gather dust unless there is a strong sentimental tie. Any piece of china is salable, although the best market may be a slow one because it is made up of collectors. Actually, there are people who collect hatpin-holders, butter pats or chips, mustache cups, and the like.

The miscellaneous china in any household often consists of a few pieces from tableware sets that belonged to mother, grandmother, or possibly a great-grandmother, for china has been made in sets for the table since the mid-1700's. Seldom is any old set still complete, even the Haviland given to a bride of the 1890's or early. 1900's. Cups and saucers are usually the first casualties.

The largest set ever made was the creamware one Wedgwood produced for Catherine the Great of Russia, *circa* 1774. It consisted of 952 pieces, each one painted by hand with a different scene, landscape, or monument in England. This was the most important piece of work ever done in creamware. Since it was a special order, neither its size nor decoration was repeated.

The inspiration for patterns has changed from time to time during the last 200 years. Only a handful have been popular enough to be made almost continuously. Pieces of these timeless patterns that are old enough to be antique are greatly sought after.

The most popular pattern of all time is Willow. It is blue decoration on white that looks as if it could have originated in China. However, it was designed in England by someone who was influenced by the Chinese porcelain he had seen, and was introduced by T. Turner in his Caughley porcelain in 1780. So popular did it prove to be that soon most English potters were producing a Willow pattern in earthenware if not porcelain. The strange thing is that although the blue might differ in shade or tint, the details of the pattern varied hardly at all. It is still being made by the Alfred Meakin firm in Staffordshire, England, who call their pattern "Old Willow," and by firms in the United States and Japan.

The traditional pattern shows a bridge, a river and islands, pagoda-like buildings, two or three figures on the bridge and one or two figures between a building and the bridge, and two birds, sometimes called doves, overhead. The whole scene is framed with trees and shrubs that are exotic if not oriental-looking. Presumably the Willow pattern depicts a romantic—and sad—tale. The figures represent a princess and the commoner whom she loves, usually shown on the bridge, her father and perhaps one or more associates of his. In fleeing from the irate father, the lovers are drowned; the two birds overhead represent the souls of the lost lovers.

The Willow pattern always has been made in a very complete set of tableware, and because of long-continued and present-day manufacture, there is

*Willow pattern, designed in England, has been made in table sets continuously since 1780. The deep saucer at the left came from an English pottery in the early 1800's; the demitasse cup and saucer from another English factory in the 1890's.*

a wide price range. Any pieces made in Japan will be difficult to sell except at a rummage sale. Most valuable are nineteenth-century pieces made in England, and the older the piece, the more it can be sold for.

Another blue and white pattern of enduring popularity is the so-called Meissen Onion from the famous Meissen porcelain factory in Germany. This pattern, made in sets consisting of as many diverse pieces as Willow earthenware in England, always was a porcelain one, at least when made by German potters. Like Willow, it was derived from Chinese porcelain—but there was no actual onion in the design. The confusion began before the pattern was introduced in 1750. The pomegranates that the Chinese used were unfamiliar to the Germans and they mistakenly called them onions. Thereafter, in the borders of their own porcelain tableware, they reproduced a motif that resembled a pomegranate far more than it did the common onion.

Meissen Onion is almost as popular today as it ever was, and pieces that can be authenticated as having been made in the eighteenth and nineteenth centuries sell for a pretty price. During those two centuries, the pattern had several peaks of popularity. It was always basically the same, but there were obvious variations at different times.

The rarest and most beautiful pieces of Meissen Onion were made during the 1700's. They had careful details in a gray-blue color. Around 1800 the design began to be simplified somewhat, and about 1820 the soft blue of the earlier years was replaced by a brighter yet dark cobalt-blue. Occasionally gilding was applied to the borders of the pattern. Large serving plates sometimes had pierced rims.

In addition to the potter's mark, there is another way to tell approximately when a piece of Meissen Onion was made: Before 1800 all onions in the border faced toward the center. After 1800 they alternated, one facing inward, the next one outward. Sets made in the Meissen factory near Dresden always have the mark that was being used at the factory at that time. Meissen marks almost invariably included crossed swords, whatever else they showed.

Some of the English factories, including Wedgwood and Doulton, also produced an onion pattern during the nineteenth century. However, their products in this pattern are not considered as fine as those of Meissen. A similar pattern in blue on white earthenware, called Blue Danube, is now being manufactured in Japan. Collectors' interest continues to run high for old specimens of Meissen Onion. Those of the nineteenth century always will remain valuable, for again after 1900 the pattern was greatly simplified at Meissen.

Another pattern derived from the Chinese porcelains is the Indian Tree. Far from being a blue and white design, this one was carried out in shades of pink and rose with some green against white. The central motif is an oriental-looking tree, and the pattern also includes flowers that could be tree peonies and carnations. The Indian Tree pattern was introduced by Coalport in the early 1800's. It was copied by other factories in both pottery and porcelain, and is still being made by at least three English firms.

Napoleon Ivy was designed by the Wedgwood firm, which supplied it as a table service to Napoleon Bonaparte during his exile on the Island of St. Helena (1815–21). This was a Queen's ware pattern with a cream background and a border of ivy leaves in green encircling the rim. This pattern, expressly designed for Napoleon, was sold generally during the nineteenth century. After a lapse of many years, the pattern is being made again currently. As in the case of Willow, Meissen Onion, and Indian Tree, it is essential with Napoleon Ivy also to identify the potter's mark and the period of years during which it was used. Nineteenth-century pieces of this dinnerware, even though not used by Napoleon, have acquired extra value.

Blue Chelsea is a famous English soft-paste porcelain pattern that has been popular since 1789 and is currently being made by the Adderly factory. Another name for it is Grandmother's Ware. Sprigs in mulberry color are

hand-applied around the rims. A great deal of tableware decorated with flower sprigs was made at many English potteries, but the sprigs on the Blue Chelsea are actually small clusters of grapes. The Chelsea factory near London has been noted for its porcelains (soft-paste in the beginning) since 1748. Before and after 1800, a pattern with grapes in a mauve-purple luster was made by Chelsea. It is generally, if perhaps inaccurately, known as Chelsea Grape and is quite similar to the Blue Chelsea pattern.

The rose was the dominant motif of several cherished patterns. The one known as Adams Rose was made by Adams & Son in Staffordshire between 1820 and 1840 and again much later in the Victorian era. The colors were

*A Chelsea plate of soft-paste porcelain with grape design. It bears no potter's mark, but the octagonal shape of the plate and a matching cup, the raised decoration, and the color indicate it was made around 1800 or slightly before.*

clearer and sharper in the early pieces of Adams Rose. Pink roses were used as the basis of a pattern in almost every English factory from Adams and Davenport through the rest of the alphabet of potters.

Rose Medallion china was decorated in Canton, China, and brought to England, Europe, and America. This one is sometimes called Rose Canton. The pieces were paneled—four and often six panels on larger pieces such as platters. The panels or medallions alternated in being decorated with people and pink flowers, birds and butterflies.

Not as old as any of these patterns, and likely to be passed by as "some more of the cheap stuff from Japan," is Imari china. This was gaudily decorated porcelain that had been made in Japan since about 1650. It was imported here mostly from the 1870's to 1900 and got its name because it was shipped from the port of Imari. The designs were red and blue florals with green foliage. A punch bowl, tray, jardiniere, or vase is as likely a find as plates.

Nineteenth-century families were likely to have a dinner or tea set in one of the patterns that have proved so popular, but they also usually had a set of earthenware or ironstone for everyday use that they kept in the kitchen cupboards. The butler's pantry or dining-room cupboards housed the "best" set of porcelain. During the 1800's, tableware was bought by the dozen and few

sets consisted of less than 93 pieces. Usually, there were more than 100. At least three sizes of plates—dinner, tea, and dessert—were included. Small butter pats or chips instead of bread-and-butter plates were general, and in the early 1800's soup dishes were desirable. Bouillon cups or cream soups did not appear until close to 1900. Cups and saucers, sauce dishes and perhaps the larger, deeper, round cereal dishes, platters, and various covered and uncovered serving dishes rounded out a basic set of tableware. This is a great contrast to the modern custom of buying tableware by the place setting, each one consisting of five pieces.

The serving dishes in dinner sets usually included one or more open vegetable dishes, a covered vegetable dish, three or more platters in different sizes, perhaps a round chop plate, a gravy boat with its saucer sometimes attached, a covered butter dish, and a sugar and creamer. Some sets included a round or square plate for serving cake and a teapot and coffeepot.

Covered butter dishes are little seen in modern china patterns. Another unusual serving dish, which is better known in rural areas, is a pancake dish. This resembled an oversized covered butter dish. The bottom was a large plate, and over it fit securely a domed cover with a knob and with small holes to permit steam to escape. Obviously it was used to carry pancakes from the griddle to the table and keep them warm until they had been served.

Oyster plates, like the oyster forks in silver flatware, have gone out of style too. Plates for oysters, clams, and snails with depressions shaped and marked like the seafood were quite common by the 1890's.

A matching plate and bowl into which a baking dish of food could be slipped for serving at the table is a nice piece to find. The inner bowl, which could withstand the heat of the oven, was some kind of unglazed pottery. The outer bowl and the plate, which was considerably wider, were often porcelain, although some probably were made in earthenware. Haviland and other·factories in Limoges made baking-serving dishes. Since they were a late-Victorian idea, the patterns are often delicate florals, with or without gilding.

Most families owned a tureen, a very old type of dish that is deep and has a cover to keep warm the soup or stew served from it at the table. This dish was not necessarily part of a full set of tableware. Tureens made in the most typical pottery or porcelain were common in every country. Meissen was producing colorful tureens in the form of fruits, vegetables, animals, or birds as early as 1750. The same sort were made a little later at Chelsea in England. A famous Chelsea tureen has the shape of a most lifelike rabbit. By 1880, tureens in more conventional shapes were common. Many of ironstone and transfer-printed Staffordshire are still around, and some of these are being reproduced.

Haviland porcelain dinner sets included butter pats until 1900 or a little later. Various kinds of pottery ones had been made much earlier. Bread platters or trays were rarely part of a set of tableware. They were made in various sizes—small enough to hold only two rolls or large enough for a loaf of bread. These trays were made from all types of china ranging from Sèvres porcelain and faïence to majolica.

Salt shakers usually were not made as part of a set of dishes. Silver or cut glass salt dishes or shakers were preferred on a dinner table set with the best china. However, many individual salt shakers were made of pottery such as Sèvres faïence and of Royal Copenhagen porcelain. Most of them are about 3 inches high, although early-nineteenth-century ones often were 5 inches tall. Only one of these large ones would be placed on a table. After 1850, pottery salt shakers became more common. The pair of matching salt and pepper shakers, identical except

*A bone dish was set at each place to receive any bones removed from meat or fish. The two at the left are Flowing Blue; the other is a later style. (1800-1870)*

*Dessert plates were frequently of a different pattern than the dinner set. And each dessert plate in a set of a dozen generally had a slightly different fan, scene, or other decorative motif from the other plates in the set. Gold highlights the pierced edges of these plates. (1875-1900)*

for the size of the holes in the top, did not come into general use until after 1875.

Trivets or hot plates to use on the table probably were not made to match sets. However, they are a pretty addition to a cloth-covered dining table. Most of them were round, about 6 inches in diameter, but a few oval ones were made. They usually were white with floral designs.

*Chocolate pots, slightly taller and straighter than coffeepots, have been made since the 1740's. The porcelain one with dainty pastel flowers and gilt was made in Limoges; the earthenware one with striking iris decoration, in the United States. (1850-90)*

A fish set graced the corner cupboard of many an East Coast dining room. In fact, such sets were common throughout the New England States as far west as Keene, New Hampshire, and Springfield, Massachusetts. A set consisted of plates from which to eat fish and potatoes, a distinctively shaped platter, a covered vegetable dish, and perhaps bone dishes. The family who did not own a fish set often had a special platter on which to serve fish at the table. As a lone piece or part of a set, a fish platter was long (more than 20 inches), oval, tapering at both ends, and narrower throughout its length than a meat platter. Luster and Old Blue were popular for the fish sets produced in England, France, and Germany.

Bone dishes also were a part of dinner sets. If they were not made to match a fish set, others were used with it. Bone dishes were small and crescent-shaped, 5½ to 6 inches or so from tip to tip. A bone dish was set in front of each place at the table and each person unabashedly piled the bones from his fish or chicken on it. These dishes were in general use until at least the 1870's. Both porcelain and earthenware were used for bone dishes; Flowing Blue and flowered patterns were probably most common.

Dessert sets or at least one dozen dessert plates, and—nearer to 1900—ice cream sets were commonly owned by families who were comfortably situ-

*A lusterware tea set usually consisted of a teapot (not shown), sugar and creamer, cups and saucers, and two serving plates. The so-called "pink" luster—actually, shades of pink and rose—was achieved with gold pigments. This set belonged to a New Hampshire family. (1820-90)*

ated. The dozen dessert plates might be accompanied by a matching cake plate, sometimes on a standard. Some sets included three sizes of cake plates or compotes. Dessert sets were made of porcelain and various kinds of pottery. Most of them had painted decoration in the center and often a colored rim, perhaps touched with gilt. A different scene on each of the plates was a popular decorative scheme throughout the 1800's. Later in the Victorian era, more romantic subjects such as fans became popular, and

often the edges of the plates were pierced. Fruit plates displaying a different painted fruit in the center of each one were a vogue in mid-Victorian days. Ice cream sets consisted of a large serving bowl with sauce dishes to match. These were made in porcelain and earthenware as well as in cut glass.

Tea and chocolate sets as well as dinner sets were made of porcelain in Germany in the 1740's. In England and the United States, tea sets became

*Tea sets of Gold Band or Wedding Ring china were common in the United States, but not all of them had white and gold rope decoration around the handles and knobs. (1850-1900)*

important before 1800. A tea set con-sisted of teapot, sugar and creamer or milk pitcher in the size and shape of the period, two serving plates, and a dozen cups and saucers. A set extensive enough to include a dozen tea plates, a dozen sauce dishes, and a small bowl evidently was intended for high tea or Sunday night supper.

Many luster tea sets were proudly dis-played and used in this country. Sprigged china ones were popular in the early 1800's, and toward the end of the century floral ones were well liked. White china tea sets with simple gold band decoration became fairly common after about 1850. In some lo-calities, these are called Wedding Ring china. Those with white and gold china rope twined about the knobs

*Family china almost always included a teapot, often with a capacity of up to 2 quarts. This one with molded rope deco-ration and sprays of colored flowers is a size and shape popular after 1850. The teacup, deep saucer, and unusually large cup plate are transfer-printed Stafford-shire made between 1830 and 1850.*

and handles are considered somewhat finer than those with plain gold trim.

Tea, coffee, and chocolate pots can be distinguished by their size. All three were considered essential in house-holds, rich and poor, throughout the 1800's. Their use dates back to the 1740's. All of them were made of por-celain and various types of pottery, as well as silver, pewter, and sometimes copper. The size and shape of each changed every so often, just as they did in the case of silver pots.

Coffeepots usually were slightly taller and more slender than teapots, and chocolate pots were taller and slimmer than coffeepots. The teapot belonging to a tea set was much smaller than the one with a large capacity made for use on the family table. Teapots and cof-feepots could be bought singly, too, and some of these separate teapots were made in very odd shapes and forms. A chocolate pot frequently came with a dozen matching cups and saucers.

Pitchers for table use varied in size from time to time, just as teapots and coffeepots did. Creamers always have been small. Milk pitchers such as the 6-inch-high one in a Gold Band tea set were taller. In the late 1800's, small pitchers became more common, and larger ones with a capacity of a quart or more were used for water. Stoneware or crockery ones were gen-erally used for milk.

*Pitchers were made both singly and to match sets. Oldest of the three shown here is the milk pitcher at the left, which is gray-blue earthenware with a molded design. The copper luster creamer has bands of transfer-printing; the squat porcelain pitcher has hand-painted floral sprays, with handle and decorative lines in honey-gold. (1800-1850)*

Pitchers in all sizes and shapes were made to be sold as single items and also to match many sets of dishes. However a pitcher was purchased long ago, it may be a collectors' piece nowadays. It doesn't have to be an apostle pitcher with a different apostle portrayed in each of the twelve panels around the sides. Or a fine porcelain one made at the Royal Worcester factory between 1820 and 1840, when dull but rich-looking "honey" gold was used to cover the handle and edge the rim and thus set off the floral design. A Belgian stoneware, a transfer-printed Staffordshire, or a copper luster pitcher can be fully as worth finding and dusting.

Cups, like teaspoons and teapots, have changed a great deal in size and shape since the late 1700's. The chances are almost as good of finding a cup without a saucer as the other way around.

If a cup is old or unusual enough, it's worth something even without the saucer.

A cup intact with two saucers is a real prize—to keep or to sell. Two saucers to accompany a handleless teacup were fashionable from about 1815 through the 1850's. It was the custom then to pour the tea or other hot drink into the large, deep saucer so that it would

*The handleless Flowing Blue cup was made with a matching deep saucer and a cup plate. (Circa 1815-40.)*

cool, and to set the cup, with some liquid still in it, to one side on the small saucer. In fact, people drank from the deep saucer. Both Flowing Blue and sprigged china handleless cups are still to be found.

The first teacups Europeans ever saw were the handleless ones common in China. European and English potters added handles before 1765. By that time, French potters had had the idea for a trembleuse—that is, a teacup whose saucer was made with a deep depression in the center into which the cup fit so snugly that it could not slip. This style was recommended for those who had shaky hands. The first teacups made in Europe and England were very small, probably because tea was so scarce and expensive. Teacups still are smaller than coffee cups, but they were being made in what we consider average size by the early 1800's.

Other types of cups became popular as the Victorian years piled up. By the 1880's, the elaborately decorated cup had found great favor as a present. It usually displayed the words "Remember Me" in gilt. These cups are hardly antiques, but they are part of the trivia that portray an era—fun to collect and colorful to display (they're easier to display without their saucers). Sprigged ware, lusterware, earthenware, and porcelain all were used to fashion the "Remember Me" cups. Many of these were elaborately decorated, others were merely gaudy. Probably most gift cups were displayed on whatnots. Today,

*"Remember Me" cups lettered in gilt were favorite Victorian gifts. Here is a coffee cup and deep saucer with colorful decoration set off with gold.*

decorators frequently buy such cups to add a whimsical touch to a room, and more than one florist has been known to buy an odd lot of them to hold small bouquets.

Mustache cups fall into the same category—not quite old enough to be antique but part of the record of an era. A mustache cup was made for drinking tea or coffee without letting the mustache touch the liquid. A part of the lip of the cup had a fixed cover with a small opening through which the liquid could drain. The decade of the greatest vogue of these cups was the 1890's. They were made in both bone china and earthenware. Some had the owner's name or the word "Father" lettered in gilt on the side. Left-handed mustache cups were made too, and these were more expensive than right-handed cups. A few years ago (1958) a Californian advertised for sale a collection of 1,000 bone china mustache cups. Whether each one was complete with saucer was not stated.

Not to be confused with mustache cups are shaving mugs, which also are collectors' items. Shaving mugs were fashionable somewhat longer (1870–1910) than mustache cups. They also were made of all types of china. Usually they were kept at a barbershop, so the owner's name invariably was part of the decoration. There were more than 150 decorative patterns that indicated occupations. These ranged from musical instruments such as an accordion or flute, to a buggy, boat, or automobile, a steel bridge, or a camera. Even the marble-cutter, surveyor, tailor, and undertaker had special designs. The owner chose the decoration that illustrated his occupation and then had his name placed on the cup too. The insignia of fraternal organizations such as Knights Templar, Knights of Pythias, and the Masonic Lodge also were popular. Occasionally a shaving mug was adorned with a deer's head, a dog, crossed United States flags, or a Gibson Girl's head.

Mugs for drinking also were made of

*Part of the rim of a mustache cup is closed in, and has a small opening through which a man can drink without dipping his mustache into the liquid. (1890's)*

china. Stoneware beer steins are almost as well known as the simply decorated mugs out of which children drank milk or cambric tea. Many mugs to be found in this country are transfer-printed Staffordshire. Some are commemorative, some personalized in some way.

Children's mugs and plates could be purchased separately or as part of a set. A set included the mug, a small pitcher, and a deep bowl with a rim about an inch high. Simple and often gay decoration was based on storybook pictures, animals, children playing games, and the like. Mugs and sets were made in transfer-printed Staffordshire, luster, Gaudyware, and other popular Victorian china.

All sets made wholly or in part of china were not meant to be used on the table. Desk sets ornamented with flowered china were an appropriate gift for a lady in late Victorian years. Such a set consisted of a rectangular desk blotter, a hand blotter that was rolled on writing paper to dry the ink, and a stamp box, each one with four ornamental corners of china in appropriate sizes. The inkstand held an inkwell of matching china and also accommodated a mother-of-pearl penholder with a gold pen or a simpler kind of pen. Whatever it was made of, the penholder and pen were not necessarily purchased with the desk set.

Inkwells and inkstands were manufactured as separate items too. Both are

A *porcelain group that can be lifted off its base to reveal an attached inkwell and sifter.*

always interesting, since they were made from many materials—cast iron, brass, silver, pewter, glass—in addition to china. China inkstands often are disguised to look like ornaments. A group of figures, for example, might be lifted from its base to disclose an inkwell and possibly also a sifter. More

*A Delft inkwell (2¼ inches square, 3¾ inches high) has a domed cover and brass bindings. The mother-of-pearl penholder with a gold pen was used by its first owner in the 1860's.*

utilitarian stands might contain one or more decorative inkwells and also have a place to rest a penholder. Old ones had a sifter too.

Individual inkwells usually were either important or attractive pieces, sometimes both. The majority of china ones had metal fittings and a hinged cover. Porcelain inkwells generally had flower and foliage decoration. The blue and white Delft inkwells are particularly stunning. Some rather grotesque pottery ones were made in the form of animals, frogs, and the like (these often were covered with brown glaze). However, all kinds of pottery, with the decoration typical of it, were used to fashion inkwells.

Dresser sets consisted of a china tray large enough to hold brush and comb, a small pin tray, one or two bottles, and a trinket box. A hatpin-holder and a hair-receiver (a two-piece globular dish with a round hole in the center of the cover) matched or harmonized with the set. Some dresser sets or pieces were porcelain, others pottery. The decoration was flowers from field or garden, portraits, and classical motifs, done mostly in pastel colors.

The washstand set was as important as the commode on which it belonged in a Victorian bedroom, and for some reason there's a fairly brisk market in these at the present time. Many three-piece washstand or chamber sets can be found, consisting of a washbowl about 15 inches in diameter and 7 inches deep, a ewer about 12 inches high, and a chamber pot. The ewer was stored in the washbowl. The chamber pot, which should have a cover, was stowed away in the small cupboard of the commode.

More elaborate washstand sets consisted of seven or eight matching pieces. In addition to the three basic ones, there were a covered soap dish, a shaving dish, a jar or vase 5 to 6 inches high for toothbrushes, a small jug for hot water, and a slop bucket. Complete sets are at a premium, and it is not too easy to find even a three-piece set without cracks, chips, or crazing.

Families had washstand sets for every bedroom. A variety of pottery was used to make them in England, Europe, and the United States—plain white ironstone, transfer-printed Staffordshire, Limoges, and crockery of uncertain origin. The decoration was as varied as the pottery but usually fairly simple.

From the earliest days of pottery-making, and in every country, many kinds of small boxes have been made of both earthenware and porcelain. Some of these boxes were carried about on the person, others were accessories in bedrooms and other rooms of the house. Cosmetic patches, snuff, powder, matches, trinkets, and candy were some of the things these boxes were meant to hold. One Victorian example is a little graniteware box 3 inches long, 1½ inches wide, and 1¼ inches high,

for wooden matches. The inside of the lid, which lifts off, is corrugated so that matches can be struck on it. On the upper surface are molded the heads of two men smoking pipes. In Staffordshire, a great quantity of miscellaneous boxes were made in such forms as bureaus, washstands, or with figures of lambs, dogs, and the like on the lids.

Other household ware included salt crocks, cracker jars, condiment sets for mustard, pickles, etc., jam jars (sometimes in pairs on a stand), and kitchen sets. The latter consisted of large covered china jars for coffee, rice, barley, smaller ones for spices, and bottles for oil and vinegar. Salt crocks were made to hang on the wall like wooden ones, and often were of stoneware that was nicely designed. Cracker jars were cylindrical, about 5 inches high and almost as wide, with a china lid. Some had silver-plated lids and handles, but most of them had only matching china covers and no handles.

Potteries in the United States were engaged in the production of these utensils for kitchen and dining room during the 1800's. They were made in England and Europe too. Except for salt crocks, the various pieces were likely to be some kind of earthenware, even semi-porcelain. Sprigs and chinoiserie were often chosen for decoration.

Other popular containers of the nineteenth century—and possibly the eighteenth — were ginger jars, potpourri jars, tea caddies, and tobacco jars.

Westerners became acquainted with ginger jars and tea caddies through imports from China. The ginger jar has a china cover that slips down over its neck. The smallest one I have ever seen is only 4 inches high, so low that it looks almost as if it were round instead of the classic urn shape. Potpourri jars, often in pairs, are urn-shaped with an inner lid of unglazed china that fits into the neck, and either a matching china outer lid with a knob or the same type of cover as a ginger jar. Potpourri jars, small or large, were made to hold the fragrant mixture of dried flower petals and spices known by that name. Tea caddies were fairly good-sized and often square.

*Pottery jars originally made for other purposes are often used now for a fragrant potpourri. This little one, only four inches tall, is decorated with lusters and gold.*

Ginger jars, potpourri jars, and tea caddies in everything from blue and white Chinese ware to English floral designs were possessions of which families were proud. Some handsome porcelain tea caddies were made in Europe. Potpourri jars were made of various kinds of earthenware and porcelain. A large, footed one entirely of pierced creamware was made at Leeds about 1780 and is now a museum piece. Royal Worcester, Sèvres, and Meissen have made exquisite ones, even in the twentieth century.

Vases always have been an important part of the output of every factory in Europe and England since the early eighteenth century, and in the United States from the nineteenth century. Chinese ones, centuries old, are priceless. The word "vase" covers a diversity of ornamental containers, from magnificent urns that were never intended to hold flowers to everyday pottery vessels.

Fine blue and white porcelain vases were imported from China in the early 1700's. Meissen, Chantilly, Worcester, Coalport, and other factories where porcelain was made produced magnificent ornamental vases and ewers during the eighteenth century. Many faïence vases were almost as elaborate. Potters and artists copied the Chinese style, form, and decoration and then went on to develop their own, with landscapes, figures, and groups of flowers or applied modeling of garlands, heads, and flowers. Colored

*Types of vases popular in Victorian days* (from left to right): *bisque, with painted decoration and handles covered in gold; stoneware, with a raised ivy garland coated with silver; transfer-printed china; green jasperware, with white decoration in relief.* (1850-1900)

glazes, hand-painting, and gilding further enriched the decoration. Many of these elaborate vases, first made in the eighteenth century, stand more than a foot tall and have their own fancy covers. Ewers proved, if not by their elaborate and colorful decoration then by their narrow necks and impractical spouts, that they were meant to be ornamental.

Toward the end of the eighteenth century, Josiah Wedgwood made some huge vases with lids from jasperware. Fortunately many of those made in the nineteenth century are smaller and more usable. By the late 1800's, the greatest amount of jasperware was Wedgwood blue or celadon green. Jasperware vases are still being made. In contrast to the simplicity of jasper, many majolica and stoneware vases of the Victorian era were quite wondrously decorated.

Vases that were more suitable for flowers began to be made about 1850. Some kind of vase was then an essential ornament for both the mantelpiece (where a pair was preferred) and the whatnot (which had room for several), and perhaps also for the center table. Many were simple enough to hold a bouquet without detracting from either the vase itself or the flowers. By the 1880's, many china vases borrowed shape, color, and decoration from the newly popular art glass. Jasperware, stoneware, Delft, majolica, and many other pottery vases that appeared during the Victorian era are worth cleaning carefully if found today.

Jardinieres and cachepots also were made during the 1700's. There are fine porcelain ones as well as those of stoneware and earthenware from the 1800's still around. Cachepots usually

*Potpourri jars, 6 inches high, decorated with pastel flowers and touches of gold. The outer cover has been removed from one to show the unglazed inner lid that fits over the neck.*

were made and sold in pairs. Many, even those of faïence, show fine work and beautiful, restrained decoration. Chinoiserie was characteristic of early cachepots. As the palm and later the Boston fern became an essential orna-

*These candlesticks of white glazed pottery fronted by a lady (left) and a cavalier (right) were made in the United States after 1860. The cavalier was brought from Virginia, the lady from Ohio, to houses next door to each other in New Jersey.*

ment in the parlor, jardinieres became more common than cachepots. These were made to hold a large potted plant and usually were quite heavy. They were made of stoneware and all kinds of pottery, and a few of them can still be considered attractive.

Many vases, urns, jardinieres, and the like were produced at the Rookwood Pottery Company, which was founded in Cincinnati, Ohio, in 1880 by Mrs. Maria Longworth Storer. Much of the Rookwood, which is an art pottery, is still attractive by present-day standards of taste. Rookwood Pottery is still in business, and twentieth-century items should not be confused with those made between 1880 and 1900, which might be classified as antiques now.

Some Rookwood pieces always have been signed by the designer or artist, and these were not duplicated. Soft coloring and mellow tones, simple and classical forms, and a good deal of naturalistic decoration became hallmarks of Rookwood pottery. During the company's history a variety of glazes has been used and some biscuit ware also produced. This pottery's experiments with glazes led, in 1884, to the famous crystalline one they called "Tiger Eye."

Candleholders could no more not have been made of clay than of various metals. Potters probably could not resist turning their skill to different types of candleholders. Many delightful chambersticks were made of pottery, from jasper to Quimper. Comparatively few wall sconces were made. Chambersticks and candlesticks of various heights were made of hard-paste and soft-paste porcelain. Often porcelain candlesticks showed floral decoration, and an English chamberstick had a socket formed like a tulip, attached to a leaf base. Candlesticks made in both Germany and France also displayed dainty, encrusted blossoms. Bolder flowers were painted on pottery.

Figures, like vases, have been an almost constant product for two and a half centuries. Certainly they were much more important during the 1700's and 1800's than they are at the present time. Meissen led all other factories in the making of beautiful porcelain figures, which are particularly noted for action poses and coloring. Many figures and groups were made of faïence

in France and Delft in Holland. In England the Worcester, Chelsea, Derby, and Bow potteries made outstanding figures and groups. Wedgwood made figures of animals and birds first from black basalt, later from jasperware, and babies from all kinds of ware before 1800.

The subjects for figures were mythical and allegorical, such as the Three Fates and Triton, and everyday persons from pastoral or military life and the like. Birds also were a favorite. Most of the factories that made figures and groups also made busts. These were not only of famous people but also of unidentified ones. Meissen, for example, made busts of children only 3½ inches high — charming ornaments. During the Victorian lusterware period, some English potteries covered busts with a luster so they would appear to be made of bronze instead of china.

*These highly colored, glazed porcelain groups (early to middle nineteenth century) were meant to be used as a pair. In one, an artist is painting one of the ladies; in the other, a game of checkers is in progress.*

Groups in porcelain, faience, and other kinds of pottery were made in England, Europe, and the United States during the 1800's. Any groups, statuettes, and busts found now are likely to have been made in the last century. China groups from Germany and Austria were the most ornate ones, but all countries made groups with at least three figures and often more.

Like figures, groups could be based on allegory and mythology. They also showed court figures and common people. Usually a group was posed in the act of doing something, such as playing musical instruments or crowding around a person at the piano.

The hard-paste porcelain figures produced in Germany and the soft-paste

*This pair of figures, 10½ inches high, is made of biscuit. The bases are the natural off-white of biscuit, but the figures are colored appropriately in muted tones. (Circa 1850.)*

ones that came from Chelsea, Bow, and Derby in England, Chantilly and Sèvres in France, faced competition from a new technique developed with clay during the 1700's. Porcelain that is fired but left unglazed is called biscuit or bisque, which proved most suitable for figures and was something different that had great appeal. Bisque could be either hard-paste or soft-paste and, truly, it is impossible for anyone but an expert to tell one from the other. Soft-paste examples tend to have a creamy tone, hard-paste ones are dead-white or sometimes chalk-white, depending on the factory. At some periods bisque was colored with pastels. Biscuit figures were a French innovation about 1769 and were soon being made in other countries; the majority were free-standing but at least a few small ones were made to be used as ornaments on clocks, for example. Since biscuit figures had to be not only sharply modeled but also flawless to be salable, less than perfect ones often were glazed and enameled so that they could be sold, too.

The Parian ware of the nineteenth century was another kind of biscuit, so called because it was believed to look something like Parian marble. Parian ware was developed and introduced by Copeland in England about 1846. It was soon being made throughout the Staffordshire District. In the United States, Bennington Pottery produced Parian figures and statuettes, pitchers and vases.

*Parian figures or statuettes, which were made of unglazed porcelain or biscuit, were immensely popular between 1850 and 1900. These Grecian statuettes are only 5 inches high.*—Ted Eastwood

Bisque or Parian ware was especially popular from 1850 to 1900. Much of it was quite undistinguished, consisting of sentimental-looking heads of children, animals, and slippers. After all, something had to be displayed on those whatnots.

Not all the statuettes and figures of Victorian days were Parian. Glazed and

colored pottery and earthenware ones continued their hold on people. Between 1875 and 1900, the Royal Bayreuth factory in Germany became noted for apple, tomato, and other fruit and vegetable figures and also for creamers and various dishes shaped like a fruit, vegetable, bird, or animal. Staffordshire figures were immensely popular throughout the Victorian age.

None of the figures were more popular than the Staffordshire dogs. Staffordshire factories made cats and other animals, too, but no animal figures were more frequently displayed or loved in more homes than the Staffordshire spaniels. It's interesting to note that the spaniels varied little in expression, whereas the cats were decidedly individual in expression and pose. Whatever their size and color, the spaniels were always posed sitting on their haunches.

Staffordshire spaniels were made in

*Staffordshire spaniels were made in various sizes, some almost as big as life. The examples shown are 3½, 4, and 5 inches tall, and are black and white, brown and white, or red and white in color.*

*Staffordshire dogs of glazed earthenware were made in pairs, always sitting on their haunches. These white ones with tawny spots wear a collar and chain like a real spaniel.*

matching pairs from 3½ inches tall to almost life-size. Some were black and white, others russet or a shade of brown and white. Occasionally, the coloring was done with lusters. Each dog wore a collar and chain. During the 1890's, Boston bulldogs were as popular in china as in reality. The Bennington Pottery also made some brown-glazed animals in addition to their Parian figures.

In a class by themselves are Toby jugs. They have been made by almost every English pottery, beginning with Whieldon and including Wedgwood, since the early 1700's. Royal Doulton and probably some other places still make Toby jugs today. During the nineteenth century some were made in the United States, notably at Bennington, with a brown glaze. The English Tobies are more colorful.

*A Toby jug covered with brown Rockingham-type glaze, made in the United States. One corner of the hat is pointed enough to serve as a pouring spout.*

A Toby is a small jug, mug, or pitcher shaped like a short, stout man who wears a cocked hat. Small ones were used for ale, larger ones as pitchers out of which liquid could be poured from the corners of the cocked hat that forms the rim. Tobies portrayed general characters such as the "Night Watchman" who carried a lantern, as well as specific characters, many from the novels of Charles Dickens. A Toby also might honor a hero or a statesman. In recent years, for example, Royal Doulton has produced Toby jugs in honor of General Eisenhower, General MacArthur, and Winston Churchill, among others. A female Toby is rare. An eighteenth-century Toby usually showed the full figure, foreshortened, but late-nineteenth-century ones showed only head and shoulders.

Rogers' statuary, referred to as "Rogers' Groups," was an American origination that became as customary in a parlor, as the horsehair-covered sofa, from the late 1800's to about 1915. Probably many of the 100,000 estimated to have been made are still in the closets, attics, cellars, and barns where they were shoved to get them out of sight in the 1920's.

John Rogers was born in Salem, Massachusetts, in 1829. He studied sculpture in Europe, but became discouraged and returned home. Not long afterward, his first group of small figures called "The Checker Players" was so well received that it started him on a new career. Rogers' Groups are not

great sculpture, but they are good folk art. The reproductions—the original was not sold—were made of plaster of Paris and painted a sort of mud color. Rogers created some 80 to 100 different groups in all. One of the largest was "Council of War," which depicted President Lincoln, General Grant, and Edwin M. Stanton. Many were based on sentimental and homelike subjects, as their names—"The Cherry Pickers," "School Days," and "The Town Pump" —imply. "First Love" showed a boy and girl with arms entwined. Rogers' Groups were too large for whatnots, and so were usually displayed on a small high table or possibly the sideboard.

Plaques to hang on the wall had been made by European and English potteries since the mid-1700's. These were porcelain, luster, and various kinds of pottery such as Delft. Wedgwood made handsome plaques of jasperware. Wall plates, which became popular in Victorian days, ranged from scenic Delft to less distinguished ones with paintings of fowl, fruit, and flowers. Finally, in the 1880's, came the smaller china plates with a pierced or lacy edge through which ribbon was threaded. The centers usually had an innocuous hand-painted design.

Bric-a-brac included highly colored pottery or porcelain houses in miniature. These were often quite complete scenes. A doghouse would have a dog peering out of the door and his dish attached to the house at one side, or a

miniature farmhouse might have a girl looking out of a window at animals around the doorstep. Miniature porcelain houses were made at Meissen and at English factories noted for porcelain. There were many Staffordshire ones. Some of the smallest houses (4½ by 2¾ by 1¼ inches) had a slot in the roof so that they could be used as banks, and these were often given to children as gifts, instead of other toys.

Porcelain and many kinds of pottery were made into cases for mantel and shelf clocks. A good many of these cases were Holland Delft and charming floral ones were made in other countries. Believe it or not, a certain number of china picture frames were made too. Oval ones in mottled brown Rockingham glaze duplicated the oval frames of mahogany and black walnut. This mottled brown glaze also was used for mammoth curtain tiebacks, different but not nearly so attractive as the pressed glass ones.

Bottles with matching stoppers were made for cologne and perfume. Corks

*China slippers were a popular Victorian novelty. The bisque slipper at the left, 4¾ inches long, bears a modeled pink rose with green stem and foliage. The other is pottery, 3½ inches long, painted salmon-color, with a green bow. (1875-1900)*

usually stopped stoneware bottles and the pottery ones in various "character" forms. Majolica bottles might be shaped like a duck or parrot, among other forms. Not yet old enough to be antique are the attractive Delft bottles in which bols, a Holland gin, was put up now and again, and the Royal Copenhagen decanters for Denmark's Cherry Heering.

It's easy to recognize a Rogers' Group or Staffordshire spaniels. However, reproductions and outright fakes are plentiful in the field of porcelain and pottery. So-called antique Meissen may prove to be quite recent Meissen, or not Meissen at all but from another Dresden pottery. The porcelain expert is guided by coloring, glaze, character of the body, modeling, and decoration. Whether a piece is marked or not, he can tell whether a figurine is eighteenth-century or twentieth-century Royal Worcester, whether a Toby jug is English, American, or a copy made in Europe or Japan. The number that so frequently is the only mark on the bottom of a vase, figure, or other china ornament is little or no help in identification.

The criteria for judging figures, groups, and other ornamental ware correspond to those for table china. A statuette or a porcelain group may have a hand, finger, or head broken off, or the piece may have been knocked over and shattered. It's unusual if some small part has not been broken and glued back in place on any figure a century or more old. In the opinion of expert George Savage, a broken figure or group that has been put together so that the damage hardly shows and that has required only minimum restoration of parts does not have to be discarded. It not only can be sold but would be worth buying. If a hand, a finger, or the rose a ballerina held in her hand has been replaced with a new one that has been carefully modeled and colored, the value of the piece should not be lessened to any great extent. The skill with which restoration or repairs have been accomplished determines how seriously the damage must be rated from a financial standpoint.

China has such a universal appeal that almost anything can be sold. A pancake dish may bring less than $5 at a country auction, but might be sold to a collector for a little more because these dishes are not common. If you get together a miscellaneous lot of pieces, including perhaps a couple of platters, a large soup dish, and a couple of cereal dishes from late-nineteenth-century tableware sets, it may be better to offer the assortment to an auctioneer or dealer. Throwing in a hatpin-holder or hair-receiver that you don't know what to do with may spell bonanza to the individual who eventually buys the lot. This is not a money-making way to sell old china, but it is a good way to get rid of odds and ends and receive a few dollars in return.

Remember that there are people who

collect hatpin-holders, mustache cups, and pitchers. Any one of these that can be classed as rare or scarce because of its decoration or the type of pottery is worth hanging on to until a customer who collects that sort of thing comes along. A shaving mug that shows a bookbinder at work could be sold right now for $40. Other occupational shaving mugs bring prices from $20 to $100 or more. Collectors also are extremely interested in cups and saucers, butter chips, mugs, tiles, and small boxes.

Platters are quite common. Tureens are not, and consequently even plain ironstone or white granite ones bring comparatively good prices. A white granite tureen can be sold for $10 to $35 depending upon the pattern — that is, if it can be authenticated as having been made during the 1800's. Staffordshire tureens start at about $50, and a rare pattern or a commemorative design sometimes can be sold for two or three times that amount.

Sets of tableware with only one or two of the dinner plates and perhaps a couple of sauce dishes missing can be sold too. Haviland sets in the dainty floral patterns so popular during the 1880's and 1890's are not fashionable in this decade, but because they are porcelain eventually find buyers. In a small city such as Glens Falls, New York, a Haviland dinner set of approximately 100 pieces might bring no more than $50. In metropolitan areas, the same set might well sell for between $100 and $200. This is a likely example

of appraisal and selling price being far apart.

A single piece or a two- to five-piece set for a washstand is readily salable. Prices will depend on the kind of china, its decoration, and condition. A five-piece set, however, could bring $25 to $35. A washbowl in good condition should be worth $5. A plain white ironstone washbowl and ewer might be sold for as much as $15, but a pair with floral decoration should bring $20. Again, prices at country auctions may be lower.

A Delft inkwell made before 1875 should not be sold for less than $20. A Royal Worcester porcelain pitcher, 5 inches high, decorated with flower sprays and honey gold, is currently worth between $25 and $30. Tobacco jars bring $15 and up, according to the kind of pottery, form, decoration, and size.

Jasperware has been made since 1775, so be sure of the span of years before making up your mind how much you want for a piece. A green jasperware wall plaque made in the nineteenth century should bring about $15 if it's 4 inches long, $25 if it's about 7 inches long. Either a blue or green jasperware box in good condition can be sold for $15 to $20 or so, depending on its size and shape. A jardiniere is worth at least $40, as would be a pair of candlesticks 5 inches or so tall.

A bust of a girl in bisque that has been

colored should be worth $10 to $15 to someone. Parian ware is worth at least as much, although the price varies with the subject. A Parian bust of President Garfield probably could not be sold for more than $15, although one of George Washington or Napoleon would bring between $20 and $30. Figurines start at about $15 and can be priced much higher depending on their intricacy.

A selling market is developing for Rogers' Groups, which have been ignored for a long time. So many were produced that prices are still modest, but at least they can be sold. Rogers' first group, "The Checker Players," brings no more than $25 in this first revival of interest in his work. His largest one, "The Council of War," is quoted at $75. The average selling price for most of his groups remains between $20 and $35.

# 13
# *Silver and Silver plate*

HOUSEHOLD SILVER for many centuries indicated the wealth of a family. It is only since about 1850, when the electroplating process was developed, that flatware for the table and holloware pieces have been priced within the budget of the average family. Nineteenth-century plated silver as well as pieces of Early American and Federal silver are as good as money in the bank today.

Silversmiths found plenty of work to keep them busy at their trade during Colonial days. Their handiwork was not seen in the average household, where similar articles were made of brass, iron, copper, pewter, or wood. However, for those fortunate enough to accumulate silver coins, the silversmith served as a sort of banker and insurance agent too. He melted down the coins, made household articles from them, and identified these pieces with the owner's monogram, crest, or coat of arms. Usually the silversmith's own mark was stamped somewhere too. Colonial newspapers often printed descriptive notices of silver pieces that had been stolen.

Nowadays, knives, forks, and spoons are the first silverware that most families invest in, but in Colonial days it was mugs, beakers, tankards, candlesticks, and other useful household articles. Covered cups, inkstands and snuffer stands, sauce boats, salts, sugar boxes, casters and dredgers, creamers, porringers, bowls and salvers, and teakettles and teapots were other likely pieces. In 1962 the Museum of the City of New York arranged an exhibit of seventeenth-century silver made in New York City. Included was the work of thirteen silversmiths, many of whom had emigrated from Holland. The earliest piece was a communion beaker made in 1678 by Ahasuerus Hendricks. Another beaker made in 1684 was the product of Jurian Blanck, Jr., New York City's first native silversmith. By far the largest part of the exhibit consisted of household silver.

Similar silver pieces were made in all the other prosperous cities and centers of the Colonies and first states. Baltimore and many smaller towns were as well able to support one or more silversmiths as Newport, Philadelphia, New York, and Boston. In all, hundreds of silversmiths worked in Colonial America. They had learned their trade as apprentices in the countries of their origin—chiefly Holland, France, and England—and they established a similar system of apprenticeship here. Before 1800, more than 150 silversmiths were working in Boston alone. Most famous of all those in Boston was Paul Revere, but he was preceded by Jeremiah Dummer, Edward Winslow, and William Rouse, among others. Some of his competitors were Jacob and Nathaniel Hurd, Daniel Henchman, and William Cowell.

In England, craftsmen's guild rules required silversmiths to stamp their wares with hallmarks that indicated the maker, his town, the year, the reigning monarch, and the sterling quality of the metal. In America, the only mark customarily was that of the maker, either his initials or his last name. And the only guarantee that all of those Spanish silver dollars had been used to make the piece was the silversmith's integrity. His mark was in relief against a depressed oval, shield, rectangle, or

some other shape. This practice continued into the early 1800's.

After 1830, either "coin," "pure coin," "dollar," or the letter C or D was usually stamped on the back. Any one of these markings guaranteed that the silverware was made of the quality of coin from the United States Mint— 900 fine, or 900 parts of pure silver out of 1,000 parts. However, it did not mean, as it would have a century earlier, that coins had been melted down to fashion the silverware.

After 1860, the word "sterling" came into use. When stamped on a piece of silver, it guarantees that the silver is .925 fine.

Silversmiths followed both the styles and decorations that had been current in their native countries. Feet, handles, and certain other parts were cast and then added by soldering.

A piece was often decorated with engraving, which might include both a design and an inscription. Engraving is done only on the outer surface and the inside remains smooth. Piercing is a form of decoration done by cutting a design through the silver. In America it was used most frequently on the handles of porringers and the raised edges of trays and salvers. Repoussé or embossing produces a design in relief and is achieved by hammering. Gadrooning is a sort of reeding, notching, or carving of a rounded molding that was much used for borders. Fluting is just the opposite, the grooves being depressed instead of raised. Chasing is somewhat similar to embossing, but is in low relief or depressed. This also was done with hammers and chisels. Cut-card decoration, which was not used as much in America, consisted of a thin layer of silver cut out in an ornamental pattern and added to the piece, for example, around the knob on a cover or around a handle.

Although all of these decorative techniques were used to some extent in this country, silver for the most part was decorated simply. Simple, classic lines and excellent workmanship with minimum decoration were the rule. Instead of the coat of arms or the crest so much used in England and France to identify silver, here an initial or monogram was much more likely.

In Colonial silver, all kinds of candlesticks as well as tapersticks and candelabra, snuffers and snuffer stands, were important. So were drinking utensils, which included beakers (handleless cups), tankards with a handle and hinged cover, mugs, and two-handled caudle cups with and without covers. Porringers were not limited to being "porridge dishes" or given primarily to children. This small dish, which is deeper than a plate or saucer and has almost upright sides and a flat bottom, was used for many purposes in Colonial homes. Those made in this country usually have only one handle and no cover.

Silver teapots were made for special customers in New York and in Boston and elsewhere in New England before 1700. By the mid-1700's, tea and coffee were important beverages and called for special equipment to use in preparing and serving them. Teapots were more general in America than coffeepots. Although a chocolate pot now in the Metropolitan Museum of Art was made by Edward Winslow, Bos-

*Eighteenth-century teapots were small because tea was scarce and expensive. Pots like the pear-shaped silver one at the right were fashionable until about 1750. Then the shape was reversed—with the bulbous part at the top. The scrolled handles are wood.*

ton silversmith, in the early 1700's, American-made ones are rare. Both chocolate pots and coffeepots followed the general lines of teapots, but were taller and slimmer.

The first teapots were very small, because tea was both scarce and expensive. They were round or globular. About 1730, pots were still small but rather pear-shaped and with domed tops. Then about 1750 the inverted pear shape became popular, and about 1780 the straight-sided oval pot with a straight spout and simple curved handle became fashionable both in England and America. After 1800, teapots and coffeepots both became much larger. Tea urns with a spigot also appeared.

Not only the first teapots were small but also the first cups and silver teaspoons. They usually were displayed on silver or china trays. Creamers and sugar bowls also were made of silver, and before tea sets or services became

*Casters were often made in sets of three, the largest one for sugar. These silver ones were made in England in the 1700's, but similar ones were also made in America.*

general, odd pieces were assembled for tea-drinking occasions. The matching set of teapot, sugar bowl, creamer, sugar tongs, and strainer, with hot water kettle and tray, began to appear in the early 1800's and gradually became popular. These tea services usually included an uncovered bowl called a dregs bowl. Tea caddies were made of china for a good many years, then of wood and other materials, but only rarely of silver.

Among the more interesting pieces of antique silver are small boxes made for tobacco and snuff and containers for condiments. Seventeenth-century salt dishes were the round saltcellar with three applied feet, the larger trencher, and a standing salt that stood 5 inches high and was shaped something like a spool. Trencher salts were oval, rectangular, or round. In the 1800's footed salts became popular and some of these had colored glass linings. Pepper boxes with a cover and handle also were made of silver. Pairs of salt and pepper shakers, however, did not appear until after 1875, and at first were not common in silver.

Casters or dredgers were shakers with pierced tops used to sprinkle sugar, pepper, mustard, spices, and, in fact, any powdered or liquid condiment for the table. They were less likely to hold salt. Casters frequently were made in sets of three, one much taller (approximately 9 inches) than the other two (about 3 inches high). The tops or domes of these casters were pierced in

*The salt dish is britannia metal with a colored glass lining. The spoons are silver. The two smaller ones (2 inches and 3½ inches) are for salt. The third one, 5¼ inches long, was made for a mustard pot.*

a decorative pattern. In some sets one of the two small casters had only simulated holes. Casters changed shape much as teapots did. That is, early ones were cylindrical. The later octagonal shape eventually was modified to vase shape.

Sugar bowls were small because sugar, like tea, was scarce and expensive. Sugar boxes, usually oval and much decorated, had hinged covers that could be locked. Mustard pots with handles often closely matched dredgers or caster sets.

In the late 1700's small spoons were made for open salt dishes. These ranged from 2 inches long with a bowl ½ inch wide, to 3 inches long with a ¾-inch bowl. Identical spoons with longer handles—5¼ inches—and ⅞-inch bowls were made for mustard pots. Spoons were the first pieces of table silver in common use. When tea-drinking became fashionable, fairly small silver

*Silver teaspoons made around 1800 were small and thin. The three at the top (note the down-turned tips of the handles) were made before 1800. The spoon at the far right has script initials on the underside of the handle; the bowl is so thin that teethmarks show.*

**290**

spoons called teaspoons were called for. Not that the spoon is not an old implement. It's mentioned in the Bible, and silver or bronze ones were made by the Greeks and the Romans. At various times spoons have been carved from wood, bone, horn, and ivory, and even into the nineteenth century of tin and pewter as well as silver. By the early 1700's in England, well-to-do families set their tables with soup and dessert spoons as well as small teaspoons. Two hundred years of change and development between the 1700's and the 1900's led to the form of the twentieth-century teaspoon, which is a comfortable one to use. The size and shape of the bowl, the style of the handle, the way the tip of the handle turns, and the placement of the initials, orna-mental engraving, or decoration are as important clues to the age of silver spoons as the mark of the silversmith.

Silver spoons were made in America before 1700. In the 1700's and 1800's, teaspoons underwent many changes.

Smaller teaspoons began to appear before 1750, and as a general rule, after 1790, spoons were thin and light. In fact, they were so thin that teethmarks often show on them and the handles may be bent from use. It is not at all uncommon to come across teaspoons made between 1800 and 1860. Some of them, even those made in the early 1800's, will have script initials or a monogram on the back. Because spoons made during this period are so

| | BOWL | HANDLE | TIP | DECORATION |
|---|---|---|---|---|
| *Around* 1700 | Large, oval | Thin, short | Three-pointed. Also round and upcurved with ridge down center back | Sometimes on back of bowl. Initials or crest on back of handle |
| *After* 1750 | Narrower and slightly pointed | Longer and wider, with more shaping | Tip turned down | |
| 1790–*Early* 1800's | Narrow and pointed | Shaped, and wider through most of its length | Tapered, rounded, or squared off to "coffin" tip | Front sometimes engraved |
| 1830–60 | Narrow, pointed | Fiddle-shaped | Upturned | Sheaf of Wheat, Basket of Flowers, also Thread outlining the fiddle shape |
| 1860— | Oval | Tapering | Upturned | Raised designs on handles. Initial or monogram on upper side of tip |

The three tablespoons and two teaspoons in this group were all made before 1840. The spoon in the center and the one at the far right, much the heaviest of the group, are marked "Pure Coin," but so is the second one from the left.

slender with very pointed handles and presumably were used to skin motes—leaf particles—from the surface of a cup of tea.

Long-handled forks with two tines were indispensable in the kitchen for cooking chores for centuries before it was considered good manners to use individual forks at the table. In Italy, where forks were first made, people made fun of anyone who used them, and the same thing happened later in other European countries. Paul Revere is said to have fashioned some silver forks in Boston. Most of those made here and in England before 1800 had two or three tines. It was the early 1800's before the four-tined forks were generally seen and used. In handles and decoration they were similar to spoons.

*Nineteenth-century silver spoons: The three teaspoons at the right are stamped "Coin" on the underside of the handles. The tablespoon has the end of the handle clipped off in the famous coffin shape. The initials P.M. in script on the front stand for Phimela Miles of New Haven, who married a Virginian and lived at Tuckahoe Plantation above Richmond. (1800-1830)*

thin and perhaps out of shape, don't think they are tin or pewter. All of them will have the silversmith's name or mark on the underside, usually somewhere along the handle. And after polishing, they will have the unmistakable patina of pure silver.

Many spoons of special design were introduced in England during the Queen Anne period (1702–20), and eventually most of them made their way to this country. These included basting spoons with handles up to 18 inches long, and serving, stuffing, and gravy spoons, which had perforated bowls to strain off unwanted bits of giblets and the like. Marrow scoops were small and narrow. Tea caddy spoons, used to measure the tea that was put into the pot, had bowls in various shapes such as a shell, bird's head, or cap, and stubby handles. Mote spoons were

It was the eighteenth century, too, before individual table knives came into general use. Originally, a knife was as much a weapon as an eating utensil, and had a sharp point. Then, as forks became generally fashionable late in the seventeenth century, knives were made to use with them and the blades were rounded. In the eighteenth century, knife blades were broad, flat, rounded and curved outward at the ends.

The earliest knives and forks had silver handles with the so-called pistol grip. This style was popular in England from the mid-1700's. Chiefly for

*Handles of mother-of-pearl, ivory, bone, and porcelain all enjoyed a vogue during the 1800's. These fruit or dessert knives and forks (circa 1850) have mother-of-pearl handles and attractive engraving on the metal parts.*

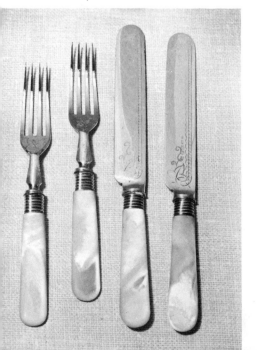

forks but also to some extent for knives, the shell, thread, and fiddle-thread were the decoration for handles during the early 1800's. Named patterns, as they are known today, did not become common until after 1860.

Knives and forks with bone handles and steel blades were widely used during the 1800's. At various times before 1800 and thereafter, ivory, mother-of-pearl, and, occasionally, porcelain handles were fashionable. Mother-of-pearl handles for dinner knives and for fruit knives and forks (the knives had decorative blades) were a Victorian fancy, and are well worth looking for.

Silver-gilt was not made to any extent in this country, although some old pieces may be found. (When silver articles are gilded, they are called silver-gilt or vermeil. Technically, vermeil may be silver, bronze, or copper that has been gilded.) Silver sugar bowls sometimes had gilded interiors and the bowls of fancy spoons sometimes were gilded. Table ornaments of vermeil, in particular, were high fashion in France from about 1764 to 1843, and especially during the Empire period. Some vermeil was imported from France and may still be found.

Almost as valuable as solid silver are old pieces of Sheffield plated silver. Sheffield, England, has been a famous center for metal and cutlery since the fourteenth century. The special process named after the town dates back to 1742 when Thomas Boulsover, a cutler, found that silver and copper could be fused by heating, then rolled out into a thin, smooth plate that could be worked as could solid silver. Old Sheffield plate is made from two sheets of silver bonded to one of copper, with the edges bound in silver. The sheets of silver in Sheffield plate are thicker than the covering of silver deposited by electrolysis on modern plated silver.

Articles of Sheffield plate were displayed proudly on sideboards, mantelpieces, and dining tables. The same pieces and the same styles that were used for silver also were produced in Sheffield plate. Candlesticks and candelabra, teapots, tea and coffee services, trays, serving dishes, and tureens were the principal large pieces. Baskets for cake and fruit, cruet stands, and epergnes were handsome and now owned by far more people than when they were made only of silver. Inkstands, small boxes for tobacco and snuff, buckles, and buttons also were used and worn proudly. Buttons were made in tremendous quantity.

Gadrooned edges were as general on Sheffield plate as on silver. Shells and three feathers were common decorative motifs and an initial or a monogram was usual. A few firms are said to have produced quite distinctive pieces that borrowed little from silver ones in design or decoration. All firms were noted for their good workmanship.

The making of Sheffield plate was a

*Sheffield plate was made between 1742 and the 1840's as a substitute for pure silver pieces. The gadroon-edged plate and the sauce boat were made in Sheffield, England, during that period.*

thriving industry for about 100 years. Some small amount was made in America, but most of the early Sheffield plate to be found in this country was imported. In the early 1800's, the fusing of silver on copper spread to France, Germany, and elsewhere in central Europe as well as Russia, but the quality is not considered to be as high as that of the Sheffield plate made in England. It's not unusual to find candlesticks or other household pieces of European plate in this country. However, the silver-on-copper ware made in Europe during the nineteenth century seldom seems to be stamped with maker's marks—certainly I have never seen any marks on pieces made in Germany.

During a ten-year period from the 1770's into the 1780's, London silversmiths succeeded in preventing firms that made Sheffield plate from marking their ware. Before the early 1770's and after 1784, identification marks similar to those stamped on silver were used. Some pieces also had the word Sheffield stamped above the hallmark.

In the 1840's, the making of Sheffield plate began to die out. It's interesting that within thirty years or so, in England, antique collectors began acquiring pieces of Sheffield plate. In 1911, action was taken and it was established in court in Sheffield that the term "Sheffield Plate" could be applied only to pieces made by the method of fusing practiced in the eighteenth and early nineteenth centuries.

Antique Sheffield plate probably represents a lost art. These pieces wear surprisingly well. However, articles with thin spots where the silver has worn down or been cut by repeated use of a carving knife so that the red copper base is exposed are called "bloody." Such pieces bring a lower price than one with its silver coatings unblemished.

Sheffield plate was less expensive than solid silver. However, it was not as much cheaper as pressed glass was in comparison to cut glass. Therefore, when the newer process of electroplating was developed in the 1840's, it displaced the Sheffield plating method in just a few years. Electroplating proved to be a far cheaper process of covering a base metal with silver (then, as now, sterling cost about three times as much as the same piece in plated silver.)

Some of the early plated silver was made by coating brass with pure silver. However, when the comparatively thin coating of silver wore off, the yellow of the brass showed, much to the owner's dismay. Some kind of white base metal, therefore, came into general use. The make-up of the base metal has varied according to manufacturer and general practice during the last century.

Only an article that is 92.5 per cent pure silver could be marked "Sterling." Plated silver, however, was made in several grades. Currently, plated silver is either standard or first quality, the latter term meaning that the pieces have a heavier coating of silver than standard ones. Quite an amount of nineteenth-century plated silver is stamped "Triple" or "Quadruple" plate. Such pieces, if they have been exposed, may be charcoal-colored and take a good deal of polishing to restore their silver tone. Of course, even triple-

*This covered butter dish, made of quadruple-plated silver after 1860, was resilvered about ten years ago. The butter knife and fork with engraved floral and foliage decoration are sterling silver.
—Ted Eastwood*

or quadruple-plated pieces that were used daily for a good many years will have spots where the silver coating has worn down to the base metal. It's worth the hard polishing that a darkened piece of plated silver needs to see just how it will look. Many of the triple- and quadruple-plated pieces are in surprisingly good condition and need only minimum polishing to look their best.

In the United States, plated silver has been made in quantity since the 1850's. Some American silversmiths made both sterling and plated silver after 1860. The same types of decoration as well as the same forms were made in plated and sterling silver. Different patterns, however, were worked out for the two distinctly different products.

Early-nineteenth-century silver relied on classical form and decoration, as did furniture. Later, extremely rococo designs and patterns were popular for both sterling and plated silver. Elaborate repoussé was done even on tableware. Patterns often were based on quite naturalistic flowers and foliage, and in Victorian days an occasional fruit motif was used. Garlands, drapery, and figures also were worked into some of the elaborate Victorian patterns. Patterns of silver-plated flatware may have been somewhat simpler than those designed for sterling flatware. However, silver-plated holloware was as ornate and decorated as sterling silver.

Often tucked away in unlikely places

and sometimes scattered in more than one hidden spot throughout a house are remnants of the set of flatware that American families gradually accumulated after 1860. The purchase of flatware by place settings is a recent fashion. In the nineteenth and early twentieth centuries, flatware was

*The ice cream forks of sterling silver shown here were part of a set given to an Alabama bride in the 1870's. The demitasse spoons with gilded bowls and lily-of-the-valley handles enameled in green and white were a well-liked style in the 1890's.*

*Some pieces of silverware common between 1870 and 1910 are no longer made. The nut spoon (far left) and orange spoon with serrated edges (far right) are sterling silver; the pudding spoon with its deep round bowl, and the pickle or olive spoon, 8 inches long, are quadruple-plated silver.*
—Ted Eastwood

bought by the dozen of each piece. Furthermore, the number of different pieces then considered essential to set a table for company is amazing to present-day brides and housewives.

Patterns of the earliest sets of flatware included five different forks—oyster, fish, dinner, salad, and ice cream or berry; four knives—dinner, luncheon or dessert, fish, and butter spreader; four spoons—soup, bouillon, tea, and demitasse or after-dinner coffee; and, finally, a dessert spoon and fork. In other words, a place setting required fifteen pieces of silver, with each knife, fork, and spoon shaped quite differently from the others. Demitasse spoons were made in flatware patterns, but often were chosen in another pattern or design. These small spoons with colored enamel decoration on the handles were popular at one time, and usually are lovely.

To round out the place settings of silver, a greater array of serving pieces was made too. These, of course, were made in the same patterns. Tablespoons were all right for serving vegetables, but a berry spoon, deeper and rounder, was essential for serving a fruit dessert. There was a different-shaped spoon for serving pudding, too, and a small spoon with its bowl often shaped like a shell to keep in a sugar bowl. Serving forks and ladles were made in at least two sizes, and there were large serving tongs as well as smaller tongs to put in the bowl of lump sugar. Then there were special servers for fish, pie, and cheese, and

both a knife and fork to serve cake. Grape scissors to be used to cut small clusters from the large bunch graced the sideboard. Nut spoons were likely to be fancy, but smaller spoons for various condiments and a long, slender-handled olive or pickle fork were made in most of the patterns.

Some patterns also included orange or grapefruit spoons. These had bowls in a much more exaggerated shape than are made nowadays. The bowl was longer, deeper, and narrower than that of a teaspoon and tapered to a point. One edge of some of these nineteenth-century spoons was sometimes serrated, the better to dig out the sections of pulp.

A few kinds of spoons were regional. One example is the Café Brûlot spoon essential in and around New Orleans. A lump of sugar was placed in this spoon and soaked with brandy, which was lighted over the coffee.

By the 1890's, every member of a family had his own napkin ring made of either sterling or plated silver. These were almost always identified with an initial or monogram, usually placed within a garland or scroll. If the napkin ring had been a gift on a birthday or some other special occasion, the date was often added, usually in script lettering. These napkin rings were cylindrical and quite wide—1½ to 2 inches (a recent fad is having them cut and shaped into cuff bracelets). About 1910 napkin rings became narrower, about an inch in width, and looked even smaller because they were nipped in at the middle. Decoration was sometimes applied. A small, inch-wide napkin ring of plated silver made around 1910, for example, was encircled with the stems, leaves, and buds of the large, open poppy that ornamented it.

At about the same time that napkin rings became a polite necessity, it became the custom to give cups or mugs with handles as gifts to newborn babies. These were made of either sterling or plated silver. They averaged between 2 and 3 inches high and at least one side was decorated. Often the handle was quite fancy too. Names and dates usually were engraved on the cups.

*Souvenir spoons of sterling became popular in the 1880's. The teaspoons at the top are from Rochester, New York, New London, Connecticut, and Toronto, Canada. The last is decorated with brilliant enamel on the tip. The demitasse spoons are souvenirs of Boston and Mount Vernon.*

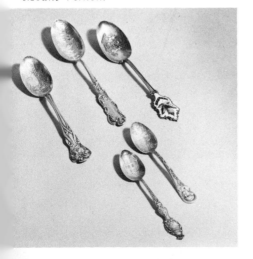

First popular during the 1880's and 1890's were souvenir spoons made in the sizes of teaspoons or demitasse spoons. Souvenir spoons still are being made, but few if any of the present-day ones compare in workmanship to those made before 1900. Nineteenth-century souvenir spoons almost invariably were sterling silver. Handles often were decorated with fine, colorful enamels. Sometimes the bowl was vermeil. Both the handle and the bowl were decorated with designs appropriate to the city, historical site, or other specific place where the spoon was purchased. Usually the name or title was engraved somewhere.

A small demitasse spoon that was a souvenir of Boston is a typical example. Appropriate motifs were used on both front and reverse. The bowl depicted the Old State House in detail but had only the word "Sterling" on the underside. The flared end of the handle displayed the State House and, successively under it, Paul Revere on his horse, a pot of beans with that word across it, and "Boston" with the letters spelled out vertically. On the reverse of the handle were Faneuil Hall, Old South Church, and Bunker Hill monument. A dozen demitasse spoons from as many places was the goal of many a young lady in the 1890's.

Not only resorts and cities such as Boston that were already considered historic by 1890 had their souvenir spoons. Many less likely places did too. New London, Connecticut, Rochester, New York, Springfield, Massachusetts, and many less notable cities and towns offered visitors the opportunity of buying a souvenir spoon of good quality. Almost anywhere a person went, whether it was for a ride up the Hudson River ("Steamer *Hendrick Hudson*") or on vacation ("1000 Islands" in flowing script on the bowl), it was possible to buy a decorated, sterling silver spoon as a memento of the occasion.

Some souvenir spoons were so fancy that they had a movable part. For example, one had a handle topped by a windmill with arms that could be rotated. Sometimes handle ends were fashioned in the shape of a bird or an animal, less often a figure. These may have been copied from the sixteenth-century style in Europe of terminating handles of the larger spoons made at that time with a figure, often a biblical personage.

Tea and coffee services as well as other pieces for serving or display always had been made from sterling silver. Later, all of these pieces were made to match the patterns of flatware. Such things as spoonholders or spoon dishes, celery dishes, and bread trays were made too. Cake plates and baskets, pitchers for water, wine, and syrup, covered vegetable dishes, and tureens also became general. Most of these

*Silver-plated tea service (post-1860) consisting of a sugar bowl (7 inches high), coffeepot (11¼ inches high), and teapot (7¼ inches high). Each one has a knob made up of leaves with a flower or fruit, which is held in place by a screw. The oval tray with a beaded edge measures 19¼ by 24½ inches. The three hollow pieces have been replated within the last fifteen years; the tray has not been but is in perfect condition. The candlesticks, silver on copper, came from Germany.—Ted Eastwood*

during the nineteenth century, from classically simple lines and decorative motifs in the early years to heavy, all-over rococo after the 1860's.

Tea and coffee services became almost as important as cut glass after 1870. They were made in many patterns other than those that matched flatware. A plated silver tea service made in the 1870's repeated, in its handles and covers, the rectangular lines of furniture made in that decade, and the decoration on the silver pieces was as shallow as the carving on the furniture. This tea service consisted of a teapot of generous size, a large sugar bowl with cover, a milk pitcher or creamer, and an uncovered bowl for dregs. A covered butter dish and perhaps other serving dishes often were made to match the tea service.

Sugar and creamer also were made in matching sets. Some sugar bowls were made with colored glass liners. After 1900, sugar bowls became smaller.

Some of the more attractive serving pieces that had come into wide use by the 1890's combined silver with glass. A cut or pressed glass jar for jelly or marmalade might have a silver cover. A glass pickle jar usually came in a plated silver stand with a handle for carrying it and a long-handled fork or tongs attached to one side. Cracker jars of satin glass or other art glass or china often were fitted with silver-plated covers and handles. Covered

*"Paul Revere · Silver Co. Boston" is stamped on the underside of this tray made of Sheffield plate, a fine example of the comparatively small amount of this ware made in the United States. A pressed glass pickle jar with a stand and fork or tongs of quadruple plate was a favorite table accessory between 1880 and the turn of the century.*

pieces were made in plated as well as sterling silver after 1860. Serving trays in various sizes and shapes were sterling, plated silver, or various plated alloys. Many attractive small dishes were made to hold candy or nuts. These were made in various styles, open or covered, footed, or flat like a basket with a handle.

Candlesticks continued to be made in various heights and not necessarily to match tableware patterns, even though lamps were used for illumination. The pair of candlesticks on the mantel or sideboard and the candelabrum on the serving table in the dining room could as well have been plated as sterling silver. Styles and decoration followed the changes that became fashionable

butter dishes of either sterling or
plated silver usually had glass linings,
and many a pottery baking dish could
be slipped into a silver container with
a cover before it was brought to the
table. Silver stands were made to hold
pottery egg cups.

Although serving dishes with glass or
pottery linings became common in late
Victorian years, a much longer history
can be traced for the many different
pieces of silver and various kinds of
plate that were designed to keep food
hot. For this purpose either a hot-water
jacket or a central hot-water compartment was fitted into the body of the
silver piece, or a hot-water chamber
into the base. Large dishes for bringing various kinds of meat to the table
often had not only a hot-water compartment in the base but also a cover
or hinged lid. Dishes equipped in this
manner were made from 1760 on, and
the Victorians also liked their vegetable dishes to have hot-water compartments. In fact, in the 1850's Victorians showed a preference for a toast
rack with a hot-water chamber in the
base. Chafing dishes first appeared during the 1700's, and by 1800—earlier in
England—tea or coffee urns were made
to fit over a spirit lamp. Any of these
old serving dishes that a person is lucky
enough to discover becomes, after it
has been polished, a practical as well
as a distinguished addition to outdoor
dining, now so popular everywhere.

There are many other odd pieces to
be on the lookout for. They may be

A cruet stand was standard dining-room
equipment until about 1900. This one of
plated silver, dating from about 1890, has
stoppered bottles for vinegar and oil,
shakers with plated tops for salt and pepper, and a squat jar for mustard.

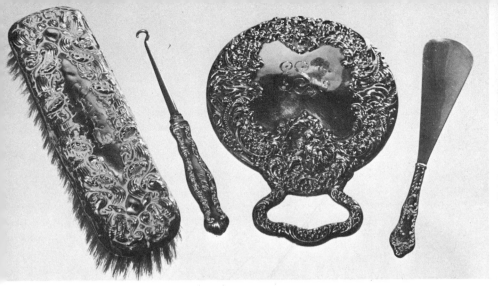

*Sterling silver accessories were common in the late 1800's. Brushes of various sizes and shapes were made with silver backs or handles. A buttonhook and shoehorn with silver handles often were part of a dresser set, which also included a hand mirror, comb, and hairbrush.*—Ted Eastwood

quite black when you find them, but polishing may reveal that they are sterling silver. This is true of buttons and buckles, toys and rattles, dresser sets and toilet articles with silver backs, covers, and handles, teaballs and tea-strainers to rest on a cup, inkstands and snuffer trays, knife rests, and buttonhooks for buttoning shoes.

The toothpick, which it was considered polite to use after meals, might be silver, gold, or ivory. More complicated but not much larger than a toothpick was a 2½-inch-long silver-plated cylinder. Turn one end and a toothpick emerged; turn the other and an equally small scoop appeared, evidently meant for cleaning wax from the ears.

Whether flatware or a tea service is sterling silver or plated, the pieces that seem odd today are the ones a person

usually finds. Considerable interest is shown in nineteenth-century plated silver. There is quite a ready market for various serving dishes. Many of the old

*A fern dish of sterling or plated silver was a prized possession of many housewives in the early 1900's. The plants and soil were put into a pottery liner that fit inside the decorative container. The example shown has a ½-inch-thick wood base. The silver is pierced in a pattern of grapes and foliage, with a matching border applied in relief.*

*The decoration of both sterling and plated silver pieces often consisted of flower or fruit motifs. The butter pat here has a design of cherries; the syrup pitcher has a strawberry motif, with foliage decorating the handle. Both pieces are plated silver made after 1860. The "Pure Coin" tablespoon is circa 1840.*

ones are no longer being made in either sterling or plate, and some that are being made were more charming in their Victorian form. A plated silver syrup pitcher, for example, with a small bunch of grapes as the knob is a delightful piece that can be sold if you don't want to keep it. First, however, be sure to find the plate into which the bottom of the pitcher fitted. A half-dozen sterling silver butter pats will be snapped up by anyone smart enough to think of having thin glass disks cut to fit into them, so they can be used for ashtrays at each place setting.

Before offering any silver articles for sale, it's important to clean them with care, at least enough so that you can distinguish markings. Plated silver, unless it is very worn off, looks somewhat like sterling. However, stand a piece of sterling and a piece of plated silver

side by side and study them. It will not take you long to recognize which one is which without turning the pieces upside down to examine the markings.

Old coin and sterling silver are not harmed by normal use and proper care, but will acquire a beautiful patina from much handling and careful polishing through the years. Even when they were new, a surface bloom gave them a warm, rich gleam or tone quite unlike that of contemporary sterling silver. The original tone of even nineteenth-century silver mellows to a warm, rich glow.

Sheffield plate also has a soft patina, although it is not as rich as that of sterling silver. Much of the old, true Sheffield plate still has its good coating of silver and little or none of the copper base shows. A piece of Sheffield plate is heavier than the same piece made of coin or sterling silver. Electroplated silver, made after 1850, is heavier than pieces of Sheffield plate and also of sterling.

Tableware and serving and decorative pieces of silver plate never gain a patina similar to that of sterling or even Sheffield plate. In fact, plated silver always has a colder, whiter, almost lifeless color. That is, until the silver coating begins to wear off, and then the plated piece looks spotty. A badly spotted or worn piece of plate can be freshly coated with silver by a professional silversmith and will look as good as or even better than when it was new.

This can be a worthwhile investment if you plan to use or display the piece in your home. If you prefer to sell it, leave it in the condition you found it.

Another form of plating produces the so-called German silver, one of many names for nickel silver. This is a white alloy of copper, zinc, and nickel used as a cheap substitute for silver. The proportions in which the metals are used to make German silver may vary. However, the more nickel it contains, the slower the piece will be to tarnish (it can't be polished as successfully as other plated silver). The quantity of nickel also determines how closely the piece resembles one of sterling silver.

German silver is heavier than sterling silver. Most of the pieces I have seen have a distinctly gray tone, which is rather dull. German silver has been used for many years for handles and other parts of dresser and manicure sets and decorative pieces, as for candy dishes. A good deal has been imported, but some amount has been made in the United States. German or nickel silver is not always marked, although pieces made in this country seem usually to be stamped "Nickel Silver" along with the name or mark of the company.

Sterling silver lasts more than a lifetime. It should be as serviceable for this generation as for the one that bought it 100 to 150 years ago. It will emerge from correct polishing as beautiful as the day it was made—more

beautiful, actually, because of its patina. Some pieces may have slight dents but they do not reduce values.

Most of the silver known to have been made in Colonial days is displayed in museums, restorations, and private collections. Should you come across a teapot, communion cup, or mustard pot that, after being polished, shows the mark of William Rouse, Bartholomew Le Roux, Joseph Lownes, or one of their colleagues, you can feel certain it is extremely valuable. Collectors will bid—and pay—high prices.

Such a find would be exceptionally lucky. But then so would finding an Apostle spoon. This is a very old English silver spoon, made in sets of a dozen with an apostle depicted on each spoon. They were presented as christening gifts. Even one Apostle spoon is worth a considerable amount of money, and settlers from England may well have brought some with them to this country. Eighteenth-century spoons such as rat-tail or coffin styles made in America are other possibilities, not as valuable as Apostle spoons but probably to be sold for more than any other old spoons. Eighteenth-century silver made in this country is scarce, for some families had it melted down and remade in the more rococo styles of the nineteenth century. There is a good deal of nineteenth-century sterling and plated silver to be found —and a market for both.

Silver does not decrease in value, but

neither does it increase as much as might be expected. Premium prices can be based only on workmanship or rarity. Thus, nineteenth-century coin and the later sterling silver do not bring as high prices as you might anticipate. At present, coin silver teaspoons sell for about $3 each, tablespoons for about $4. Spoons that are badly bent, dented, or misshapen will bring less money.

Pieces of sterling silver flatware made after 1860 can be sold for only slightly more than the same pieces would cost to buy today. Serving pieces that are less commonly made now but are still useful can be sold for slightly higher prices. Patterns that have been discontinued also should bring a slight premium. A great many of the sterling silver flatware patterns made between 1860 and 1900 have been discontinued by manufacturers, and there always are people who want to fill in an old set. You may stumble on possible buyers, or prefer to dispose of pre-1900 flatware quickly by selling it to one of the dealers who specializes in stocking old patterns.

Sterling silver holloware, candlesticks, tea and coffee services, pitchers, serving dishes, and the like, made in the nineteenth century can be sold, but most of it for only slightly more than contemporary pieces. There is a market also for plated silver pieces. A four- or five-piece tea or coffee service of plated silver may be blackened and need resilvering, yet in either condition it can be sold for $35 to $50. Most of the plated flatware—forks, knives, spoons —is unlikely to be in good enough condition to be sold unless you run into a collector.

There is no real market for napkin rings. Surprising as it may seem, it's usually possible to sell children's cups, even blackened ones of plated silver. Some people collect them because they are small and easy to display; others, because they are nice containers for bouquets of small garden flowers.

Many triple- and quadruple-plated serving pieces can be sold readily. A syrup pitcher with its plate might bring $10 to $15, depending on the condition. A pickle jar in its plated silver stand ought to be worth close to $10; a covered butter dish that needs resilvering, perhaps $7.50.

Old Sheffield plate is more valuable than early electroplate. A Sheffield sauce boat made before 1840 will be worth $25 to anyone who appreciates this product. A tray, approximately 16 by 25 inches, can be sold in most parts of the country for $50 to $75.

Boston and other cities where silversmiths were kept busy during Colonial days are not the only places where a person can expect to find old silver. As families moved westward in the 1800's, silver was one thing that could be taken along. After all, silver frequently represented a family's assets, even if it was silverware and not coins. Really old silver and Sheffield plate may be found almost anywhere in the country, far away from the place where they were made.

After 1850, when the making of household silverware and tableware became an industry instead of a craft, New England became the largest center of its manufacture. Connecticut, Rhode Island, and Massachusetts are still important, although Maryland is an exception that keeps New England from maintaining a monopoly.

## GLOSSARY

### TYPES OF SILVER

*Silver:* any piece marked "Sterling" consists of 92.5 per cent pure silver. Before 1860, pieces marked Coin, Pure Coin, Dollar, C or D contained 90 per cent pure silver.

*Nickel silver:* a white alloy consisting of copper, zinc, and nickel, which is an inexpensive substitute for sterling silver.

*Plated silver:* any piece that has a coating, which may vary in thickness, of pure silver over a base metal, which is usually white. Electroplated silver has been made since about 1850.

*Sheffield plate:* a piece made by fusing pure silver on the top and bottom of copper and sealing the edges with pure silver. The only true Sheffield plate was made from 1742 into the 1840's.

*Vermeil:* silver, bronze, or copper that has been gilded. Silver that has been gilded is called either silver-gilt or vermeil.

*Wirework:* articles made of wire, usually silver over copper, which is interwoven, and having only a solid base or rim.

### TYPES OF DECORATION

*Chasing:* a design created on the exterior with sharp instruments, in low relief in comparison to repoussé.

*Cut-card:* a thin layer of silver cut out in an ornamental pattern and added as decoration on a silver piece—under and around the knob on a cover, for example.

*Engraving:* decoration that is incised on the outer surface only. Inscriptions or lettering also are engraved.

*Fluting:* one or a series of curved grooves that are depressed instead of raised.

*Gadrooning:* ornamentation of a rounded edge or molding by means of notching, reeding, or the like.

*Piercing:* a design made by cutting through silver, used chiefly on handles and rims.

*Repoussé:* a raised design formed by hammering from the underside. Also known as embossing.

### ANTIQUE ARTICLES

*Beaker:* a deep vessel with a wide and open mouth for drinking.

*Caddy:* a small box used for storing tea.

*Caster:* a shaker with a pierced top, 3 to 9 inches high, used to sprinkle sugar, pepper, mustard, or any condiment; often made in sets of three for the table.

*Caudle cup:* a low cup with a wide and open mouth and two handles, originally used to drink hot, spiced wine known as caudle.

*Cruet:* a stand that holds several small glass bottles for vinegar, oil, and the like.

*Dredger:* a small container with perforated top for sprinkling sugar and the like; same as dredging-box, caster.

*Epergne:* a table centerpiece usually with several branching arms to hold fruit or flowers.

*Muffineer:* a dish in which muffins can be kept hot; also, a shaker with perforated cover from which sugar, spices, or the like can be sprinkled on muffins.

*Porringer:* a small dish, deeper than a plate or saucer, with almost straight sides, a flat bottom, and one or two handles, originally used for porridge or cereal. Open or covered.

*Salver:* a plate or tray, often footed, for offering cakes or other food to guests.

*Tankard:* a tall cylindrical cup with one handle and a hinged cover.

*Trencher:* a large container for salt, used on the table.

*Tureen:* a large deep dish with two handles and a cover from which hot soup, stew, or the like is served at the table.

### GENERAL TERMS

*Flatware:* articles for the table that are flat, referring chiefly to knives, forks, and spoons but also including plates, platters, and other flat pieces.

*Holloware:* pieces shaped so that they have a cavity, such as teapots, sugar bowls, pitchers, and the like.

*Hallmark:* the official stamp identifying maker, town, year, and sterling quality of the silver, required on every article of silver or gold as evidence of its genuineness. Originally required by Goldsmiths' Hall in London, England; now, any similar mark of identification.

## FOR FURTHER INFORMATION:

BOOK OF OLD SILVER by Seymour B. Wyler. New York: Crown Publishers, Inc.

DICTIONARY OF AMERICAN SILVER, PEWTER AND SILVER PLATE by Ralph M. and Terry H. Kovel. New York: Crown Publishers, Inc.

EARLY AMERICAN SILVER (A Picture Book). New York: The Metropolitan Museum of Art.

SMALL ANTIQUE SILVERWARE by G. Bernard Hughes. New York: The Macmillan Company.

# 14
## Indispensable Metals

THE BRAZIER, THE BLACKSMITH, the tin-smith, and the pewterer performed inestimable services not only during Colonial days but until well along in the nineteenth century. The metal craftsman, settled or footloose, ranked only behind the farmer and the merchant in his importance to every-day living. Yet though many of them lived in one village or town all their lives, most of them are nameless. It's rarely possible to credit the brass can-dlesticks, copper teakettles, iron trivets, and painted tin boxes as made 150 years or so ago, however handsome these things still are. The only excep-tion is pewter pieces, for many pew-terers are almost as well known as silversmiths. Save for pewter, identifica-tion seldom extends beyond the ma-terial itself, the span of years during which an article was made, and the area or locality where it originated. As for the tinker who traveled around re-pairing pots, kettles, and other things made of metal, he is only a legend.

These craftsmen made everything from the pots in which food was cooked and the spoons with which it was stirred to the plates from which it was eaten. Many common items were made in more than one kind of metal. Candle-sticks might be made of pewter, iron, or tin as well as brass. Teakettles were made of all these metals except the soft pewter, which would melt over heat. So indispensable were metals and so skillful the men who worked with them that the buttons that fastened a Sunday coat and the buckles that flashed from a lady's slippers might be made from almost any one of them.

Just about anything that could be made in silver could be made from one or more other metals and sold for very much less. As a result, a vast number of articles essential to everyday living, as well as luxurious things, were made of the less expensive metals. Bronze was worked with least of all metals or alloys. Pewter and britannia were more

Tin, iron, and brass were all used for household implements. Here an iron skillet is suspended from a chain in the fireplace, and dippers and ladles of both iron and tin hang ready for use. On the bench are a tin lantern with pierced sides and pointed top, a foot-stove of pierced tin, and a brass teakettle. This photograph was taken at Marlpitt Hall, Middletown, New Jersey.

popular here than in England and were made in this country longer than they were in England. Iron is a short-lived metal because it rusts and corrodes so easily. Tin also may be rusted, unless it was painted, and may be dented. Brass was the pride of many a housewife and homeowner.

Examples of useful things made in each of the common metals and rather frivolous ones made from some of them during the nineteenth century are still to be found in all parts of the United States. However insignificant

the article may seem, some collector somewhere will seize on it.

### PEWTER

Pewter was more generally used than silver or brass in American households from Colonial days until about 1850. Yet enthusiastic collectors, who became legion during the 1950's, consider pieces made between 1810 and 1860 excellent finds. At that, there are hardly enough to go around and many collectors are satisfied with European-made pewter.

In Europe and England, pewter had been made for centuries when America was being settled. Yet here pewter became more popular than in any other country. American housewives evidently liked it and used it whether or not they could afford silver.

Pewter is duller, darker, and softer than silver. When new or after polish-

A metal inkstand containing two inkwells with a small drawer between to hold pens. The rest at the back is for penholders.

ing, pewter has its own special luster. Unlike silver, which is a precious metal, pewter is an alloy made of several metals. Tin is the chief constituent, and other ingredients may be copper, bismuth, antimony, and lead in varying proportions.

Because pewter is so much softer than silver and brass, it can be bent, dented, and scratched easily. It also corrodes and develops tiny pockmarks. It melts if it is placed directly over heat. One reason early pieces are so scarce is that worn and badly scarred pewter was melted down and gleaming new things made from the old.

Britannia resembles pewter so closely that one can be mistaken for the other. It also is an alloy of tin, chiefly with some antimony and copper. Britannia was considered an improvement over pewter, not only because it was brighter in appearance (still not as gleaming as silver), but also because it did not bend as easily and was more durable.

The name *britannia* was natural since this alloy was originated in England. Its introduction to the United States was so successful that, after 1825, britannia for the most part replaced pewter.

Both pewter and britannia were in great demand for all sorts of household articles. Mugs, tankards and a variety of drinking vessels, measuring cups, pitchers, creamers and sugar bowls, plates and bowls of all sizes, salt and pepper shakers, and open salts were most common. Not uncommon were buttons and buckles, door latches, and picture frames.

Tankards were a notable output of the many pewterers who earned their living in New York City. These drinking vessels varied in the design of the cover, handle, terminal of the handle, and thumbpiece according to whether they were made by Frederick Bassett, William Kirby, Cornelius Bradford, Peter Young, or other pewterers whose names are still known. Frederick Bassett produced the largest tankards (3½ pints) ever made in this country before the Revolution. One is displayed in the pewter collection at the Brooklyn Museum. A dolphin terminal on a handle was made only in New York City. So important was the New York Pewterers' Society that it marched in the parade celebrating the ratification of the United States Constitution in 1788.

*Pewter plates, mugs, bowls, pitchers, and other articles for kitchen and table were in general use in the United States until about 1850.*

Porringers were popular for a variety of purposes until about 1850, which was much longer than this article remained in favor in Europe. The handle is likely to be a clue to where a porringer was made. Pierced or openwork handles were popular in New England, especially Rhode Island and Connecticut. The more handsome "flowered" handle, which was scrolled, was skillfully turned out by pewterers in New York. The Pennsylvania Germans favored a solid handle formed like a tab, whereas craftsmen in Newport, Rhode Island, for a time at least, turned out porringers with solid pear-shaped handles.

Small pear-shaped pewter teapots, which were made by Thomas Danforth Boardman and his brother Sherman Boardman in Hartford, Connecticut, in the early nineteenth century, are as prized by collectors as the teapots made by William Will in Philadelphia in the previous century. It would be unusual to find a complete tea set, but they were made. There are nineteenth-century coffeepots to be found, too, made to some extent wherever pewterers worked.

Candlesticks and chambersticks were as handsome as those made of silver. Chandeliers and sconces also were made of pewter, as were some of the earliest oil-burning lamps. Pewter also was considered sufficiently decorative to be used for inkstands.

Other pieces of pewter and britannia followed the shape, size, and general styling of comparable silverware. Styles for candlesticks, teapots, and the like not only changed more slowly in America than in England but also were simplified here. American pewter, for example, was less likely to be engraved or otherwise decorated than English and European pieces.

Spoons were made in all sizes and for all purposes. There were cooking spoons and ladles, teaspoons, and small salt spoons. Sugar scoops are a delightful find and eminently usable.

*Objects made of pewter, which was once called "poor man's silver," followed the styles of those made of silver. The plate is the oldest piece in this group, but all the pewter on the mantelpiece was made before 1825. (The framed "picture" is actually Delft pottery in shades of brown and cream.)*

Plates, spoons, and other tableware were made in one piece. Teapots, tankards, measures, porringers, mustard pots, and other items that had to be cast in two or more pieces and soldered together became known as holloware, as were similar pieces in silver.

In this country it was not essential that pewter be marked by the maker, as it was in England. However, makers' marks were general here. Early pewterers copied various symbols common in England for hallmarks, but after the Revolution the eagle in various poses was adopted. Both the pewterer and, often, the place where he worked can be identified by the marks he used. Instead of identification, some pieces have a quality mark on the underside to indicate the grade of the metal alloy. Holloware made closer to 1850 often has the word "Britannia" or the initial B stamped on the underside in addition to the firm or maker's name and a number.

Some of the companies that first made pewter and britannia went on to make plated and sterling silver. The Meriden Britannia Co. or Meriden B. Company of Meriden, Connecticut, made plated silver between 1852 and 1898. Reed and Barton, a firm that still produces both sterling and plated silver, also made britannia ware during the nineteenth century.

A certain amount of pewter is still being made, although not for general household use. Authentic reproduc-

tions of eighteenth-century pieces also can be purchased.

The best way to identify genuinely old pewter is by its surface. The piece may look smooth but will feel rough when it is touched because it is bound to have become scratched from daily use. The surface also will be slightly uneven, since pewter is soft.

Unlike silver, pewter and britannia did not gain a patina with use and age. Although any that is found today undoubtedly will have been made no earlier than 1825 and perhaps as late as the 1860's, it certainly will have no luster and probably will be darkened. Some pitting and corrosion are as inevitable as dents. Such signs of use are as helpful as a maker's mark in authenticating age. When pewter and britannia were purchased a century and more ago, they were clear and burnished. There's no reason why pieces shouldn't be cleaned carefully to restore some of the original gleam.

Reaction to pewter is always definite. A person either likes it a lot or wouldn't have it in the house. This attitude seems to be as true of old as it is of modern pieces. Fortunately, enough people are interested in pewter to collect it. Thus any piece, however blackened and dented, will find a buyer. Because of collectors' interest during the 1950's, prices have been rather higher than might be expected.

Antique porringers sell for between

$25 and $100, depending on condition, workmanship, type of handle, and the maker. A porringer that can be identified positively as having been made by the Boardmans in Hartford will be worth at least $50. Unmarked and unidentifiable ones, even with a crown handle, will be worth only about $25.

Teapots average between $30 and $75, depending on size, maker, and condition. An unmarked plate may sell for only $10, but marked ones may go as high as $50—an 8-inch Boardman plate should sell for $35 to $40; a plate by Bassett, who worked earlier, for $40 to $50. Bowls will bring higher prices.

Teaspoons can be valued at $3 to $4 each, tablespoons at $5 to $6. Small boxes for snuff are worth $10 or more, and even buttons may bring a dollar or more.

### BRASS

Brass is not as important to the smooth running of a house nowadays as it used to be. When the United States was a young nation, a caller gained admittance to many houses by clanging the brass knocker on the front door. Indoors, candlesticks and chambersticks, the andirons and fender at the fireplace, the pots and kettles hanging around it, were softly gleaming brass. The tools to tend the fireplace also often were tipped with brass handles. In the fireplace corner stood at least one long-handled brass bedwarmer. Ten to one, the key to the front door was made of brass too.

Brass added a cheerful gleam to any room then as it does now. It was not used for a wide range of tableware—spoons, plates, and serving pieces—as was pewter. The teakettle and other handsome kettles, the long-handled fork for cooking at the fireplace, ladles, dippers, and milk pans probably were brass. But although brass was used for a host of essential articles and many decorative ones, people did not eat from it.

Brass is an alloy consisting chiefly of copper and zinc in variable proportions. Unlike pewter, brass is not soft. A kettle or pot may have been dented accidentally, but candlesticks, andirons, and the like generally are in excellent condition. Although brass will tarnish, it can be polished with little effort to its original sheen.

A considerable amount of brassware always has been imported. Undoubtedly many settlers brought some pieces with them from England and Europe. Nevertheless, braziers are known to have worked here in Colonial days. One of the earliest ones was Henry Shrimpton, who died in 1665. During the early 1700's braziers came here from England, Holland, and Germany.

A few of the silversmiths did a certain amount of brass work (the Revere family in Boston was one example). Cop-

*Antique brass can be recognized by its rich golden-yellow color. It does not turn red when tarnished. The candlesticks shown, 4½ inches tall, were made in New England between 1810 and 1820.*

persmiths also worked with brass. Still, there were thousands of braziers working here by the end of the eighteenth century and during the early years of the nineteenth century. Although their work was quite as beautiful in its own way, braziers were far more self-effacing than silversmiths and pewterers.

Most braziers kept busy turning out useful articles for the households in their communities. They made bullet molds, bootjacks, and powder horns for the men, sewing birds for the ladies. But the greatest part of their output was for the house itself and the chores that had to be done in and around it. Of candlesticks, kettles, and pots there seems to have been no end.

The first glimpse of the brazier's work, as mentioned before, was often seen on the front door. As early as the 1700's, knockers were made of brass as well as iron. For the more handsome brass ones, such classic motifs as a shell or an elongated vase were preferred, with a brass hoop attached. By 1790, eagles were as popular a form for knockers as for furniture decoration; some were simpler than others, and the poses varied. Brass knockers continued to be made during the 1800's.

Candlesticks and other articles followed the styles that braziers had known in their native countries. Brass as well as pewter candlesticks were fashioned after the more expensive silver ones. It is safe to say that no new styles were developed in this country.

Candlesticks, made in pairs, ranged from short ones about 4½ inches tall, to high and quite elaborately shaped ones. Heights of 6½, 8¾, 9½, and occasionally 12 inches were common. Candlesticks had square, octagonal, or round bases during the eighteenth century. A distinctive and not too common style was a round base with swirling. Sometimes a small saucer was attached just under the socket or at mid-height of the stick to catch drippings so that they did not mar the table.

Chambersticks, perhaps no taller than 2½ inches, with saucer bases and ring handles were a style made over and over again between 1750 and 1850.

*Chambersticks were short candleholders with a saucer base and a ring handle. Some, like the brass pair here, had a knob that could be raised upward in a slot, to dislodge the candle stub.*

Chambersticks are short candlesticks meant to be carried about the house and particularly to light the way to the bedchamber.

Chambersticks and some candlesticks have a slot with a knob jutting from it at one side. By pushing up the knob, the stub of the candle can be dislodged effortlessly.

Sconces, or brackets to attach to a wall and hold a candle, were widely used during the eighteenth century. Like candlesticks, sconces were often put up in pairs. Many sconces held only one candle, but those made to hold two candles were also popular and some held a group of candles. Occasionally a sconce was made to hold a globe protecting a candle much as glass hurricane shades were made to slip over tall

brass candlesticks. Backplates varied in height from about 6½ inches to almost 12 inches. The backplate usually was quite simple in design, and if the projecting arm for the candle was scrolled, this also was simple.

Candelabra and double-armed candlesticks were made in brass as well as silver. The arms on the latter in some cases could be adjusted at different heights, as could the later brass lamps. During the eighteenth and nineteenth centuries, brass also was well-liked for chandeliers and hanging lanterns for indoors. Chandeliers held from four to a dozen long candles, and many lanterns held two to four shorter ones.

Two essential accessories for candlesticks and other styles of candleholders were a snuffer or extinguisher and the combination snuffer and trimmer. They

*A candle snuffer both extinguished the flame and trimmed the wick. The trimmings were caught in the box attached to the blades. The snuffer in this photograph, 5½ inches long, is made of brass; small brass mounts on the long blade and the handles serve as supports.*

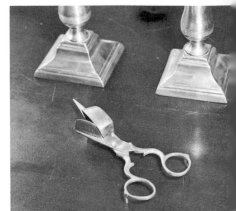

*The little brass teakettle was made in the United States after 1860 but the mortar and pestle are older. They were brought here from Bohemia in the 1850's and were used for grinding cinnamon sticks and other spices.*

could be made of tin, iron, or copper, but brass ones were made for brass candlesticks. Old brass ones are particularly nice.

The extinguisher, which is often called a snuffer, is nothing more than a small cone of metal to be held or dropped over the candle to extinguish its flame. Some of them are exceedingly plain, others are tipped with knobs or finials and have a ring handle attached to one side at the base.

The combination snuffer and trimmer is sometimes called a scissors candle snuffer. This often stood on a small matching tray. If not, small mounts were attached to the underside of the handles and the long blade. This type of snuffer was a scissors-like tool between five and six inches long, with an open box an inch or so long attached to the one pointed blade and the

fourth side of the box on the other short blade. Its purpose was to clip off burnt portions of the wick so the candle would burn more evenly and brightly. The clippings were caught in the box so they did not fall to mar the wood or the cloth under the candleholder. While doing this, the tool also snuffed out the candle.

Perhaps even more important than lighting devices were kettles and pots. They were produced in a vast array of shapes and sizes and were prized highly by housewives. All manner of cooking utensils were made of brass. So were teakettles, and trivets on which to stand these and other hot dishes. Some brass pails were made too. Incidentally, most brass trivets are handsome, whether they are the cyphers and simply scrolled designs, many of which were imported from England during the 1700's, or the fancier patterns of the 1800's similar to those of cast-iron trivets.

A brass mortar and pestle was essential in an apothecary shop. Many of them were also put to good use in kitchens to grind herbs and spices.

In the old days, the cooking pots and teakettle used to hang from the crane, which was fastened securely to a wall of the fireplace. The iron crane could be pushed into different positions in order to keep the gleaming pots over the fire. However, other brass was considered desirable in or near the fireplace, which for so many years was doubly important because it was both the source of heat indoors and the center for cooking. Andirons too were needed, although they were not as indispensable for the fireplace as the crane and kettles. Less prosperous homes during the eighteenth century managed without them and supported logs on a couple of stones. When a family moved into a larger house, each room had its own fireplace for heat. Although not every one of these necessarily had a full complement of tools and equipment, all were furnished with enough so that a fire could be started and tended in safety.

Until quite late in the nineteenth century, many pairs of handsome brass andirons were made and used. Probably as many as andirons of all other materials, for brass was preferred for all but the most utilitarian ones. A good many andirons had both shaft and horizontal bar of iron, with the shafts tipped with a knob or finial of brass. As families could afford them, they liked andirons with brass shaft and legs. A good many andirons had small brass balls or finials on low shafts about three inches behind the tall brass shaft, and the bar between the two overlaid with brass. This, plus brass shaft and legs, is an

*Andirons topped with large balls are a style made between 1810 and 1840. The legs, shafts, and the small balls about 3 inches behind them are brass too, and the space between shaft and small ball is overlaid with brass. The fireplace tools (right)—tongs and shovel—are iron with brass handles and hang from all-brass jamb hooks screwed into the wall.*—Ted Eastwood

indication of quality.

Some slight changes in design are noticeable in brass andirons. During the eighteenth century, brass shafts were usually baluster-shaped and tipped with an urn or pointed finial. Occasionally the brass column would be square and tapering. Then in the early nineteenth century when all furnishings showed Empire influence, the shafts became rounder and heavier-looking and were topped with sizable round balls.

Fenders probably were never as popular in this country as they were in Europe. They were so low that they were not much of a guard for the fire, but even today they are still often used decoratively in front of a fireplace. Although they had given service in England and Europe much earlier, fenders were little seen in this country until the late 1700's and then only in the wealthier homes. A fender was curved at the ends or serpentine, between 6 and 8 inches high, and pierced in a decorative pattern.

A set of tools for the fireplace consisted of a small shovel, tongs, and poker. More often than not, these tools were made entirely of iron, but at least one room in the house was likely to have a handsomer set with brass handles. Sometimes brass tool-handles were made to match the brass shafts of andirons. The tools were hung on either side of the fireplace by means of jamb hooks, also made of brass. Two holes in the brass plate of each jamb hook enabled it to be fastened to the wall. The stands used nowadays to hold fireplace tools are a modern idea. Jamb hooks, on the other hand, belong to the days when a fireplace and its equipment were essential to comfort in a house.

By about 1850 when coal, and then gas, began to be used for fireplace heat, grates were needed instead of andirons. These grates or firebaskets made of iron sometimes finished with brass finials and facings. Coal scuttles or coal boxes were made of brass to stand beside the fireplace. Both boxes and scuttles often were hammered to form a pattern on the surface.

Braziers were such a versatile group of workmen that they could go from making a pair of beautifully turned candlesticks to such everyday small items as buttons and thimbles, spurs, stirrups, and pony brasses. Pride could be taken in making keyhole escutcheons, other furniture hardware, eagle finials, and curtain tiebacks. Trivets, inkstands and inkwells, and an occasional sundial were made from the early 1700's.

Bells were another important order. Not all of the old bells were made of brass, but there's never any question about selling one that is. Size and to some extent shape varied with the purpose of the bell. Ship's bells are among the larger brass ones. Cowbells, almost rectangular instead of round, were made in more than one size. School bells and dinner bells were attached to wooden handles, and the small sleigh bells were fastened along leather straps. Brass bells differ in tone, but their ring is always a pleasant one.

In spite of the number of braziers who worked steadily in America, a good deal of brass continued to be imported. A great number of candlesticks and many cooking utensils were sent here from England. Brass milk cans as well as decorative tobacco boxes came from Holland.

It often is difficult to tell whether a piece of old brass was made in this country or abroad. Just as there are almost no records of braziers' names, so also was brassware seldom marked. However, it is not difficult to tell whether brass is antique or modern. The color is a true indication.

Antique brassware is a beautiful shade of golden yellow. It never turns red when it becomes tarnished, as do later pieces. It also has a soft patina as does old silver, and this is as impossible to reproduce as the color. Seams are another indication that brassware is old. Each article was cast in two pieces and joined together. Then it was polished and finished by hand.

Old brass consistently sells for good prices. The umbrella stand that is not really old enough to be an antique because it was a late-Victorian idea will bring $10 to $15. The very much older and smaller curtain tiebacks are worth

$15 to $20, and a brass bootjack in the neighborhood of $7.50.

Since collecting bells is a popular hobby, there's always a market for them. A large cowbell can be sold for $6 or so, a 6-inch-high school bell with a wood handle for about $10. Sleigh bells are at such a premium that dealers frequently cut a leather strap into sections, each with two or three bells, and sell these small pieces for $1 or so. A 24-inch strap, intact, may bring $25.

Much of the fireplace equipment made only yesterday copies the styles of antique andirons, fenders, and the like. Andirons made between 1830 and 1850 and topped with brass balls are worth

*This bronze candelabrum (circa 1840) on a marble base has three arms supported by a grapevine that appears to be growing out of an urn. Each socket is fitted with a deep bobeche.*

at least $35. Those from other periods range from $25 upward. A large coal scuttle with a hammered design might be priced as high as $50.

Brass kettles sell for $10 to $20, depending on their capacity. A small mortar and pestle can be priced at about $12.

Antiques made of brass have not deteriorated as have those made of many other metals. Brass is sturdy and, like silver, acquires beauty with its age. Furthermore, any article of old brass was the product of a craftsman, not a factory. It was handmade and its color is unmistakable.

### BRONZE

Still another alloy is bronze. It consists of tin, copper, and zinc, and is both strong and malleable. As a rule, bronze pieces were finished by being cleaned in acid and then lacquered or gilded.

Bronze was not particularly important in America until the Victorian age. In France, bronze for many centuries had been almost as important as the products of the silversmith. Elaborate chandeliers, candlesticks, boxes for snuff, and other things frequently were outstanding when made of bronze.

Among the things that made Empire furniture look different were its bronze mounts and ormolu decoration (ormolu is gilded bronze). They ornamented Empire furniture made here as well as in France and the rest of Europe. The long Victorian era that followed the Empire period saw more things of bronze made here as well as imported. For example, American clockmakers turned out ornate clocks that combined bronze with marble. Candlesticks and candelabra either were all bronze or bronze mounted on marble bases. Bronze animals and busts took their deserved share of space among Victorian bric-a-brac too.

### COPPER

More extensive deposits of copper exist in the United States than in any other country in the world. The Indians of the Plains States and Rocky Mountain area used copper to make implements and ornaments. White settlers in the East and Midwest also liked articles made of copper. This metal was not easy for them to obtain. Although Paul Revere is known to have been a coppersmith as well as a silver-

*The copper cooking pots with curved handles shown here measure, respectively: 7½ inches in diameter and 4 inches deep, 8½ inches by 4½ inches, and 10½ inches by 5¾ inches. Copper was used to fashion many utensils for kitchens, dairies, and shops after 1830.—Ted Eastwood*

smith, most articles of copper as well as brass were imported during Colonial days. Records show that sheets of copper were hammered and rolled out in this country by 1800 or a little earlier. However, little of the copperware still to be located was made before 1830.

Raw copper is red, and polished copper pieces are distinguished by their pink glow, sometimes almost a golden pink. Copper, incidentally, is not affected by dry air, but in moist air containing carbonic acid it develops a green coating known as verdigris.

*The copper piece at the left is a shaving mug, with a lip inside the rim opposite the handle. The other two are measures (pint and half-pint), which were used in an Ohio drugstore around 1880.*

*Copper measures (these are 1 pint, 1 quart, and ½ pint in capacity) were preferred everywhere except in taverns. These date from the middle of the nineteenth century.*

Many of the same utensils were made in copper and brass. It seems to have been a matter of personal taste during the 1800's whether a teakettle, chocolate pot or coffeepot, pans, dippers, pitchers, and mugs were bought in copper or brass.

Candlesticks, andirons, and furniture hardware were usually made of brass. On the other hand, copper seems to have been the first choice for pudding molds, measures except those used in taverns, and utensils for dairies and shops such as those that sold drugs.

Unusual things of copper to be on the lookout for are the cone-shaped ale warmers that were stuck between the logs in a fireplace, and small copper pots with lip and handle, for heating liquids over the coals. You may discover, after polishing them, that many everyday items such as funnels, dippers, and skillets are copper. If they were used from 70 to 100 years ago, they are valuable now.

The oval wash boiler used for laundry work in the early 1900's can be sold for a good price if it is made of copper. This is a container about 3 feet long and 20 inches high, with a handle at each rounded end and a tight-fitting cover. It was used to boil clothes in order to get them clean. A copper one can be sold now for $12 or so. Copper chafing dishes, also popular in the early 1900's, bring good prices too—$25 or more, depending on condition.

*The copper teakettle at the left is older than the coffeepot with its wooden handle. The latter piece was not made before 1880.*

A copper teakettle was a welcome Christmas gift as late as the 1870's. One can be sold now for $25 to $35, depending on its age, the type of handle, and the shape. Coffeepots of copper, if in poor condition, sell for about $7.50; those in excellent condition, for as much as $15. Teapots, which often are beautifully shaped, sell for somewhat higher prices. Most valuable of all is a copper weathervane, but even a funnel or dipper in good condition can be worth $5 or $6.

IRON

The first successful ironworks opened in 1644 at Saugus, Massachusetts, to supply New England blacksmiths. From the beginning, iron ore (in Saugus it was obtained from a nearby bog) was needed for many essential things. It is said that some of the daily production of raw iron taken from the available ores was cast immediately into pots, firebacks, and the like. Then the rest was reheated and converted into wrought iron, from which tools and other necessities could be made.

**321**

Cast iron, one of the three products obtainable from suitable ores, is hard, comparatively brittle, and readily fusible, but it cannot be forged or welded. It is poured molten into a mold to solidify in the desired shape. Although it is easy and cheap to produce, old articles of cast iron are often quite valuable because they are no longer being made or are curiosities.

Wrought iron by comparison is soft, malleable, and ductible. It can be forged or welded. However, it also is a tough product and resists corrosion. Wrought iron generally is not made directly from the ore but from iron that has been smelted. The third product derived from iron is steel, malleable and weldable and, most important, capable of being tempered to a high degree of hardness.

In Colonial days, settlers depended on the blacksmith for nails, latches, hinges, and locks for the houses they built. The blacksmith worked with wrought iron in the form of bars (bar iron), which he obtained from ironworks that were close at hand in Pennsylvania, Virginia, and other areas as well as New England. From these bars he worked or wrought an almost unbelievable number of things that made living possible. For housewives, he produced cooking, fireplace, and sewing equipment. For the men, he made tools, wagon axles, and weapons. He also shod horses and oxen and forged runners for sleighs. As families settled down, they wanted many things to make life more comfortable, and again the blacksmith found work making candleholders and candlesticks, toddy irons, doorstops, and hitching posts.

The blacksmith produced so many things for housewives that he must have been busy from morning to night and even later. A crane for the fireplace and pots to hang from it were indispensable. When a family owned a good many pots, S-hooks and trammels (notched rods that permitted pots to be hung at different heights over the fire) were needed to hang them from the crane. He made skillets and the long-handled frying pans called spiders, skewers, spits, and a long-handled tool called a peel for putting things in and taking them out of the ovens that were part of the main fireplace. He also was soon making toasters, waffle irons, and broilers.

Early toasters made to be used in a fireplace may seem crude, but often they are excellent examples of the blacksmith's craft. For many a black-smith was a fine ·craftsman who was not satisfied with making a plain object. His toasters and the long-handled forks and spoons for cooking frequently were ornamented with designs formed from wrought iron. Such a blacksmith would also take time to make a cooking pot in a pleasing shape and to give even the most functional object a harmonious design. Thus, we have strap hinges with tips shaped like a bean, ball and spear, heart, or leaf.

Tools for tending the fire also were made from iron. More often than not, during the 1700's, andirons were too. Wrought-iron firedogs or andirons were simple but not unattractive, for the legs were well formed and the shaft tipped with a finial or knob. Around 1800, some andirons were cast with the shaft or upright in the shape of a Hessian soldier or George Washington. These were popular well into the 1800's and are being reproduced to-day. Firebacks of cast iron were important to reflect heat and protect the back wall of a fireplace. Some of them were quite simple in design, others were most ornamental. Patriotic, religious, floral, and conventional motifs were worked into low-relief designs on these firebacks.

Door knockers have been used in this country since the days of the Pilgrims. The first ones of wrought iron were fairly simple, perhaps only a small back plate with an attached ring. In spite of the popularity of brass knockers, cast-iron ones were made in quantity during the 1800's. Those in the form of an eagle, lion's head, or a leaf were common in the early part of that century. By 1850 knockers displaying Masonic emblems or with a hand clasping the knocker had become familiar. The iron foot or boot scraper that was placed by the door was comparatively simple.

Indoors, trivets were an important item. These three-legged stands were placed over the fireplace coals to keep the food in the pots and kettles hot. A quad had four legs and often was much simpler in design and construction. Smaller, simpler trivets were used under irons. Now even cast-iron reproductions of all sorts of trivets are used on dining tables and for decoration. Wrought-iron trivets were made during the eighteenth and part of the nineteenth centuries. Cast-iron trivets appeared about 1850.

Many trivets were round. Others were almost square or rectangular with a projecting piece to serve as a handle. Those that were shaped like an iron with a handle were not necessarily meant to be used under irons. Because of the shape these trivets were known as the cathedral type, probably because they called to mind the arched Gothic windows.

Whatever the shape of a trivet, it had an openwork design. Simple patterns— a cross within a circle, for example— became traditional during the 1700's. They continued to be made during the 1800's, but by 1850 much more elaborate designs began to appear. Among the numerous ones that proved popular were heart and tulips, hearts, arrows and heart, entwined hearts, peacock, horseshoe, geometrical circles, spade and star. These designs also have become traditional, and many of them are being reproduced. There are many more. Not forgotten were flower and fruit motifs, the insignia of fraternal organizations, and portraits of presidents, other patriots, and famous people. In the late 1800's, when stoves were replacing fireplaces, many manufacturers made cast-iron trivets to give or sell to customers at modest prices.

The blacksmith supplied carpenters and builders with hinges, latches, nails, and tools. The farmer was another customer, and almost all workmen not only obtained tools from the smith but also had them repaired at the smithy. An old adze with a wood handle may be recognizable to modern eyes, but wrought-iron shears in various sizes, wrenches, and a screwdriver may not look familiar at all. When hammers were made by hand, they were sometimes shaped amusingly and with considerable individuality.

Even though most of the old tools that a person comes across now were made and used during the nineteenth century, there still are a good many that puzzle even collectors. An ice hatchet or bow drill might baffle anybody. So might an implement that combined the functions of a ruler, screwdriver, tack hammer, and tack puller. One authority has divided tools into fourteen categories to help the people who have started to collect tools recently. Since collecting and displaying old tools has become popular, it is always possible to sell any you find.

Many of the things that were made of iron during the eighteenth century continued to be made during the nineteenth. Local blacksmiths did less diversified work as iron manufacturing became an industry. Between the smith and the factory, more things than ever —some of them bulky and heavy— began to appear.

For one thing, stoves began to compete with fireplaces during the 1800's. Benjamin Franklin had invented the Franklin stove in 1742. This was a big improvement over the open fireplace because it conserved wood, produced better heat, and kept rooms free of smoke and flue gases. By the 1830's, the cast-iron stoves that were to be much more widely used than Franklin stoves began to replace fireplaces. As late as the early 1900's (and perhaps in a few places in this country even today) these iron stoves were used to heat rooms. They were made in various sizes, some of them very small, and one stove heated one or more rooms. A parlor stove usually had fanciful decoration on its cast-iron surface. Sometimes quite fantastic ornaments surmounted these stoves.

In the late 1800's, miniature stoves became common. Some of these were manufacturers' models; others were play stoves with lids that could be lifted and grates that could be shaken. Play stoves were made until about 1920.

The Victorians found many new uses for cast and wrought iron. For one thing, about 1850 they started to make furniture from iron. Cast-iron bedsteads, chairs, and tables with marble tops became common in bedrooms and parlors, and hatracks with arms in the front hall. Small sofas and chairs with intricate grapevine and floral designs are now copied for outdoor furniture, but if you find any authentic Victorian pieces, they are really salable.

Iron appealed to Victorians, and they decked their houses with it inside and outside. Railings, balconies, and trellises along porches were made in complicated designs. So were fences. In southern cities such as New Orleans this decoration is referred to as "iron lace." However, houses in New England and on the West Coast also had their quota of iron trim. A surprising number of people, realizing that its like will not be made again, salvage this sort of trim when old houses are being torn down, (either free if a person carts it away or for a small purchase price). The finest houses in any town had a cast-iron deer or dog on the front lawn and a cast-iron hitching post in the shape of a horse's head, a jockey, or a Negro boy. A jockey or boy usually was painted in gay colors, a horse's head in black.

"Iron lace" was carried indoors in the form of scrollwork shelves, brackets to support wood or marble shelves, and wall brackets to hold lamps. The latter often are used now for potted plants. Both shelf and lamp brackets are being duplicated at the present time. A round twine-holder of "iron lace" was made to be hung from the wall. It consisted of two halves that could be separated to insert the ball of twine, which was threaded through a hole in the bottom. Then there were match-holders to hang on the wall or keep on a table or shelf. Both twine-holders and match-holders were often made in designs somewhat like those of trivets.

A clock might be housed in a swollen cast-iron case, pictures were sometimes displayed in scrolled iron frames, and a few lamp bases were lacy iron. Iron kitchen implements included a tea-kettle, a coffee grinder, a pea sheller, and a cherry pitter. There were also hanging spring-scales about 6½ inches long and 1½ inches wide—some were of iron with a brass face—that registered a weight up to 24 or 50 pounds. Another type of small scale was the steelyard, which had a long horizontal arm with a counterweight that could be moved from notch to notch.

*The flatirons that were in general use 50 to 100 years ago often serve today as door-stops or bookends. Sometimes their present owners decorate them with folk motifs. The numeral 6 on the top of one of these indicates that it weighs six pounds.*

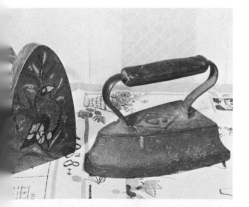

Irons had always been a necessity for the weekly household chore that traditionally was done on Tuesdays. During the 1800's they began to be made in greater variety. Regular flatirons were made in several weights, the better to press different materials. A numeral impressed on the upper surface of an iron indicated how many pounds it weighed. The housewife usually kept some half-dozen irons heating at the fireplace or on the stove. It was quite a feat always to have one ready at the desired temperature.

Heavy cast flatirons with handles of various shapes were known as sadirons. These were tiring to use. Still other cast irons were hollow so that they could be heated by filling them with hot coals. Special irons, oddly constructed, that rocked or rolled were fluting irons, indispensable during Victorian days to flute or ruffle crisp fabrics.

Old flatirons are snapped up quickly at church fairs and auctions. Contemporary owners use them for bookends, paperweights, doorstops, and almost any purpose except the weekly chore of ironing.

During the last half of the nineteenth century and particularly in the 1880's and 1890's, mechanical and pull toys were made of cast iron or tin. They may not seem quite so ingenious as the mechanical toys carved or whittled from wood, but they were gaily painted and lifelike in miniature. Cast-iron circus wagons were made in such variety after 1890 that a whole circus parade could be assembled. The various cage and band wagons were modeled after those used by circuses of the time. Fire engines, wagons, carriages, and even the post-1910 toy automobiles are also now collectors' items.

So keen are toy collectors that they often will be satisfied with toys made as late as the 1920's. Especially valuable are the Schoenhut toys, made by a firm of that name in Philadelphia from 1872. Schoenhut is still manufacturing toys, although quite different ones from those made just before and after the turn of the century.

Penny banks made of cast iron were popular between the 1860's and 1910.

Originally, the mechanical ones were made as toys, but because of the American belief in thrift, particularly strong during Victorian days, they also were given to children to encourage savings. Cast-iron banks in the shape of buildings, animals, men, or other figures, with a slot for dropping in coins, are known as still banks. Much more fun are those that are animated in some fashion when a coin is inserted.

Some of these mechanical banks are as simple as a dog that jumps through a hoop in order to deposit a penny in a drum. Somewhat more complicated is the one on which a cow kicks over a bucket and a boy when a coin is inserted. A baseball bank on which a coin is caught by the catcher as the batter misses was first made in 1870. A

*The mechanical bank collection at the Seamen's Bank for Savings in New York City has these examples of the Kicking Cow bank (left) and the Girl Skipping Rope, which were animated by depositing a coin.*

*The popular cast-iron mechanical bank had some part that moved when a coin was deposited. More than 250 different ones were made between the 1860's and 1910. The three shown are from the collection at the Seamen's Bank for Savings, New York City.*

1909 bank titled "Teddy and the Bear" consisted of a small cast-iron figure of Theodore Roosevelt, which fires a gun to deposit the coin and causes a bear to pop out of a tree stump.

"Teddy and the Bear" is one of the many mechanical banks that are now being reproduced. One made recently from original molds and hand painted sells for about $16, but one made in 1909 sells for $75. That is, if the mechanism still works. Old mechanical banks range in price from $40 or so to several hundred dollars, depending on their rarity and condition.

According to the Seaman's Bank for Savings in New York City, which has the largest collection of cast-iron mechanical banks, many of them sold for as little as a dollar in their day. There are no records of their having been given as premiums. They were manu- factured chiefly at small iron foundries in New England, New York, Pennsylvania, and Ohio. However much they were used, these cast-iron mechanical banks usually still work, and that is more than people in the next century will be able to say of the plastic ones made during the last ten years.

Mechanical banks are not the only things made of cast iron that are being reproduced at the present time. Trivets in many of the traditional patterns, lamp and shelf brackets, Franklin stoves, firebacks, andirons, and some Victorian furniture are being manufactured. Some craft places are reproducing hinges and latches, fireplace and cooking equipment. It is often difficult to tell whether or not trivets, S-hooks, and many small things are one or 100 years old.

Nineteenth-century lamp brackets sell

for $5 to $10 if they are complete with wall plates. Similar patterns or copies are priced at $5 to $6. A match-holder sells for $5 and up, and a twine-holder for about $7.50.

A simple pair of andirons with knobs topping the shafts should bring about $16.50, an S-hook $1.50 or so. The cherry pitter that seems so unnecessary now can be sold for close to $5. Toys in good condition sell for comparatively high prices. On the other hand, tools in which collectors' interest is fairly recent still sell for modest prices even if two or three unfamiliar ones are included in an assortment. A good many of the cast- and wrought-iron pieces that would seem to be white elephants actually can be sold.

### TINWARE

Tinware and ironware were an important part of the stock carried by the peddlers who traveled the highways and byways during the eighteenth and a great part of the nineteenth centuries. Much of the tinware is still around, and neglected because it is rusty, dented, or battered. If tinware was painted originally, such decoration will be faded and perhaps peeling too. None of this tinware, plain or painted, was expensive. People pay much more nowadays for a faded and battered piece than the original owner did when it was shining and new. Sometimes tinware also was decorated by piercing, punching, or crimping.

No deposits of tin exist in the United States, so the colonists were dependent on supplies from England, where tin mines in Cornwall have been worked from the days of the Romans. Because England was niggardly about shipping this metal here, it was not until after the Revolution that much tinware was made in this country. By 1830 tin-smiths—or whitesmiths, as they were often called—were well established and their products were keeping many a housewife happy. One of the chief centers of production for peddlers was the state of Connecticut.

Tin is not an alloy but a metal almost as white and lustrous as silver, although inferior to silver. It is essential to making such important and beautiful alloys as bronze, pewter, and britannia. However, utensils, boxes, and cans were made from tinplate, which is sheet iron or steel covered on both sides with tin. The iron or steel gives strength, the tin a pleasing luster and protection against corrosion under normal conditions of exposure. The making of tin-plate is complicated and requires great skill.

Much of the nineteenth-century tin-ware that is still around consists of cooking and kitchen utensils. Pots and pans of all sizes, dippers, mugs, cups and measures, spoons, cooking forks and ladles, pudding and candle molds, cookie cutters, teapots, coffeepots, tea-kettles, and plates were sold everywhere. Spice boxes and nutmeg graters made a century or more ago may still be usable. Pie cupboards with door

*Tin kitchen utensils like these were often purchased from itinerant peddlers. The smaller coffeepot and the little teakettle are older than the large coffeepot at the left, but all date between 1850 and 1880.*

panels of tin pierced in a decorative pattern are interesting finds that most often turn up in rural areas.

Tin was important for lighting too. Candlesticks and chambersticks of tin, plain or painted, were inexpensive and hence in great demand even during the 1800's. So were sconces. Sconces with round shields were often crimped or scalloped along the edges. A higher, narrower, shield-shaped back might be punched so that the "buttons" raised thereby caught and reflected the light. Cone extinguishers of tin were plainer and much cheaper than similar ones made of brass. Like old oil lamps, sconces now are sometimes electrified, and electrified reproductions are made to hold candle-shaped light bulbs.

Lanterns to provide light outdoors after dark were made of pierced tin. Lamps to burn whale oil were made of tin from the 1820's to the 1860's. They might be tall or low, with or without a handle, and some had saucer bases. Chandeliers of tin belonged to the eighteenth century. They were not plentiful because tin itself was not plentiful here then. Those that were made usually had six arms, each one holding a candle. On the whole, tin chandeliers were simpler in design than those of pewter or brass.

Fireplace equipment included footstoves, which were square or rectangular boxes with a handle. The sides were pierced tin. A box for wood also might be tin. Tin match-holders were common.

Painted tinware, also called japanned ware, toleware, or tole, has been popular for a good 200 years. About 1700, experiments in Pontypool, an iron town in England, resulted in the successful painting of tinware to resemble the lacquered pieces imported from China. By 1730, a flourishing business had been established.

Tole, painting on metal, was done not only professionally but also by amateurs. Metal painting became a lady's hobby between 1750 and 1800, just as china painting did about 1900. In America, where metal painting did not become fashionable until the early 1800's, and in England, tole was largely painted tinware. In France, where it was fashionable and popular in the late eighteenth and early nineteenth centuries, it was sometimes done on copper. These countries and Holland, too, developed their own style of tole. After 1840 when electroplated and papier-mâché articles became the fashion, little was heard or done about tole for another 100 years or so.

The backgrounds for the designs painted on metal were usually dark—black, brown, deep red, or tortoiseshell. The designs themselves were done either freehand with brushes and oil paint or by means of stencils. Colors and bronze powders (metallic tones of gold, silver, and colors) were equally favored. Decorations ranged from oriental scenes and designs copied from oriental lacquering, peacocks and other birds, to country scenes taken from prints or possibly an oil painting. Garlands, large and natural-looking flowers as well as smaller sprigs, and fountains were used again and again.

Probably more trays and boxes than anything else were painted. Serving trays with a lacy or pierced edge were popular in this country around 1800. Later, both large rectangular trays with rounded edges and octagonal ones became more common. Bread trays were smaller. Boxes in all sizes were painted.

Many that had handles were large enough to hold a lunch. Some were called document boxes. Then there were tea caddies and small trinket boxes. Even coffeepots, teapots, and mugs sometimes were painted tin. Nothing but the most utilitarian tinware was immune while tole was at the height of its popularity, particularly when amateurs dabbled at it.

The fashion of making a utensil in the form of a person, animal, fish, or other "character" caught the public's fancy during the first half of the nineteenth century. Although most of these character pieces were made of pottery or

*Now used as a cookie jar, this piece of character tinware is actually a canister dating from the first half of the nineteenth century. It is shaped like a Toby jug; the hat is a tight-fitting cover. Note that the colorful old paint is scarred.*

glass, a few were made from tin and painted—especially cookie jars and other covered pieces. Some of the character tinware resembled the Toby character jugs or pitchers of earthenware.

It doesn't pay to be hasty about throwing out a long-empty tin or canister that once held cookies, biscuits, or other foods sold or displayed in a store. It may be useless from your viewpoint, but there are eager collectors of gaily decorated tin boxes. Some firms made a series of them that, in spite of any advertising included in the decoration, were the kind people just couldn't throw away. Leaders in the decorating of tin cans and boxes with bright lithographed designs instead of paper labels were the Somers brothers, metalworkers in Brooklyn, New York, in the 1870's. Some businessmen designed containers for their products. For example, Schepp's coconut was sold in a tin pail with a fantastic design featuring monkeys (later Schepp's put up their coconut in glass jars with a coconut as a knob on the cover). The Hercules Powder Company used a decorated flask that could be attached to a hunter's belt. Most of these lithographed designs included self-advertising.

Tobacco companies were especially fertile in ideas. Green Turtle Cigars were packed in a lithographed tin lunch box with an appropriate design that incorporated a green turtle on the sides. One of the containers for Continental Cubes tobacco had a richly colored standing portrait of George Washington.

All sorts of household necessities as well as drugs and cosmetics were packaged in tins. Among those sought after now are the Huntley & Palmer's biscuit tins. This is an English firm that packed their products in tins of unusually imaginative shape prior to 1900. Examples are a pedestal topped with a sundial, a 12-inch grandfather's clock, and a set of "leather-bound" books. The tins were covered with lithographs that carried out the idea of their shapes. People bought such tins eagerly and, in fact, the public was urged to "collect" the variously lithographed tin boxes for tobacco and candy. Many firms brought out a series in distinctive shapes and colorings.

The canning industry grew from an award given in 1810 by Napoleon to a Frenchman who had perfected a method of preserving food by cooking it partly and then sealing it in bottles with cork stoppers. Also in 1810, an Englishman was granted a patent for preserving foods in "vessels of glass, pottery, tin and other metals or fit materials." A canning factory in New York was set up about 1812 by Thomas Kensett, an Englishman. At first he used glass containers, but after 1837 Kensett and others who had entered this new industry used tin cans. Both the California Gold Rush in 1848 and the War Between the States gave an impetus to using food from tin cans.

Not that people save old tin cans. However, it is interesting that tin, which was once so scarce and precious here, has been the basis of an enormous industry for more than a hundred years. By the 1880's, tin was plentiful enough for the manufacture of toys. All of these were painted and many of them were animated. Some of the mechanical ones would seem to have supplemented the cast-iron circus wagons, for they were performing animals. Collectors are interested in tin toys, if they are in reasonably good condition.

Both painted and unpainted tin can be sold for surprisingly good prices. Tin boxes and containers, even with self-advertising on them, will sell for $5 to $10. Rarity, unusual shape, and the condition of the lithograph covering influence the price that may be asked and expected. A tole box, however small, commands higher prices. A painted coffeepot in good condition is worth about $7.50; an unpainted one, equally good, perhaps $5. Large tole trays starts at about $15 and go very much higher, depending on their age and condition.

Tin articles made during the eighteenth century are worth about twice as much as those made during the nineteenth century, if the condition is good. An eighteenth-century wall sconce, for example, can be valued at about $30; a nineteenth-century one, probably machine-made instead of handmade, may be worth no more than $10 or $12, and current reproductions sell for $10 to

$20. A tole sconce might be worth $50. An unpainted candlestick with saucer and push-up knob should be priced at about $5, or more if the condition is really good.

A tin mold for making candles probably goes back to the late 1700's or only the earliest years of the 1800's. A mold for making a dozen candles sells for about $8.50 at the present time. Pudding molds with fluted or tapered sides and a design in the bottom were much used throughout the nineteenth century, but any that are in good condition will bring at least $5 and perhaps as much as a candle mold. The tin wash basin kept in a kitchen is worth a dollar or so, and the portable tin bathtub may sell for close to $10, although neither one may be more than 75 years old and the purchaser probably has no intention of using them for their original purpose.

During the last two centuries, candleholders in various styles, sconces, teapots, coffeepots, and teakettles have been made not only in precious silver but also in pewter and britannia, brass, copper, iron, and tin. An iron candleholder may be older and more unusual than one made in any of the other metals. In spite of these two merits, it will not be as easy to sell an iron candleholder, even for less money, as the more attractive ones of pewter, brass, or painted tin.

Weathervanes were made chiefly of metal during the 1800's, with copper, brass, iron, and tin all used to some extent. After 1850, the vane of copper or other metal was shaped by means of a mold of cast iron.

A sewing bird might be made of brass, iron, or, more rarely, silver. Both brass and iron birds sometimes were plated or lacquered to disguise their basic material. Most of these birds either carried a velvet pincushion on their backs or stood on a cushion, and a few had two pincushions. Victorian sewing birds sell for $7 and up.

As already mentioned, during the 1800's two metals sometimes were combined in one object, such as the scales for store and home use that might be tin or iron with brass face or pans. An old steelyard sells for about $5.

Other metal alloys of which nothing is heard nowadays were used for decorative accessories and personal articles after 1850. A jewel or trinket box of hard metal that is golden in color might well be what was called jeweler's bronze.

## GLOSSARY

*Alloy:* a substance composed of two or more metals.

*Brass:* an alloy, golden in color, consisting chiefly of copper and zinc in variable proportions.

*Britannia:* an alloy of tin, chiefly with antimony and copper; it so closely resembles pewter that it largely displaced the latter after 1825. More durable than pewter.

*Bronze:* an alloy of tin, copper, and zinc.

*Chamberstick:* a low candlestick with saucer base and ring handle, made to be carried about the house and especially to light the way to a bedchamber.

*Fender:* a low metal frame, usually decorative, placed on the hearth before an open fire, presumably to prevent sparks or coals from jumping into the room.

*Fireback:* a cast-iron plate attached to the back wall of a fireplace to protect the wall and reflect heat.

*Firedog:* one of a pair of supports for wood in the fireplace; same as andiron.

*Iron:* an important metal extracted from rock or other ore. Cast iron results from pouring the molten metal into a mold to solidify. Wrought iron has been worked or formed by a blacksmith from iron that has been smelted.

*Peel:* a long-handled flat implement of iron for taking hot bread or other food out of a fireplace oven.

*Pewter:* an alloy of tin and other ingredients such as copper, bismuth, antimony, and lead, which is a soft material yet lustrous.

*Quad:* a small stand with four legs to place under hot dishes and pots.

*Sadiron:* a heavy, cast flatiron.

*Sconce:* a bracket attached to a wall

by means of a backplate, for holding a candle or a group of candles.

*Steelyard:* a portable scale or balance for determining weight; properly, a steelyard is a balance consisting of a long horizontal arm divided into notches and provided with a weight that can be moved along it and a hook from which the object to be weighed is suspended; the horizontal arm itself hangs from a short vertical arm. A hanging spring-scale is often incorrectly called a steelyard.

*Tole:* metal, usually tin, which has been painted decoratively in colors.

*Trammel:* an implement hung in a fireplace to support cooking pots, either a notched rod or often two parts so it can be lengthened or shortened. Trammels were hung from the backbar or a crane.

*Trivet:* a small stand with three legs placed over the embers in a fireplace to keep food hot; also used to support irons for pressing and smoothing.

FOR FURTHER INFORMATION:

AMERICAN PEWTER by J. B. Kerfoot. New York: Crown Publishers, Inc.

# 15

## Wood Necessities and Pleasures

ONCE UPON A TIME, every man and boy whittled at his own fireside and around the stove at the general store. Their whittling amounted to more than shaving a stick with a good pocketknife. Things like toys and whirligigs and spools carved in the shape of crosses from applewood were not taken for granted 200 years ago because they could not be bought at a store then. Spools might seem a minor convenience, but these oddly shaped ones undoubtedly influenced some people's lives, for young men used to whittle them and give them to girls they admired. Many a young lady estimated her popularity according to the number of spools given her (thread was purchased in paper envelopes and had to be wound on these handmade spools).

Working with wood was not just a pastime. In towns, it was an occupation for the carpenters who built the houses, the skilled joiners who did the finishing on a building (doors, stairs, etc.), the coopers who made barrels and casks, the wheelwright who for so many years made wheels of wood, the wainwright who made the wagons, the cartwright who turned out the two-wheel vehicles (at least one nineteenth-century carriage-making firm could furnish any one of 500 different models), and the shipwright who hammered together the vessels that sailed on voyages lasting several years. Then there were the cabinetmakers, whose specialty was fine furniture.

These men knew their woods. A wheelwright made his choice as carefully as a cabinetmaker. The wheelwright's selection, for example, might be black or sour gum for a hub, oak or ash for spokes, hickory for the rim (felly), because in his opinion this combination made a wheel that was most durable as well as most comfortable for riding.

The average homeowner and farmer knew woods too. Women also knew something about wood, if only which kinds made the best fire for cooking and baking. In the new settlements of the eighteenth century and on the farms that were so numerous well into the nineteenth century, men had to be knowledgeable about woodworking and handy at repairing all of the wooden objects used in the house, barn, or carriagehouse.

Early wooden houses were held together with wooden nails or trunnels (tree nails). Wooden pins or pegs were used for paneling and furniture long after metal nails became plentiful, and pegged floors in old houses that need renovating are such a selling point that in some newly built houses the floor-boards are pegged. Trunnels and pegs, incidentally, never cause cracks—probably because they swell and dry out just as does the wood around them. Plain round wood pegs driven into the wall—and not the fancy brasses in the shape of eagles, shells, and the like that are now so popular—preceded closets for hanging coats and clothing.

Wooden water pipes for a house were still being manufactured quite late in the nineteenth century, and wooden pumps to obtain water from wells were still common in rural areas in the twentieth century. The first bathtubs that were not portable were built in place by carpenters and then lined with sheet lead. These tubs first took people's fancy between 1840 and 1850 but re-mained uncommon until about 1900.

Its surprising how many homes, not far from modern cities, still have one of these old built-in wooden tubs. Some of them were handsomely encased in mahogany or cedar, but most of them were oak. If you have to clear out a house that still has one of these old-fashioned bathtubs, or if you buy a vacation house in the country that still boasts an old wooden pump outside, you may as well resign yourself to the fact that there is no selling market for these two things. You may want to leave the pump as a landmark or a proof of the age of the property. If not, probably the best way to dispose of it, or the bathtub, is to offer them to one of the museums in various parts

*This small trunk (30 inches long, 15 inches high) was made between 1830 and 1850. The top is basswood, the lock and nailhead initials are brass. About 1930, the trunk was attached to a stand with legs, to make it more accessible for storing mittens, scarves, and the like in a hallway.*

of the country that collect farm or house equipment, or to an old house that is being restored (the number grows every year in all parts of the country).

Shutters are a different story. There's an amazing demand for all kinds of shutters and louvers. Even early-twentieth-century ones with a few loose slats sell quickly—to be made into folding screens and who knows what else. Nineteenth-century styles, either those used on houses or the kind shopkeepers put up against their store windows at night, also find a ready market and bring fairly good prices, whatever their ultimate destination.

Wood was used in the greatest amount and in the most varied ways during the seventeenth and eighteenth centuries in America. By the mid-1800's, other materials started to displace it for many purposes. Wood tools, implements, and utensils as well as small decorative and practical objects that were made during the 1800's are still to be found. You may not recognize some of them, and when they are identified you may find you have no use for them, but they are salable if only for their value as curiosities.

It's important to identify unknown wooden objects and discover what purpose they served. Anything made of wood represents handwork that, except in some of the crafts that are still maintained, is now a thing of the past. Wood was handled in many ways, from simple cutting to whittling and carving, in order to produce essential items. Splints, very thin pieces of wood, were either interwoven as for chair seats and baskets or applied to a solid backing as in the case of sugar buckets and boxes.

Some men so enjoyed working with wood that they not only built cradles for the young ones but also carved the paneled sides. It's also probable that some of the wooden candlesticks common during the 1700's and even a carefully shaped and marked yardstick of the 1800's were turned out by the men of the household.

Many of the old wooden candlesticks were tall enough to stand on the floor. They consisted of a crossbase supporting a turned pole so that the crossbar that held the candles could be adjusted to various heights. Many of the wooden candlesticks and candleholders made during the eighteenth century were cleverly worked out in the ways the light could be adjusted and the holder carried or set down safely. Some of them could be taken apart and put together again easily, perhaps because in that century travelers usually carried a candleholder in their luggage since only the finest inns provided illumination for their patrons.

Indispensable to bedrooms in both country and town during the eighteenth century—and sometimes still found in dusty corners—were patter paddles and wrench. The wooden wrench, sometimes amusingly carved, was needed to tighten the ropes of a rope bed. Patter paddles with handles that slant to one side instead of extending straight outward were used to pat and pound the featherbed (it needed this treatment after every night's sleep on it). If a pair of patter paddles is initialed and dated, they were probably an eighteenth-century wedding gift.

Bed steps, two steps high, were needed to climb into the high four-poster beds, and night caps and slippers were stored in them. These steps can be as useful elsewhere in the house today.

It's quite likely that anyone would recognize wooden nutmegs, which presumably were carved in Connecticut and were foisted on unsuspecting housewives by nineteenth-century peddlers. However, a bootjack might be puzzling, since most people now have no need of one. The bootjack—a V-shaped device for pulling off boots —was essential up to a century ago, when travel by horseback was general and farmers and other men wore boots as protection against the weather and wet land.

Woodenware or treen, as it is sometimes called, was used in many households, especially in rural and newly settled areas, until well along in the nineteenth century. The word "treen," the ancient plural of "tree," is correctly applied to plates and dishes made of wood. Trenchers, which were wooden plates or platters on which food was carved, served, or eaten, were used far longer than most people imagine. In their simplest form, they were merely flat pieces of wood or board, either round or square.

*Woodenware common in kitchens throughout the 1800's included useful items like the knife box at the left, as well as bowls of various shapes and sizes. This knife box was almost black when found, but careful refinishing revealed that it was made of glowing pine and constructed with precise mortising. The maple bowl, approximately 18 inches long, 11 inches wide, and 4 inches deep, evidently was used for chopping food.*—Ted Eastwood

The plates, platters, and bowls classified as treen were a little more elegant and showed finer work than trenchers. Also common in nineteenth-century households were wooden mugs and dippers, all kinds of spoons, ladles, rolling pins, and cutting and pastry boards. These were used long after wooden plates and platters had been discarded. Cookie molds and molds for butter were popular in some regions of the country. Measures and sifters, perhaps with splint sides, were common in both kitchens and barns.

The trouble with finding a spoon rack is that it's hard to tell whether it is antique or merely a battered reproduction from the last fifty years. Wall brackets and corner shelves, however, are identifiable by their lines. Classic simplicity marked eighteenth-century examples, but those of the Victorian era showed carving, often naturalistic, and curlicues. These small shelves were important during the 1800's both for shelf clocks and bric-a-brac. Hatracks that could be folded up like an accordion and newspaper racks, both to be hung on the wall, were other Victorian contrivances. Much more attractive are the wooden tiebacks that were whittled or carved in the early years of the century to hold back curtains and support mirrors or pictures.

Churns, washing machines, spinning wheels, and looms were needed for the never-ending chores of making butter, doing laundry, and providing the clothes for a family. Churns and spin-ning wheels are highly salable items, although both are sometimes converted to odd uses.

Although cranberries are harvested in only a few relatively small areas of the country, the cranberry scoop is a well-known tool. So great has been the demand for these scoops that they are being made and sold currently in quantity for decorative purposes. Many a scoop that has never touched a cranberry vine holds pipes, plants, or the like. An oxbow, which is equally easy to recognize even though few people have seen oxen hitched with one, is fast reaching the popularity status of the cranberry scoop.

The utmost skill shows in the whittling, shaping, and joining of the innumerable tools that were made entirely, or in large part, of wood for so many years. A man took such great pride in the tools he fashioned for himself that, until the early 1800's, he often marked them with his name and the date. Such tools, of course, bring a better price in the antique market than similar ones unmarked.

Handles for various kinds of axes, augers, and frows (an L-shaped tool for splitting shingles or cleaving) and the handles or frames for saws and other tools with essential metal parts were carefully fashioned to fit a man's hand. A good handle was shaped to fit so precisely that it was almost a work of art. Essential tools made entirely of wood include clamps, the carpenter's square, the mallet, plane, and brace, and a good many others that usually have a somewhat familiar look to those who know their present-day counterparts. Quite a find would be an architect's compass, which is exactly the same shape and works the same way as modern ones made of metal.

It is not always easy to figure out the purpose of all the tools unearthed in a dilapidated barn or the cellar of an old house. To cite one example, an old-fashioned hayfork with three long curving tines reinforced near the handle by two wood crosspieces looks very different from contemporary hayrakes.

Sugar buckets covered with splint are considered primarily a Vermont product. However, similar buckets, if not exactly the same kind, were used elsewhere in New England as well as in New York State, Pennsylvania, Ohio, and wherever maple sap became a spring harvest. Where sugar maple trees do not grow, it might be worthwhile to look for other styles of wooden buckets that are typical for certain products or chores of the region.

New England sugar buckets have sides of splint, bottom and cover of solid wood. Two or more bands of splint

*Wood splint was used for making all kinds, shapes, and sizes of boxes. The splint container (left), 13¾ inches high and 11¾ inches in diameter, in which spices were packed for shipment to general stores, was appropriated by the storekeeper's wife, who added her own label—Black Pieces—and filled it with leftover bits of black lace and black silks. The maple sugar bucket (right) has been dressed up for household use by attaching a hooked mat to the lid.—Ted Eastwood*

encircle the bucket, depending on its depth. Handles were either curved splint, or metal with a wooden spool grip in the middle. Probably few nineteenth-century wooden buckets are still to be found, but so many uses have been thought up for buckets of this kind that more than one factory is busy making them at the present time. A large bucket is advertised as a receptacle for magazines. Various other sizes are mounted on tripod legs and recommended as sewing baskets (with hinged covers) or as storage places for a pipe-smoker's paraphernalia or knitting or shoeshine equipment.

### BOXES

At least a dozen different kinds of boxes have been popular enough to be made for both the poor and the rich during the history of this country. At one time or another, some of these boxes were made from silver or other metals, china, glass, or papier-mâché, instead of wood. But the wooden ones always are charming. Many of them were painted, sometimes with decoration in more than one color added to the basic coat. Wallpaper was another means of adding bright colors to a simple wooden box. Carving and occasionally inlay were other types of decoration. However, marquetry or inlaying woods in two or more colors to form a pattern was less often done on boxes made in the United States. Old lacquer, ivory, or cloisonné boxes may be discovered by families whose forebears included sailing men.

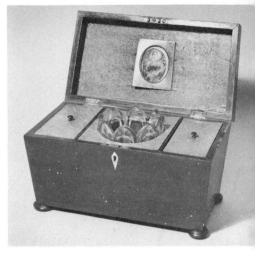

*Boxes of rosewood or mahogany for storing different kinds of tea were fashionable in the late 1700's and early 1800's. Here is a metal-lined mahogany one with compartments at either end. The glass for mixing teas that fit into the center has long been lost, but a pressed glass tumbler has been inserted to display small bouquets. The miniature inside the cover is also a recent addition.*

*Kitchen salt boxes have been made of many materials. This crude one of wood, to hang on the wall, has a back 12 inches high, with a container 11 inches long, 5 inches wide, and 4 inches deep.—Ted Eastwood*

Bible boxes and most Bride's boxes were made of wood. The rectangular Bible box is perhaps the oldest made in this country for a specific use. The first ones were brought from England by the early settlers and others continued to be made, especially in New England. Bible boxes were imposing enough to be as important as any piece of furniture. They were quite deep rectangular boxes with hinged lids, made of heavy wood and decorated with carving and perhaps also paneling. In the Pennsylvania German section, Bible boxes usually were painted. Wherever they were made, the family name was either carved or painted on the cover.

Bride's boxes were a Pennsylvania German custom, probably brought from Europe. They were painted in typical colors and designs and were meant for storing wearing apparel. Such a box was often given to the bride by her intended husband.

The Shaker colonies were especially noted for simple yet distinctive and well-made boxes. These were as likely to be round or oval as rectangular. Shaker boxes of wood splint were made in graduated sizes from as large as the biggest hatboxes today to very small ones.

During the latter part of the eighteenth and the early years of the nineteenth century, handsome boxes were made to hold an assortment of teas. The box itself might be mahogany or rosewood. It was divided into from two to ten or twelve compartments, with a special compartment in the center that held a glass for blending the teas to a guest's taste. The box and its compartments were lined with metal, and each compartment had its own cover. The box could be locked to keep the precious teas safe.

For kitchen use there were salt and sugar boxes. The plain wooden salt boxes to hang on the wall still adorned many kitchens in the early 1900's. Their slanting covers were responsible for houses with steeply sloping roofs being called "salt box" houses. Both salt and sugar boxes usually were made of pine and were extremely plain in most parts of the country.

Spice boxes varied greatly. If they had six, nine, or twelve drawers they usually were called spice chests, but both boxes and chests were made to stand on a shelf. Sometimes they were small copies of larger chests in the house. Some were quite plain, others were painted or carved, and many were initialed and dated, which would seem to imply that they were gifts. Oak, walnut, cherry, and maple were used. Sizes varied from six inches to about two feet in height, with the width in proportion.

Knife boxes of two kinds are known. Handsome urns or boxes with slanting covers were carved from mahogany to stand on sideboards and hold the table silver. These are not plentiful. How-

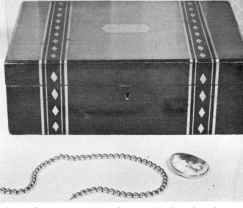

ever, the shallow rectangular box made of pine or maple and divided lengthwise into two or three compartments was common in kitchens throughout the nineteenth century.

Quite as useful as any of these boxes but much gayer and more personal were the bandboxes that became popular during the nineteenth century. Bandboxes originated in New England and had their first great popularity from 1825 to about 1850, at which time they were made of thin wood and decorated with bright paper, either wallpaper or other paper with scenes, historical and otherwise. Later, they were made of pasteboard.

Bandboxes were generally round or oval and were made in several sizes. Both men and women used them to keep hats dust-free. Women used them also to store various kinds of clothing, not just collars, caps, and lace. Bandboxes were carried on trips too. Really old bandboxes can be sold for infinitely more money today than they cost originally. Incidentally, always look inside a bandbox—they were customarily lined with old newspapers and these may be valuable now.

About 1850 to 1860, Victorian ladies became fond of writing boxes. These were not as large or as heavy as the writing boxes or lap desks that preceded full-size desks. Victorian writing boxes were approximately 12 inches long, 7 to 8 inches wide, and 3 to 4 inches high. They were mahogany,

*A mahogany writing box with bands of black and gold stenciling that was treasured by some Victorian lady is today being used as a jewel box. Dimensions are 11½ by 7¾ by 3¾ inches. The box has a trough for pencils and pens and a compartment at one end for an inkwell. There is also a slant-top, felt-lined inner cover that was used as a writing surface.*

rosewood, or black walnut, the favorite woods for furniture at that time. Bands of inlay or shallow carving were the usual decoration. These boxes, of course, could be locked.

The interior of a Victorian writing box was fitted with compartments. The arrangement often consisted of a 2-inch-wide trough across the full width of the front for pencils and penholders, with one end squared off to hold the inkwell securely. The rest of the interior space, where paper, envelopes, and perhaps letters could be kept, was closed off with a thin, slanted, felt-covered piece of wood. This provided a writing surface. The lid had a tight-fitting inside cover that made a concealed or secret place to keep important papers and letters. Sometimes writing boxes were lined with decorative colored paper.

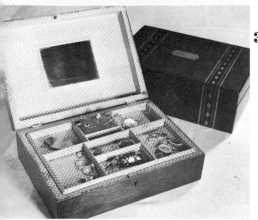

*A trinket box was as popular with a Victorian lady as her writing box. This one of black walnut, 11⅛ inches long, 8 inches wide, and 3½ inches deep, was made after 1870, for the cover has an incised floral decoration. The box is completely lined with wallpaper, including the shallow tray divided into compartments. (The jewelry shown all dates between 1860 and 1890.)—Ted Eastwood*

Still other wooden boxes of about the same size and outward appearance were evidently made for trinkets or possibly cosmetics. In these, a small mirror was inserted into the paper lining of the cover. A paper-covered tray divided into shallow compartments fit into the box.

Trinket boxes of wood splint were common in Pennsylvania and some parts of New England, also during the nineteenth century. The covers and sometimes the sides of these boxes were painted. In Pennsylvania the painted decoration usually had Pennsylvania German motifs. Elsewhere, flowers and birds were done freehand. Trinket boxes were 12 to 18 inches long, usually oval but sometimes shaped like a small trunk.

Sewing was such an essential accomplishment 200 and even 100 years ago that boxes as well as accessories for this occupation were likely to be attractive. Women had to sew whether they liked to or not, and probably it helped to have nice equipment. Sometimes each female in a household had her own sewing table made in the style of the period. Boxes—usually they were called work boxes instead of sewing boxes—were important for keeping sewing necessities together and carrying them wherever the lady chose to sit. Some boxes were decorated tinware, but most probably were of wood. The Shakers made plain sewing baskets

*A New Haven, Connecticut, bride took this wood sewing box with inlay trim to her new home in Virginia in the late 1700's. The top tray is indented to hold her large cutting shears. There is an emery bag in the shape of a red strawberry, and at the rear are two spools hand-carved from applewood.*

on the order of their splint boxes.

Sewing boxes ranged from the simplest sort, made from whatever wood was at hand, to elaborate ones of fine hardwood handsomely decorated. Inlay and veneer were used frequently. However plain or fancy the box, its interior was lined with bright paper or fine fabric. Most sewing boxes had a shallow tray to hold thimble, needles, scissors, and the like. This could be lifted out to get at patches and bulkier materials stored underneath. Some boxes were divided into compartments.

Accessories for sewing often were handed on from mother to daughter. Very nice accessories also were given to little girls to encourage their learning to sew. Needlebooks or needlecases were essential. A needlebook had leaves of flannel in which to insert needles; the covers often were of wood (occasionally one with mother-of-pearl covers or an odd-shaped case of silver is found). Cases for knitting needles, shuttles for netting or lace-making, and darning eggs were other accessories made of wood.

Ingenious boxes for spools of thread were made during the nineteenth century, and anyone can be excused for not recognizing what they are. One example is a small chest with a drawer at the base and two shallow cupboards above (the drawer has a wooden knob in the center, the two cupboard doors similar knobs at the left-hand side). The proof that this is a thread chest is the two rows of holes (5 per row), pierced alternately across the front of each cupboard door, through which thread could be fed to hang outside without snarling or tangling. In other words, ten spools of thread could be stored in each cupboard. Simpler wood boxes such as a small round tub with a tight cover also were made for storing spools of thread.

Many small boxes were made for various purposes, and more often than not were carried. Snuff and tobacco boxes, patch boxes for the ladies, toothpick cases for both ladies and gentlemen who carried their own toothpicks, often were made of wood. They also might be made from silver, pewter, brass, and other materials. However, the wooden boxes made for personal use were not necessarily crude or unattractive. Sometimes two woods in contrasting colors were worked together. Then again, veneer, inlay, or other decoration was applied.

These small boxes to be tucked into a waistcoat pocket or a lady's reticule were made in many amusing shapes. A snuff box of wood might be shaped like a shoe, not the Dutch wooden shoe but the sort Americans wore—complete to the buttons. One toothpick case for a lady was fan-shaped.

Most of these small boxes have become outdated. So has a powder shaker for gloves, which was shaped like a large perfume bottle and often was made of wood. Such a shaker was essential on the dressing table or bureau of every Victorian lady to enable her to pull on her long, tight-fitting kid gloves. Just as baffling is the much smaller pounce box. This also was a sort of shaker, filled with sand or other coarsely ground material; it was a necessary writing accessory before blotters were invented.

Boxes were made for so many purposes that every person is likely to find at least one made before 1900—at some time during his life. Probably all of the very old Bible boxes have been accounted for, and Bride's boxes also are rare. Should you chance to come upon one of the latter, it would have to be in very poor condition to sell for less than $100. The mahogany knife boxes

*An oak box that displayed packets of flower seed in a general store circa 1880 became a button box after it was cleaned and waxed. The fancy clasp, hinges, and brackets are good brass, and the varicolored lithograph inside the cover is in perfect condition. (In front of the box are buttons of carved jet and hand-painted china, and brass ones from a Civil War uniform.)*

displayed on sideboards were never common in this country. However, everyday knife boxes as well as salt boxes and other kitchen containers, fancy writing boxes, and the small personal boxes so popular during the Victorian era are all too frequently found —and ignored.

A Victorian writing box in good condition should bring $10 or more. Sewing and thread boxes can range from $10 up to around $100, depending on their condition and rarity, the quality of the wood and workmanship, and the number and intricacy of the interior compartments and fittings. The smallest boxes or curiosities of wood will be worth a minimum of $3.00 to anyone who collects wooden articles or some specific class of wooden equipment.

Equally salable are some of the wooden boxes in which things were shipped to, or displayed in, stores. The packaging to which Victorians were accustomed may not have had the sanitary aspects of current plastic bags and wrappings, but the workmanship of their ordinary wooden boxes is astounding and their display boxes were often further enhanced with colored lithographs. When such boxes are found in the cellars, attics, or closets of old houses, they deserve a good dusting and a second look before being thrown away.

Several dirty, dusty boxes found in a Pennsylvania cellar about ten years ago proved to be as sound as the day they were made. The clue to the age and original purpose of one of them (made of oak with brass hinges and clasp) was the picture of garden carnations that lined its lid, the colors fresh and the print unmarred. It carried the lettering of D. M. Ferry & Co., Detroit, Michigan, a seed firm that opened for business April 1, 1856, and in 1930 merged with another firm. The box had displayed packets of seed in the early 1880's in the general store that had been owned and operated by the owner of the house two generations before.

Boxes in which tea, coffee, grains, cereals, and the like were packed or displayed often are fine enough that, even with their advertising lettering, they suggest several possible uses today. If not to the person who finds them, they will to someone who becomes fascinated with them. One such seed box, 11½ by 7 by 4 inches, now is a button box.

The clutter out of which a seed box and similar finds are dredged may also contain the store sign. By 1880, most signs had fairly prosaic lettering, but throughout much of the nineteenth century many special shops had extraordinarily graphic signs.

### CARVING

Shop signs, cut, whittled, or carved from wood, so clearly identified the wares or services dispensed within that a person had no need to ask directions or know the name of the shopkeeper. Giant eyeglasses, a large boot or high-buttoned shoe, and a mortar and pestle indicated respectively an optical shop, a shoemaker, and a drugstore. Smaller trade signs cut in the shape of a fish and a ram's head called attention to the store that sold fish and the one that sold meat. These trade signs owed as much to the painter as to the wood-carver or carpenter.

The wood-carver really came into his own with figures, even though those made during the 1800's were painted too. In fact, carved figures now are ranked as folk art. In spite of their size, they are collected eagerly by people who display them in recreation rooms and elsewhere in their homes or some place outdoors.

Barber poles are more common than other old-time barbershop signs that announced the barber also was a surgeon. One of the latter had a basin hanging from a pole. The spiral stripes of red and white on a pole represent a bleeding arm wrapped with gauze.

Tobacco shops had fully as many typical figures as barbershops. The painted, life-size wooden Indian is the one usually associated with tobacco or cigar stores. The Indian was a standing one, but not always in the same pose or garb. Or the figure might be a sultan in robes and turban, or a sailor smoking a long-stemmed pipe. So enthusiastic were the Victorians about these figures that many shops displayed beside the door any carved and painted wood figure large enough to attract attention. A sailor holding a sextant announced the wares of a nautical instrument maker in New Bedford, Massachusetts. However, a Captain Jinks complete to handlebar mustache was little more than a come-on.

Inside shops, busts were placed on counters. Often these were of nationally-known persons. Figures also ornamented the common or public room of taverns.

Figureheads, which projected from the prow of a ship, comprise another important group of carvings. They were busts or three-quarter or full-length figures. Subjects ranged from a goddess to a Dutch girl, from Columbus to Admiral Dewey, and included animals. The figurehead often interpreted the name of the sailing vessel. If no figure was used, the head of the ship usually was finished off as a scrollhead or a fiddlehead.

A carver who turned out eagles had no trouble selling them, particularly in the late 1700's and early 1800's. Wooden ones invariably were covered with gilt paint or gold leaf. They were made in all sizes—small ones to top flagpoles, furniture, and mirrors, large ones with wings spread to display against walls and over entrance doors.

Ducks and other waterfowl were carved life-sized, as decoys, from solid blocks of wood, starting about 1750. There recently has been a revival of interest in these old and weathered objects,

even those with the wood cracked or chipped and the paint faded. Strange things are done with them—they turn up as lamp bases, bookends, doorstops (after being weighted), or merely ornaments to be set on shelves or mounted against the wall.

Weathervanes and whirligigs were still another outlet for wood-carvers. Whittling the weathervane figure was a pastime for the first winter new settlers spent on land anywhere in the country. Only in America were weathervanes so original that they became a branch of folk art. The first weathervanes were whittled or carved from thin pieces of pine, and few—if any—made before 1800 are still in existence.

What possibly may be found are the carved (rather than whittled) wooden vanes that served as a pattern for the cast-iron mold in which the long-lasting figures were made. Before 1850, a metal vane was made by soldering together at the edges two convex pieces of metal to form a figure in low relief. After 1850, the custom was to make a cast-iron mold from a detailed wood carving of the figure. The finished vane of copper or other metal, when taken from the mold, was in high relief and displayed more and sharper details than did the older metal figures.

The earliest figures for weathervanes and the simpler ones made in the early 1800's were flat profiles of wood, tin, or iron. Such a profile of a rooster or other farm animal might be no more than 9 to 12 inches high. During the nineteenth century, the figures became larger and more elaborate—from 24 to 30 inches high and proportionately wide.

The carver who specialized in decoys or made the patterns for metal vanes, as well as the blacksmith who cast the iron molds, usually remained nameless. Their selection of figures ranged far beyond the rooster, which was popular in Europe, and well-known farm animals like the horse and cow. Fancy stretched also to fish, whales, and dragons. One of the most original figures that became popular here was a huge grasshopper.

Subjects varied also with different regions. Probably the coiled serpent was popular wherever any of the several Revolutionary flags that featured a rattlesnake and the words "Don't tread on me" was introduced. An arrow, although ornamented with carving, was simple in comparison to an Indian paddling his canoe or the full figure of an Indian topped with war feathers. The angel Gabriel, ships, and—later on—a horse-drawn sulky were other popular motifs.

Whirligigs—some parts of which can be made to twirl or rotate rapidly—usually are considered toys. But whirligigs 2 to 4 feet high also were mounted on the roof of a barn, a fence post, or elsewhere where the wind would put them in motion. They did not indicate the direction of the wind, but pre-sumably the velocity of the wind could be approximated by their moving parts.

These good-sized whirligigs were figures with paddle arms that rotated in the wind. They are believed to have been introduced in Pennsylvania, probably in the Pennsylvania German farm country. However, their use spread at least as far as New England. Certainly the figure of a sailor was more likely to have been a New England idea. The sailor was dressed in the garb of his day and wore a cap; he stood, with sleeves rolled up, so that he looked as if he instead of the wind were turning the paddles he held in his hand. Most whirligigs were more formal figures, carved and painted to be quite recognizable.

Although whirligigs were not as generally common as weathervanes, they bring almost as good prices. Even if the paint has faded and one paddle is missing, a whirligig is probably worth a minimum of $150. A person is more likely to find a twentieth-century copy of a weathervane that gave service a century or so ago, either an outright reproduction or one made from an old mold. If a carved wooden pattern or a cast-iron mold could be found, either could be sold for an astronomical amount to the right person. Wooden or metal vanes that can be authenticated as nineteenth-century ones can be priced starting at about $100 and moving upward according to the condition and rarity of the figure, how it was made, workmanship, etc. Many old vanes have been sold for several hundred dollars. A decoy showing signs of use brings $25 to $50.

Least expensive of the shop figures are barber poles, and a good one with traces of its red and white paint sells for $50 or a little more. Life-size figures such as Indians start in the hundreds of dollars and move up into the thousands—some bring $2,500 or even $3,750. A ship's figurehead is likely to sell for more rather than less than $1,500.

Small wooden toys, especially those made before 1860, bring prices that seem fabulous too. A jointed doll of wood and pewter sells for not less than $100. Animated or mechanical toys can be priced much higher, and even simple little carved animals are out of the "couple of dollars" class. Of course, many people collect dolls, soldiers, and other kinds of toys and thus create a ready market.

The whittlers in a family produced what toys children had during the eighteenth century. Often these were made as much for the whittler's as for the youngsters' pleasure. Many toys showed the remarkable skill and imagination of their creators. Dolls were inclined to have rather severe expressions, but even wooden dolls by the early 1800's were likely to have jointed arms and legs that could be moved.

Animals perhaps were easier to make

in miniature. All the familiar ones—cows, horses, oxen, dogs—were shaped from solid wood. A Noah's ark was a project that probably took more than one winter to complete, for it accommodated innumerable pairs of tiny animals and had room for Mr. and Mrs. Noah too. All the pieces were painted. Toy animals were made everywhere, but Noah's arks probably gained their popularity in Pennsylvania.

Extra-clever whittlers went in for mechanical toys. The simplest of these were the jumping jack on a stick and the bird with head or tail that could be moved by weighted strings. More elaborate mechanical toys began to be made in the early 1800's, but they were always based on familiar occupations. Some performed their tasks when the toy was pulled. One pull toy on wheels consisted of two woodcutters using a saw to cut planks from logs. Considerably more intricate was another nineteenth-century toy that showed four carpenters building a house. When set in motion, the carpenter on the roof laid shingles, two others attached clapboards to the walls, and another sawed wood laid across sawhorses.

Goodness knows how long the hobbyhorse has been beloved by children. Early ones were no more than a stick with a profile of a horse's head attached to one end. As the nineteenth century progressed, hobbyhorses became more realistic and worked on rockers.

By the middle of the nineteenth century, fewer toys were made in homes. Itinerant wood-carvers who traveled about the countryside carved toys in exchange for a night's lodging. Then, too, peddlers carried toys as well as wooden nutmegs. As toys began to be produced outside the family circle, they became more plentiful and diverse.

In the 1800's animals and many other wooden toys were painted even when they had been whittled or carved by hand. A small unpainted wooden animal probably is older than a painted one, and therefore more valuable. Good collections or displays of old toys have been acquired by several museums in different parts of the country. A visit to one of them can be interesting as well as helpful in establishing approximate dates for any toys you find. In setting a price for any you wish to sell, remember that the period when children played with them is as important as the woodworking skill and present condition.

## GLOSSARY

*Carving:* an article shaped and cut out artistically.

*Hardwood:* wood from any broad-leaved deciduous tree such as maple, birch, and the fruit trees. On the whole, hardwood is heavy and close-grained.

*Louvers:* sloping, narrow boards set in a frame in such a way that they shed rain outward and permit ventilation, or can be adjusted to do so.

*Papier-mâché:* a hard, strong substance made of a wood pulp mixed with size, rosin, or the like.

*Pasteboard:* a stiff material made by pasting together sheets of paper; hence, a board of paper.

*Peg:* a small pointed piece of wood used to fasten boards together.

*Pounce:* a powder of cuttlefish bone used to prevent ink from spreading; a powder (charcoal dust, for instance) used for making stencil patterns.

*Shutter:* a wooden cover for a window, either solid wood often with a cut-out design or narrow strips of wood in a frame.

*Shuttle:* a small tool used in weaving, lace-making, and tatting, with a bobbin centered between two small pieces that taper to a point at either end; made of bone, shell, ivory, or metal, as well as wood.

*Softwood:* wood from a cone-bearing tree, most of them evergreen, generally light in texture and easy to work.

*Splint:* a thin strip of wood.

*Treen:* woodenware, especially plates and dishes. The word is a very old plural of tree.

*Trencher:* a flat, round or square platter or plate on which food, especially meat, was carved or served.

*Trunnel:* a wooden peg set in place hot and dry so it will swell with normal moisture; also called a treenail.

*Whittling:* paring or cutting off chips from the surface of wood with a knife.

*Whirligig:* a figure or toy with parts that can be twirled or rotated; specifically, carved figures 2 to 4 feet high with paddle arms that rotate in the wind.

FOR FURTHER INFORMATION:

AMERICAN YESTERDAY by Eric Sloane. New York: Wilfred Funk, Inc.
EARLY AMERICAN WOODEN WARE by Mary Earle Gould. Rutland, Vermont: Charles E. Tuttle Co.

# 16
## Personal Belongings

FROM THE FIRST VENTURESOME colonists to the last great waves of migrants in the late nineteenth century, a bundle of personal possessions was all that many persons were able to bring with them to America. It was not until they found a place to settle down and earn a living, perhaps to establish a farm or a business, that they began to own more material things. Yet personal possessions remained important.

Anyone who has ever had to clear out a house in which a family has lived for fifty years or more knows that odd and unexpected things are certain to be found. "Why did she save this?" and "What on earth will I do with that?" are questions to which there are no answers.

Both questions are superfluous when it comes to old clothing. "Old" does not mean necessarily the bustles and bonnets worn a century ago. It can mean

clothes worn in 1910, 1915, and even the 1920's. For some reason or other, most antique dealers are eager to buy clothing that was fashionable during any decade from the 1920's back through the nineteenth century. Women's and children's clothing is easiest to dispose of, but the stovepipe hats, vests, and other sartorial items favored by Victorian gentlemen disappear too—and bring some cash money. Tucked in the bottom of some chest are bound to be some hand-stitched and embroidered baby clothes, but for all their sentiment, these are less redeemable.

It is well to look over clothing that has been saved for many years. Furs are less likely to be worth money now, for the skins have a way of drying out and becoming too brittle to be handled and made into something more up-to-date. (This can be true of a beaver muff or fox neckpiece only thirty-five years old.) However, taking time to go through a closet or trunkful of clothes may bring to light an evening dress *circa* 1912 or a ball gown of the 1890's and all its accessories. The attention of possible buyers certainly should be called to a costume with several pieces, even a suit with the blouse and the hat that was worn with it on the street. Bridal dresses, whether a simple apple-green silk one with dainty white lace collar and cuffs or an elaborate one of Paris muslin or peau de soie with a train and yards of fine lace trimming, are certain to find buyers.

Look through trunks and chests of clothing for shawls and laces, miser's purses and calling card cases, parasols and umbrellas (the handles of the latter are the most valuable part and appeal to collectors). Who knows, you might even find, tucked down among the hemstitched and lace-ruffled petticoats, a buskboard—a stiff wood or whalebone board worn by a woman to make her figure flat in front. Calling card cases are small and slim, and fold over either once or twice. Many of them were covered with silk, but ivory, tortoiseshell, papier-mâché, or silver were not uncommon.

Many kinds of purses may still be found. Most interesting and one of the oldest types is a miser's purse. This was crocheted or knitted, with an opening in the middle and rings to keep the contents in either end secure. A miser's purse 12 inches long was carried in the

hand, and sometimes they were long enough to be carried over the arm. On the other hand, men carried much shorter and narrower ones in their pockets. Those carried by ladies often were embroidered or had tiny beads crocheted in a pattern along their length. They also might be finished with bead fringe at either end.

Any dealer or other buyer of period clothing and accessories should be interested in combs, barrettes, and large,

*Victorian purses: The miser's purse (below) trimmed with cut steel beads was carried by a lady, but smaller, plainer, knitted or crocheted ones were commonly used by men. The silk bag (above) is distinguished by a 5½-inch-deep band of very fine beadwork in various colors. The coins are (left to right): a large one-cent United States (1850), a Canada one-cent (1886), a United States Flying Eagle cent (1858).—Ted Eastwood*

ornamental hairpins. Sometimes these were merely shell or horn; then again they were silver or were ornamented with silver or gold, and for special occasions, with semiprecious stones such as rose quartz and turquoise.

A complete outfit of lady's or gentleman's clothing, not necessarily made expressly for a wedding, may be of interest to a restoration or museum in your state or county. Since such organizations usually are non-profit ones, they are more interested in suitable gifts than in purchases, and most of them reserve the right to decide what is suitable for their displays. The prestige of having some of their ancestors' clothing and accessories on permanent display will offset the lack of any financial gain for many persons. Less historic clothing and accessories may be sold for cash, either to antique or second-hand dealers.

Shawls were an essential article of dress for ladies until the early years of the twentieth century. Shawls were not only needed indoors before the days of central heating but also were worn on the street. Solid-color or plaid woolen ones also were worn by men as they walked about the town and cities on their business during the 1800's.

The word "shawl" is of Persian origin and refers to a large square or oblong article of dress that has appeared in many forms and under different names all over the world. Pre-eminent among the shawls worn by American women were those known as Kashmir and Paisley.

An India or Kashmir shawl was a prized possession of many ladies during the 1800's. Such shawls were brought to this country as early as the 1780's, and no one could estimate how many came into United States ports on clipper ships. All of these shawls made in India are noted for glowing and enduring colors and intricate patterns. They were made from a fine, soft, short under-wool found on the shawl goat, and the finest of all came from the goats in Kashmir.

The "cone" pattern dominated the elaborate design of most Kashmir shawls and of Indian textiles generally. The shawls were woven on hand looms, sometimes in one piece but more often in small sections that were sewn together so precisely the seams are almost impossible to detect. Another type of Kashmir shawl had an intricate

*In the mid-1800's, a clipper ship captain delighted one of his Virginia relatives by bringing her this Kashmir shawl of soft red wool with an embroidered pattern.*

pattern embroidered over the plain woolen background.

Paisley shawls were machine-woven in Scotland in imitation of Kashmir shawls. A Scotch textile manufacturer by the name of Paterson first succeeded in copying the pattern of the treasured shawls from Kashmir shortly after 1800. The pattern was multihued, but black and white, red, yellow, or some other one color predominated. Shawls have not been woven in Paisley, Scotland, for years, and nineteenth-century ones of fine wool are highly prized.

Beautiful shawls of silk with silk embroidery were brought from China during the 1870's. Embroidered silk shawls always have been a favorite in Spain. The Spanish shawls invariably were edged with long silk fringe. The typical floral patterns were embroidered either on silk or silk net in gay color combinations or in black on black for mourning wear.

Small shawls of silk or wool were worn over the head upon occasion. The mantilla, usually of lace and meant to be a head covering that falls down over the shoulders, has been worn in Spain and the Spanish colonies as well as in Genoa, Italy, for centuries. Comparatively few old family trunks except those in California, the Southwest, Mexico, and possibly Florida are likely to yield a lace mantilla unless a sea-going captain brought one home to his wife. However, it is a rare family whose

*A lace bertha, made in Belgium from linen thread, that adorned a bridal gown worn during the 1890's.*

female members did not own some good lace.

Real lace, handmade, was used for many things other than wedding veils. Fortunate indeed is the person who finds a Mechlin, rose point, or Brussels lace wedding veil first worn by a bride in the 1700's or 1800's. During the 1800's, good lace was used on the caps generally worn by grown women indoors, on fichus, collars, some aprons, and handkerchiefs. Battenberg lace, for example, might edge a handkerchief or set off a luncheon set or bureau scarf. Dainty, fine lace also was essential on christening robes.

It would be a pity to cut into a lace bertha (a large, shaped collar) made during the nineteenth century. If it cannot be used as is, by all means sell it. Handmade laces common during the 1800's have all but disappeared. Actually, according to the *Encyclopedia Britannica*, lacemaking was developed to its highest art in Belgium during the 1700's. During that century and the next one, linen thread was the basis for a great many kinds of lace. Cotton, silk, gold or silver, and mohair threads, also aloe fiber, were used to some extent.

Mechlin, one of the famous Belgian laces, is a bobbin lace. It can be distinguished from other famous bobbin laces such as Binche and Valenciennes by the cordonnet, a flat silky thread that outlines the pattern. Typically, the pattern is floral, the border a shallow scallop or a slight wave. Mechlin lace, even in the 1700's, was costly. The same type of lace made in Italy was called Vermicelli. Not all kinds of lace were made in all countries, but from Italy to Ireland each country was noted for at least one type until the early years of the twentieth century.

*Mechlin lace wedding veil made in Belgium and worn in 1792 by Elizabeth Randolph when she married William Berkeley at Wilton on the James River in Virginia. (Six generations of brides, her descendants, have since worn the veil.) Mechlin has a flat, silky thread outlining the floral pattern.*

Incidentally, the lace made in Ireland, which is correctly known as Irish crochet lace, imitates some of the much older Venetian and other Italian laces. The roses are one of the things that distinguish this Irish lace from others. Each rose, leaf, and other motif was hooked separately and then chain-stitched in place on the pattern of the lace. This is a slow method of producing crocheted work but a much faster method of lacemaking than the ancient bobbin and needle methods. Irish crochet lace became popular about 1850 and continued to be so until quite recently. Although it is such a late addition to handmade laces, this Irish crochet type should not be disdained. Who knows when it may again become the height of fashion?

Anyone who is a button collector will find it hard to resist snipping the buttons off an old dress or Civil War uniform. This is a mistake, if the clothing looks as though it might be at all valuable either because of its age, style, or fabric. Sometimes a decision will have to be made between the buttons and the garment.

Buttons in themselves are valuable, and the interest in collecting them is nationwide. It is such an engrossing interest that there is a national button society as well as regional and local branches, all of which schedule regular meetings. The society has its own official publication. In addition, several other magazines frequently publish articles on button collecting and there are books on the subject. All in all, it is not difficult to obtain reliable information.

Buttons can be sold in bulk, or any that prove to be rare can be sold individually or in sets of four or more. To sell buttons in bulk, those which are found in old boxes tucked in various places around a house as well as those in a sewing table may simply be tossed into a bag or box. Of course a lot of the buttons will be ordinary ones.

Many materials and styles have been used for buttons since they became the practical means of fastening clothing, as early as the fifteenth century. China, glass, various kinds of metal including silver, copper, brass, and cut steel, wood, ivory, shell, horn, jet, mother-of-pearl, and cloth all were popular during the nineteenth century. Buttons were enameled, hand-painted, inlaid, jeweled, carved, and embroidered to make them ornamental.

Carved jet buttons were popular with Victorian ladies. So were the china buttons called calicoes, which displayed a spotted or figured pattern similar to the cloth of that name. Hand-painted china buttons in various sizes were popular during the 1700's and 1800's and some of these are decidedly valuable. Delightful, and less common than carved jet and china calicoes, are mille-fiori buttons that resemble in miniature the varicolored glass paperweights.

Military buttons are a field in themselves. They usually were metal. Many pretty metal buttons, some quite small, were made for women's clothing. A half-inch one taken from a dress of the 1850's consists of a sparkling cutout leaf fastened to a shallow cup of brass.

Don't discard passementerie (the buttons and trimmings of braid or silk cord) or sets of studs. The latter consisted of two or three studs and possibly a matching pin of china, hand-painted in a floral pattern or with a female profile or a head. They were used in the 1890's to fasten the starched pleated, ruffled, and fluted white shirtwaists, which had collars so high they covered the neck. Some collectors of buttons will be as much interested in stud sets and possibly belt buckles. Buckles of the same vintage as stud sets were large and fancy. They usually were metal with a decorative pattern and sometimes, in addition to the prongs to hold the material, had a pin across the back.

Because of the tremendous interest in buttons, it is not surprising that a good many museums feature displays of them. More surprising, perhaps, is the number of museums of fine arts—not just restorations and folk art collections—that include among their treasures various kinds of needlework. The fact that crocheted or knitted lace is no longer fashionable on clothing does not detract from its intrinsic beauty. Hooking rugs is almost as popular a pastime now as it was 200 years ago, but with a difference. Colonial women had to make rugs in order to have floor covering, and they used scraps of cloth from the rag bag and dyed them with colors obtained from plants, berries, and nuts. Then the cloth was cut into strips and fashioned into a rug on a backing from a West Indies sugar sack, with a hook whittled from wood, bone, or porcupine quill. Today, hooked rugs are a hobby to which manufacturers cater—with a machine-made hook, burlap backing stamped with a pattern, and cloth or yarn precut into ready-to-work lengths. Braided and woven rag rugs are much later than hooked rugs and not nearly as valuable.

Spinning and weaving, sewing, and all kinds of needlework were household arts for pioneer women. They made clothing and household linens as well as curtains and coverings for beds and chairs. Only wealthy families, even during the 1700's, could afford brocades, damasks, and velvets from Europe. All kinds of sewing and needlework continued to be an important part of the education of every girl throughout the nineteenth century. She started to learn as soon as she was able to hold a needle, and practiced at home and at school. The ability to monogram her own household linens and embroider doilies was one mark of a well-brought-up young lady until at least 1900.

Hooked rugs made during Colonial days were worn out long before museums and restorations thought of saving them. They continued to be made through the 1800's, even for sod houses

on the prairies. Most of the needlework, too, that is still to be found will have been made during the nineteenth century. Although machine-made bedspreads and coverlets could be purchased fairly reasonably by about 1850, most women took pride in their own hand-knitted or candlewick bedspreads and in their hand-sewn quilts.

The patchwork quilt probably is the most truly American development in needlework. Not that American women originated either patchwork, which presumably was done as early as biblical times, or quilting, which dates back to at least the Middle Ages in Europe, when garments, bedspreads and coverlets, hangings and curtains, were quilted for warmth. In America, the quilt became a synonym for a bed covering. Actually, the quilt combined two different types of needlework: first, small pieces of cloth in various colors and shapes were stitched together in a pat-

*Close-up of a Basket pattern quilt. This one was made in New Hampshire in the 1860's. Triangular pieces of gay calico form the baskets, which were sewed to 8¼-inch blocks of white muslin.*

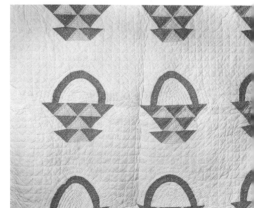

tern to make the quilt top; then the quilting itself consisted of the sewing together—by means of fine running stitches—of the fancy top layer and a bottom layer of plain material with a filling of wool, cotton, or down in between.

The English and Dutch settlers along the East Coast established the art of quilt-making in the Colonies; in truth, the cold winters made quilted things a necessity. However, the fact that American women, between the 1600's and the 1800's, developed a characteristic style of their own and invented more than 300 patterns as original as the names they gave them is evidence of the inherent artistic ability of these pioneer women. As families moved westward, the women continued to make their quilts and added many more patterns, which often were variations of an old one inspired by the new surroundings. Incidentally, the only regions where quilt-making was not common were the warmer areas settled by the Spanish. Quilting is by no means a lost art today, but unfortunately many contemporary quilts are machine-made.

The pieced or patchwork quilt started with small pieces of brightly colored material cut into the shapes necessary for some particular design or pattern. The requisite pieces were sewed together to form a square block, which was an integral part of the pattern.

When enough blocks had been com-

pleted, these in turn were sewed together in strips; finally, the strips were sewed together lengthwise to make the quilt "top."

Almost as old as pieced quilts are those with appliquéd tops. Both types were made in Colonial times, and appliqué in this country became as distinctive as piecing and unlike similar work done elsewhere. For an appliquéd quilt, small pieces of colored cloth were cut into the various shapes required for a pattern, but in this case the snippets were not sewed together but were stitched into place (appliquéd) on blocks of background material, and the blocks then put together to form the over-all pattern of the quilt top.

Women took great pride in their patchwork and the patterns originated for it. Whatever their skill at the fine stitching preferred for the actual quilting, everyone was welcomed to the quilting "bees," which in the old days were the social events of the winter. Then all the women for miles around would gather at one home to quilt the coverlet whose top their hostess had pieced or appliquéd during the preceding months. When the menfolk joined them in the evening, the quilting bee became a festive occasion. Those were the days, too, when a bride's chest was supposed to contain a baker's dozen of quilts. Twelve were for everyday use; the thirteenth or bride's quilt was more elaborate. While she was growing up, a girl worked at piecing quilt tops during her leisure time. When friends were invited to quilt a girl's tops, it was considered a sign of her approaching engagement. The bride's quilt, however, was not started until her engagement had been announced.

One of the all-time favorite motifs of quilt-makers was the star. No less than fifty-eight different named patterns were based on it. Most of them were for pieced quilts, but about 1835 Feather Star with Appliqué combined the two methods of quilt-making, and about 1850 Prince's Feather and Rising Star displayed appliquéd feathers and pieced stars. (Two other names for this handsome pattern are Princess Feather, and Ostrich Plume and Rising Sun.) The first quilt pieced in a star pattern is believed to have been made in New England. The wives and daughters of seafaring men copied their eight-pointed star from a ship's wheel and gave their pattern that name. Mariner's Compass, also of New England origin, featured a sixteen-point star in each block. Four Doves in a Window was a variant of the eight-pointed star. The doves that gathered at openings under the eaves of the high Pennsylvania barns inspired some woman to cut geometric patches, which she sewed to form four doves in the star of each block.

Another version of the eight-pointed star, developed in New Orleans and called the LeMoyne Star, was based on the crest of Jean Baptiste LeMoyne, founder of that city. After 1803, American women called the design Lemon Star. Among later variations of the pattern was "Pineys," made by making six points in red or orange, two points in green, then adding stems and leaves in appliqué. Lemon Star also was the basis for some lily and tulip designs. From new homes on the Plains came Harvest Sun, an eight-pointed star pieced of bright-colored patches. Lucinda's Star originated in Indiana. Star of the Bluegrass, Stars of Alabama, Star of Texas, St. Louis Star, Star of the West, Chicago Star, and California Star trace the progress westward. Each one is undeniably a star pattern and quite different from any other. When innumerable small pieces were sewed together to form one large star that covered most of the quilt, the pattern was known as Lone Star or the slightly different Star of Bethlehem or Star of the East.

Many of the flower patterns were appliquéd, also known as patched or laid-on work. Roses dominated at least two dozen quilt patterns, some of which can be traced back to the early 1800's. Radical Rose, of Civil War days, had one flower and four buds per block. Tulips, peonies, sunflowers, and other big, bold garden flowers inspired many a quilt pattern. Although women loved lilacs enough to carry a bush or roots with them from New England or Pennsylvania to Ohio, Missouri, and Colorado, the blossoms were too fine and airy to inspire a quilt pattern.

Current events inspired the naming of many a pattern. Typical were Kansas

*Like all crazy quilts, the one shown here consists of snippets of various materials sewed together hit-or-miss. It was made in New Hampshire before 1850. Wool, silk, and velvet were used indiscriminately, and flowers were painted (as here) or embroidered on some of the larger pieces.*

Troubles, Old Tippecanoe, Washington's Plumes, Union Calico, Whig Rose and Harrison Rose, Rocky Road to Kansas and Rocky Road to California, Little Giant (named for Stephen A. Douglas), and Lincoln's Platform. Log Cabin, a famous pattern, was an arrangement of rectangular pieces within a block. Squares, triangles, and other geometrical snippets were pieced together in innumerable original ways to give rise to dozens of different patterns.

Most quilts were, and still are, made of cotton. But leftover pieces of other fabrics—silks and satins and velvet—were often cut into odd-shaped pieces and sewed together to form the Crazy quilt. The name applied to any quilt put together in a hit-or-miss fashion without a distinct pattern. It is believed to be one of the oldest types of patchwork quilt, but was made through-

out the 1800's. A Crazy quilt with a stenciled design painted on some of the larger pieces or with a flower or other motif embroidered, usually with wool, here and there was meant to be used only as a "throw" that was draped on a piano or the back of a sofa during Victorian days.

Among the most treasured and valuable quilts today are the all-white ones of fine muslin, woven linen, or homespun, with a thin interlining, which were made until the late 1800's. Over a period of more than a hundred years, every woman aimed to own at least one of them to use as a bedspread. The beauty of these old white quilts was in the quilting design and the fine stitching that held the three layers together. Most favored was a large central panel, with smaller designs in the corners, taken from the central one. Around the decorative sections, the background was so closely quilted as to resemble woven fabric and to throw

*Martha Bond finished this sampler in 1836. It is an ambitious one, but flouts tradition in not including the alphabet.*

the design into low relief. On some all-white quilts, the main design was emphasized by stuffing all the important motifs, such as flowers and leaves. Stuffing was a tedious chore accomplished by making tiny holes on the underside and pushing cotton in with a large needle.

A century or two ago, fully as important as piecing a quilt top was the sampler required of every little girl. The completion of her sampler—after countless hours of painstaking stitching —was a milestone in her girlhood. This piece of needlework was well-named, for it was a sample of a girl's skill at sewing. Some of the samplers now displayed in museums were the work of little girls between six and ten years old.

Samplers are rectangles or squares, usually of hand-woven linen, filled with designs in cross-stitch. Part and parcel of all samplers was the alphabet, cross-stitched first in small letters, then in capitals. A two- to four-line motto to live by was surrounded usually by naturalistic motifs. Sometimes a cat, probably a pet, was the central feature, or it might be an urn of flowers. During the nineteenth century, samplers became more pictorial and were likely to include a little girl's interpretation of the house in which she lived or a small scene, probably glimpsed from a window. Most samplers were enclosed with a border, usually a garland. All of them were signed with the needleworker's name worked in cross-stitch and, often,

*This needlepoint garland, worked by a country woman between 1860 and 1880, recently was transferred from its worn black-wool background to a new one of velveteen. It was made originally for a rather crude footstool of wood, 14 inches long, 7½ inches wide, and 4¾ inches high, with legs stained dark.*—Ted Eastwood

under it the date and her age. A few crooked letters in the alphabet do not downgrade a sampler, for usually the youngster was sewing more skillfully by the time she got to the garland border.

Other types of needlework based on that customary with the ladies of Europe and England were continued in this country. Needlepoint, worked with wools on canvas, had been an occupation for the ladies of the manors and castles. So had crewel, but the women who helped to settle this country started to do a far different kind of crewel embroidery than their betters in their native lands. The motifs in Early American crewel embroidery were brighter, gayer, more informal and naturalistic than any done abroad. American women used simple stitches such as seed, outline, couching, lazy daisy, and feather-stitch to embroider,

*An example of an 1880's tidy, made of white muslin rounds stitched by hand. The 3-inch fringed border was crocheted from white cotton thread.*

but not cover, wool, linen, or cotton cloth with flowers and foliage, birds, and trees loaded sometimes with fruit. Crewel embroidery was used on chair seats, bed valances, hangings and curtains, and coverlets.

Less old crewelwork survives than needlepoint, but more plentiful than either is the more varied embroidery usually done with silk floss on fine cotton or linen in the late nineteenth century. Then every girl and young woman embroidered. Usually she bought the material stamped with the pattern to be worked, for this was the time when pattern companies established their business. Floral and fruit designs were popular and were applied on both household and personal linens. Durings these years, too, almost any woman could put a hemstitched hem in her full white petticoat or her fine linen handkerchief. She monogrammed towels, pillowcases, and sheets, and embroidered pillow shams to cover the bed pillows during the daytime.

A typically Victorian piece of needlework was the tidy or antimacassar made to protect the back or headrest of a chair, sofa, or couch from wear or soil. Narrow matching pieces usually were made for the arms. Tidies might be knit, crocheted, or sewed. If fabric was used—perhaps muslin—it might be cut into small rounds, on which a narrow hem was sewed by hand. Next, each round would be gathered with a thread into a small pouch, leaving an open center, and flattened out by hand. Finally, enough of them were sewed together to make a tidy of the desired size.

Pillow covers or coverlets were made of scraps of silk or velvet in the same manner as the tidy of muslin. Sometimes these finer materials were sewed over small hexagonal pieces of heavy paper or cardboard. The covered pieces were stitched together openwork-fashion, or on all sides for a solid cover.

The chenille bedspreads that are so popular today are machine-made versions of the candlewick ones that used to be made by hand. This combination of weaving and embroidery, which calls for a special needle, was being done before the Revolution. Few examples displayed merely simple tufting. Many were worked in elaborate patterns called Leaves and Swags, Prince's Feather, Eagle, Medallion, and Sunflower. Some patterns such as Robbing Peter to Pay Paul copied those of patchwork quilts of the same name. Crocheted bedspreads are later than knitted ones, but they also copied some of the quilt patterns such as LeMoyne Star, the points of the star being worked out in popcorn stitch. As 1900 approached, handmade bedspreads began to be replaced by Marseilles bedspreads. These were machine-woven of stiff cotton with raised figures.

Homespun sheets and pillowcases were made all over the country. The majority of them probably were used until they were worn out, for fewer of them are still being found than of the cherished knitted or candlewick bedspreads. However, silky linen towels with long, elaborate knotted fringe, banquet cloths of Irish or European damask linen, the red or dark blue and white woven cloths with simpler fringed edges—all of which were the pride of many a Victorian housewife—are still treasures even if they were not woven by hand.

So are the yards of knitted or crocheted lace that a lady made herself to edge her petticoats. Strangely enough, centuries ago knitting was man's, not woman's, work. Of course knitting has been used to make all sorts of things from rugs to stockings. Knitting was almost as important as needlework for the early American women—so important that little girls learned to knit almost as soon as they could hold the needles. At some time during her schooldays, a girl knit a sampler too, a piece about six inches wide and a yard or so long displaying any number of patterns, each one carried on for a few inches and never repeated.

Not all knitting was strictly serviceable. American women knitted lacy, delicate stockings and mitts of white cotton thread to wear "for best"—on Sundays and special occasions. Almost as fine as the personal wearing apparel that they knit were the doilies and table sets.

Although the crochet stitch itself is very old, having been used by some American Indians as well as inhabitants of the Near East, the art of crocheting is comparatively new to American women. It probably received its greatest impetus from the patterns published by Sara Josepha Hale in *Godey's Lady's Book*, starting in 1846. In a sense, crocheting is lacework, but unlike the old traditional laces, it is hooked, freehand as it were, in the air. Pinwheel, popcorn, spiderweb, filet— innumerable stitches and delicate patterns are created by the person who crochets. Weaving and knitting patterns also can be duplicated by crochet.

Bedspreads usually were crocheted of cotton thread but warmer coverlets were crocheted of wool. Bonnets, mufflers, mittens, and caps also were crocheted from various types of woolen yarns. Doilies for many purposes, tray cloths, piano covers, and tablecloths might be crocheted entirely or at least edged with a lacy crocheted border. Even rugs were crocheted. And of course yards and yards of crocheted laces were made to adorn clothing.

Incidentally, the trunks and boxes in which clothing, laces, and household linens were packed away and forgotten may also contain a few lengths and remnants of old textiles. Most desirable would be a Toile de Jouy, a linen or cotton fabric printed with a scenic design in one color on a light background, and chintzes with copperplate printed designs made in England during the 1700's and 1800's. Calicoes and some of the old silks are worth looking at twice.

With all the work there was to be done by hand, it might seem that a woman never could sit still and fan herself on a hot day. Nevertheless a fan was as important on a summer day as a shawl on a cool one. Fans are said to have been invented in Japan as early as A.D. 670, and were common in China and Europe during the sixteenth century. During the 1600's Paris became a center of fan manufacture, and the next century saw fans reach a peak of popularity as well as fine workmanship. Incidentally, at that time fans were carried by both men and women. By 1800, cheap printed fans began to appear.

Fans were carried by ladies in Europe and America during the eighteenth and most of the nineteenth centuries. Surviving examples are not necessarily of great value, for the material and decoration depended on what a family could afford. Many old fans that were not originally high-priced ones seem charming today. It is hard to date a fan accurately unless it is a family heirloom or can be documented by some means or other.

During the 1800's, fans were made of many materials. Lace, ivory, silk, feathers (peacock, ostrich, turkey), fragrant sandalwood or other rare wood, parchment, and paper all were common for folding fans. Often the material was painted or embroidered. Some famous artists of the period painted fans. Wood, ivory, and other fine materials were used for the sticks and mounts, and if the material permitted, were sometimes carved.

Special fans were made for ladies in mourning. These were black, with jet decoration and with sticks of dark tortoiseshell or polished black wood. Black lace fans, sometimes embroidered with sequins or beads, were a little too fancy for mourning but not for an elderly lady to carry to church.

The screen fan, a different type, often was woven of straw, cane, or reeds. This style also was made of parchment or silk and decorated.

Novelty fans included the rosette type that folds into the handle, the mask, and the mirror fan. In the 1890's, young ladies sometimes decorated their own fans. They would paste cutouts

*Most ladies of the 1800's and early 1900's possessed at least one or two fans—some, many more. These examples were all used in the late 1800's. The cutouts pasted on the black silk one in the center were put there by its owner.*

of college pennants, headings from writing paper at resorts, and similar mementos on the heavy silk or paper of a folding fan.

If you think you have found a fan that is valuable or unusually attractive, it deserves the best of care. Old fans must be protected from excessive heat and cold, both of which can cause discoloration and separation of the parts. Opening and closing a fan subjects it to strain and may cause wear and tears. It's best to keep an old fan opened out in a glass case or frame. In this way, one or more frequently are used for room decoration. Poor condition detracts from the beauty of a fan, and even in the case of a rare one, reduces its salability.

Every woman also treasured some jewelry, particularly during the Victorian era of peace and prosperity. Not all of this jewelry was expensive. Coral, turquoise, amber, jet, onyx, garnet, and moonstone were prized, and these at best are semiprecious stones. The miscellaneous jewelry that was not considered valuable enough to mention specifically in a will probably has some cash value today. For one thing, coral and turquoise are fashionable again. So are charm bracelets and the bangle bracelets beloved by Victorian ladies. The long chains on which they wore their watches are frequently turned into bracelets with the slides as ornaments. The earbobs worn in pierced ears can easily be converted into screw or clip earrings.

The fact that you fail to turn up any diamond rings, pins, or bracelets is not necessarily anything to bewail. As much money can be realized from other old jewelry as from a piece with any but a very large diamond, because

*The oldest pieces in this typical collection of Victorian jewelry are the gold beads and the cameo pin, first worn about 1810. The pin-on gold watch was ornamented on the back with a jeweled butterfly. Victorian gentlemen favored stickpins like those at the lower right.*

the diamonds in old pieces are likely to be "old mine cut." This cut admittedly is unusual now, but there is little market for these diamonds. They cannot be sold for their full appraised value because some of the stone will be lost when it is recut in one of the several currently fashionable shapes.

Old mine cut is a recognized shape for diamonds, slightly oval with a pattern of facets and a deep point below. A rose cut diamond, another old style, varies more than old mine cut. Oval, oblong, and square diamonds with rounded corners are old cuts that are more acceptable nowadays than old

*Victorian ladies wore small gold watches on long chains with ornamental slides. The garnet pin (lower left) and the ring made from its matching earbob were part of a bridal set in 1867. The other rings are garnets with moonstones or pearls. The enamel decoration is almost worn off the round gold pins.*

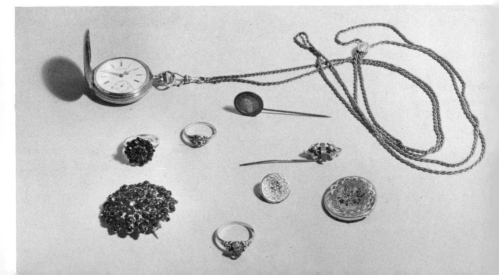

mine and rose. Pear and heart shapes also are old, but are newly fashionable; the marquise or boat-shaped diamond is not much more than 75 years old.

Adult as well as young Victorian ladies were fond of rings of lovely, softly gleaming old gold set with small diamonds, sapphires, and emeralds alone or in combination. A band of five or six sapphires or of some other gem stone is currently enjoying a revival of popularity. Combinations of small emeralds and diamonds, of pearls or moonstones and garnets, are charming rather than salable curiosities.

Bridal sets of jewelry were important to Victorian couples. A set usually consisted of earrings for pierced ears, two bracelets, and a breast pin or brooch, possibly a necklace. Sets of seed pearls or pearls on mother-of-pearl probably are the most valuable today. Around 1870, sets of garnets were popular. Similar sets of jewelry often were given on other important occasions. They ranged from simple gold with black enamel decoration to onyx with pearls and more valuable stones.

Mourning jewelry was made of jet. Bracelets, pins, and other personal ornaments woven from human hair were memorial pieces or mementos of a loved one.

One of the charms of Victorian jewelry is the rich, soft, real gold color of the gold in which stones were mounted and of which chains, watchcases, and

the like were made. A gold locket an inch or two long, often set with one stone, was worn on a long chain, as was a watch. Chokers of gold beads, usually all the same size, may be too snug for today's women to wear, but they were invariably of excellent quality. A considerable amount of jewelry —bracelets, earrings, pins, and lockets —was gold with colored enamel. Cobalt blue and black were favorite colors.

In spite of the excellent workmanship, many pins that Victorians wore proudly seem to have no particular distinction today. Cameos, however, often are interesting, sometimes unusual. The classic profile always has been common, but some old cameos were carved to display groups or a scene. Cameo pins were mounted in beautiful, quite plain gold settings.

Pins and earrings of millefiori and mosaic often are delightful. The rose was a favorite motif for mosaic, usually delicate pink inlaid in a polished black background. The detail is sometimes so sharp that the flower can be identified as a Cabbage rose.

Men wore jewelry, too, probably more than at the present time. Their watch fobs and seals have a ready market for the charm bracelets women wear today. Few stickpins, unless they are set with a precious stone of fairly good size, can be sold for more than a very small sum. However, stickpins are enjoying some popularity among women, who group several on a lapel or have them mounted together to make an important pin. Cuff links were as varied as stickpins, and if they are not appealing for their original purpose, can be converted quite easily and inexpensively to earrings.

As might be expected, jewel cases were cherished by Victorian ladies. The small, hinged box or coffer for storing jewelry was turned out in a wealth of shapes and materials and was invariably decorative. Sometimes a jewel box was included in a dresser set of silver or other material. More often, individual boxes were made of various metals, papier-mâché or tortoiseshell, glass or china, or were covered with velvet, plush, or occasionally leather. Ormolu mounts were common before 1850.

Cut glass jewel cases, which became popular between 1876 and 1900, often had sterling silver covers. Opaline glass boxes in delicate blue, green, or pale pink are still charming. Some opaque glass boxes, like those of china, were painted with landscapes or figures.

Some jewel boxes were made in fanciful shapes. Small opaline glass ones might be egg-shaped and mounted in brass. Others in the shape of a suitcase or clover of glass cannot be considered unusual, in view of all the whimsies made to hold matches and toothpicks.

Jewel boxes were not likely to be decorated with enamels, but many smaller boxes such as those for snuff and patches, and also cases for personal toothpicks, often were. Perfume

*Jewel cases dating between 1875 and 1900: The larger one, made of opaque white glass, is decorated with a landscape painting, a border in amber and brown, and ormolu mounts. The other is hard metal in a golden shade, with scrolls framing classic heads of women.*—Ted Eastwood

bottles, spoons, and buttons as well as mirror knobs were other favorite subjects for enamelwork or European cloisonné.

Generally referred to as enamels are objects covered with colored enamels fused on a metal base, less often on glass or pottery. Until the close of the fifteenth century, surface decoration with enamels was properly called cloisonné. This term stemmed from the fact that wire fillets attached to a base formed cells or *cloisons* into which the enamel was sunk. Cloisonné as well as later methods of enameling was practiced in both Europe and the Orient. Some of the most exquisite cloisonné was made in China in ancient times.

About 1750 in Battersea, England, a process of painting and then fusing enamels on copper was discovered. It was done in several large factories, for only a few years. Afterward, some amount was produced in the Staffordshire District. France also produced admirable enamels before the Revolution and during the Empire period, and Russian craftsmen under the Czars did outstanding work. Boxes, bowls, vases, occasionally an inkwell, plate, or jardiniere, were the chief items in both oriental and European work. Enamels always have been expensive and still are, as antiques.

An enamel or silver toothpick case may still have the owner's toothpick in it. Toothpicks have been carried by men and women since Elizabethan days. The Victorians went one step further and had decorative cases in which to carry their toothpicks carved from bone, ivory, or a quill or, more rarely, of gold.

The social and economic history of the United States has been influenced tremendously by tobacco. The American Indians were the first to smoke tobacco and the Portuguese and Spanish introduced the custom to Europe. Probably because not only the Dutch who settled New Amsterdam but also those who stayed at home so greatly enjoyed their smoking, Holland more than any other nation devised accessories to help make this habit a pleasure. And, of course, tobacco became the financial mainstay of the colony of Virginia.

Pipes are the oldest method of enjoying tobacco. The Indians held the tobacco that they smoked in shells or horns. The white settlers used long-stemmed clay pipes, many of them made in Liverpool and Scotland. Steel pipes, introduced in the eighteenth century, became popular with sailors and stagecoach passengers because they did not break as easily as clay ones. Meerschaum, porcelain, and ivory were used for the bowls of pipes, which often were carved or painted.

Because tobacco was a costly luxury, pouches were made to carry and keep safe any small amount. Then came tobacco boxes. Narrow brass boxes, em-

*This oval silver box with a hinged cover is decorated in a style linked to Holland during the 1880's. Since the Dutch made many smoking accessories for export, it probably was meant to hold snuff or tobacco. (Height is 3½ inches, width 2¼ inches.)*—Ted Eastwood

bossed, were exported everywhere from Holland during the seventeenth century. Lead and pewter ones came from England.

Other accessories included long tongs with which to pluck a coal from the fireplace to light a pipe. These appeared during the 1700's, as did tinder boxes with flints and steel, often designed in the shape of a pistol. Then there were pipe tampers. That century also brought the introduction of smoking stands and hanging pipe racks. The latter usually had a drawer at the base for tobacco.

Tobacco jars also have been made since the 1700's. Usually these were not only a container for pipe tobacco or cigars but a humidor as well. Although tin,

pewter, and some other materials were used for tobacco jars, the greatest variety was made in pottery and porcelain. Delft, majolica, bisque, and porcelain became common. Most of them had appropriate decorations. Some were shaped in the form of an animal or of an Indian or a white man smoking, and appropriately colored. On others, only the covers or knobs had shapes linked to smoking.

Cigars did not become generally popular in America until about 1850, although Spaniards had smoked them almost since the discovery of tobacco. Cigarettes date back to the Aztec Indians. However, the modern style of cigarette was hand-rolled in the 1850's and has been mass-produced since the 1880's. Cigar and cigarette accessories include cigar cutters, clippers, and cases, and the cards found in cigarette packages *circa* 1900.

Firearms are a highly specialized field as well as a popular one that attracts many collectors. Their interest ranges from the early blunderbusses, flintlocks, and muskets to the long rifles called Kentucky or Pennsylvania rifles. These long rifles were made first in the vicinity of Lancaster, Pennsylvania, where they were adapted from Yeager hunting rifles brought to that area by settlers from Germany. Because these rifles were taken over the mountains by hunters and explorers, they became better known as Kentucky rifles. A Kentucky rifle was a prized possession

*Old sewing accessories are often most attractive. The thread boxes and needlebook (they belonged to a New Haven girl of the late 1700's) were mother-of-pearl with carved covers. The tiny envelope of thread (left) came from England, but was rewound on spools carved from applewood.*

that often was handed on from father to son. It always was kept within easy reach in case of trouble.

Firearms used during the War Between the States are of particular interest in the 1960's. Collectors also are attracted to those bearing such important names from the 1880's onward as Sharps, Springfield, Winchester, and Remington. Colt was a significant name in pistols and revolvers. Then there are derringers as well as pistols identified by such descriptive words as dueling, gambler, and muff.

Sidelines for those interested in firearms are bullet molds and cartridges. Powder horns are a mere decorative accessory nowadays, though once they were a necessity. They were first made in Europe, later in America, to carry gunpowder without damage to it. The earliest ones were made of horns from a cow, bullock, or ox. Later, in this country, buffalo horns were used. The natural curve of these horns made them fit nicely on a person's hip. Since the horns were impervious to water, they kept the powder dry. A tiny opening to form a spout was made in the tapered end, and this as well as the wide end were plugged with wooden stoppers cut to fit tightly.

*This Volcanic Rifle, .38 caliber, was made in the late 1850's by the New Haven Arms Company, a forerunner of Winchester Repeating Arms Company.*—Courtesy of Winchester Gun Museum

Many a hunter, trapper, farmer, and settler in the United States made and carved his own powder horn. Engraved ones made in this country are at a premium now. The engravings were forts, maps, town buildings, animals, or birds, and the lines sometimes were colored with black, green, or red. It was not unusual for the owner's name and a date to be carved on the horn.

Powder horns began to be displaced by flasks in the 1830's. These small flasks, often with a measure to dole out the powder, were made from pewter, brass, or copper. Although flasks were inexpensive in their day, a powder flask in excellent condition can be sold for $10 or more at the present time. Plain, undecorated powder horns sell for $5 or so, but engraved ones run from $20 up, depending on the theme of the decoration and the quality.

Any kind of firearm, like jewelry, had best be taken to an expert or a specialist for appraisal and sale. The financial return from miscellaneous Victorian jewelry may be disappointing. Actually, more money may be obtained for a gun or pistol, even one that is less than a century old. But it's important to find out whether any kind of firearm is worth a few dollars or good deal more. Lace and buttons also are specialized fields in which it is important to find the right customers. Of course, a Mechlin lace wedding veil made dur-

*Small boxes for trinkets, keepsakes, and essential little articles often were made of glass or china. The opaque white glass box (left), 4⅛ inches long and 2⅝ inches wide, had flowers, now worn off, painted in the center of the lid and the scrolled edges gilded. The china box at the right is a late-Victorian whimsey that is shaped like a fireplace, complete to the fender painted with gilt. The mantel, which serves as a lid, is all one piece, including the little girl peering into a mirror framed in china, the cup and saucer and the pitcher. One exactly like this in every detail recently brought $13 at a country auction.*—Ted Eastwood

ing the 1700's and worn by several generations of brides is priceless. On the other hand, a Battenberg lace handkerchief made during the late 1800's should be worth about $5, and several yards of delicate hand-knitted or hand-crocheted lace for edging fully as much.

Again, with household linens, it's a case of finding the customer. A red or blue and white cloth with fringe should bring in the neighborhood of $10, depending on its size and condition. Towels with long, knotted fringe sell for about $3. In view of all the hand stitching that went into them, quilts and samplers sell reasonably. A person is fortunate to receive between $20 and $50, unless the piece has some historical significance.

In this diverse field of personal belongings, it is often the little things that bring surprising returns. Ordinary paper fans with simple wood sticks can be sold for $1 and the ostrich feather ones for about $5. A very old fan with carved ivory sticks and hand-painted silk or a paper fan made in France should be worth about $50 if it is in good condition. The unusual handle of an umbrella or parasol also brings good money.

The tobacco jar, perhaps of majolica, that you wouldn't have around your house is likely to sell to someone for $10 or more. Many china ones are worth twice as much. Pipes, particularly those with carved bowls or painted china ones, sell for as good, if not better, prices than the tobacco jars.

Any kind of box, large or small, always finds a buyer. Perhaps this is because boxes are fully as useful today as when they were made, even though the present-day use may be quite different. The whimsically shaped jewel box sells as readily, and perhaps for as high a price, as the attractive one of fine workmanship. Glass ones bring particularly good prices.

A Battersea enamel box no more than 3 inches long and 1¼ inches high will almost certainly sell for about $135, or possibly a little more, if it has not been chipped or otherwise damaged. French and Russian enamels bring good prices. The work of certain artists is more valuable than that of others, so it is important to have enamels appraised or examined by an expert who has studied them and perhaps also knows something about the current market.

*A fine example of a Battersea enamel snuffbox (1750-56). The scenes in pastel tints are framed in gold scrolls against a deep blue background.*

Although many personal belongings sell for only modest amounts and probably for far less money than you think they should bring, the sum-total realized should be quite satisfactory. Particularly since, at first glance, many of them seem silly things to have been saved for so long. It may take time to dispose of these diverse articles here and there, but in the long run some of the most baffling things you find will delight a new owner.

## FOR FURTHER INFORMATION:

FIREARMS by Howard Ricketts. New York: G. P. Putnam's Sons
THE FIRESIDE BOOK OF GUNS by Larry Koller. New York: Simon & Schuster, Inc.
WOMAN'S DAY BOOK OF AMERICAN NEEDLEWORK by Rose Wilder Lane. New York: Simon & Schuster, Inc.

# 17

# Family Possessions

THE BOOKS PEOPLE READ, the games they played, and the kind of pictures they hung on their walls are as important as the clothing they wore and the furniture they used, in reconstructing how they lived in years gone by. Many people nowadays like to acquire these and other minor appurtenances of daily living. A book, an aquatint, a greeting card, a toy, or stamps and coins can be interesting on their own account. Cachet is added—and the value increased—if the first owner was a celebrity or honored person.

There are tales—some true, others apocryphal—of letters written by historic persons a century or more ago or the stamp on an old envelope having been sold for a fabulous amount of money. Certainly it is smart to scan each letter in a ribbon-tied packet to be sure that no autographs of financial worth or contents of interest to historians or the public are thrown out with the love notes and report cards from schooldays.

The monetary rewards from the miscellaneous accumulation in most households will be modest. For the number of people who find a rare or valuable stamp or autograph, there are hundreds who turn up only routine correspondence, books, and the like that have little interest even for direct descendants. Still, it is always sensible to call in one or more antique as well as second-hand dealers. They may realize that what appears to you to be run-of-the-mill stuff has some attraction for certain collectors of memorabilia.

First, however, any item that looks promising should be set aside for the advice of a collector or expert in that field. Letters, books, coins, prints and pictures, the old cribbage or domino set, paper dolls, and the ship in a bottle may well entrance someone else and prove more valuable than you thought at first glance.

Generally recognized is the importance of costume and textile collections to designers and manufacturers. Equally valuable for researchers in many fields are city directories, telephone books, almanacs, and such books as a profusely illustrated history of a town or county. Libraries and museums, both cultural and industrial, may give welcome acceptance, if not payment, to offers of such things.

Every attic and many cupboards and chests have pictures of some kind, framed and unframed. Of course, there is always the chance that the frame may be more valuable than its contents. But that's all right, for no one can keep the likeness of every one of his ancestors. If you should gather together a nondescript lot of framed photographs taken during the last two or three decades, by all means destroy the photographs before you send the box of frames to the rummage or auction sale held by your church. Pictures of any kind that originated during the 1800's should be gone over more carefully.

A few American painters made their names famous during both the 1700's and 1800's. But in spite of the growing wealth of innumerable families during the 1800's, the majority could not afford to have portraits of their children or elders painted by important artists.

In the days before photographs and even after daguerreotypes and tintypes were accepted, an oil portrait was the thing to own. Most of these were done by journeymen artists, many of them little more than hacks.

Oil paintings must have been one of the status symbols of the Victorian era. Fully as popular as portraits were still lifes of fruit, flowers, and game birds. They adorned the living-room and dining-room walls of homes that were comfortable rather than wealthy.

*A portrait of George Washington (part of a set which included Martha Washington and Abraham Lincoln) is painted on the back of the glass and enclosed in a gilded frame. Reverse paintings on glass, particularly of men of historical or national prominence, ladies of fashion, and children, were popular from 1820 to about 1860. Many were smaller than this picture, which measures 25½ by 21½ inches.*
—Ted Eastwood

Most of these still lifes were no more skillfully painted than many of the oil portraits. Yet the panel of pansies in a wide gold frame that hung over the sliding doors between two rooms, or the pheasant in oils in an equally rococo gilt frame on the dining-room wall, was extraordinarily natural-looking.

Landscapes painted to order by itinerant artists were usually less skillfully done than either still lifes or portraits. Some of them are pretty bad; others have a certain vigor or colorful quality that makes them deserve a second glance at least. All three types, either in oil or water color, are now classed as primitive or folk art. Thousands of such pictures were painted throughout the 1800's. Of them all, portraits probably are the most salable. Many an "ancestor" painting has been bought at auction and hung proudly in the home of its new owners.

Almost certain to be valuable—probably more so than large oil paintings—are miniatures. These are just that: small portraits painted on ovals 2 to 4 inches high. The art of miniature painting is a fine and delicate one, and many museums display miniature portraits of Washington, Lafayette, and other statesmen.

Miniature portraits go back to the sixteenth century and probably earlier in Persia and India. They were produced in quantity in Europe and England starting in the early sixteenth century;

notable artists in every country have produced them. They became popular in America among those who could afford them in the 1700's and continued to be very much so through the early 1800's. One of the first miniature painters in this country was John Watson. Other important ones were Charles Willson Peale in Philadelphia, Henry Bembridge in Charleston, John Ramage of New York City and Boston, and, later, Archibald and Alexander Robertson. Two of the finest miniaturists were Edward G. Malbone, born in Rhode Island, and Robert Field. Just possibly one of your ancestors was portrayed on a bit of ivory, if not by one of these painters then by a lesser-known artist.

Miniatures were painted in oil or water colors. Enamel ones are more rare. Gold, silver, copper, possibly pewter, ivory, glass, vellum, and heavy, thick paper of good quality were the materials used as background. Probably more miniatures were painted on ivory and vellum than on any other material, particularly during the late 1700's and early 1800's. Some miniatures were small enough to be fitted into a locket. Most of them had gold frames, and occasionally, if a family was wealthy enough, a frame was ornamented with pearls or other precious stones. Then again, a miniature with or without a frame was mounted in a velvet case.

In the late 1800's and early 1900's, miniatures were not always hand painted. Instead they were photos colored and mounted on ivory. These may as well be kept for their sentimental value. Certainly they cannot be appraised highly and are not, at least at the present time, of interest to collectors of miniatures.

Popular in this country until 1850 or thereabouts were silhouettes. These were much less expensive than miniature paintings, although they were cut by many famous artists. Like miniatures, silhouettes have special charm.

A silhouette is a cutout portrait in profile, either a bust or a full-length figure. Two kinds were made. The hollow-cut had the head and figure cut

*A silhouette or profile cut from paper and mounted against paper of contrasting color became a popular kind of portrait in the United States during the early 1800's. The frame here is gilded and Victorian Rococo in style.*—Ted Eastwood

away, leaving a white paper frame silhouetting a hole. This frame was mounted against black paper or cloth or possibly painted glass. The second and more usual type had the head or figure cut from black paper and then mounted on white or light background paper. Less commonly found are the black paper silhouettes mounted against an appropriately painted or lithographed background, with the cutout embellished with ink, water colors, or gilding.

Portrait silhouettes were most popular. In addition, flowers, eagles, and more conventional designs were cut out and mounted purely as decoration.

Most silhouettes were unsigned and were done by unknown artists. At that, they are quite good. Charles Willson Peale, the well-known artist, left behind some silhouettes as well as miniatures. Another name worth looking for is that of Augustin Edouart, a Frenchman who traveled throughout the United States in the 1840's and produced portrait silhouettes with sepia backgrounds.

Silhouettes, if not portraits in oil, were perhaps supplanted by daguerreotypes. The daguerreotype, named after Louis J. M. Daguerre, one of the two Frenchmen who perfected the process during the 1830's, was an early type of photograph. This process was practically pushed aside by the 1860's. A far cheaper method of making portraits called tintypes had been developed by that time.

*Tintypes, like the older daguerreotypes, were usually mounted in a leather case with the picture framed in gold-colored metal and the cover lined with velvet. By the 1880's, most families owned a handsome album covered in leather or plush, with gilt-edged pages and fancy gilt clasps, to hold pictures of relatives and friends.—Ted Eastwood.*

It is difficult to tell, by looking at one of these little pictures, whether it is a daguerreotype, a tintype, or an ambrotype (made by another one. of the methods that led to photography as we know it today). Even a professional photographer usually has to take the picture out of its case to identify the process. However, a daguerreotype is likely to be a much better and less faded picture. The process called for care and skill, but the results could be excellent.

Daguerreotypes were made on a silvered copper plate, ambrotypes on glass, and tintypes on an iron plate. By far the majority of all three are rather stiff portraits of a family or some one or two members of it. All three types usually were mounted in cases of real or imitation leather with a plush or velvet lining into which the picture was fitted, perhaps framed with gilt.

Prints or lithographs to hang on walls became immensely popular during the Victorian era. Lithography provided pictures, of which Victorians were so fond, at far lower cost than hiring an artist, even one who may have worked for only overnight lodging and board. Lithography was a comparatively inexpensive as well as a fast way of making prints of the same picture in quantity. The process of lithography was worked out by Alois Senefelder in Germany before 1800. It consisted of putting designs on stone with a greasy material, often with crayon, and from this producing printed impressions. Senefelder took out patents in England in 1801, but by that time Englishmen had worked out a similar process.

Lithographs can be excellent. At first, all prints were black and white. Later came the chromolithographs, which were printed in colors from a series of stones prepared by the lithograph process. The shortening of this term to chromo, usually spoken in a derogatory tone, can be attributed to the harsh coloring of many of these prints. Some, of course, were of good quality.

The most famous firm in the United States to produce lithographic prints was Currier & Ives. Nathaniel Currier went into business in New York City in 1834; then in 1857 James Merritt Ives became his partner. Both retired in the 1880's, but the firm continued in business until 1907. There were many other lithographing firms, not only in New York City but also in such cities as Hartford, Boston, and Buffalo.

Currier & Ives produced a tremendous number of prints. Their subjects alone totaled more than 7,000. The early lithographs from Currier & Ives were printed in black and white. If color was called for, it was applied by hand by means of water colors. By 1880, this firm printed in various colors.

The subjects of the prints produced by all the lithographic firms appealed greatly to Victorians. There were American views and scenes, artists' conceptions of historical events, country and garden scenes, portraits of prominent persons, family groups idealized and sentimentalized, cartoons including political ones, horses and horse racing, hunting, fishing, and other sports including boxing and baseball, railroad and Mississippi River themes, religious subjects, fires, and other current events. In other words, these inexpensive prints covered all phases of living and the outlook of the time. One of the notable Currier & Ives prints, and a great favorite today, was titled "Home for Thanksgiving."

Any lithograph is worth taking to an expert for his opinion of its value. It need not be a Currier & Ives. Those from this as well as other firms differed greatly in quality. Subject matter is as important in determining a lithograph's present cash value.

Other types of "pictures" appealed to Victorians. An example would be an aquatint, made by an etching process so that the print imitated the broad, flat effect of an India ink or sepia drawing or a water color. Another process of engraving (on copper and steel, by scraping or burnishing a roughened surface to produce light and shade) gave the mezzotint. Then, of course, there were wood and steel engravings and etchings. But these were more expensive and hence not as commonly found today as the lithographs.

Prints were turned out in quantity by several processes, and are a specialized field in themselves. Bird, animal, flower, and fruit prints can be important; also prints of Indians and the American West. Some flower and fruit prints may come from nursery catalogues of the 1880's. Prints of John James Audubon's famous paintings of birds and animals (quadrupeds) of North America were expensive even in their day. Mark Catesby and Alexander Wilson were also noted for their paintings of birds, reproductions of which illustrated their volumes of natural history. From the portraits and documentary sketches of American artist George Catlin came prints of the Indians of the Plains and western mountains, and Alfred J. Miller, who traveled to Wyoming about 1837, immortalized the trappers and fur traders of his time. Charles Bodmer, Edward Borein, and Frederic Remington are others whose fame rests on Western themes.

Not of as widespread interest as prints but currently attracting many collectors are lithophanes. These are porcelain transparencies, first made at the Berlin Royal Porcelain Manufactory in 1828. They continued to be made elsewhere in Germany and in France and England until about 1900. These unusually translucent porcelain pieces were used as shields for candlelight, lampshades, and plaques to be placed in windows. Children and pets, groupings of a father and child, figures, and flowers were typical designs.

Much older than this type of room decoration were the old hand-lettered and hand-decorated pieces called *Fraktur,* the work of the Pennsylvania Germans. These were primarily certificates of birth, marriage, or baptism or perhaps house blessings, with lettering and decoration consisting of flowers, birds, hearts, and angels in color. During the 1700's the work was done entirely by hand, but in the 1800's many were printed, with blanks for filling in names and dates. The coloring of the designs might have been done by hand. These pieces were large enough to be framed and hung on the wall.

Needlework pictures were stitched by adults during the 1700's and 1800's, and were unlike the samplers which were done by children. Needlepoint, cross-stitch, and embroidery with silk floss were in and out of favor for these scenic, floral, or sentimental groupings, or possibly copies of famous paintings. Painting on glass was an acquired art for young ladies, especially in Pennsylvania and New England, during the early 1800's. Also fashionable among young ladies were theorems or stencil paintings with water colors on paper or with oils on velvet. The vase of flowers or bowl of fruit was not done freehand but by the arrangement of variously shaped stencils. Then there were pinpricked pictures, and shellwork wreaths and bouquets in frames and under glass domes.

Much of the fancy art work done by young ladies was inspired by such

*Old periodicals recorded the fashions and customs of their day. Here, all the 1850 issues of* Godey's Magazine and Lady's Book *have been bound together to make a single volume. The framed fashion print is from the August 1859 issue of* Peterson's Magazine.—Ted Eastwood

magazines as *Godey's Magazine and Lady's Book* and *Peterson's Magazine. Godey's Lady's Book,* as it is usually now called, was a tremendously successful monthly publication that was started in Philadelphia in 1830. Fashions, household hints, sketches and floor plans for houses and cottages, continued stories, short stories, essays, and verse all contributed to the "high moral tone" claimed by Louis A. Godey, the publisher. Among the famous writers whose work was published were Washington Irving, Oliver Wendell Holmes, Henry Wadsworth Longfellow, and Edgar Allan Poe. But the most famous name of all was that of Mrs. Sarah Josepha Hale, editor of the magazine and this country's first woman editor. She was not only a successful editor but also a prolific writer of novels, essays, and poems.

Nineteenth-century magazines such as *Godey's Lady's Book* and *Peterson's Magazine* are a wonderful guide to the fashions, furniture, customs, and activities of the time. Issues were lavishly illustrated with full-page lithographs, many of them bearing the printer's name. A single print, cleanly cut from the magazine, means cash in hand. In fact, many of the fashion prints of the 1800's came from these magazines. However, a complete issue and particularly a full year of issues are considerably more valuable.

Magazines and periodicals that were printed monthly began to be published in the United States as early as 1741. Most of them were short-lived and unimportant until *The American Museum* was launched in 1787. Many magazines in addition to the two designed primarily for the ladies were started during the 1800's—for example, *Harper's Magazine* (1850) and *The Atlantic Monthly* (1857), which are still being published. An occasional issue of many of these magazines may be valuable to collectors, libraries, and the like because it marks an anniversary or contains articles on special events. Complete files for a year or longer, not only of general magazines but also any on specialized subjects such as chemistry, botany, nature, and the like are fairly easy to sell.

Almanacs have had a longer and much livelier history than monthly publications in the United States. The most famous publisher of an almanac was Benjamin Franklin. The first appearance of his *Poor Richard's Almanack*, which he wrote and then published in his own printing shop in Philadelphia, was in 1732. So widely sold and so thoroughly read were the issues of this almanac, which Franklin published for twenty-five years, that it was the foundation of his fortune.

Almanacs antedate newspapers, for the first ones were printed here in the late 1600's. From the 1680's through the 1700's and a great part of the 1800's, the average American depended on an almanac to keep track of the days and weeks, the phases of the moon, and weather predictions, to decide on planting times, and to calculate volumes and measures. Almanacs provided reading matter and amusement, for they included riddles and short articles, which writers often were glad to furnish free of charge in order to get into print. Of the innumerable almanacs published over a period of two centuries, Franklin's *Poor Richard's Almanack* takes all the honors for being the most witty and pithy.

As a matter of fact, some almanacs were propaganda for various causes. Some supported the temperance movements; some were for Freemasonry, others against it. Some almanacs were practically religious tracts, except for their calendar of the days, weeks, and months of the year, the listing of ecclesiastical and saints' days, and the presentation of astronomical data and phenomena. In Utica, New York, in 1832, Edward Giddings published a 64-page anti-Freemasonry almanac that was offered for sale in New England, as far west as Detroit, Michigan, and in Charleston and Macon in the South. Almanacs were published in many states. In Connecticut, for example, between 1783 and 1800 they were published in three towns: Norwich, New London, and Hartford.

Almanacs are not as indispensable nowadays as they were a century ago. Then they were kept in kitchens for ready reference. By the end of the year, these little paper pamphlets were pretty well worn out. It is unusual to find an almanac 100 to 150 years old that is in good condition.

The two largest collections of the almanacs published in the United States are owned by the American Antiquarian Society in Worcester, Massachusetts, and the library of Indiana University in Bloomington, Indiana. In the latter collection, which includes 7,000, one almanac is dated 1696. Of the many currently being published, *The Old Farmer's Almanac*, which still makes its annual appearance from New Hampshire, is said to have been established in 1792.

Many newspapers in the United States have observed a full century of continuous publication; a few, 150 years or more. Widely credited as the first newspaper published in this country was the *Boston News-Letter*, in Boston on April 24, 1704, but it was preceded by the *Master William*, which was first published as a daily newspaper by the French who settled the Isle St. Croix, now Dochet's Island, near Calais, Maine. James Franklin, the elder brother to whom Benjamin Franklin was apprenticed to learn the printing trade, established the *New England Courant* in Boston in August, 1721. After Benjamin Franklin had settled in Philadelphia, he purchased (1729) the weekly *Pennsylvania Gazette*, for which he succeeded in building up the largest circulation of any newspaper in the Colonies.

The word "gazette" as a synonym for a newspaper comes from the Venetian coin *gazetta*. This was the amount a person had to pay to hear the news read publicly in Venice, Italy, after 1563, when the first newspapers were issued there by the government.

Newspapers are chiefly valuable for stories of some far-reaching event or history-making episode. Unless they are editions that were printed on rag paper, most of them will now be fragile and yellowed. This makes little difference if they can still be read and the story is sufficiently momentous.

A much more valuable type of printed matter than almanacs or newspapers would be original wallpaper, 100 or more years old. Very old wallpapers usually can be removed successfully without damaging tears because they were mounted on canvas or some other fabric. However, anyone who suspects that the old wallpaper in a room may date back a century or more should certainly get the opinion of an expert, and also his advice on how to handle it.

Scenic wallpapers included landscapes, seascapes, and historic scenes. Many of the late eighteenth- and early nineteenth-century papers had architectural motifs, and floral designs also were popular. Wallpapers from China first were hand-painted, later printed, but most of those dating back to the early nineteenth century came from France, where they were hand-printed from wooden blocks, one for each color. Many contemporary wallpapers draw inspiration from the designs of old ones, and a few authentic reproductions of eighteenth-century wallpapers are now being printed and sold as such.

Books are another specialized field. There is always some market for old ones of all sorts—not just the first editions, limited editions, and copies autographed by the author. For example, there are collectors who hunt for the Frank Merriwell stories, the rags-to-riches novels written in such abundance by Horatio Alger, and the eighty-odd books of adventure written for boys by George A. Henty in the late 1800's. One resident of the Hudson River Valley haunts country auctions in summer looking for nature books written by authors who were better known on other subjects (one of his finds was a nature book written by E. P. Roe, the Presbyterian clergyman who wrote such properly sentimental novels during the 1870's and 1880's).

Don't count on too great a return from the leatherbound sets of Balzac, Thackeray, Scott, Ruskin, Dumas, and others that were published and sold in profusion between the 1860's and 1910 or thereabouts. During this same period, a lavishly illustrated and decorative leather-covered copy of the poems of Elizabeth Barrett Browning, James Whitcomb Riley, Eugene Field, or their contemporaries or the essays of Elbert Hubbard was a highly acceptable gift. Sets of books are not exactly easy to dispose of, and the individual volume, however handsome, is not of any great value.

Light novels and books of lending-library caliber are best sent on to the nearest rummage sale. It will be wise to make a list of all other books, including title, author, illustrator if any, publisher, and year of publication. The list then can be submitted to second-hand book dealers. The age, rarity, and condition of a book as well as the author and subject matter determine its value both to collectors and in the second-hand book market. Dealing in old books is a flourishing business in almost every city throughout the country.

It was a rare household that did not own one to a half-dozen Bibles. Perhaps the most interesting are the Family Bibles, which were conspicuously important to Victorian families. These Bibles usually were large books, four inches or more thick with pages approximately 9 by 12 inches. They contained not only the Old and New Testaments but also supplementary material such as a history of the books of the Bible, stories of the Bible for young people with references to the book in which each was related, great deeds of Bible heroes, perhaps a history of the coins and denominations of money used in the Bible. Line drawings and full-page illustrations in color enlivened the finer Bibles. Most important, however, were the few pages of heavy, decorated paper on which could be written data concerning all the members of a family—names, place and date of births, and dates of marriage and death.

A Family Bible was prominently displayed in the parlor. Therefore, it usually had a rich-looking binding of leather, possibly velvet or plush. What a person who is not interested in keeping a Family Bible does with it, is strictly his or her business.

Scrapbooks can be a gold mine. The keeping of a scrapbook was a popular hobby for adults during the 1800's, not only in the United States but also in England and European countries. Often these scrapbooks were nothing more than ledgers, with every page carefully pasted over with clippings. Some, of course, were especially made for the purpose, with blank pages and fancy covers.

Some scrapbooks contain nothing more than newspaper clippings pertaining to the history of a family between, say, 1850 and 1900. More fascinating are books of miscellaneous clippings. These included events, disasters, memorials, observances, verse, etc. Sometimes the columns of black-and-white type were broken up with a flower cluster clipped from a seed catalogue, or something similar and colorful.

Included in many scrapbooks was delightful handwork—water colors, prints colored by hand, needlework pictures, silhouettes and other cutouts, feather work, and pressed flowers, as well as the clippings from newspapers and magazines. Friends often contributed to scrapbooks and usually signed their names to the pages on which their offerings were pasted.

A scrapbook is an "iffy" find. An antique dealer will leaf through it in hopes of finding at least one prize. It might be a small Currier & Ives print, a fashion plate from one of the ladies' magazines, a page of cutout flowers gracefully mounted on a dark background, or anything else that is decorative and unusual. For such finds he will pay some money, remove the page from the scrapbook, and probably frame it to sell.

Diaries, including those kept by soldiers during the War Between the States, seldom prove to be the basis for a best-selling novel or non-fiction book. However, don't discard these until someone has looked through them to find out whether they might be of interest and value, and hence something to be turned over to a historical society, a research group—or an author.

City directories, county atlases, and local maps belong to the group termed "ephemera" by collectors. Mail order, seed, and nursery catalogues, posters, and handbills can be even more interesting or may have possibilities as colorful decoration. Stop and look over any piles of such material. They might have historical value to libraries and the like, in which case you would probably have to donate them as gifts, for research use. On the other hand, it may be worth your while to call in antique dealers who specialize in maps, old books, prints, and the like.

Then there are advertising cards, many of them as charming and amusing now as the greeting cards mailed at St. Valentine's Day and Christmas during the nineteenth century. The advertising cards displayed some copy about a product of the firm that issued and distributed them. These printed and lithographed cards called attention to all sorts of things, such as dentifrices, coffee, thread, dye, stove polish, corsets, organs, cologne, cough drops, soap, and cleaning fluid (such as Pearl-

*Greeting cards of the 1880's: The card with a bird is a Valentine; it has a verse and a drawing printed inside the folder. The others are Christmas cards. Each consists of two cards with the same design (printed in different colors), pasted back to back and edged with silk fringe.*

ine, also advertised in *The Ladies' Home Journal* of the 1890's). Often, a series of scenes, animals, people, or the like were issued for one product or by one firm.

The exchange of cards on St. Valentine's Day is a much older custom than exchanging Christmas greeting cards. Valentine cards were being exchanged during the 1700's. The earliest ones were handmade. The first commer-

cially made Valentine cards, probably available during the late 1840's, were about as elaborate as those that were made by hand. Although Victorians inclined toward sentimental cards, the first comic or caricature ones appeared during the 1840's too.

The custom of exchanging decorative cards at Christmastime originated in England. The first one is attributed to W. C. Dobson, one of Queen Victoria's favorite painters. In 1845 he sent lithographed copies of one of his paintings to friends. Printed Christmas cards were made first in this country in Roxbury, Massachusetts, in 1874. There Louis Prang had established his lithographing and printing business, for which he perfected the use of as many as twenty colors. Prang's cards were noted not only for their excellent coloring but also for their good design.

Victorian Christmas cards seem to turn up in smaller quantity than Valentine cards and do have at least a nominal market value. In the 1880's, few cards displayed the motifs now considered typical of Christmas. In fact, some of them could be mistaken for Valentine cards. Many sent at Christmastime were double-faced cards pasted back to back, with a silk fringe edging them. Less elaborate ones were printed on paper.

The habit of sending picture postcards seems to have been much more widespread and general around 1900 than it is at the present time. A one-day excursion on a trolley car was enough to warrant mailing a card to the folks at home. Yes, there are people who collect postcards too. For this reason, cards have been classified, somewhat as buttons have been, into groups, such as early airplanes, automobiles, boats, California before 1900, state capitols, comics, expositions and fairs, horseshoes, views or areas, Tuck postcards, etc. Only cards printed before 1915 have monetary value. A postcard dis-

playing an early airplane may sell for as much as 45 cents now, and those in other categories have a market price from 5 to 20 cents each. If you don't want to take time to sort out an album or box stuffed with old postcards, the whole thing can be sold for a dollar or two.

Once in a great while, the canceled stamps will have more value than the postcard or letter to which they were affixed. If you think this may be the case, leave the stamp on the envelope —do not cut it off or attempt to loosen the adhesive. No one but an expert can tell you whether or not a stamp has any market value, let alone whether it might bring a premium price.

Stamps were first used in England in May, 1840, and in the United States in 1847. The first adhesive United States stamps were a five-cent one with Benjamin Franklin's picture and a ten-cent one with George Washington's portrait. Nowadays, it is possible to buy an 1847 Franklin stamp of high quality for $25 or a little more, and a Washington one in excellent condition for perhaps $75. The fact that a stamp is old or rare does not necessarily mean that it can be sold for a sum of money much greater than its face value. Certain issues are in demand because they are scarce, and at the present time collectors are interested in stamp oddities. However, the situation may change in another year or two.

It is true that an 1856 one-cent stamp

of British Guinea, which is insured higher than any other stamp at shows and exhibits, was found by Vernon Vaughn when he was looking through old papers in an attic in 1873. Such finds occur perhaps once in a century. Legends have flourished about the value of stamp collections, perhaps because some famous persons are known to have had extensive ones.

It's entirely possible that a book in which has been placed every stamp of every country might have no interest except to another stamp collector. Every stamp in the book might be worth no more than face value—or less if it has been canceled—because all of them are common stamps. By the same token, sheets of commemorative stamps also have been mistakenly though commonly regarded as an investment. Commemoratives are especially designed and usually are colorful. Therefore, they are attractive, particularly when blocks or sheets are filed in a stamp book. Billions usually are printed of each commemorative stamp, so (in the words of one stamp collector) they may as well be used up for postage. For a sheet of 100 four-cent commemorative (United States) stamps, a dealer's offer is likely to be only $3.

Both stamps and coins are time-honored hobbies. In recent years, coin collecting has grown phenomenally, spurred perhaps by occasional newspaper stories of an exceptionally high price paid for a certain coin. To find

one that can be sold for more than its face value, a person has to develop the habit of looking sharply at loose change in pockets or purses and all coins that pass through his hands. The usual accumulation of circulated coins from foreign countries and old ones minted in the United States is as likely to contain only odd ones worthy of use as lucky pieces or pocket pieces as it is anything of real financial value. How much a coin can be sold for depends on rarity, condition, and demand. Many inexpensive coin catalogues are available that will alert a person to possible values. Catalogues quote prices for the several conditions in which a coin may be found, but it must be remembered that these are selling rather than buying prices. Furthermore, according to some dealers in old coins, the average retail selling price is a little less than that quoted in catalogues.

Cleaning or polishing an old coin will not increase its value. As a matter of fact, unless cleaning is done by an expert, the coin may be damaged and its value reduced. Dealers usually pay higher prices for coins left in the condition in which they were found.

With reference to condition, dealers classify coins as poor, fair, good to very good, fine, very fine, extremely fine, uncirculated, and proof. "Proof" is a carefully and especially struck coin with a brilliant mirrorlike surface. A coin is considered to be in poor condition when the design, inscription, and date are almost illegible. A coin in this condition must be very rare indeed to be worth more than its face value.

On United States coins the mint mark may add to the value. These marks are "CC" for Carson City, where a mint was in operation between 1870 and 1893, "C" for Charlotte, North Carolina, where only gold coins were struck from 1838 to 1861, "O" for New Orleans, opened in 1861 and discontinued in 1909. "D" on a gold coin stands for Dahlonega, Georgia, where a mint was in operation from 1838 to 1861. "D" on other coins means Denver, where a mint opened in 1906 and is still operating. "S" refers to the San Francisco mint, which opened in 1854 and closed in 1955. Coins struck in the mint at Philadelphia, which opened in 1793, may be stamped "P" but are likely to have no identifying mark. A mint set of United States coins consists of a cent, nickel, dime, quarter, and half-dollar struck in all three mints—Philadelphia, Denver, and San Francisco—in the same year (in some years not all mints struck all of these coins).

There is considerable interest now in Indian head pennies, which were made of copper and nickel or bronze from 1859 to 1909. For example, a 1909 "S" mint Indian head penny may be worth from $3.50 to $10, depending on its condition. A Lincoln penny minted in 1909 in San Francisco with the initials VDB, for the designer Victor D. Brenner, is worth more than other Lincoln head cents of the same

year. One of these may be sold for as much as $10.

It's fun to find one of the large cents coined from 1793 to 1857 except for the year 1815. Those minted in certain years are worth, according to condition, from 50 cents to $50, but the majority with other dates only 25 to 50 cents. A smaller one-cent coin known as the flying eagle is worth from $50 (good) to $150 (the latter for a proof coin) if minted in 1856; an 1857 one, from 40 cents to $1 or more according to condition. (Millions were minted in 1857). Half-cent pieces, large cents, two-cent and three-cent pieces, and half-dimes are now obsolete but not rare coins, and their value depends on their condition.

Half-dollars struck between 1807 and 1836, with the exception of 1815, can be purchased for only a few dollars. This is true also of commemorative half-dollars such as the Illinois Centennial piece struck in 1918, the Alabama and Missouri Centennial ones in 1921, the Lynchburg, Virginia, Sesquicentennial in 1936, and dozens of others. Many of the commemorative half-dollars are handsome pieces, but the prices quoted are for extra fine or uncirculated coins, and at that you can hardly expect to sell one for quite as much as the catalogue price.

Silver dollars still are given in change in Rocky Mountain and West Coast states, and banks elsewhere in the country can supply them on demand in return for a one-dollar bill. Silver dollars were coined from 1794 to 1935 with the exception of 1805 to 1835, 1837, 1874 to 1877, and 1905 to 1920. A silver dollar stamped in one of the years of the 1800's may still be worth no more than one dollar, or if the condition ranges from good to extremely fine, may bring $2 to $5 or more.

A coin marked "Trade Dollar" on the reverse side under the eagle has not been accepted as legal tender since 1887, but it does have value among collectors. Trade dollars were minted from 1873 to 1885 for export use, chiefly in China.

Gold coins do not have to be turned in to the United States Treasury Department if you have only a very few of them. They may be kept or may be sold. There is an almost constant demand among dealers for gold coins, which, of course, are no longer minted. The market prices fluctuate.

Civil War tokens, about the size of present-day pennies, were issued by various merchants as a patriotic gesture. About 14,000 kinds exist, all of them dated 1863, 1864, or 1865 and displaying various slogans. Dealers sell these tokens for about 25 cents each, so you would be paid less than that by a dealer. A "Hard Times" token or "Jackson cent," struck during 1837 and 1838, is about the size of the large cent. Like Civil War tokens, these were minted privately to alleviate the short-

age of United States cents. Wooden nickels also were issued from time to time by various counties, cities, and organizations, usually as a commemorative item. Actually, they could be used at face value in place of money where they were issued. Because they are colorful and unusual, wooden nickels appeal to collectors.

Roman coins 1,500 years old may be worth less than a rare American coin only 150 years old. As a matter of fact, the rare coin that can be sold for a good price looks at first glance no different from the run-of-the-mill coin. It takes a numismatic or coin expert or dealer to point out the differences.

The tokens issued during the War Between the States (1861–65) are the least valuable and important of the mementos that may be found packed away, North and South. Now, a hundred years later, collectors are interested in almost anything issued to, worn by, or made by a soldier on either side. Federal or Union items are more plentiful than Confederate ones. This is understandable, since so much of the Confederate soldiers' equipment was surrendered or destroyed. Furthermore, anything still serviceable was put to good use in the South after the war.

One example is buttons, although the Federal or Union ones certainly are not scarce. Buttons on the uniforms of Federal soldiers were issued by the government. They displayed an American eagle with a shield bearing a "C" (Cavalry), "I" (infantry), or "A" (artillery). State militia troops were issued buttons with the seal of the state. Metal could not be spared for buttons in the Confederate States, for it was desperately needed for weapons, so their soldiers' buttons were likely to be made of bone or leather. Some Confederate soldiers used buttons taken from the uniforms of Federal prisoners and defaced.

Military belt buckles were made in many designs. The United States and Confederate government buckles had the initials U.S. or C.S.A., respectively. Other belt buckles had the state seal, motto, or name of the state imprinted on them. Belt buckles worn by army officers often had different decoration from those worn by enlisted men; a naval officer's buckle probably bore an eagle and anchor.

Military leather goods, in addition to belts, included holsters, saber straps, and ammunition pouches. All are popular among present-day collectors. Canteens, tin mess kits with knife, fork, and spoon, knapsacks, and bullet molds are also desirable. Federal soldiers carried metal stencils cut with their name and unit to mark all of their belongings. Not only are the stencils a collector's item, but anything so marked is more valuable than a similar piece unmarked.

Soldiers, like sailors on long voyages, carved as a pastime. One popular product was neckerchief slides carved of bone in heart, shield, or round shape. Pipes also were carved, probably by prisoners of war, and some of these were quite elaborate.

Clothing is a field all by itself. It probably will be no trouble to dispose of any uniform or part of one, particularly if it is in fairly good condition. A hat band can be sold for $3 or $4, an officer's hat for three times as much. The sword carried by a Union officer is worth at least $25, one that belonged to a Confederate about $50.

Drums are another item now much sought after by collectors, who, when they find them, do not necessarily use them as a drum was made to be used. About the oldest drums anyone is likely to find are those from the Civil War period. Federal drums had painted on their sides the United States shield and eagle, and the words *Regiment* and *Company*, with space for the designations to be filled in. State militia and volunteer units for the War Between the States had special decoration painted on their drums by way of identification. When a drum was retired from service, its head was sometimes painted with a commemorative scene.

The snare drum was preferred in this country for military units. The bass drum, a much larger instrument that is beaten at either end, appeared chiefly in military parades. The heads of old drums were parchment, the sides usually maple, although other wood was sometimes used.

The cords on the side of a drum are for tuning it when it loses its resonance either from long use or being wet. By tightening the cords, the tone quality is improved. These cords are one method of estimating the age of a drum. Before and during the Civil War, the cords were inserted through holes in the top and bottom hoops. Afterward, they were held in place by metal hooks attached to the edge of the hoops by metal clips.

The military drum found in an attic is almost certain to be more valuable than the violin with broken strings or the battered clarinet. Making music was a favorite form of entertainment at home among Victorians. In late Victorian days the guitar, jew's harp, mouth organ or harmonica, and the ocarina or sweet potato were popular. It may even be possible to sell the banjo, which was the instrument to own during the early 1900's. Accordions are perhaps more popular nowadays than they were 75 years ago, but this does not necessarily mean that the old one will be salable except as a curiosity.

Important stringed instruments such as the various styles of piano need the advice of an expert. So probably would a harp, which was a much more popular instrument a century ago than it is today. There is considerable interest in melodeons, harmoniums, and various other types of organ. Player pianos, which were so popular in the late 1800's, are being manufactured again, and so it's quite possible that an old one could be sold without much difficulty. Certainly the rolls which enabled the player piano to make music are salable. There is some market also for hymnals and songbooks.

Music boxes entrance so many people that it is never necessary to hunt long in order to find a new owner for one you don't want to keep. Their tinkling tunes seem to have some kind of special appeal, whether the box itself is large or small, decorative or not. Many kinds and sizes were made. The Swiss have long been noted for the production of music boxes, but they were manufactured in other European countries and later in this country. Old Swiss music boxes of the cylinder type often play six, eight, or ten tunes; later ones—but still antiques now—have interchangeable cylinders or perhaps attachments such as bells or drums. Boxes that produced their music by means of disks were made under several trade names; some played more than 20 disks, others changed disks automatically, and any of them might have been equipped with attachments that ranged from bells to a zither. Miscellaneous objects such as steins, jewel boxes, and carved wooden plates have been made with tiny music boxes concealed in or under them so that one or more tunes can be played after a spring mechanism has been wound with a key.

The "talking machine" or phonograph

that was invented by Thomas A. Edison in the 1880's was being manufactured by several firms before 1900. The Columbia Gramophone was patented in 1885. Victor was not the only make with a large horn flowering full-blown, like a morning glory, from its top. Many old phonographs no longer produce music, and the sounds produced by those that still function cannot be rated as good music. Old phonographs are chiefly curiosities, but even so, one that works can be sold for $25 or better.

However, there is quite a cult for collecting old phonograph or Victrola records. Early jazz records bring the highest prices, for there are many jazz buffs. There also is a market for opera records made by such golden stars of the past as Enrico Caruso, Alma Gluck, Marcella Sembrich, Frieda Hempel, Nellie Melba, Johanna Gadski, and such later artists as Maria Jeritza, Amelita Galli-Curci, and Geraldine Farrar. Master records are most valuable.

Before the days of the talking machines, probably during the era of the melodeon, it was the fashion to pass many an evening looking at views through a stereoscope. This device, invented in England a few years previously, first captivated Americans around 1850. It worked this way: Dual pictures, mounted on a card side by side, of the same object or scene (taken from slightly different angles) were placed in an adjustable rack before dual eye-

pieces. As a person looked through the eyepieces, the pictures blended into a single, striking, apparently three-dimensional image — of Niagara Falls, the Pyramids, or the canals of Venice, for example. The picture cards, which came in sets, chiefly showed famous places, natural wonders, and the like, although there were some sets on such subjects as Rogers' statuary groups, whaling, the Alaskan gold rush, and transportation.

Magic lanterns were not introduced from Germany until about 1890; they continued to be popular until 1910 or a few years later. The name came from the fact that the first ones housed a kerosene lantern inside the machine. Colored glass slides were inserted between the lantern and the lens, and were projected as pictures on a wall or a sheet. The condition and size of an old magic lantern will determine whether or not it can be sold. If you find a buyer, you might as well throw in any slides too.

Games were another way Victorians passed the evenings, and many of their favorites are still popular. Sometimes a person is lucky enough to come across a beautiful set of dominoes in a handsome case. The finest dominoes were made from ivory or ebony or carved from bone. Cribbage boards and chess sets also ranged from beautiful carved pieces of Chinese ivory to rather primitive homemade ones of wood. Boards for backgammon and other games may still be quite handsome, or may be scarred, commercially-made ones of inexpensive materials. Whether the old pin-on games that were a staple of children's parties, and the wherewithal for tiddlywinks, fish pond, old maid, and snap, which adults played with gusto between 1890 and 1914, are to be turned over to youngsters, sold, or thrown away is a decision for the finder. Bible games, played with cards, were permitted in the most strict households, and some of these sets may be quite old and are certain to be prized by a collector or restoration.

Playing cards are an ancient pastime that came to Europe from either China or India. Extremely old round cards from India, for example, are displayed in museums. Playing cards certainly were common in Europe during the fourteenth century, for in 1397 in Paris an edict forbade working people to play at tennis, bowls, dice, cards, or ninepins on working days. The symbols on playing cards have changed a great deal through the ages. Old playing cards can be most interesting, and collecting and studying them fascinating. The chips used with playing cards were ivory, bone, or sometimes mother-of-pearl. Card-playing or "gaming" was so general in American cities by the mid-1700's that most homes included tables for the purpose. If you find a table, then look also for cards and chips.

That dirty old bag of marbles is nothing to toss away or give to the children. Adults who no longer play marbles, but who remember the game nostalgically, collect them. Long, long ago marbles actually were made out of marble. During the 1800's they were made of clay, porcelain, and glass. Those made from clay were properly called migs. An aggie was a large marble made of real agate. Many old marbles were made of colored and striped glass, and sulphides were glass with a small silvered figure encased in the marble. Crockies were made of pottery with a shiny brown or blue glaze, and steelies were steel ball bearings. Crockies and steelies are not as valuable nowadays as migs and aggies. One mig may sell now for more than a bagful cost 50 to 75 years ago.

The many fascinating hours which grown-up Victorians spent indoors with a stereoscope and view cards were matched by the time youngsters spent gazing into a kaleidoscope. This was a tube about a foot long that had bits of colored glass in the bottom, and a fixed lens. When the tube was turned, a child could watch endless, varicolored geometrical patterns as they formed. If you come upon a kaleidoscope, you'll find it hard to put down.

Toys undeniably were made originally for children, but old toys have become almost a mania with adult collectors. Pull toys and mechanical toys, squeak toys and rattles, circus toys and vehicles, and all other kinds of vehicles—these and many more have had their day. Toy soldiers for boys, dolls for girls, were the usual gifts.

Toy soldiers have enjoyed world-wide popularity for about 200 years. The first ones were modeled on the armies of Prussia's victorious, eighteenth-century Frederick the Great. Napoleon's army, the British Redcoats, Federal and Confederate soldiers, and World War I troops and equipment are some of the noted groups that were reproduced in miniature as toys. Toy soldiers in reasonably good condition with some of their paint still evident should be salable, for they are considered a popular collectors' item.

Dolls are rated as the perennially popular toy. There are, in fact, doll societies, and doll shows are held regularly. Many museums have fine doll collections. If you are interested in collecting dolls—or even if you have a group of them to sell—it's a good idea to study a little about them and to visit any exhibits within a reasonable distance. Dolls from foreign countries dressed in native costumes are interesting, but so are the dolls with which American children have played for so many years. Of the latter there are more than two dozen classifications.

The nineteenth- and early-twentieth-century dolls are the ones for which most collectors search. Part of their appeal lies in the fact that they are dressed in the styles adults and children wore at the time. Incidentally, boy dolls were made, but the proportion of boy to girl dolls probably is about one to ten.

Wooden dolls go back to the early 1700's and up to the early 1900's. Wax dolls were made from the 1700's to the late 1800's (one English firm made them continuously from 1791 to 1935). Papier-mâché dolls were popular from the late 1700's to about 1825. China dolls were common throughout the 1800's. The early ones had wooden or cloth bodies with a china bust attached to the shoulders. Many of these china busts had glass eyes and molded, painted hair. Later china dolls had wigs, and some could close their eyes

A circa-1850 *doll with exquisitely painted features on her china head. The molded hair is painted black. The calico dress and other clothes are new but made in the appropriate style.*

to sleep or have their necks moved. Among the most beautiful dolls are those of Parian and bisque. Many handsome bisque dolls were imported from France and Germany during the 1800's.

Dolls also were made with tin heads and entirely of celluloid. Then there are rag dolls, both homemade and commercially manufactured. Dolls have been made from apples, rawhide, leather, and rubber and gutta percha too.

Baby dolls have been popular for at least 150 years. Those made during the 1800's are especially coveted by collectors. Not just the materials, but also the appearance, of baby dolls has changed a good deal from time to time, and those made even in the early twentieth century are quite different from the older ones.

Portrait dolls representing such famous persons as Jenny Lind and Queen Victoria, fashion dolls with papier-mâché heads (they were sent to America from Europe between 1820 and the 1870's to display the latest fashions in clothes), religious dolls, and mechanical dolls that moved or made music or both are some of the most important classifications.

Pedlar dolls, which appeared in the late 1700's and remained popular until about 1850, are greatly coveted. These were made in England, Mexico, France,

Russia, and many other countries. There were many versions and the dolls were made of various materials. Some were rag dolls with embroidered faces; others had wax, china, bisque, or papier-mâché heads or were made of wood. In any case, they were more likely to be displayed as ornaments than played with as toys.

A pedlar doll was dressed for the street and carried a basket with combs, shells, watches, pocketbooks, playing cards, fruit, flowers, or other merchandise. An English pedlar known as the Portsmouth doll wears a black dress, white apron, red coat, and a frilled cap topped by a black poke bonnet, and carries a basket of tiny wares. Other names for pedlar dolls are Notion Nannies and Haberdash dolls. More rare was the pair of door-to-door pedlars, male and female. Some doll collectors dress nineteenth-century dolls in pedlar costume, and some reproductions are being made at the present time.

Paper dolls had been popular for 200 years or more when they went out of fashion about 1930. If you find any magazines dating from 1900 into the 1920's with pages of Dotty Dimples and Little Colonel dolls, there should be a ready market for them. Strangely enough, paper dolls were first made as an adult diversion. During the 1700's, French ladies and gentlemen amused themselves with jointed paper dolls, manipulated by pulling strings attached to the arms and legs.

Children took over the paper dolls in the 1800's. There were both homemade and commercial ones. The dolls were named and had many changes of costume. Raphael Tuck made some well-known English ones and *Godey's Lady's Book* included cutouts of paper dolls.

Both real dolls and paper dolls were likely to have many clothes as well as accessories such as earrings, fans, gloves, and parasols. There were dishes and furniture modeled on the materials and styles popular for grown-ups' houses, and also carriages, dollhouses, and stores. The tiny piano made for a dollhouse was much smaller than the miniature pianos made for children to play. Both upright and grand pianos were made.

Doll furniture came in sets just as the Victorians bought furniture for their houses. A bedroom set might consist of a bed, a bureau with mirror, a tin washstand, a table, and two chairs. Parlor sets often were upholstered with velvet. The furniture was made in perfect scale. Everything was made in miniature for dollhouses. There might be a kitchen stove with tiny skillet and pots or a parlor stove, all made of iron. Dishes, made in sets, reflected the preferences of the time for the family table. They ranged from spatterware and Old Blue to everyday crockery.

The manufacture of miniatures as toys became a big business. Some of the furnishings and accessories — in fact, some dolls—originally had been made as salesmen's samples.

Traditionally, dolls and other toys are what every youngster hopes to find under the family Christmas tree. So, along with the toys stored in an attic, you also may find relics from long-ago Christmas trees. The decorating of a

*After 1860 or so, pressed glass candleholders similar to the one at the left were used on many Christmas trees. A china bank was a popular Christmas gift during that era; on the front of the one shown here, Santa Claus is holding a tree. A pincushion was also a common gift. This polygon pincushion, made of scraps of silk sewed to cardboard, was a gift in 1858 and was always an ornament on the tree.*

tree at Christmastime is not an old American custom, for except among those who came here from Germany, it has not been common longer than a century. Especially appealing to collectors are the Christmas-tree lights, colored cups made of pressed glass to hold candles. Some few of these were made in recognizable patterns. The colored balls used to decorate early Christmas trees were made of blown glass. These are scarce.

Figures from the *Putz* or Christmas village set up by the Pennsylvania Germans in their homes, and crèche figures of ceramic or carved wood from Nativity scenes set up anywhere in the country, are other things that find a market. A Santa Claus of whatever material does not have to beg for a new owner—the figure may be iron in an iron sleigh drawn by iron reindeer, or it may be a pottery bank or a bottle in the shape of the jolly saint. Some music boxes play only Christmas carols. The blue and white Danish Christmas plates have been made in an annual edition for more than fifty years, and some of the early designs are no longer easy to purchase. Limoges also produced a holly-decorated china during the 1800's that seems rather scarce.

Bells, too, are popular with collectors. Many different kinds of bells common during the 1800's contributed less nerve-shattering sounds to the cities, towns, and countryside than their present-day substitutes. There were church bells, school bells, bells that tinkled when the

*Bells with various pleasing tones were used for many purposes during the 1880's. In this photograph are two schoolbells (center and right). The one with the wood handle is brass, 3⅛ inches in diameter. The other, with its handle broken off, is nickel, 3⅝ inches in diameter. The little sleighbells (only 1¾ inches) are attached to a leather strap, which was originally much longer.*—Ted Eastwood

door to a store was pushed open, doorbells for houses, bells for the horses that drew the carriages and wagons, and bells for cows and oxen, sheep, and cats. On the teacher's desk there probably was a bell with a push-down button to make it ring. On the dining table a dainty table bell made of silver, brass, glass, or china was set at the place of the mistress of the house.

Heard throughout the land were sleigh bells in winter, harness bells the rest of the year. The Conestoga wagons that took families across the Plains had their special set of bells made of brass on a wrought-iron frame to be attached to the collars of the horses or oxen. Other bells linked to transportation were those on railroad engines, on ships and fire engines.

There are two possible outlets for a bell from fire-fighting equipment: the collector of bells and the enthusiast who likes old fire equipment. The fire buffs also look for the old leather buckets that were used for carrying water, for horns and trumpets, lamps from old fire engines, shields from uniforms and hats, and buttons and helmets. Any of these may be found in an attic if your grandfather or some other male relative belonged to a Volunteer Fire Company.

Firemarks appeal to almost everyone. In fact, they are so popular that many old ones are being reproduced in miniature as wall ornaments or paperweights. Firemarks were made of iron, lead on wood, or terra cotta; reproductions usually are iron. Before the days of professional firemen (the first groups were hired by cities in the 1850's), every insurance company had its own insignia and furnished its plaque to each client, who fastened it somewhere on the front of his house or business building. The firemark indicated to the amateur firefighters that the house was insured, and therefore it would be worth battling a blaze there because a financial reward could be expected. First to issue a firemark—clasped hands against a shield—was the Philadelphia Contributorship For The Insurance of Houses From Loss By Fire, formed in 1752 with Benjamin Franklin as one of the directors (the firm is still in business). This firm would not insure houses surrounded by trees, but the Mutual Insurance Company of Philadelphia, organized in 1784, would, so its device featured the now-famous "flowering

tree." Popular with the many other insurance companies formed during the next hundred years were motifs such as firefighters in uniform, speaking trumpets, hydrants, and various pieces of equipment. Also often used was an eagle. The Eagle Insurance Company of Cincinnati in 1855 issued an oval plaque to be mounted horizontally, with an eagle and the name of the company on a ribbon below. Another oval, to be mounted vertically, showed an eagle whose pose has been changed several times since the first one was issued in 1792 by the Insurance Company of North America.

Telescopes or spyglasses, binoculars, and compasses may be fully as serviceable now as they were when they were first used a century or more ago. Spyglasses were little used by mariners until the late eighteenth century, and compasses were not common until the nineteenth. Barometers, clocks, and lanterns, as well as bells, ships' logs, and old navigation maps and charts are other nautical accessories to be set aside for appraisal and sale.

Models of ships old enough to be antique may be worth considerable money to people who study and collect them. However, everyone is fascinated by a ship in a bottle. The art of inserting a miniature ship into a bottle and creating a scene around it originated in the early 1800's. British sailors presumably started this hobby, but soon sailors of all countries were trying their skill. All kinds of vessels traveling the oceans during the nineteenth century were re-created to ride their bit of sea made of tinted clay or plaster fastened in a bottle. Scenery included sea and possibly a lighthouse or a shoreline with village and trees.

Another seaman's art, scrimshaw, was peculiarly American. Scrimshaw is the term for small things carved from the tooth or bone of a whale. Every member of a crew from captain to cabin boy is said to have passed time on the whaling voyages that lasted two, three, and sometimes five years by making scrimshaw. It is a natural art to have developed among New Englanders, who on land were noted for whittling. A ship model or small chest for keepsakes or jewelry was an ambitious project known as large scrimshaw. More numerous are the innumerable small gadgets and useful objects, such as but-

*Scrimshaw was a favorite pastime on whaling voyages. Ship models necessitated the carving of countless small pieces, which then had to be skillfully fitted together. The photograph shows a ship from the scrimshaw collection of the Seamen's Bank for Savings in New York City.*

tons, clothespins, handles for canes, a pie crimper, a corset stay or buskboard, even picture frames. There also are a good many examples of a sperm whale's tooth carved into an artistic piece such as a wreath, emblem, or figure.

Some scrimshaw is finer work than others, for the quality varied with the skill and patience of the seaman. Only the simplest tools were used. Files of varying coarseness and sometimes sharkskin smoothed and polished the rough, ribbed surface of the sperm whale's tooth. This was followed by rubbing with the fingers and palm of the hand for a shining, smooth surface. The seaman's knife, awls, and needles were used for carving the bone or tooth into the desired shape and then decorating it with an elaborate and detailed, yet often delicate, pattern.

The best way to identify scrimshaw or a piece you suspect to be scrimshaw is to visit one of the maritime museums such as those in New Bedford, Massachusetts, and Mystic, Connecticut, on the East Coast or in San Francisco, California, on the West Coast.

Anyone who counts the captain of a clipper ship or a whaler among his ancestors may find ivory carvings which he brought from the Orient. Miniature ivory carvings used to be displayed on the whatnot. Or his preference may have been for netsuke, the small fastenings like a knob or button that have been carved for generations in Japan.

Ivory, bone, jade, wood, and other materials have been used for netsuke, which were often elaborately carved in such forms as dogs, frogs, figures, and gods. Some of them were inlaid, lacquered, or enameled.

Articles have been fashioned from animal horn in America as well as in countries all over the world. In addition to the indispensable powder horns, drinking cups, small dishes, boxes such as those for snuff, and napkin rings were carved from horn during the 1800's.

Finding an Indian arrowhead is comparable to plucking a four-leaf clover. Some people can look down on a Long Island meadow and pick up either one; others never see them. For those whose eyes are sharp enough, there are still probably some other Indian artifacts to be found. Stone arrowheads and spearheads are quite plentiful, but differ in size, shape, and color of stone. Don't scorn anything from arrowheads to flints or drills that sharp-eyed relatives may have found and displayed in their homes. If you don't want to keep them or the children are not interested, by all means give them to a museum or local historical society, or sell the lot to a dealer for whatever he offers.

Artifacts from the world the white man created on North America may be worth gathering together for possible sale. Relics of old political campaigns, for example, might include flasks made

with the likeness of William H. Harrison when he was running for president, and posters, banners, torches, campaign buttons, and badges from other local and national elections during the last 100 years. A Currier & Ives print depicting a favorite candidate may have been hidden away too.

The elaborate wicker or wire birdcage that has not been used in goodness-knows-how-many years can be disposed of for a few dollars. A decorator who buys it undoubtedly will charge a client many times what you receive for it. Wire cages made in the shape of figures, Chinese pagodas, and various styles of houses may not be in the best condition but probably can be sold for at least a couple of dollars. Or suppose that in clearing out a house, you have piled up a group of eggs, such as a darning egg whittled from wood, a china egg that formerly was placed in a hen's nest, a rather grimy but still glittering Easter egg with a peephole for viewing the scene attached inside, and an old perfume container in an egg. Well, some people collect all kinds of useful or decorative eggs and anything else that featured or was used in connection with eggs.

Just as Victorian birdcages are taking on whimsical importance in contemporary decoration, so are lavaboes. These wall basins with faucets and bowls were made of many materials, from about 1400 up until 1890. Silver, Sheffield, iron, pewter or painted tin, wood, earthenware such as majolica, and ironstone or other stoneware were used with varying degrees of skill. Most of them are quite decorative.

People have even been known to buy at an auction—and bring home to set up in a recreation room—an old post-office cage that formerly stood in one corner of a country store. That being so, there is no reason to think you cannot sell a monster of an old-style typewriter, a cash register worked by hand, an early style of checkwriter, scales from butcher or grocery shops long since closed, or early fountain pens (but not those in use just before ballpoint pens displaced them).

A few cents for an old style of fountain pen, a few dollars for the typewriter that has not been used for years, will satisfy most people. Unless you want to keep it for sentiment's sake, a set of ebony and ivory dominoes that is complete in its original wooden box ought to sell for $7.50, even if no one intends to play with it. Chess sets will be priced according to the materials and workmanship, playing cards according to age and rarity. A magic lantern, even in the best condition, probably cannot be sold for more than $20, or a stereoscope that still works for much more than $5. Cards for a stereoscope in a set of approximately 100, may bring another $5.

It is much easier to set a price on imported ivory miniatures than on scrimshaw. Not that scrimshaw sells for fabulous prices, but a person would have to have some knowledge of scrimshaw in general to appraise any one piece. A carved ivory napkin ring may be worth $5, a letter-holder with elaborate carving perhaps $5. Netsuke vary from about $15 to $40 or more depending on the material, decoration, and workmanship. A horn napkin ring may sell for no more than $1, but a horn snuffbox should be worth at least $5.

Dolls in good condition bring excellent prices, particularly if any of their original clothing is available. A fashion doll is certain to sell for more than $100. A doll with a china head, hands, and feet that are not chipped may sell for about $75, wax dolls for $50 or less. Dolls with bisque heads range from about $50 to well over $100, and perhaps more if stamped with the name of the maker or country.

Considerable financial return may be netted from selling prints and pictures. Silhouettes range from a couple of dollars to $50, according to whether they were signed by the artist and depending on their condition and the identity of the person depicted. Miniatures painted on ivory or porcelain vary in quality. Again, the signature of the artist affects the value as much as the skill with which the painting was done. Many miniatures that are not outstanding sell for $40 to $75; others bring considerably more. Daguerreotypes that are authenticated as such bring a few dollars—as much for the case, if it is in good condition, as for the picture. Of course, a daguerreotype of a famous person such as Abraham Lincoln will bring considerably more money than one of an unknown grandfather. Tintypes have no particular value.

A lithophane plaque or picture may bring as much as $25. Prints sell for less — and a great deal more, since prices can range from a few dollars to hundreds and, in some cases, thousands. The subject matter as well as the condition of the print helps to determine its market value. It is a mistake to try to clean a very dusty or a stained print. This chore should be tackled only by an experienced person. An expert should be consulted about price, too. So many reproductions have been made of Currier & Ives and of Audubon bird prints that it is important to be certain you have originals. A subject for which there is constant demand will sell for a higher price than less popular ones. Some Western prints by such specialists in this field as George Catlin and Charles Bodmer may be sold for no more than $35 to $75, whereas a rare one by either artist may bring several hundred dollars.

The fact remains that it is possible to sell almost anything that deserves the qualifying word "antique."

## GLOSSARY

*Ambrotype:* an early type of photograph made on glass.

*Aquatint:* a picture made by an etching process so that the print imitates the broad flat effect of an India ink or sepia drawing or a water color.

*Chromo:* a chromolithograph or a picture printed in colors from a series of stones prepared by the lithographic process.

*Daguerreotype:* an early type of photograph produced on a silvered plate; generally much better and less faded than an ambrotype or a tintype.

*Fraktur:* hand-lettered and hand-decorated pieces, usually birth, baptism, or marriage certificates or a house blessing, to be hung on the wall.

*Kaleidoscope:* a tube containing a fixed lens, and loose fragments of colored glass so arranged that changes of position show the glass fragments in an endless variety of multicolored patterns.

*Lithograph:* a picture produced by lithography, a process of putting designs on stone with a greasy material and from this obtaining many printed impressions. Lithographs were used for illustrating publications, as framed pictures, and for covering tin boxes and cans.

*Lithophane:* a decorative transparency of translucent porcelain.

*Magic lantern:* a machine with a kerosene lantern and a lens, for projecting colored slides.

*Mezzotint:* a print produced by a process of engraving on copper and steel so as to produce light and shade.

*Stereoscope:* an optical instrument with two eyepieces through which two pictures of the same subject, taken from two slightly different angles, are viewed in depth.

*Tintype:* a photographic mount made on a thin iron plate; a less effective as well as cheaper type of photograph than a daguerreotype.

## FOR FURTHER INFORMATION:

THE DOLLS OF YESTERDAY by Eleanor St. George. New York: Charles Scribner's Sons.

GUIDE BOOK OF UNITED STATES COINS by R. S. Yeoman. New York: Whitman Publishing Company.

INTERNATIONAL COIN CATALOGUE AND PRICE LIST. New York: The Coin and Currency Publishing Institute.

MINKUS NEW WORLD WIDE POSTAGE STAMP CATALOG. New York: Minkus Publications, Inc.

Volume 1: United States and possessions; British Commonwealth countries; United Nations; independent nations of Asia, Africa, Central America, South America.

Volume 2: European countries and their colonies.

MODEL SOLDIERS by Henry Harris. New York: G. P. Putnam's Sons.

MUSIC BOXES: THEIR LORE AND LURE by Helen and John Hoke. New York: Hawthorn Books, Inc.

# 18

# Fakes and Reproductions

So many kinds of antiques are to be found in all parts of the country that there should be enough for everyone. After all, the person who likes trivets may be glad to get rid of an early-nineteenth-century chair, and someone who hunts Staffordshire china in two colors is likely to be happy to part with any pressed glass in her cupboards.

Antiques, however, have become fashionable. People who heretofore regarded anything in an attic as junk are beginning to shake out minutely stitched patchwork quilts and use them as wall hangings, to refinish the black walnut commode and use it for a side table in living or dining room, and to polish all the old brass or quadruple-plated silver they can find and display it on the mantelpiece or room divider. Young married couples with no great-aunt to give them a Wedding Ring tea set are browsing around antique shops for old china or silver to lend cachet to

their handsome storage chest. Moreover, neither age nor budget need keep any interested person from owning and enjoying antiques.

One natural result of both the vogue for and the genuine interest in antiques is that many of them are being copied or reproduced as fast as Dior frocks and Chanel suits were. Like copies of clothing, many pseudo-antiques are so cheap-looking as to be obviously shams. But there are clever copies, too, on which time and effort have been spent to make them look authentically aged. Because fakes and reproductions look so much like antiques themselves, particularly to those who know little about the real ones. people who want to sell old things should do all they can to learn how genuine or false they are.

Pseudo-antiques fall into one of three groups: cheap imitations, clever fakes, and sound reproductions. All three have been made to such an extent during the twentieth century that probably every major group of antiques has been subjected to their inroads. It is easy to be fooled, particularly if the article was made with intent to deceive, but the most careful fake is no more comparable to the antique on which it was based than the garish imitation.

Imitations of fine old china and lamps are sold in many kinds of stores. The quantity in which they are displayed is one clue to their recent origin, the details that have not been copied carefully enough for them to be reproductions is another. On the other hand, a clever fake is sometimes offered as a genuine antique, particularly in the case of furniture, if the tales of cabinetmakers who have taken old wood from an antique chest and combined it with new wood to make another piece are to be believed. However much effort has been expended to copy characteristic details of style and to simulate aged materials, a fake is still a counterfeit. There is, of course, nothing wrong with a good reproduction so long as the owner doesn't try to pass it off as a genuine antique. Many reproductions are such faithful copies that it would be difficult to tell the difference, if it were not for the lack of wear; years of use and care add special character to any antique.

Price is no guarantee of authenticity. Some people buy reproductions, particularly in furniture, because they think they cannot afford genuine antiques. Actually, reproductions that are careful replicas are about as costly as the originals. This is as true of a mirror in American Chippendale style and a brass hanging lantern as it is of important pieces of furniture. The cost of the labor necessary to produce even a clever fake built of wood, of which only one-fourth is old and the remainder treated to look old, is so great that the price must be nearly as much as that for an antique. Anyone who thinks that a pine spice chest a century or so old is overpriced at $25 to $35 has only to consult cabinetmakers or repairers about mending a broken drawer or replacing a missing one to realize that a reproduction would cost more than an original. Still, however much a reproduction costs, it cannot be expected to sell for as high a price as the antique on which it was modeled.

Reproductions have been popular for a great many years, but the number of antiques being reproduced and sold as such has never been greater than at the present time. Furniture is most widely represented, for there is not only a great deal of it but also the examples range from certain styles of the seventeenth century through the eighteenth and into the early Victorian era. All sorts of household furnishings and accessories from wallpaper and textiles to pressed glass, silver, and numerous things made of other metals have proved popular as reproductions too.

Pre-eminent examples are the reproductions of eighteenth-century furniture and accessories made under the auspices of Colonial Williamsburg. Every care has been taken to duplicate the furnishings of the buildings and homes in that famous Colonial town. An original has been used as the model for each reproduction. Other restorations specialize in equally authentic nineteenth-century antiques of one kind or another.

Furniture is available in the widest range. There is furniture of contemporary manufacture that is referred to as traditional because its design is based on details characteristic of various eighteenth-century styles. Such furniture is not an actual reproduction. Authentic replicas are most common in eighteenth-century styles, and a few earlier pieces also are available. One type of reproduction that is usually excellent is the piece made by a skilled cabinetmaker—there are still a few of them working—from old wood. It is often possible to obtain from him a pre-Victorian piece of the early 1800's. Generally speaking, the furniture reproductions sponsored by restorations are about as close as a person can get to antiques. The choice extends from finished pieces such as those distributed by Colonial Williamsburg, to equally authentic furniture kits that can be assembled and finished, according to instructions, by the purchaser.

Furniture illustrates the broad range of reproductions with which many people are content. It breaks down into two main groups: entirely machine-made or made by hand. In weighing a reproduction versus an antique, remember that the originals were hand-made until 1830 and in some cases for many years thereafter. Accurate as the current "furniture store" reproductions of early Victorian sofas, chairs, and tables may be, they are factory-made. The original models were turned out individually in cabinetmakers' shops. The details of construction and carving, therefore, appear quite different to knowing eyes. And any reproduction, however accurate, lacks the inimitable patina wood acquires through years of use and polishing. If you find it hard to discern patina, the kinds of wood and details of construction common to the period when the style was first made are discussed in the chapters on furniture.

Equally good examples of the two chief methods of reproduction are found in hardware and pressed glass. Strap hinges tipped with a bean, ball and spear, or a heart, which probably were the first type made in America, and H and HL hinges can now be purchased in almost any neighborhood hardware store. However, the examples of these pieces of hardware that are available in the average retail store have been machine-stamped. Nevertheless, it is possible to buy old-style hinges as well as latches, bolts, and other household hardware at a restoration such as Old Sturbridge Village in Sturbridge, Massachusetts, where they are forged or hand-hammered by a working blacksmith. The difference between machine-made and handmade hardware may be so subtle as to be unnoticeable to anyone except an expert, but the handmade replicas are certainly preferable for an old house that is being restored and perhaps also for a cupboard or other piece that has been a do-it-yourself project for a house of any age.

Pressed glass frequently is advertised as having been made recently from old— meaning nineteenth-century — molds. However genuine the molds, the resulting glass cannot be compared with the original pieces. Both the glass and its color are somewhat different. The present-day manufacturer who uses nineteenth-century molds does not go to the trouble of mixing a batch of glass according to nineteenth-century formulas. As a result, his clear glass is not an exact counterpart of last century's, and the red, green, blue, or other colored glass pieces rarely have the same tints and tones as the originals.

In addition to reproductions, many fakes are being made in pressed glass. One telltale sign of a fake is a slight difference in pattern. During the 1800's, variants of popular patterns became common, but a variant made by a glasshouse other than the one that introduced the pattern shows some alteration in the motifs or their arrangement. A fake, on the other hand, is an attempt to reproduce a pattern of the 1800's without bothering to copy every detail exactly. Twentieth-century imitations of the popular Wildflower pattern, for example, have fewer leaves and flowers in each motif. The band of pressed daisies also is narrower. Moon and Star, a pattern that probably was not made before the 1880's, can be confused with an inaccurate contemporary version in which the sawtooth-like cutting around the moon is smoother and flatter than in the originals. As a matter of fact, any colored Moon and Star pieces are definitely fakes, for the nineteenth-century pattern was offered only in clear or clear and frosted glass. Dimensions of pieces also differ, but this is impossible to judge unless you have access to an authenticated nineteenth-century piece.

Pattern glass was made after 1850 in large sets for the table. Reproductions of even the most popular patterns, however, seldom include the entire set. Goblets are the most widely reproduced pieces, with tumblers, mugs, salts, match-holders, and other small pieces likely in some patterns. Considerable lacy glass with its stippled background, first made by the Boston and Sandwich Glass Company in the 1830's, also is being made now. Lacy glass never was made in a complete table set. Other specific clues for distinguishing between antique pressed glass and this century's copies are discussed in the chapter on pressed glass.

Cup plates, which were generally used until about 1850, and dolphin candlesticks, which were made from the 1830's to the early 1900's, have been so popular that fakes and imitations found a ready market. Dolphin candlesticks made between 1900 and 1910 can hardly be classed as antiques yet, but most of the late ones are much finer work than the more recent fakes and reproductions. Again, some dolphin candlesticks are said to be made from old molds, but the glass is not the same quality or the color a duplicate of the original.

Dolphin candlesticks were made by many glasshouses, from the Boston and Sandwich Glass Company, which introduced them, to firms in Pennsylvania and the Midwest. The earliest Sandwich glass ones had a single square base. Then came the double square or square stepped base, also made at Sandwich and widely reproduced before World War II in the United States and Europe. Other glasshouses during the 1800's produced candlesticks having the dolphin shaft but with bases and sockets differing from those made at Sandwich. A hexagonal base, for example, introduced by a Pittsburgh glass firm in the 1850's has been reproduced widely too. There is also the petticoat dolphin with a high round base first made in the 1850's or 1860's. All styles were made in clear, opalescent, and some colors, also opaque white and opaque blue.

Anyone who looks carefully should be able to recognize copies of dolphin candlesticks. Those made within the last thirty years have sharper, clearer details (fins in particular are sharper

to the touch). The sockets, whether ribbed or petaled, usually do not flare outward. The glass is of poorer quality and the colors more garish. The proportions are not so good either, for the dolphin is likely to be larger, and many of the copies are shorter candlesticks.

In spite of the large number of patterns in which cup plates were made in the 1800's, comparatively few are being reproduced. Since the originals were early pressed glass, the quality of the glass was good enough to give a bell-like ring when the little plate was tapped lightly. Reproductions or twentieth-century imitations sound dead or dull. A classic example of a fake, imitation, or reproduction—call it what you will—that can confuse all but the most knowing is the Butterfly pattern cup plate, first made by the Boston and Sandwich Glass Company in clear and colored glass. The butterfly that gives the pattern its name stands out in the center against a stippled background. Flower sprigs encircle the rim and the edge is scalloped. During the 1930's, Butterfly cup plates were reproduced from a new mold that was not an exact duplicate of the original one. On antique Butterfly cup plates, the stems of the two leaves below each blossom are at least ⅛ inch apart, but on this century's, the stems are almost opposite each other. One blossom on the old Butterfly plate has seven petals; all the blossoms on the recent plates have six. It's particularly easy to be fooled by a blue Butterfly cup plate, for this color as made in the 1930's compares favorably with that of the 1830's.

Imitations of curtain tiebacks and furniture knobs also were made in quantity and sold cheaply during the 1930's. Old patterns, including some of the Sandwich ones, were copied in both clear and colored glass. Neither the quality of the glass nor the workmanship are any more comparable than the colors to those made during the 1800's.

Fakes are not confined to pressed glass. Bottles and flasks, for example, frequently are made in imitation of typically American styles of the nineteenth century. A "golden amber" bottle in the shape of a fish, made recently in Italy, "queen of the glass-making industry for generations," is not worth any more than its retail price. Only the amber fish bottles made in this country to hold Dr. Fisch's bitters are antiques. For holiday sale in 1961, a liquor company packaged its spirits in colored glass flasks made in the style of a century or more ago. A tiny booklet attached to each one summed up the background of historical flasks and explained the company's choice of motifs for their reproductions. Although these 1961 flasks are not exact reproductions, perhaps fifty years from now someone will think one of them is much older than it really is.

Milk-white glass is still being manufactured in quantity, and many pieces copy or are reminiscent of the forms and decorations used during the late 1800's. However, the character and appearance of nineteenth-century milk-white glass are quite different. The slightest acquaintance with any piece of antique milk-white glass should enable a person to distinguish between the old and the contemporary.

To tell the difference between a nineteenth-century pressed glass goblet and a twentieth-century reproduction or fake, a person must be alert to the patterns and pieces that are currently being manufactured. Equally important are a knowledge of the authentic motifs, as well as of their make-up, proportions, and placement to form the patterns, and the ability to judge the quality of stippling and frosting.

Cost prohibits the reproduction of cut glass as it was made throughout the 1800's. Its surface distinctions are the sharpness of the decorative motifs to the touch and the heaviness of the piece. Other characteristics of cut glass as it was made at various times, as well as the traits of hand-blown, blown-molded, and blown-three-mold have been outlined previously.

Fully as rich a field as glass for reproductions and fakes is provided by the diversity of household and personal items made from silver, pewter, brass, copper, and iron. It is easy to say that old silver (coin and sterling) has an unmistakable patina, old brass is a quite different color from twentieth-century reproductions, and old pewter always feels slightly rough to the touch. Outstanding and essential as each of these characteristics is to the metal in question, more knowledge is required to identify antiques.

Old silver is not nearly as plentiful as pressed glass or even cut glass. Consequently, it is an active field for faking. The purpose is to make a piece more salable and at a higher price. But excellent and acknowledged reproductions also are being made of both antique silver and the pewter pieces that were used in American homes.

The style of the lettering and the decoration are clues to the age of silver. So are the marks, although a considerable amount of old American silver carries no mark. There is a good deal of nineteenth-century silver and plated silver around, much of it of interest to owners, finders, and collectors. Probably faking is practiced more often on English and European silver, which finds a ready market in this country. Adding a fake hallmark, shifting a hallmark from a spoon or other small piece to a larger piece, and removing or altering decoration are sometimes attempted in order to make a silver piece more valuable. Because styles in handles, finials, and spouts changed as often as did decoration, discrepancies can be spotted by anyone who knows something about shifting fashions in silverware. Furthermore, although decoration may be hammered, buffed, or otherwise removed from the outside of silver, its outlines cannot be destroyed on the underside.

It is not too difficult to distinguish between an antique and a fairly recent reproduction of pewter (see the chapter on metals). Fakes are more confusing. Always check any mark on pewter, for the faker may have added an earlier mark to increase the value of the piece or forged a mark which, upon investigation, proves to be somewhat different in size, design, or some detail than any recorded pewterers' marks. Some knowledge of style, decoration, and workmanship at various times is another safeguard against fakes.

No material, however, has been too lowly to exploit by copying, to judge from the many reproductions of trivets, match-holders, string-holders, and other common household gadgets made from iron between 1850 and 1900. Clues for distinguishing between the antique and the copy, whatever the material, are suggested in the preceding chapters. Even without specific clues, it should be evident that the wooden cranberry scoop with teeth that are not rounded and worn down and the tin sconce that shines brightly and has no dents are not antiques. Signs of wear come only with use and are as typical of things, large and small, in any material as they are of furniture. It takes too long to fake this kind of aging and, anyway, it is next to impossible to do successfully.

In china as in glass, a person must know the characteristics of the old wares in order to avoid mistakes. A collector of porcelain will have to learn, for his own protection, when factories made hard-paste and when they made soft-paste porcelains if he is to be fairly sure that a piece is the age claimed for it. This information is equally important to anyone who has a porcelain to sell. The type and quantity of decoration, as well as the colors that were used and the changes that took place from time to time, are essential knowledge for judging the age of porcelain and pottery.

Potters' marks may be helpful, but are not necessarily conclusive. They can, and have been known to, be erased or altered. Crossed swords have been incorporated into the Meissen mark since that factory first made porcelain in the 1740's. From time to time the overall appearance of the Meissen mark was changed somewhat, although the two swords were retained. But crossed swords—or what seems to be crossed swords, at first glance—have been used by other factories for their marks. If the intention was to fool buyers into thinking they were getting porcelain of Meissen quality, it probably succeeded some of the time. A person who likes Haviland china should become familiar with the various marks used by this firm during the 1800's so that he can date a piece fairly accurately.

Some patterns of tableware have been made continuously or intermittently for 100 to 200 years. In the case of Meissen Onion, a popular pattern among collectors, it has been made by the same factory. However, the basic pattern differed slightly from time to time, as did the mark of the factory. Awareness of changes and of what they were is essential to identifying early- and late-nineteenth-century examples. The Willow pattern was made by many different potteries. Here again, the mark—or lack of one—can be important in judging the antiquity of the piece.

Graniteware, often called ironstone china, was popular in the United States between 1850 and 1890. Reproductions of many of the pieces that made up a set of tableware have been made during the last decade. The person who comes across some pieces and would like to sell them cannot determine a fair price without consulting someone expert enough to decide whether they are antiques or reproductions. The collector also will want to learn enough about graniteware to be reasonably certain of buying nineteenth-century pieces.

Quite generally copied in china are the old figures, flowers, vegetables, and fruits, and tureens in the form of birds or animals. Sometimes the reproductions are made from old molds and the decoration done by modern methods. Antique gilding, for example, is a rich gold color, not brassy or bright. The hand-painting on antique pieces is so skillful that details appear sharp when they are looked at under a magnifying glass.

Reproductions of figures and other ornaments are one thing, imitations something else again. The Delft of Holland has been imitated in other countries, and the copies may be almost impossible to recognize unless a person checks the potter's mark or unless the country of origin is stated under the potter's mark. Perhaps no kind of pottery has been more widely imitated than jasperware. The finest examples always have been made by the Wedgwood pottery in England, where this ware was perfected. The quality excels even that of jasperware made by European potteries during the eighteenth century, and of course the blue and white unglazed stoneware from Japan in this century is in no way comparable.

Comparatively few people know enough about more than one field of antiques to tell a fake or reproduction from an authentic piece. This is as true of antique dealers as the general public. An antique dealer who is an authority on seventeenth- or eighteenth-century furniture may have only superficial knowledge about the glass made during those years. By the same token, the pressed glass expert may know little about silver and china.

What, then, can the average person

do? He can study exhibits and collections, learn from books and other people, look and listen before and during auctions, compare a questionable piece with an authenticated one. Above all, he can ask questions of a reputable dealer, of experts such as curators and others who work with antiques, and of collectors or anyone who has studied some special field. Collectors usually admit to having bought one or more fakes or reproductions while they were learning the distinguishing characteristics of their chosen item. The person who thinks he knows more than he does about antiques, who closes his mind to the fact that fakes, imitations, and reproductions exist, is the one who is disappointed about his discoveries or who is fooled in his purchases.

The characteristics, styles, and decoration of articles made in the seventeenth, eighteenth, and nineteenth centuries will be explained in any general book on furniture, glass, silver, or other category of antiques. Books with a positive approach are easier to find than those that contain a negative discussion of fakes and reproductions. On glass, however, the following book is worth while:

ANTIQUE FAKES & REPRODUCTIONS by Ruth Webb Lee. Wellesley Hills, Massachusetts: Lee Publications.

# INDEX

French furniture, 24
French influence, 28, 33
French Empire period, 38
  furniture, 29
French provincial furniture, 24
fretted plate hardware, 39
fretwork, 17, 18, 39, 40, 75
  frames, 84, 85
  mirrors, 84
    prices for, 94
Frosted Circle pattern, pressed glass, 193
frosted glass, 198
Frosted Ribbon pattern, pressed glass, 193
Frosted Stork pattern, pressed glass, 180
frosting, 179, 180, 189
Frothingham, Benjamin, 26
fruit and flower paperweights, 212
fruitwoods, 24
Fry, Henry C., 148
  Glass Company, 146, 148
furniture
  American Eastlake, 75
  American Empire, 32, 37, 68
  background of, 7-41
  bamboo, 75
  Belter, 75
  Biedermeier, 68
  Chippendale, 9, 17-30, 32, 38
  country, 42-64
  determining age of, 35, 36
  doll, 400
  Dutch (Hudson River), 44
  fakes, 409
  French, 24
    Empire period, 29
    provincial, 24
  hardware for, 32-34, 39
    brass, 317
  Hepplewhite, 20-24, 32, 38
  iron, 324, 327
  Jacobean, 37
  knobs, imitation, 413
  Late Victorian, 75
  Maryland, 28
  mass production of, 65, 66
  New England, 42
  Pennsylvania Dutch, 42, 44, 52, 58, 59
    characteristics of, 44
  Primitive, 42
  reproductions, 409, 410
  Scandinavian, 44
  Shaker, 42, 44
  toy, 400
  Victorian, 63-81
    Jacobean, 72
    Louis XVI, 72
    Oriental, 75
    Turkish, 75
gadroon, 40
gadrooning, 286, 305

gallery, 40
games
  backgammon, 396
  chess, 396
  children's, 397
  cribbage, 396
  dominoes, 396
    prices for, 405
  Victorian, 396
gateleg tables, 10, 12, 38, 46
gather, 166
Gaudy Dutch, 244, 245
Gaudy Ironstone, 245
Gaudy Welsh, 245
gemels, 223
*Gentleman and Cabinet Maker's Director, The*, 17
George Duncan and Sons, 156, 171, 180
German silver, 303
Gibson, Charles Dana, 252
Gibson Girl plates, 252, 253
Giddings, Edward, 385
gilding, 17
Gillinder, James & Sons, 149, 171, 179, 180, 187, 211, 216
Gilman, B. C., 103
ginger jars, 273, 274
girandoles
  clock, 104
  lamp, 118
  lightholder, 125, 134
  mirror, 88
glass, 136-244, *see also* art glass, cut glass, pressed glass
  agata, 150, 155, 156
  amberina, 150, 155, 156
  Amelung, 136, 137
  American Bristol, 150, 159
  aurene, 150, 160, 161
  black, 158
  blown, 137
  blown-molded, 137, 139
  blown-three-mold, 137, 139, 140
  Bohemian, 152
  bottle, 138
  Burmese, 150, 153
  Cameo, 151, 152
  cased, 152
  carnival, 151
  chips or cracks in, 165
  clear, 138
  colored, 159
    brides' baskets, 159
  crackle, 151, 159, 160
  cranberry, 6
  Crown Milano, 151, 155
  crystal, 138
  cut, 6, 141, 142, 145, 146, 148, 205, 206, 218
  cutting on, 141